CURRENT CONTINENTAL THEORY
AND MODERN PHILOSOPHY

D0770208

Northwestern University
Topics in Historical Philosophy

General Editors David Kolb
      John McCumber

Associate Editor Anthony J. Steinbock

CURRENT CONTINENTAL THEORY AND MODERN PHILOSOPHY

Edited by Stephen H. Daniel

Northwestern University Press
Evanston, Illinois

Northwestern University Press
www.nupress.northwestern.edu

Copyright © 2005 by Northwestern University Press. Published 2005. All rights
reserved.

Printed in the United States of America

10   9   8   7   6   5   4   3   2   1

ISBN 0-8101-2201-4 (cloth)
ISBN 0-8101-2202-2 (paper)

Library of Congress Cataloging-in-Publication Data

Current continental theory and modern philosophy / edited by Stephen H.
Daniel.
     p. cm. — (Topics in historical philosophy)
   Includes bibliographical references and index.
     ISBN 0-8101-2201-4 (cloth : alk. paper) — ISBN 0-8101-2202-2 (pbk. : alk.
paper)
   1. Philosophy, European. 2. Philosophy, Modern. I. Daniel, Stephen H.
(Stephen Hartley), 1950– II. Northwestern University topics in historical
philosophy.
B791C87 2004
190—dc22

                                                                2004012211

MY 24 '06

⊚ The paper used in this publication meets the minimum requirements of the
American National Standard for Information Sciences—Permanence of Paper
for Printed Library Materials, ANSI Z39.48-1992.

Contents

Preface

Stephen H. Daniel

For decades continental theorists known for their work in critical theory, psychoanalytic structuralism, feminism, deconstruction, semiotics, philosophical hermeneutics, poststructuralism, and postmodernism have engaged in provocative, penetrating, and often extensive examinations of modern philosophers from Machiavelli to Kant. Because they have not presupposed many of the historiographic assumptions that inform standard accounts of sixteenth- through eighteenth-century philosophy, they have opened new ways to think about figures such as Descartes, Spinoza, Leibniz, Locke, Hume, Rousseau, and Kant. Accordingly, by focusing on the often overlooked historiographic presuppositions that guide interpretations of modern philosophers, recent continental theorists have revealed how the study of modern philosophy is typically framed in terms of particular strategies developed by those thinkers. However, rather than use Cartesian or Lockean doctrines as filters to interpret modern philosophy, continental theorists often invite us to read modern texts with a sensitivity to how such pronouncements ground ways of thinking that are only retrospectively characterized as modern. Instead of providing anachronistic readings of texts, continental theorists thus attempt to recover aspects of modern philosophy that have been systematically overlooked.

Much of the work by continental theorists on sixteenth- through eighteenth-century thinkers has been ignored by commentators interested more in how their twentieth-century strategies engage current philosophic questions. For example, Jacques Derrida's deconstructive critique attracts much more attention than his interpretations of Condillac or Rousseau. Gilles Deleuze is much more widely known for his seminal works in poststructuralist thought than for his book-length analyses of Spinoza, Leibniz, Hume, and Kant. Michèle Le Doeuff's and Luce Irigaray's treatments of Descartes, Julia Kristeva's review of the Encyclopedists, and Louis Althusser's discussions of Spinoza and Hume all are generally subordinated by commentators to their more theoretical, less historical writings. This book is an attempt to correct that imbalance.

No doubt, part of the reason that scholars concerned with current continental philosophy have shied away from extensive discussions of the moderns (and even discussions by major continental thinkers of the moderns) stems from the fact that such discussions require researchers to straddle two subfields of philosophy—a tall order in these days of disciplinary specialization. Besides, recent continental theory has made all but thematic its ongoing critique of many of the doctrines associated with the mindset of modernity. To develop a research program that draws on continental insights to expound on "modern" or "modernist" topics might seem a bit perverse and require a split academic personality, one willing to play both sides.

For their part as well, historians of modern philosophy (in particular, English-speaking historians) have been reluctant to embrace current continental movements and have ignored their impact on our understanding of the issues and approaches of the moderns. More often than not, critical theory, psychoanalytic structuralism, feminism, deconstruction, semiotics, hermeneutics, poststructuralism, and postmodernism are considered by historians of modern philosophy so recondite that the effort to mine whatever gems might be found there seems to involve more of a commitment than it is worth. In some quarters the very mention of some of these approaches is dismissed as unworthy of philosophy, and in such places it would indeed be a brave soul who invokes the insights of a Le Doeuff or a Deleuze to clarify the ideas of Descartes or Hume. In those environs, raising questions about the historiographic presuppositions of the study of modern philosophy would be considered less a concern of philosophy than one of history or literature. For current continental theorists, though, such disciplinary divisions are no constraints at all because they highlight presuppositions that need to be exposed and critiqued in the first place.

This collection of essays aims to bring the two areas of philosophy closer together by showing how new ways to study modern philosophy are being opened by current continental research. Some of the essays are largely expository: They explore how major continental theorists explicate the ideas of classical modern thinkers. Other essays draw on recent continental insights to examine the doctrines of modern philosophers. Some are written by established thinkers; others are by scholars early in their careers. Each shows how current continental theory reinvigorates the study of the history of modern philosophers by transforming not only how we interpret their answers to questions with which we are still struggling but also how we understand the formulations of the questions they raise.

All but three of these essays have been written specifically for this collection. Of those three, two previously published essays appear here in English for the first time, and the third has been substantially revised. Half of the essays are based on presentations given at an international conference, "Recent Continental Thought and Classical Modern Philosophy," held at Texas A&M University in College Station in September 2000. Without the support of the Office of Graduate Studies, the Melbern G. Glasscock Center for Humanities Research, the College of Liberal Arts, and several departments and programs at Texas A&M, neither the conference nor this volume would have been possible.

Finally, as with all my efforts, this book is dedicated to my wife Breaux. Her support of my projects seems to know no bounds. I could never thank her enough for all the little things that help bring the big ones like this book to fruition. Whenever you look at this volume, know that there is a Cajun businesswoman who is largely responsible for it.

Introduction

Stephen H. Daniel

By focusing on the principles by which the history of philosophy is described, current continental theory redirects the study of early modern philosophy by replacing the attempt to explain the arguments of sixteenth- through eighteenth-century thinkers with an account of the presuppositions of those arguments. In particular, it rejects the classical (especially Platonic-Aristotelian) assumption that the structural differentiation of words, ideas, and things is a timeless given and instead emphasizes how such differentiation emerges. So rather than simply assume that there are true propositions about how words, ideas, and things are related, continental thought reveals the historical and social practices that channel the desire for truth into creating structural differences.

The history of modern philosophy can thus be chronicled either as a "modern" (Cartesian-Lockean) extension of the classical, ahistorical mindset or as a field for research in which philosophies are understood in terms of culturally and historically conditioned presuppositions about structures of reality and knowledge. Because the shift from the first perspective to the second raises questions not only about historiography but also the nature of philosophy, it is no wonder that some historians of philosophy sometimes have doubts about the philosophic credentials of continental thought itself.[1]

However, as the essays in this collection attest, the second approach addresses modern philosophy in terms of the material or practical strategies that establish such structural commitments. Drawing on the ideas of Derrida and Deleuze, Miguel Vatter explains how the discussion of historical beginnings is central in Machiavelli's thought. The question of origins arises as well in Warren Montag's discussion of Althusser, which explores how Locke's notion of property is based on material labor, and in Robert Bernasconi's exploration of how Locke's theory of property is clarified by Heidegger's treatment of artistic creation.

Pierre Macherey, Jay Conway, Joel Reed, and Susan James indicate how the ontological status of matter is enhanced (though complicated) by interpreting materialism (and in the case of Hume, empiricism) critically, that is, in terms of practice rather than simply theory. That switch, according to Macherey, affects how we compare Pascal and Spinoza on the question of the vacuum (void). It also explains, as Conway shows why, at the level of *praxis*, Deleuze treats Hume's fictions as creative concepts rather than as objects of theoretical appropriation. Following Althusser, Reed argues that this makes Hume's materialism all the more "aleatory" (contingent) and less theoretically dogmatic—a point reinforced by Susan James, who shows how Althusser's "materialist" notions of ideology and science are transformed by his apppropriation of the Spinozist understanding of imagination, reason, and intuition.

This theme of material activity forms the backdrop for: Etienne Balibar's exploration of whether the body politic is (for Spinoza) a true ontological individual; Todd May's Deleuzean account of Spinoza's One as difference itself; and Daniel Smith's description of how, for Deleuze, Leibniz's metaphysics of the calculus provides a principle of conceptual difference and a theory of singularities that makes representation possible. Balibar's discussion of the individual also has resonances with: Leslie MacAvoy's consideration of Levinas's treatment of how the subject, for Descartes, is conditioned by alterity (and how the infinite exteriority of Descartes' God is foundational for Levinas's ethics); Anthony David's summary of how, for Le Doeuff and Irigaray, Cartesian wonder makes room for a doctrine of the body (and the feminine); and Constantin Boundas' review of Deleuze on how the Kantian subject is divided and riddled with desire.

This internal division of subjectivity, epitomized according to Deleuze in Kant's third *Critique*, signifies philosophy's ability to create ever-new concepts. Endorsing the importance of the third *Critique*, Dennis Schmidt turns to Heidegger and Gadamer to show how, for Kant, the materiality of language frees things from the bounds of concepts. Katherine Arens notes that Julia Kristeva makes a similar point in claiming that the Encyclopedists' treatment of language as a deep-structured system ignores the historical discursive practices that, according to Deleuze and Félix Guattari, characterize philosophy. And as Penelope Deutscher maintains in her discussion of Derrida's recent work on hospitality, those same practices raise issues surrounding the purity, perfectibility, and pervertibility of Rousseau's concept of nature and the prospects for a future open to possibility and the Enlightenment notion of progress in general.

The strategies employed in these essays amount to what I refer to as *poststructuralist historiography*, by which I mean a way to study the history of philosophy in which philosophic strategies, categories, and theories are understood in terms of material, ideologically conditioned practices that express differentiations of desire and power. Since the practices themselves cannot be understood in any more fundamental terms, it is the task of poststructuralist historiography to reveal the meaning of philosophic texts ultimately in terms of those practices. That, I suggest, is what these essays do.

This approach can also be characterized as broadly "postmodern" in that it diagnoses the modern condition as one filled with the sense of its own novelty, its independence from the past, its affirmation of itself apart from any cultural, historical, or linguistic heritage. It thematizes the discrepancy between, on the one hand, sensual, political, and linguistic experience and, on the other, attempts to provide a transcendent or transcendental rationale for experience independent of historical or ideological contingencies.[2]

Poststructuralist historiography differs from classical-modernist historiography for the same reasons and in the same ways that poststructuralism or postmodernity differs from modernity.[3] In claiming to have transcended the socio-economic and historical prejudices of the contingent present, modernists see no need to question the authority by which their self-critique proceeds. Rooted in the Enlightenment project of social, cultural, and political rationality, even their mechanisms of reform and resistance (for example, liberalism or Marxism) are presupposed as part of a progressive and unified effort to achieve increasingly clearer ideas about our current situation and about the past (including the past of philosophy). Appealing to a new set of strategies to understand the history of philosophy, poststructuralist historiography challenges this Whiggish account by reframing the way in which canonical texts are interpreted.

For example, for some time historians of philosophy have recognized how, for Diderot and Rousseau, the confidence placed in reason by the Enlightenment was ill-founded.[4] For Diderot and Rousseau, no binary opposition of reason—between materialism and idealism, determinism and freedom, nature and culture—offers any promise of a closer approximation to the truth, since the notion of truth is itself a product of positing such oppositions. In modernist historiography, such challenges to dialectical reason are appropriated as the dialectical opposition to rationality. So, a Diderot, a Rousseau, or a Kant could be interpreted as speaking for the Enlightenment's own rational self-critique. So even challenges to the Enlightenment project of universal or totalizing appropriation could themselves be appropriated by the project.

But postmodern theorists point out that Diderot, Rousseau, and Kant are not only critical and suspicious of the material and ideological conditions of their own philosophical environment but also are misinterpreted if understood apart from the psychoanalytic or ideological exchanges that characterize the institutional systems in which their discourses are articulated. In this way of thinking, as Gilles Deleuze notes,

"Everything that happens and everything that is said, happens or is said at the surface," and the purported depth of the inner psyche and height of Platonic ideas are reinscribed in the folds of sensation.[5] There is nothing beneath or beyond the surface, because notions of beneath or beyond are intelligible only in terms of bodily, political, or textual differentiations. Central ideas of modernist thought (for example, the self, certainty, rationality) here are no longer allowed in philosophic discourse without acknowledging their sensual, ideological, and rhetorical heritage. No longer are we allowed to imagine the mind of Montaigne beyond or beneath his text, for as he himself says, "It is not deeds that I write down; it is myself, it is my essence. . . . I have no more made my book than my book has made me—a book consubstantial with its author."[6]

For a poststructuralist, this kind of claim cannot be dismissed simply as a metaphorical use of language, for that would assume that one has a self-grounding way of speaking which is unambiguously nonmetaphorical and able to distinguish itself from that which is derivative. But, of course, that is precisely what cannot be done. So when Francis Bacon declares his independence from the past, he must know that his claim cannot be thought without appealing to the culture, history, and language of what it claims to displace.[7] Otherwise, as Kant observes about the Enlightenment in general, he speaks in a way that transcends history, and in transcending it ends it. The only way to reaffirm the historicity of modernity is to argue (following Michel Foucault) that Kant himself acknowledges the Enlightenment as that *historical* moment when reason's pretensions to universality and transcendence are unmasked.[8]

In the hands of poststructuralists, even Descartes (the archetypal modern) is transformed from the disembodied defender of the cogito to a *literateur* who inscribes philosophic reflection within the self-acknowledged fabrication of a fable. By placing the pursuit of truth itself into question, Descartes' feint of a world and a self is thus permeated by (and hardly independent of) the sensual and linguistic constraints he pretends to doubt away.[9] Michèle Le Doeuff goes so far as to depict Descartes' effort as a bona fide poststructuralist (indeed, feminist) enterprise by noting how his provisional morality provides the material that can only be dreamt of as the other to an epistemology bent on certainty.[10]

In like manner, Louis Althusser, Antonio Negri, and Pierre Macherey describe Spinoza's apparently nonpolitical masterpiece (the *Ethics*) as a rigorous immanent critique of the ideological character of metaphysics and epistemology.[11] For them, Spinoza's subordination of the individual self indicates his suspicion of the ideology that justifies private enterprise, liberal political institutions, and bourgeois morality.[12] When combined with his historical and scriptural hermeneutics, Spinoza's philosophy thus becomes an argument against the monolith of reason that it is traditionally portrayed as exemplifying.[13]

These few examples are part of a much wider continental movement to retrieve modern thinkers from the modernist ways in which they have been described since the nineteenth century. Collectively, these reappropriations constitute (to use Foucault's term) a counterdiscourse to the discourse of modernist historiography. Theirs is a poststructuralist historiography, with its own countercanon or counter to the possibility of a canon.[14] Together they extend the pivotal reassessments of Hegel, Marx, Nietzsche, and Freud by Derrida, Foucault, Deleuze, Althusser, and others which defined the poststructuralist enterprise originally.

No doubt, the import of the challenge to modernist historiography represented in these examples is just beginning to be appreciated by English-language students of the history of modern philosophy. Postmodern criticisms of humanistic beliefs (for example, about the value of individuality, autonomy, and authorial intention) strike at the heart of philosophic historiography. So Deleuze's call to reconceptualize the texts of the moderns must be seen as a call to reengage in philosophy itself. But in this kind of poststructuralist historiography, his "Don't ever interpret, experiment!" does not mean that we should ignore texts but rather that we should be aware of not only how our preconceptions determine our reading but also how our notions of philosophy and its history often prevent us from appreciating what a text masks. Discerning ways of detecting such masks is what this volume is about.

Notes

1. See Richard Campbell, "The Covert Metaphysics of the Clash Between 'Analytic' and 'Continental' Philosophy," *British Journal for the History of Philosophy* 9 (2001), 341–59.

2. See my introduction to *Contemporary Continental Thought* (Upper Saddle River, NJ: Prentice-Hall, 2004).

3. Some of the following remarks are taken from my "Postmodernity, Poststructuralism, and the Historiography of Modern Philosophy," *International Philosophical Quarterly* 35 (1995), 264–67.

4. See Karlis Racevskis, *Postmodernism and the Search for Enlightenment* (Charlottesville: University Press of Virginia, 1993), 1, 13, 73.

5. Gilles Deleuze, *The Logic of Sense*, trans. Mark Lester and Charles Stivale, ed. Constantin V. Boundas (New York: Cambridge University Press, 1990), 7, 9, 132.

6. Michel de Montaigne, *The Complete Essays of Montaigne,* trans. Donald M. Frame (Stanford: Stanford University Press, 1979), 274, 504. Cf. Anthony M. Cascardi, *The Subject of Modernity* (New York: Cambridge University Press, 1992), 63.

7. Cf. Charles Whitney, *Francis Bacon and Modernity* (New Haven: Yale University Press, 1986), 159–60.

8. See Michel Foucault, "What is Enlightenment?" in *The Foucault Reader,* ed. Paul Rabinow (New York: Pantheon Books, 1984), 32–39, 49–50. Cf. Mark Poster, *Critical Theory and Poststructuralism: In Search of a Context* (Ithaca: Cornell University Press, 1989), 74–77.

9. See Jacques Derrida, "Cogito and the History of Madness," in *Writing and Difference,* trans. Alan Bass (Chicago: University of Chicago Press, 1978), 48–63; Stephen H. Daniel, *Myth and Modern Philosophy* (Philadelphia: Temple University Press, 1990), 65–85; and Sarah Kofman, "Descartes Entrapped," in *Who Comes After the Subject?* ed. Eduardo Cadava, Peter Connor, and Jean-Luc Nancy (New York: Routledge, 1991), 183.

10. See Michèle Le Doeuff, *The Philosophical Imaginary,* trans. Colin Gordon (Stanford: Stanford University Press, 1989), 68, 97.

11. See Louis Althusser, *Essays on Ideology* (London: Verso, 1984), 49; Christopher Norris, *Spinoza and the Origins of Modern Critical Theory* (Oxford: Basil Blackwell, 1991), 43–44, 122, 135–59, 231; and Antonio Negri, *The Savage Anomaly: The Power of Spinoza's Metaphysics and Politics,* trans. Michael Hardt (Minneapolis: University of Minnesota Press, 1991).

12. Cf. Norman O. Brown, *Apocalypse and/or Metamorphosis* (Berkeley: University of California Press, 1991), 123–39.

13. See Brown, *Apocalypse,* 95–116; Norris, *Spinoza,* 138, 205–23.

14. See, for example, Jean Starobinski, Réda Bensmaïa, and Michel de Certeau on Montaigne; Jacques Derrida, Foucault, Le Doeuff, Jean-Luc Nancy, and Luce Irigaray on Descartes; Paul de Man, Louis Marin, and Lucien Goldmann on Pascal; Negri and Max Horkheimer on Hobbes; Deleuze, Althusser, and Derrida on Spinoza; Deleuze and Michel Serres on Leibniz; de Man on Locke; Hans-Georg Gadamer, Theodor Adorno, Max Horkheimer, and Hayden White on Vico; Derrida on Condillac; Philippe Lacoue-Labarthe on Diderot; Deleuze on Hume; Derrida, de Man, Starobinski, and Althusser on Rousseau; Foucault, Jean-François Lyotard, Deleuze, and Derrida on Kant; and numerous feminist commentaries on these and other seventeenth- and eighteenth-century thinkers.

CURRENT CONTINENTAL THEORY
AND MODERN PHILOSOPHY

Machiavelli, Historical Repetition, and French Philosophies of Difference

Miguel Vatter

Historical Repetition and Modern Historical Consciousness

The development of modern historical consciousness, from Vico and Rousseau through Hegel and Marx to Nietzsche, Heidegger, and Benjamin, betrays a single-minded fixation on historical repetition, which appears far more important in its formulations than any schema of linear temporal progress. By "historical repetition" I do not mean the belief that similar events occur throughout history but rather the belief that those events which are historically effective ("make history") seem to be thinkable only through logics of repetition. In this paper, I argue that the first expression of modern historical consciousness through a theory of historical repetition is found in the *Discourses on Livy* of Niccolò Machiavelli.[1] To elucidate how a theory of historical repetition functions philosophically and politically, I bring to bear on my reading of Machiavelli two of the latest and most explicit logics of repetition, namely, those found in Deleuze's *Difference and Repetition* (*DR*) and Derrida's *Of Grammatology*.

Throughout modernity, historical becoming is thematized in connection with the phenomenon of revolution. Revolutionary events are comprehensible only as breaks with the linear unfolding of tradition and authority.[2] Revolutions make for historical beginnings that open the future in the real sense of the term, that is, as a temporal horizon in which what happens can do so without being predetermined by what came before. Conversely, tradition and authority assign to historical beginnings the status of origins that antedate, anticipate, and forestall what is to come. It does not seem so strange, then, that modern revolutions, in order to emancipate the future from the grip of the past, would enact a historical repetition to counteract the effects of origins and wrest the power of beginning from their authority. In short, modern revolutions are those events in which repetition and innovation coincide, in which historical repetition can be said to be *originary* without being *origin*. Walter Benjamin gives the most succinct formulation of such revolutionary praxis: "to Robespierre ancient Rome was a past charged with the time of now which he blasted out of the continuum of history. The French Revolution viewed itself as the return of Rome. It quoted ancient Rome exactly in the way that fashion quotes a costume of the past."[3]

Historical Repetition
and the *Discourses on Livy*

Prior to the French Revolution, the first example of an explicit call to repeat the Roman past in order to detonate its charge in a present ripe for revolutionary change is found in Machiavelli's *Discourses on Livy*, where the desire "to find new modes and orders" and the decision "to take a path as yet untrodden by anyone" coincide with the need to imitate "the examples of the ancients."[4] Motivating Machiavelli's call for imitation is the lack of "true knowledge of histories" found in his contemporaries, whereby "the infinite number who read them (the histories) take pleasure in hearing of the variety of accidents contained in them without thinking of imitating them—as if heaven, sun, elements, men had varied in motion, order, and power from what they were in antiquity."[5] What Machiavelli attacks, then, is precisely the alleged impossibility of "returning" to the ancients—but this is nothing short of the alleged impossibility of destroying the linear temporality of tradition and authority in and through a revolution of the present by bringing up the past. Machiavelli's famous, and famously misread, analogy with the motion of natural objects ("as if heaven, sun, elements, men had varied in motion, order and power from what they were in antiquity") employs the "universal equality" of such motion, that is, the fact that the sun moved for the ancients as it does for the moderns, for the express purpose of destroying the aura, the sense of pure origin and unbridgeable distance, caused by the naturalization of historical situatedness of both ancients and moderns, that so captivates, at the aesthetic level, and so paralyzes, at the political level, his contemporaries.

That one is not dealing with a nostalgic return to the Roman past can be gathered from the text of the *Discourses on Livy* that is itself structured to pit the Roman exemplar against itself. In the first part of the text, Rome functions as origin, which is why the "beginnings" of political orders and the grounds of authority are Machiavelli's subjects of discussion. By the third and last part of the work, Rome functions as repetition, which is why the grounds of political revolution are explicitly addressed in terms of a praxis that "returns to beginnings" the political body. Such ambivalence of the Roman exemplar is possible because Machiavelli describes both authority and revolution as bound up with historical repetition. But whereas authority is constituted by an external relation between repetition and beginning, revolution is constituted by the internal relation of these terms.

Authority, or the External Repetition of Beginnings

As do most thinkers in the main tradition of Western political thought, Machiavelli views the Roman system of authority as the most significant solution to the problem of providing political rule with a stable foundation. Roman *auctoritas* institutionalizes the complementary beliefs that whatever is "first" ought to rule and that ruling is the "ground" of all things. Machiavelli shows that the institution of authority works by positing the beginning of a political form as an absolute origin of that form. The beginning is absolved from historical becoming by requiring that every political action be turned around to (*re-legere, re-ligio*), or repeat, the initial moment of form-giving to carry out and augment the form of rule. All authority (whose root is *augere*, augment) is in this sense fundamentally religious and traditionalist: History is preformed whereas the political forms themselves are prevented from being historicized in turn.[6]

On this account, the effects of authority are possible only on condition that the relation between repetition and beginning is an external one. A beginning functions as an origin whenever it conditions the repetition of "itself" without the act of repeating's being capable of beginning anything new. The externality of the relation between the founding act and its repetition by "other" beginnings simply reinforces the originality of the foundation, effectively granting it its authority. Authority augments the grasp that forms have over events through a process of "continuous constitution-making" or "reconstitutions" whose very continuity is designed to prevent new beginnings.[7]

The external relation between beginning and repetition that constitutes the system of Roman authority also explains the most basic foundational political relation in Western political thinking: one founder gives the form (*agere*) that many citizens augment (*gerere*).[8] For, as Machiavelli explains, "if one individual is capable of ordering, *the thing itself is ordered to last long* not if it remains on the shoulders of one individual but rather *if it remains in the care of many and its maintenance stays with many.*"[9] The political form can last through time only if the "many" are set on supporting it. But this support requires that the "many" be deprived, a priori, of the possibility of beginning something radically new, of breaking with the first beginning, with the foundation, which, on the contrary, they must carry out. Hence when Machiavelli considers the figure of Romulus, the founder of the Roman state, he argues that Romulus had no choice but to kill his brother in view of instituting a senate alongside a king.[10] The founder has to remain alone at the moment of founding the state because in this way the many can sever themselves from the violence inherent in the first establishment of political form so as to accede to the privileged position of a nonviolent legal and routinized form of rule. The founder is "one" always already in relation to those "many," whom the founder's isolation allows to accede to a position of authority, an authority which is followed by the founder itself.

> That Romulus was one of those ["who has the intent to wish to help not himself but the common good"], that he deserves excuse in the deaths of his brother and his partner, and that what he did was for the common good and not for his own ambition, is demonstrated by *his having at once ordered a Senate with which he took counsel and by whose opinion he decided.*[11]

It is difficult to find a clearer formulation of Machiavelli's belief that the system of authority fashions for itself a founder and not vice versa. In Machiavelli's Romulus, the routinization of charisma is at work in the charismatic agent itself since the founder's charismatic origin of rule is retroactively supposed by that political subject who wants the practice of ruling to appear a matter of routine.[12] Machiavelli identifies this political subject, for the sake of whom the founder is required to "have authority alone," as the nobility. In his main theoretical works, Machiavelli always characterizes the nobility as that political subject whose "only desire [is] to rule and command."[13] In the *Discourses on Livy* he shows why this "desire to dominate" needs to find its political organ in the Senate, responsible for the *auctoritas* that assures the well-founded nature of the orders and laws of the state.

Republican Freedom
and Historical Repetition

In Roman society, as in every society, there exists another subject position, that of the people, characterized by the "desire not to be ruled or commanded."[14] Perhaps the most fundamental thesis shared by the *Discourses on Livy* and *The Prince* is that the conflict between these two political subjects determines historical becoming.[15] The uniqueness of the *Discourses on Livy* with respect to all previous and posterior political thinking based on the Roman paradigm consists in its claim that civil life (*vivere civile*) becomes a free life (*vivere libero*) only if politics transcends and transgresses the ideal of well-founded rule, modeled on the Roman system of authority.[16] The claim is made and defended throughout the third part of the *Discourses on Livy*, where it is argued that a political body can live freely only if it undergoes what Machiavelli calls a reduction or return to beginnings (*riduzione verso il principio*).[17] Both in content and in form a "return to beginnings" denotes a revolution.[18] A return is made to the same "origin" of authority, the absolute beginning of founding, in order to strip it of its capacity to impress a political form on historical becoming and instead reveal the radical contingency of all political forms.

Machiavelli condenses the political significance of revolution in the actions of Lucius Junius Brutus, who "begins" the republic by expelling the Roman kings and later killing his own sons for attempting to bring the monarchy back.[19] For Machiavelli, the "sons of Brutus" represent the nobility, for whom "the freedom of the people seemed to have become their slavery."[20] Indeed, the actions of Brutus prepare for the entrance of the people into political life, just as the actions of Romulus prepared for the entrance of the nobles. The emergence of the republic or political freedom occurs as a revolutionary event that breaks with the process of founding the state through the system of authority. Republican freedom "begins" when political life cuts itself off from the absoluteness of beginning that imposes the augmentation of the form of rule as the sole end of political action. The symbolic value of the actions of Brutus is to show that the political body augments its freedom by reducing its forms of rule; it does so by not only getting rid of its head (the monarchy) but also killing "the sons of Brutus" who stand for all those who grow to have privileges (and thus become "noble") under a given political and legal order. The actions of Brutus cut open a political space and time in which neither the founder-legislator nor the nobility (the two subject positions operative in the system of authority) have a place. To clear such a space that cannot be occupied by some as opposed to any others, a space in which the desire for no-rule is offered recognition with and against the desire to rule, is the sole purpose of actions that "reduce to freedom" the political body and its form. One can say that Machiavelli's Brutus is symbolic of the emergence of freedom in an event that reduces the political body to its principle, or returns the body to its beginning, *riduzione verso il principio*,[21] in the sense of reducing (diminishing) the principle of the nobility, that is, the desire to dominate, and thereby discloses a space and time of radical political equality. This is the public space of a plurality or multitude, of the many-without-one: the event of the republic.

For Machiavelli, civil life becomes politically free when the orders and laws, before which the state considers its citizens to be equal, emerge out of a public space where all can equally participate in the making of those laws. Machiavelli redefines the republic as an isonomical space-time from which all political forms must emerge and into which they can be led back or reduced (Ital. *riduzione;* Lat. *reducere:* a leading-back or returning to) whenever the privilege or inequality that a given political form establishes begins to corrupt those who grow under it and are favored by it. Time brings out the inequality implicit in the application of any political form and legal order: *veritas filia temporis.*[22] This is why the reduction to the equality and freedom of the public space can occur only in an event that "returns to beginnings," that is, revolutionizes the political form and counteracts the process of corruption in the political body. Corruption means the reification of inequality that occurs through the fixation and perdurance of any given political form of domination.

Revolution, or the Internal Repetition of Beginnings

When political bodies are returned or reduced to their beginnings, they undergo a movement that is designated as counternatural. Natural bodies, as Machiavelli says, are mortal because they follow "the course that is ordered for them by heaven [*ordinato dal cielo*]," a course that can be completed only by "those things that do not disorder their body [*disordinano il loro corpo*] but maintain it in an orderly way so that either it does not alter or, if it does alter, it is for the sake of its health and not to its harm."[23] The natural course moves bodies across their aionic lifespan, from youth to old age, from vigor to weakness, and in general through the stages of birth, growth, acme, and decadence. Counter to this natural course is the return to beginnings in which political, but not natural, bodies can "renew themselves frequently by means of their orders, or indeed that through some accident outside the said order come to the said renewal. *And it is a thing clearer than light that these bodies do not last if they do not renew themselves.*"[24] The very change of form that is to be avoided by natural bodies falling under the ordainment of the heavens must be embraced by political bodies. Only a body that changes itself by going against the times, that is capable of negating what has been naturalized in it, is able to break with heteronomy and live in freedom.

The idea of a counternatural revolution is already found in Plato's *Statesman*. Discussing the myth of Kronos, Plato says that "the god himself at times joins in conducting this all and making it circle as it goes along, and at times he just lets go, whenever the circuits have obtained the measure of the time appropriate to the all, and it then gets to turn around spontaneously in the contrary direction."[25] The primary consequence of returning the cosmos to its beginning is the interruption and then inversion of the natural course of time so that things originate as old and move forward into youth.[26] Machiavelli's formulation of the return to beginnings is a "citation" from Plato's myth that simultaneously rewrites its political meaning.

Plato believes in the possibility of rebirth and renewal, in a rather transparent allegory of radical political change, in terms of the backward motion of time. Indeed, rebirth can be conceived as a process of moving from old age back to infancy and even of coming back from the dead.[27] But for Plato this kind of rebirth has completely negative connotations: It occurs when Kronos, who oversees everything, suddenly lets go of control. The risk of this counterchronological motion is that all order will be dissolved and "sink into the limitless sea of dissimilarity,"[28] that is, into the space of simulacra, of differences that are not themselves identities. Thus for Plato the revolutionary motion through which order is brought to its degree-zero and a complete renewal becomes possible is itself the manifestation of the "sickness" of the cosmos, by the well-known Platonic identity between health and order.[29]

In the myth of the *Statesman*, Plato situates the possibility of revolution as the mythic event that signals the end of the Golden Age (the age of Kronos) and the transition to the age of human beings (the age of Zeus). The latter is an age in which action can no longer correspond to what the times demand because humans have lost their divine guidance, their *daimones* or "divine shepherds," of which the myth speaks.[30] It is because of this loss that human beings, after the revolution that brings to an end the age of Kronos, must supplement their lack of a truly "political" activity (the capacity to always do the right thing at the right time, which accounts for the state of peace and plenty found in the Golden Age) by the activity of legislation and the empire of the law.[31] In Plato the laws stand as a frail, "human all too human" attempt to contrast the overwhelming power of time over individuals and peoples in the age of Zeus.

Machiavelli is fully aware that the law, and in general the fixity of any political form, cannot withstand the change of times: "if laws vary according to the accidents in a city, its orders never vary, or rarely; this makes new laws insufficient because the orders, which remain fixed, corrupt them."[32] For this reason he brings back the possibility of changing the times, of revolutionary action, that Plato had both opened and closed by placing it at the gate of the mythical Golden Age: "if Rome wished to maintain itself free in corruption, therefore, it was necessary that it should have made new orders, as in the course of its life it had made new laws."[33] The start of the third book of the *Discourses on Livy* makes the point that without change of political form, no political life can survive in time. Revolutionary change is essential to the political body; it is not an inconvenience or indeed something intrinsically negative as it is for classical political philosophy. Machiavelli's thesis marks the beginning of modern political thought: Political life is constituted in and through an essential relation to its historicity. It is a contradiction for a political body to have a "natural" lifespan.

For Machiavelli, and against Plato, the revolutionary and countertemporal motion has a positive value: Without it, no political body could survive historical becoming. The return to beginnings is the name given to the necessity of revolutions when political life gives up on the Platonic dream of a Golden Age in which a "divine shepherd" demonically rules over everything. To renounce this dream is to banish from politics the idea that "ruling is everything," an idea that leaves no space for the expression of the desire for no-rule represented by the people.[34] Similarly to Plato's account, in which time "eats itself up" and thus makes the "elders" into "children," Machiavelli's return to beginnings moves against the grain of history in order to bring something radically new to light, but the innovation in question coincides with an anarchic practice of repetition, with a politics of simulacra.

If my reading of Machiavelli is correct, then it follows that discourses on historical repetition are the privileged sites where modern political thought carries out its critique of foundationalism in politics and expresses its anarchic vocation. If every instance of beginning or origin can be solicited by a practice of returning to beginnings or historical repetition, then it is impossible to establish the difference between what is original (the one, the founder) and what is a copy (the many, the citizens), and consequently also the distinction between copy (the citizens) and simulacrum (the multitude without form; the people), on which every system of authority depends.[35] The theory of return to beginnings subverts the foundational schema according to which one founder must begin to rule by setting up the form, and many citizens must augment the beginning and support the form by carrying out its orders. This subversion perhaps explains why the third book of the *Discourses on Livy* is preoccupied exclusively with developing a theory of political action that requires citizens to learn how to become princes and princes' citizens; that is, a theory that defines politics as a function of the change of positions between self and other.

But the system of authority is not all that founders in the practice of returning to beginnings. In the revolutionary event, the people translate their desire for no-rule back to the site of foundation. The event of no-rule does not itself, however, become a new foundation for whatever new order emerges from it because the people as a plurality, in returning to and occupying the position of the one founder, are thereby released from the obligation that characterized them in the position of the many citizens, namely, the obligation to support and carry out the first orders. For Machiavelli, a revolution may result in new orders but it does not found them. The revolution does not, as such, create an obligation toward these orders. Rather, what becomes fundamental about the revolutionary experience is precisely the experience of not being obligated to (any) order.

After every beginning issues from a return to beginnings, no beginning can function as a pure or ab-solute origin. In a revolutionary event, the traversal of the historical distance from past to present destroys the aura of first beginnings, turning the act of beginning into the only thing, paradoxically, that can be made again and again, that can be reproduced further along, mechanically as it were, and whenever needed. Falling to the wayside are the twin ideas of an irrevocable order of things and of a final revolution. With his theory of historical repetition, Machiavelli shows that a modern political order must have a revolutionary origin that is both unavoidable and radically contingent.

Logics and Politics of Repetition in Derrida and Deleuze

The concept of originary, historical repetition is central to the thought of Deleuze and Derrida, yet the direct connection between repetition and politics in these two thinkers, judging by the most recent commentaries, still remains unthematized.[36] I conclude this essay by attempting to make that connection perspicuous by indicating some points of intersection between the conceptions of repetition found in Derrida and Deleuze and the explicit politics of repetition found in Machiavelli.

A first point of intersection is the essential reference to Plato's myth of Kronos, against which Machiavelli stakes his own modern conception of repetition. This reference explicitly appears in Deleuze's *Difference and Repetition,* where it functions as a foil to his reading of Nietzsche's eternal return.[37] A reference to Plato's myth is also found in Derrida's *Of Grammatology* even though it is never expressly acknowledged or named. Without giving the source of the citation, Derrida reports a remark by Rousseau to the effect that "after every catastrophe" a return "to the presence of the origin" occurs thanks to the intervention of "a divine finger which turns back the order of the world by inclining the axis of the globe on the axis of the universe, thereby making man 'sociable'."[38] The "catastrophe" that is set right again by the "divine finger" signals the Platonic motif. And it is against Plato that Derrida tries to show Rousseau's equivocal recognition of the originary character of the "catastrophe." For such a catastrophe is "the signifier, what represents. Likewise, the signifier is always in itself 'new,' irrespective of the epoch in which it appears. It is the essence of modernity."[39] Derrida reads Rousseau's seemingly antimodern "return to origins" as a reactive recognition of the inescapable "modernity" of representation or repetition, which is thereby essentially linked to the advent of the "new," of historicity itself.

Here emerges a second point of intersection: Modern historical consciousness, for instance in Rousseau, can be understood only in terms of some variant of originary repetition. Derrida's variant turns on the claim that Rousseau's abortive attempt to repeat the origin reveals the originary effects of historical repetition. That repetition can actually give rise to effects of origin is shown through the "logic of supplementarity." For modern repetition must be understood, as Rousseau's failure teaches, both as the way in which an origin (repeatedly) establishes its presence and, conversely, as the way in which an origin never attains presence (and, by the same token, presence never becomes originary). The logic of the supplement maintains both possibilities in play. What makes historical repetition originary for Derrida is its capacity to function both as the condition of possibility and the condition of impossibility for the presence of origin.[40] Historical repetition enters into relation with origin always duplicitously: subverting it by establishing it and establishing it by subverting it.

According to this logic of the supplement, then, something would be inescapably revolutionary about the system of authority and inescapably authoritarian about the event of revolution. Derrida's variant of the logic of repetition accounts for Machiavelli's thesis that repetition is both the condition of possibility of political form (in that it establishes its foundation through a system of authority based on the "external" relation between supplement and origin) and the condition of impossibility of political form (in that it subverts this foundation through the revolutionary "return to beginnings" based on the "internal" relation between supplement and origin which reveals the absence of the latter).

At the same time, we must also acknowledge that Derrida's logic of historical repetition as supplementarity falls short of accounting for one central feature of revolutionary practice. Conceived as a logic of conditions of possibility and impossibility, deconstruction describes the double bind in which the origin stands with respect to its attempt to command temporal unfolding, but it cannot itself open the future as a future, which is precisely a characteristic of every revolutionary event. Perhaps one could even say that if any major development of Derrida's thought occurs since the period *Of Grammatology*, one should look for traces of it in his later, explicit and sustained effort to think historical repetition as revolutionary practice, principally in *Specters of Marx*.

In *Specters of Marx*, Derrida again returns to the problem that haunts him from the beginning: the coincidence of repetition and innovation or alterity. "Repetition and first time: this is perhaps the question of the event as question of the ghost."[41] Why the question of the event must be phrased in terms of "repetition and first time" is by now clear. What may seem at first puzzling is the relation between the event and the ghost or the quasi-phenomenon of "spectrality." The ghost in this text serves two principal functions. At the ontological (or, as Derrida says, "hauntological" level), the ghost is another figure of *restance*, the spectral "presence" of absence in presence and of presence in absence which Derrida has previously named *différance* or supplementarity: It is the ontological pendant to the logic of iterability. But the (non)figure of the ghost comes into its own, so to speak, only in relation to what one may call the problem of the inheritance of revolutionary spirit. For the question posed by *Specters of Marx* is, What of the inheritance of Marxism today? In other terms, How is one to inherit the revolutionary spirit that Marx conjures up? Derrida gives his answer with and against Marx: The revolutionary spirit (*Geist*), if it is to have revolutionary effects, must remain a ghost (*Gespenst*), that is, must resist the temptation to realize itself and instead serve to de-realize (de-reify) the given forms of domination.[42] For Derrida the attempt to maintain the spirit of revolution as a ghost is identical to the project of understanding the phenomenon of revolution as an event, as something that lacks a proper form, essence, and presence. Hence the circular relation between ghost and event: "Each time it is the event itself, a first time is a last time. Altogether other. Staging for the end of history. Let us call it a hauntology."[43]

It remains a question whether, in fact, Derrida's later work successfully displaces that interpretation of repetition in terms of the "quasi-transcendental" condition of possibility and impossibility of transcendental forms in general,[44] which prevents deconstruction from being what Derrida later claims deconstruction to be: nothing short of "Marxist" revolutionary practice.[45] For deconstruction to be revolutionary practice it would have to show that it is no longer the absence of Origin (or, better: the "presence" of Origin, but as radically other to presence) that distracts and sunders internally every present and every presence, as in *Of Gram-*

matology. Instead, as in *Specters of Marx*, this same sundering of the present occurs in and through its being distracted and pulled by an unrealizable future, a to-come that never advenes. In other words, Derrida would have to show that he no longer thinks of the coincidence of "first time" and "repetition" as what is made possible by the action of a past that can never be present, that is, the past as (other) Origin; rather, it is made possible by the action of a future that can never be present. No longer would it be a question of "repeating" away (from) the Origin but rather of "repeating" (into) the future as future.

A year after the publication of *Of Grammatology*, Deleuze published *Difference and Repetition*, in which modern historical repetition is from the start conceived as revolutionary practice. As does Derrida, Deleuze thinks that the concept of originary repetition is the crucial trait of the situation of modernity; but in contrast to Derrida, he casts this situation in terms of the possibility of modern political revolution. He does so for two reasons. First, he understands repetition in opposition to law: "If repetition is possible, it is due to miracle rather than to law. It is against the law: against the similar form and the equivalent content of law. If repetition can be found, even in nature, it is in the name of a power which affirms itself against the law. . . . In every respect, repetition is a transgression. It puts law into question, it denounces its nominal or general character in favor of a more profound and more artistic reality" (*DR* 2–3). Second, Deleuze identifies the essence of morality with habit; consequently, the power to innovate, to break from habit, comes to have that extramoral character that is associated, ever since Machiavelli, with revolutionary action.[46]

The variant of originary repetition that Deleuze defends is the one he associates with Nietzsche's doctrine of the eternal return of the same. Deleuze's interpretation of this doctrine offers a new way of understanding the function of the "return" itself.

> Eternal return cannot mean the return of the Identical because it presupposes a world (that of will to power) in which all previous identities have been abolished and dissolved. Returning is being, but only the being of becoming. The eternal return does not bring back "the same," but returning constitutes the only Same of that which becomes. Returning is the becoming-identical of becoming itself. Returning is thus the only identity, but identity as a secondary power; the identity of difference, the identical which belongs to the different, or turns around the different. Such an identity, produced by difference, is determined a "repetition." (*DR* 43)

Only what becomes also thereby returns; or, better, it returns to the extent that it becomes; it acquires an identity only to the extent that it differs from that which it thus repeats. The possibility of return, or repetition, is like a filter through which passes all becoming. The filter maintains (by assigning it "being" or "identity") only the kind of becoming that makes a difference.

The republican revolutionary event, in which political life "returns to beginning," exemplifies the two meanings of the formula "the identity of the different" through which Deleuze considers originary repetition. The first meaning of the formula can be rendered as follows: in the republican understanding of revolution, "identity" refers to the equality of all, of the plurality, to make the law (isonomy) before which one is to be equal. This isonomic equality of all to make the law requires the recognition of those who are "different" or "unequal" as much as it requires granting them access to the public space because of their "difference" or "inequality." Mere "equality before the law," on the other hand, recognizes those who are "different" only as a function of what makes them "identical" to each other—for instance, their shared status as "citizens." Whereas the equality before the law already presupposes the existence of public space, isonomic equality is the kind of equality or identity that is required to disclose such public spaces. The equality before the law is the equality of already constituted citizens, whereas isonomic equality is the condition of possibility of citizenship. The second meaning of the formula "identity of the different" is that an "identity" is assignable only on condition that a radical change and subversion of a previous identity has occurred. As I showed previously, for Machiavelli no revolutionary event exists otherwise than through the becoming-princes of citizens and the becoming-citizens of princes.

But what kind of "becoming" owes its paradoxical identity to its power to "make a difference"? What does such an event of difference look like? For Deleuze, radical innovation occurs only if one can change the times in an event that is not predetermined by any form of change. Indeed, the change of times is revolutionary precisely because it contains in itself the possibility of emergence and dehiscence of form as such. In what is perhaps the central passage of *Difference and Repetition,* Deleuze says that any event of revolution must contain time "as a totality," in its past, present, and futural dimensions. "The idea of a totality of time must be understood as follows: the caesura, of whatever kind, must be determined in the image of a unique and tremendous event, an act which is adequate to time as a whole" (*DR* 89). Deleuze explicitly understands historical repetition as the event of time's temporalization, the opposite of time as an empty continuum in which events happen. And he does so by understanding repetition as a revolutionary act, in ways that, at least in my opinion, seem to match with the modes in which Machiavelli's theory of return to beginnings thematize the thoroughgoing historicity of form.

Repetition is constitutive of the past because, as Deleuze says, "there is always a time at which the imagined act is supposed 'too big for me.' This defines a priori the past or the before" (*DR* 89). In the *Discourses on Livy* Roman history is also described at first as a function of an unrepeatable origin, of founding acts which are "supposed [to be] 'too big for me'" and that serve to model political action as the maintenance of pregiven forms and habits that must be passed down in time. This is the mode of experiencing historical distance that corresponds to the system of authority and to Romulus as its mythical founder.

Repetition is constitutive of the present as "the second time, which relates to the caesura itself . . . the present of metamorphosis, a becoming-equal to the act and a doubling of the self, and the projection of an ideal self in the image of the act" (*DR* 89). The theory of return to beginnings in the *Discourses on Livy* describes Roman history as a function of breaks with the tradition, of events in which political life transcends the process of maintaining political form and aims at radically changing that form. This mode of experiencing historical distance corresponds to the symbolic value of Brutus and the emergence of the republic in a "present of metamorphosis, a becoming-equal to the act and a doubling of the self," in which the very division between founders and citizens, those who initiate orders and those who carry them out, is suspended.

Last, repetition opens the future as a future in "the third time, [when] the event and the act possess a secret coherence which excludes that of the self; [when] they turn back against the self which has become their equal and smash it to pieces, as though the bearer of the new world were carried away and dispersed by the shock of the multiplicity to which it gives birth" (*DR* 89). Machiavelli's return to beginnings describes Roman history as a function of the event-like, contingent character of both the authoritarian founding of political form and the revolutionary subversion of its foundation. In this mode of experiencing historical distance, history itself, the difference between past and present, is reoriented toward the dimension of the future as a future, toward that event which opens historical becoming from the outside and keeps history open ended.

The early Deleuze and the late Derrida, therefore, coincide on this basic point: Only if the revolutionary event can be shown to contain all time can the future be disclosed as future. The temporal ekstases of past, present, and future must be understood from the praxis of revolutionary events and not the other way around; this is true because only if time itself is an eventuality can a future as future-to-come advene. The kind of politics that is to articulate this futural mode of originary repetition, the only mode of repetition that can give history a future, remains the decisive topic of investigation for both Derrida and Deleuze. At the beginning of modernity, Machiavelli sketched the minimal requirements of a politics of the future: the irruption of the people, the plurality without unity, into political life in order to question the legitimacy of rule from the standpoint of no-rule. Machiavelli formulates this irruption as the event in which citizens become princes and princes citizens, the event in which every political position can be indiscriminately occupied. To consider the future of democracy from the bases established by Derrida and Deleuze seems to necessitate a return—before Nietzsche or Marx or Rousseau—to Machiavelli.

Notes

1. For all matters pertaining to my interpretation of Machiavelli in this essay, I take the liberty to refer the reader to the extended discussion found in my *Between Form and Event: Machiavelli's Theory of Political Freedom* (Dordrecht: Kluwer, 2000).

2. On the "pathos of novelty" in modern revolutions, see Hannah Arendt, *On Revolution* (London: Penguin, 1990), chapter 1.

3. Walter Benjamin, *Über den Begriff der Geschichte,* thesis XIV, in *Gesammelte Schriften* (Frankfurt: Suhrkamp, 1974–89), vol.VII.

4. Niccolò Machiavelli, *Discourses on Livy* (Chicago: University of Chicago Press, 1996), I, Preface. For the idea that the Renaissance, and in particular Machiavelli's return to the ancients, was the matrix of modern revolutionary thinking, see Pocock: "It can be shown that the American Revolution and Constitution in some sense form the last act of the civic Renaissance." (J.G.A. Pocock, *The Machiavellian Moment* [Princeton: Princeton University Press, 1975], 462.)

5. Machiavelli, *Discourses on Livy,* I, Preface.

6. Arendt speaks of the Roman senate as an institution in which one finds a "presence" of the founders "and with them the spirit of foundation was present, the beginning, the principium and principle, of those *res gestae* which from then on formed the history of the people of Rome." (Arendt, *On Revolution,* 200). "The very coincidence of authority, tradition, and religion, all three simultaneously springing from the act of foundation, was the backbone of Roman history from beginning to end." (Ibid., 201). See also on the Roman sense of *religio* as *relegere,* Emile Benveniste, *Indo-European Language and Society* (London: Faber and Faber, 1973), 521; and Jacques Derrida, "Faith and Knowledge: the Two Sources of 'Religion' at the Limits of Reason Alone" in *Religion,* eds. Jacques Derrida and Gianni Vattimo (London: Polity Press, 1998), 36–7.

7. Arendt, *On Revolution,* 200, 208. See also 202: "The very concept of Roman authority suggests that the act of foundation inevitably develops its own stability and permanence, and authority in this context is nothing more or less than a kind of necessary 'augmentation' by virtue of which all innovations and changes remain tied back to the foundation which, at the same time, they augment and increase."

8. See the discussion of this political relation in Plato found in Hannah Arendt, *The Human Condition* (Chicago: University of Chicago Press, 1958), 222 ff.

9. Machiavelli, *Discourses on Livy*, I, 9. Emphasis mine.

10. *Ibid.*: "So a prudent orderer of a republic, who has the intent to wish to help not himself but the common good, not for his own succession but for the common fatherland, should contrive to have authority alone; nor will a wise understanding ever reprove anyone for any extraordinary action that he uses to order a kingdom or constitute a republic. It is very suitable that when the deed accuses him, the effect excuses him; and when the effect is good, as was that of Romulus, it will always excuse the deed" (emphasis mine).

11. *Ibid.* Emphasis mine.

12. On the routinization of charisma, see Max Weber, *Economy and Society* (Berkeley: University of California Press, 1978), 1121–22. In these passages Weber suggests that, in spite of their formal opposition, charisma and the process of routinization are at bottom connected by a common "religious" character: "The two basically antagonistic forces of charisma and tradition regularly merge with one another. . . . Both charisma and tradition rest on a sense of loyalty and obligation which always has a religious aura" (ibid.).

13. Machiavelli, *Discourses on Livy*, I, 5; idem, *The Prince*, IX.

14. *Ibid.*

15. *Ibid.*, 4–6.

16. For an excellent discussion of the Roman and neo-roman theories of the state, see Quentin Skinner, *Liberty before Liberalism* (Cambridge: Cambridge University Press, 1998).

17. Machiavelli, *Discourses on Livy*, III, 1.

18. For other interpretations of Machiavelli's theory of "return to beginnings" as a theory of revolution, see Claude Lefort, *Le travail de l'oeuvre Machiavel* (Paris: Gallimard, 1972) and Antonio Negri, *Insurgencies: Constituent Power and the Modern State* (Minneapolis: University of Minnesota Press, 1999).

19. See Livy, *Ab urbe condita*, I, 58–60; II, 1–5.

20. Machiavelli, *Discourses on Livy*, III, 1.

21. *Ibid.*

22. "When any malignity remains hidden for a time, this proceeds from a hidden cause, which is not recognized because no contrary experience has been seen. But time, which they say is the father of every truth, exposes it later" (ibid., I, 3).

23. Machiavelli, *Discourses on Livy*, III, 1.

24. *Ibid.* Emphasis mine.

25. Plato, *Statesman* (Chicago: University of Chicago Press, 1984), 269d–270e.

26. "Many different circumstances, marvelous and strange, coincide, *but here is the greatest one and a consequence of the unwinding at that time of the all whenever it goes into the turn that's contrary to the one which obtains at present. . . . First of all, the age, which each and every animal had, came to a halt,* and everything that was mortal stopped its advance toward looking older, *but, in altering, each genus grew back in the contrary direction, younger as it were and suppler. . . .* And from that point on they began to wither away and vanish utterly and completely" (Plato, *Statesman*, 270d–e). Emphasis mine.

27. "The elders go into the nature of the child and, on the other hand, it is from the dead, who lie in the earth, that they get put together there once more and live again" (Plato, *Statesman*, 271b–c).

28. Plato, *Statesman*, 274d.

29. For this reason, Kronos "once more takes his seat at its rudder, and by twisting round of the things diseased and sprung in the former circuit by itself, he makes it a cosmos and in correcting it, works it up into something deathless and ageless" (Plato, *Statesman*, 273d–e).

30. Plato, *Statesman*, 271d–e.

31. *Ibid.*, 292a–302b4.

32. Machiavelli, *Discourses on Livy*, I, 18.

33. *Ibid.*

34. For the expression of the "divine shepherd," see Plato, *Statesman*, 275c. On the use of *daimones* to rule over all living things, see ibid., 271d–e. In this sense, Machiavelli does not think of revolutions as a process that will bring the world back to the purity of archaic origins, to the "Golden Age" of Kronos, as is often thought in the interpretations of this myth in the context of modern revolutions. See Hannah Arendt, *On Revolution*, 205–211 for another reading of the myth.

35. On the concept of the simulacrum, I refer to the discussion in Gilles Deleuze, *Logic of Sense* (New York: Columbia University Press, 1990).

36. See Paul Patton, *Deleuze and the Political* (London: Routledge, 2000) and Richard Beardsworth, *Derrida and the Political* (London: Routledge, 1996). Both of these otherwise noteworthy works miss the importance of the problem of historical repetition for the political thought of Deleuze and Derrida.

37. Deleuze, *Difference and Repetition* (New York: Columbia University Press, 1994), 59–62; hereafter *DR*.

38. "Le discours et les questions de Rousseau ne sont possibles qu'à anticiper une re-naissance ou une réactivation de l'origine. La re-naissance, la résurrection ou le reveil se réapproprient toujours, dans leur fugitive instance, la plénitude de la présence revenant à soi. Ce retour à la présence de l'origine se produit après chaque catastrophe dans la mesure du moins où elle renverse l'ordre de la vie sans le détruire. Après qu'un doigt divin eut renversé l'ordre du monde en inclinant l'axe du globe sur l'axe de l'univers et eut ainsi voulu que 'l'homme fut sociable,' la fete autour du point d'eau est possible et le plaisir est immédiatement présent au désir." Derrida, *De la Grammatologie* (Paris: Editions de Minuit, 1967), 437 ff.

39. Derrida, *De la Grammatologie*, 418.

40. "Et il ya une nécessité fatale, inscrite dans le fonctionnement meme du signe, à ce que le substitut fasse oublier sa fonction de vicariance et se fasse passser pour la plénitude d'une parole dont il ne fait que suppléer la carence et l'infirmité. Car le concept de supplément . . . abrite en lui deuz significations dont la cohabitation est aussi étrange que nécessaire. Le supplément s'ajoute, il est un surplus, une plénitude enrichissant une autre plénitude. . . . Il cumule et accumule la présence. . . . Mais le supplément supplée. Il ne s'ajoute que pour remplacer. Il intervient ou s'insinue à-la-place-de; s'il comble, c'est comme on comble un vide" (Derrida, *De la Grammatologie*, 208).

41. Jacques Derrida, *Specters of Marx* (New York: Routledge, 1994), 10.

42. And thereby also the figures of the "New World Order"; hence the reason for Derrida's polemic with Fukuyama, which runs throughout *Specters of Marx.*

43. Derrida, *Specters of Marx,* 10.

44. For the most persuasive reading of the practice of deconstruction in these "quasi-transcendental" terms, see Rodolphe Gasché, *The Tain of the Mirror* (Cambridge: Harvard University Press, 1986).

45. "This attempted radicalization of Marxism called deconstruction" (Derrida, *Specters of Marx,* 92).

46. For Deleuze, the application of the moral law exhibits the generality of "habit as second nature. . . . It is the form of habit . . . which is essentially moral or has the form of the good" (*Difference and Repetition,* 4).

Truth and Evidence in Descartes and Levinas

Leslie MacAvoy

The objective of Levinas's philosophy is to describe and establish the priority of an ethical subjectivity that is constituted in responsibility for the Other. Crucial to his position is the claim that such a subjectivity is not self-constituting but is constituted in subjection to the Other who is "exterior" to the subject and who makes a claim on the subject's freedom. So, against a tradition that promotes the autonomy of subjects, Levinas emphasizes a subjectivity founded on heteronomy.

To establish this point, Levinas explores and develops possibilities embedded in the work of important figures in the philosophical tradition. This method is exemplified in the well-documented reading of Descartes in which Levinas appropriates Descartes' idea of the infinite.[1] This idea is a moment of heteronomy which not only disrupts the tradition's reading of Descartes as an unambiguous thinker of autonomy but also runs counter to Descartes' own efforts to establish the autonomy of the subject, a concern which is clearly manifest in his discussion of truth. Levinas tries to move beyond Descartes' position by unfolding the possibility of a heteronomous subjectivity that is suggested by Descartes' idea of the infinite but which Descartes himself does not develop. This paper explores how Levinas, in his effort to "heteronomize" subjectivity, introduces elements of heteronomy into Descartes' conception of truth. In my discussion, I focus largely, although not exclusively, on Levinas's earlier thought—that is, the thought which culminates in *Totality and Infinity* (*TI*)[2]—because this is where the engagement with Descartes is most pronounced.

In "Philosophy and the Idea of Infinity" ("PII"), Levinas claims that philosophy tends to characterize the pursuit of truth in two manners.[3] The first characterization focuses on the subject's relation to a reality which lies beyond it or transcends it. If that of which knowledge is to be obtained is external to me, then my knowledge of it must involve experience, so truth becomes a matter of experience. As Levinas puts it: "Truth would thus designate the outcome of a movement that leaves a world that is intimate and familiar . . . and goes toward the stranger, toward a beyond" ("PII" 47). Truth is a consequence of the subject's relation to a reality that outstrips its own. This reality might refer not only to the external, physical world of particular things but also a metaphysical, ideal world, for example, a world of physical laws or of Platonic forms ("PII" 47). In such cases, truth could also be considered an experience of the ideal. Philosophy that is concerned with the ideal is metaphysics, and the tendency which guides such philosophy is called heteronomy because it construes truth as experience in relation to the Other or the transcendent.

The second characterization emphasizes that truth lies not in a relation to the other but in an act in which one freely judges that something is true. Levinas notes that "truth also means the free adherence to a proposition, the outcome of a free research. The freedom of the investigator, the thinker on whom no constraint weighs, is expressed in truth" ("PII" 47–48). Judgments that are made freely are considered to be unbiased or true because they are not made under conditions of interference. Such conditions include interference not only from or by other people but also with the proper functioning of the rational faculty by factors within the subject, such as passion or self-interest. In other words, thought that is not led astray leads to a clarity of apprehension which ensures true judgments. Objects are brought into view, grasped, and understood according to the laws of thought. Levinas calls this philosophical tendency autonomy because it stresses the subject's liberation from the influence of the other and the subject's mastery of the other in that objects are known when they are made to conform to the laws of thought located in subjectivity.

As described in "PII," heteronomy and autonomy can be considered modes of epistemological subjectivity because each offers a picture of how a subject can be said to "have" knowledge and how that knowledge can be considered true. On the one hand, truth is said to lie in laws of reason and thought that only relations with the Other can interfere with and corrupt. In this case, pursuit of truth demands independence and self-sufficiency. Levinas maintains that this tendency toward autonomy, which he considers to entail a "*reduction of the other to the same*" ("PII" 48), is predominant in the western philosophical tradition. On the other hand, truth might lie in heteronomy. It might be the experience of the ideal and the transcendent that exist exterior to the subject and with which the subject may enter into relation.

Clearly, however, Levinas is concerned not only with the epistemological implications of heteronomy and autonomy but also with these as modes of ethical subjectivity. His choice of terminology invites thoughts of Kant's distinction and the ends toward which he puts it in his moral philosophy. For Kant, ethical subjectivity is fulfilled in autonomy because in autonomy the subject is self-legislating, acting in conformity with the moral law as given by reason. Moral or ethical autonomy, then, is connected to rational autonomy or autonomy of thought. Levinas draws attention to heteronomy and autonomy in the epistemological sense in order to make the important point that our metaphysical and epistemological accounts of the subject are bound up with our ethical accounts of the subject. Moreover, Levinas's philosophical aim is generally to trouble the discourse on autonomy. He often argues that autonomy is grounded in something more primordial, and he takes pains to explore the phenomenon of heteronomy and the role it may play in constituting subjectivity.[4] The emphasis that Levinas places on heteronomy, then, should be seen to have consequences for our thinking about ethical subjectivity; indeed, it is motivated by such concerns.[5] In this regard, Levinas is mapping out a position that counters Kant.

Here, however, we are primarily concerned with Levinas's relation to Descartes, who, along with Plato and Husserl, is a thinker whose work is generally considered to exemplify autonomy. Levinas tends to read these philosophers in order to pinpoint moments of heteronomy in their texts and arguments, thereby isolating points of ambiguity from which alternate philosophical possibilities might be developed.

In reading Descartes' *Meditations,* for example, he draws attention to how the subject is concerned above all not to admit the truth of that of which it is not completely certain. Methodological doubt discourages the subject from accepting the truth of what is given in sense perception, and that which is grasped by the mind alone is taken to be self-evident and certain. This reliance on what can be grasped indubitably in thought is a marker for autonomy, and Levinas comments on this aspect of Descartes' thought when he writes that "when Descartes comes to discern an acquiescence of the will in even the most rational truth, he not only explains the possibility of error, but sets up reason as an ego and truth as dependent on a movement that is free, and thus sovereign and justified" ("PII" 50). Although Levinas views Descartes primarily as a thinker of autonomy, he sees potential in the idea of the infinite for undermining the autonomy for which Descartes argues. When the subject thinks the infinite, it attempts to think more than it is able to think because the finite subject's idea of the infinite can never be adequate to the infinite itself (*TI* 49–50; "PII" 53–54). Thus, the infinite can never be comprehended, and the fact that we have the idea shows that we are not alone and implies that we are not wholly sovereign because we are not capable of producing the idea ourselves. Moreover, in Descartes' thought the possibility of knowledge itself rests on this idea and, more important, on the other of whom it is an idea. For Levinas, then, the idea of the infinite challenges the autonomy of the subject and suggests its heteronomy.

The force of this point, however, does not appear to be reflected in Descartes' claims regarding truth in relation to subjectivity in the *Meditations*, where the discussion is primarily oriented toward securing the possibility of knowledge by establishing the autonomy of the subject. Descartes most explicitly discusses truth in the Fourth Meditation. By this stage in the argument, he has established that God exists and that he is not a deceiver. Now that we are assured that the faculty of judgment is not inherently flawed, we must ask how false judgment is possible. It is explained that each judgment consists of an act of understanding through which an idea is presented to consciousness and an act of will in which this presentation is affirmed or denied. Since the faculty of understanding is limited whereas the capacity to will is unlimited, we sometimes affirm or deny that which we do not completely understand, and false judgment results. True judgment occurs when the will is guided by the understanding, and since this understanding is the subject's own, truth in this case is guaranteed through a kind of self-control or self-mastery.

If understanding guides the will, then we need to know when we understand something, and the criterion that Descartes provides is clear and distinct perception.[6] One grasps the truth of the thing when it is clearly and distinctly perceived because only in this case does one grasp what the thing is; only in this case is the thing self-evident. Since one is justified in affirming or denying the truth of some state of affairs only if one grasps that state of affairs clearly with the understanding, the truth of understanding must underlie the truth of judgment. This implies that the truth of judgment, which is a truth asserted of objective states of affairs, is grounded in the clarity of the subject's mental perception. Both the truth of judgment and the truth of understanding are bound up with the autonomous activity of the rational subject. Descartes uses the idea of the infinite to ensure the possibility of that autonomous activity, but he does not explore the consequences of this idea for the notion of truth.

If clear and distinct perception can be construed as an *experience* of truth in the subject, then the possibility emerges of rethinking this idea in accordance with the tendency toward heteronomy. One might think that Husserl moves in this direction when he construes clear and distinct perception in terms of the notion of evidence in the *Cartesian Meditations*. To speak of truth as evidence is to emphasize the *experiential* aspect of that truth. Evidence consists in experiences in which the thing is present in itself,[7] and in Husserl's view, for something to provide evidence it must confirm an intention which one already had. This idea is further elaborated in *Logical Investigations*.[8] That something acts as evidence indicates that the subject has a prior intentional orientation that is fulfilled or adequated by the object given. In other words, objects intended in acts of signification are attested to by objects given in acts of intuition. The object given in intuition acts as evidence for the object intended. Truth is experienced in the adequation that results. In Husserl's view, evidence grounds judgments because the truth of judgments depends upon their expressing the things themselves, but this cannot be determined without evidence.

In recasting clear and distinct perception as evidence, Husserl emphasizes the *intuitive* dimension of the experience of truth. But evidence remains, as was true for Descartes, primarily *self*-evidence. The self-evidence of truth in both thinkers remains a marker of autonomy; it guarantees that one's understanding is not prejudiced or corrupted by outside influences. Levinas rejects Husserl's account of the experience of truth because it makes that experience dependent upon the subject's intentional orientation, which the object either does or does not fulfill. Evidence can only ever satisfy or fail to satisfy the subject's intentional expectation. It does not throw that expectation into question.[9]

Nevertheless, the notion of evidence is suggestive, and in Levinas's hands the concept undergoes a transformation which is important to his own account of truth. As characterized so far, evidence is proof that justifies judgments which express knowledge claims. But as Levinas puts it in *TI*: "We may also say that to know is to justify, making intervene, by analogy with the moral order, the notion of justice" (*TI* 82). The interpolation of justice into a discussion of knowledge and truth is not surprising, given the relationship Levinas is interested in establishing between ethical and epistemological accounts of subjectivity. Moreover, Levinas contends that truth *presupposes* justice (*TI* 90–101), so to fully address the question of truth in relation to subjectivity we cannot limit ourselves to the connection between truth and knowledge; we must ask about the place of truth in ethics. In such a context, evidence takes on a special meaning, for evidence is something one gives as testimony at a trial. Levinas employs the imagery of the trial to great rhetorical effect in his work (cf. *TI* 240–247). The court is the place of judgment where individuals who have been accused must face their accusers and must justify themselves before the judge, jury, or both. Evidence is presented: Those accused must answer for their actions; witnesses may be brought forward to testify. One is pledged to speak nothing but the truth because the witness that one bears to events is necessary to establishing the facts so that a verdict may be made. Sincerity or speaking truly is consequently necessary to the rendering of true judgments and therefore also to the rendering of justice.

Evidence in this framework differs from that of Husserl's in two important respects. First, to give evidence is to give something that is not self-evident. The truth of evidence is not apparent. One's belief that the evidence is true depends upon one's belief in the honesty of the one who gives it. Second, evidence does not affirm or confirm anything that we already had in mind. It is meant to establish the facts of a case: Evidence proposes the world.

I argue that rethinking evidence in this ethical or juridical context allows Levinas to introduce an intersubjective dimension to the two moments of truth identified in the Cartesian account. This intersubjective dimension disrupts the autonomy that permeates that account and allows Levinas to develop the possibility of heteronomy in these two moments. For Descartes, the truth of objective states of affairs is established through judgment in which the will is guided by the understanding. There are two important aspects to this claim. First, the will is not free to will whatever it pleases. Its spontaneity is curtailed by the understanding, therefore the truth of judgment is guaranteed through a kind of self-critique by the understanding. Second, for this self-critique to work, the understanding itself must be true, and as I have said this entails clear and distinct perception. Thus, the subject must truly apprehend the thing itself before passing judgment on it and thereby asserting its objective truth. Two moments of truth can be identified here: an objective moment in which a claim is made concerning some state of affairs which is asserted as true, and a subjective moment which involves the apprehension of evidence in virtue of which the truth of that state of affairs is grasped. The subjective moment provides the criterion for the objective moment. As discussed previously, Descartes describes both moments in terms of autonomy.

Levinas employs the insights drawn from consideration of evidence as testimony to assist him in showing that truth is established heteronomously in relation to the other. The objective moment is located in the attestations of one person to another concerning some state of affairs. The objectivity of this state of affairs is established intersubjectively in that objectivity is accomplished in language through one person's speaking to another. Moreover, the critique to which such claims are submitted at this stage is not self-critique, as in Descartes, because the evidence is not given to oneself, it is given to another, and the evidence is not *self*-evident to the Other. Thus, the truth of judgments based on the evidence given depends in turn upon the truth of the evidence provided and the good faith participation of the one who testifies. In other words, it depends upon a truthfulness in the subject. The truth of evidence for Descartes is guaranteed by self-critique and the belief that the subject's perception, as long as it is clear and distinct, cannot be wrong. In Levinas's new formulation, matters are complicated by the fact that evidence is given intersubjectively and not intrasubjectively; the truth of evidence relies to a much greater degree on the goodness of the witness. But such goodness requires that the subject understands its ethical responsibility through understanding that it is responsible before the infinite. Thus, the subjective moment of truth is also established in relation to the other—this time the other as the infinite or transcendent. These two moments of truth—the objective one in which a state of affairs is asserted to be true, and the subjective one in which the one who so asserts speaks truly—occur heteronomously in Levinas's formulation.

Let me fill this sketch in a bit. According to the position in *TI*, truth requires separation, or the differentiation between interiority and exteriority, because there is no truth without the possibility of error, and that possibility is guaranteed only if that which one would know is beyond oneself (*TI* 60–61). The pursuit of knowledge, then, consists in a movement beyond oneself toward the other. Truth is a particular modality of the relation between this interiority and exteriority—between the same and the other (*TI* 64).

We often characterize knowledge and truth as pertaining to the subject's grasp or comprehension of the object. This characterization suggests that what is known, which is initially situated in exteriority, is drawn into the interiority of the subject. Levinas explicitly challenges this formulation by suggesting that truth pertains more to the relation between the interiority of the subject and the exteriority of what lies beyond the subject and which the subject desires to know. That which is exterior always presents itself as being exterior, as having a depth that outstrips the content of what is presented. It withdraws or withholds itself; it appears as beyond the interiority of the subject.[10]

If truth is the experience of the relation with exteriority (perhaps even an experience of exteriority in which the exteriority of the other is preserved), then a relation of heteronomy between interiority and exteriority is required for truth. Levinas insists that the distance between the two not be reduced. Nevertheless there is contact between interiority and exteriority. But how is this irreducible, seemingly untraversible distance traversed? Through language. Truth, we are told, rests on language.[11] While it is customary to say that truth is linked to propositions, this does not exhaust what Levinas has in mind in linking truth and language. Propositions are linguistic forms that signify something by thematizing or objectifying it. But propositions, Levinas says, are proposed by someone; they are spoken or uttered by a speaker. There are two important consequences of this claim. The first pertains to the idea that propositions are to be thought of as utterances. Ordinarily one would say that a proposition expresses an objective state of affairs because it represents that state of affairs. So, one can verify the truth of a proposition by looking for a correspondence between the content it expresses and the "objective external world." But Levinas maintains that "the world is *offered* in the language of the other; it is borne by propositions" (*TI* 92, my emphasis), and that means that propositions do not *represent* the world. The proposition is a sign or a string of signs issued by one who signifies. The object of the sign is its meaning—what the signifier meant in speaking. Objectivity is produced through the signification that occurs in propositions. Levinas claims that objectivity is "*posited* in a discourse, in a *conversation* which *proposes* the world" (*TI* 96). So, the objectivity of what is expressed in a proposition does not consist in its reference to an objective external world. Objectivity consists in the positing of something as an object in an utterance; through expression something is thematized and thus rendered objective.[12] This idea can be rephrased in the language of *OTB:* propositions are a kind of "saying" with reference to which their content or object is a "said." Consequently, propositions resemble statements of evidence given in the juridical context which are used to establish the facts of a case. Statements in which evidence is given do not represent a special type of proposition; rather, they exemplify qualities typical of all propositions.

The second important consequence of the insight that propositions are proposed by a speaker pertains to the signifier or speaker who is the source of the sign and who signifies by it. A proposition does not signify only what it thematizes. The signs that are given also signify the speaker without thereby thematizing or objectively giving the speaker him or herself (*TI* 96). In this manner, persons are manifest in language through speaking but are manifest as exterior. The claim that propositions are utterances of a speaker through which the world is proposed makes the question of the truth of these propositions considerably more complicated. If their truth cannot be determined by referring them to an objective external world, then their truth needs to be determined by referring them back to the speaker. A proposition is true if the one who utters it speaks the truth. But because the Other is exterior to us and is not given in the proposition, we do not have access to what is required to ascertain whether the speaker does speak the truth, and a real possibility of duplicity presents itself. What is given—what is said or expressed—may or may not be true. While for Descartes a proposition is true if it reflects what the understanding grasps, in this case, we are dealing with something that the understanding *cannot* grasp. So, we have to take the speaker at his or her word. The speaker stands in the position of a witness whose word must be taken.

Paradoxically, however, the presence of the speaker, who in being beyond our epistemological grasp makes us doubt the truth of what is said, also provides us with what is required to restore our confidence. We believe that the speaker is sincere in speaking because the speaker *attends* what is said and stands ready to be questioned and to respond to those questions. In speaking, the speaker signifies his or her presence and thus indicates that he or she is there to stand by what has been said and to vouch for it. According to Levinas, "speech is always a taking up again of what was a simple sign cast forth by it, an ever renewed promise to clarify what was obscure in the utterance" (*TI* 97). Thus, what the speaker says can be submitted to critique, or, if you like, to cross-examination, and one pays attention to the Other by attending to what is said. Truth thus involves an ethical relation, a situation in which one person faces another. The face-to-face approach in conversation wherein one speaks sincerely is justice because such an exchange is truthful and attests to the ethical character of those involved.[13]

So, the speaker's uttering of a proposition is analogous to a witness's giving of evidence, and this point is important for rethinking the objective moment of truth in terms of heteronomy. Propositions—claims regarding what is objectively true—are expressed by speakers to Others, and those statements may be subjected to critique. What is objectively true now is not a judgment made intrasubjectively but intersubjectively. The heteronomy involved here is apparent when it is seen that ultimately those to whom evidence is given must rely upon the sincerity of the speaker because one can never be certain that the speaker speaks the truth. One *trusts* that the speaker does, but in the final analysis one does not *know*.

But how is the truthfulness of the subject to be established? One could argue that the possibility of critique guarantees this truth because the speaker may be called upon to defend what she or he says. But I am not sure that this is sufficient to ensure that the speaker tells the truth, for an artful liar will be able to respond in a manner consistent with the original falsehood. What is really required to guarantee the truth of what is said is the sincerity of the subject, and this requires the subject to have grasped its ethical responsibility, which is disclosed in the face to face. Levinas never says how the truthfulness of one person can be established by another. Indeed, this is something one never can establish because of the exteriority of the Other. Moreover, whereas Levinas develops at length the possibility of how one can be held accountable, he is less interested in providing an account of reciprocity in which the Other's accountability is discussed.[14] Nevertheless, I think the question does make sense because it is relevant to something with which Levinas is concerned, namely, why I should ever speak sincerely. Levinas's claims regarding the asymmetrical relation between myself and the Other do not preclude my making the valid inference that if the Other's mental states are inaccessible to me, then my mental states are inaccessible to the Other. In other words, if I cannot know that the Other tells the truth, then the Other cannot know whether I tell the truth. Thus, if I am a good liar, I can deceive the Other. Why shouldn't I bear false witness? Why should I speak truly? In unpacking the answers to these questions, we will illuminate the subjective moment of truth in Levinas's reformulation.

Clearly, Levinas's response will be that one has an ethical responsibility not to lie. This responsibility is experienced as a constraint on one's spontaneous free activity. In understanding oneself as an ethical subject, one understands that one is not free to do whatever one wills. But the constraint that one experiences here is not like the restraint of understanding on the will that Descartes describes, nor is it like the constraint that Kant says dictates of reason such as the categorical imperative place upon the will of imperfectly rational humanity. Such restraints are placed by reason and our rational nature upon our subjective inclinations; they exemplify autonomy. Levinas would say that these are instances of self-control or self-mastery. The will is curtailed by me, not by something transcendent and beyond me.

Ethical responsibility for Levinas is grounded heteronomously in the relation to the Other. According to the idea of the face to face developed in the early works, one experiences the ethical as something to which one is subjected before the Other. One should be cautious, however, of thinking that the law to which one finds oneself subjected is the law of the other person, for such a criterion permits submission to arbitrary imperatives. The command of the Other is not necessarily a command to act in accordance with the good. The law to which one submits oneself must be construed as a higher law. In other words, I am responsible for the Other, and when I speak I must respond to the Other, but ultimately I am responsible to the infinite. The ethical imperative is to be good, and this means experiencing the constraint that the good places upon oneself. But Levinas thinks, along with Plato, that the good is transcendent and an ideal. It is beyond me, and that is why I must strive to reach it. If it were already in me, then I would neither need to strive for it nor would I desire it. Being in a relation with the good is being in a relation with the other. It is heteronomy. The idea of the face to face adds another aspect of heteronomy to the picture in that the ethical imperative announces itself in the relation to the Other. In fact, the general tenor of Levinas's text suggests that the responsibility through which ethical subjectivity is born is experienced and announced in the face to face.

So, the ethical imperative to take up one's ethical responsibility—to be ethical—is announced heteronomously in the relation with the Other. And the law to which one is to submit oneself in order to establish one's truth and goodness is not the law of the other person, but of the good. Yet since the good is itself transcendent and ideal, it, too, is other, and the subjectivity through which goodness and truth are achieved is consequently heteronomous.

Levinas expands on the view that the truth of the subject is established heteronomously with reference to a higher other in "The Truth of Disclosure and the Truth of Testimony" ("TDTT").[15] In this essay Levinas elaborates on the truth of speaking or of signifying. If we were to locate truth in disclosure, then we would focus on what is given or disclosed in the event of disclosure. Within such a framework, testimony would consist in the "confession of some knowledge or of an experience by a subject" ("TDTT" 100), and this would make testimony about what is thematized in it. But Levinas asks whether testimony might signify something other than a content or a said ("TDTT" 101). Consistent with his claims in *TI* and *OTB*, Levinas maintains that testimony signifies the saying of the one who gives the testimony. Testimony signifies beyond its content; speaking to the Other, which might otherwise be construed as a banal transmission of words, is shot through with ethical significance. It signifies that one *is for* the Other ("TDTT" 102). That one is for the other has a double signification. On the one hand, and perhaps most obviously, it means that one is responsible for the other, that one is to care for the Other. This is in contrast to the idea of being selfish or "out for oneself" (*OTB* 111). On the other hand, the "one-for-the-other" is also meaning itself because it is the very signifyingness of meaning ("TDTT" 102). Such a claim sounds obscure until we realize that Levinas has taken a familiar philosophical locution and inverted it. Often we speak of phenomena as being "for us" and by this we mean that they signify, that they have meaning. Thus, to be for the Other is to signify for the Other. It appears that Levinas derives the first signification from the second, for the second spurs us to ask, What do I signify for the Other? What does my presence to the other mean? Levinas's reply appears to be that its meaning, its significance, is ethical. In other words, my presence signifies for the Other not merely in the sense of being intimated along with the sign given but in the ethical sense of being responsible for the Other. The truth of testimony is concerned not so much with what is said but with the saying and what is signified in that saying, precisely my ethical responsibility. This is not a responsibility which I freely assume; it is one to which I am summoned by the transcendent. Levinas writes: "My responsibility for the Other is precisely this relation to an unthematizable Infinity. It is neither the experience of Infinity nor proof of it: it testifies to Infinity" ("TDTT" 103). Thus, in speaking, I bear witness to my relation to the infinite, to my relation to something beyond myself, which is paradoxically within me, as an other within me which has ruptured my autonomy and solipsistic integrity. This "other within" resembles the intimation of the infinite implied by the presence of the idea of the infinite, and here Levinas appears to be elaborating the ethical implications and significance of the presence of this idea. The words that I speak to the Other do more than give the meaning which they explicitly carry. They also carry an implicit ethical promise. In speaking, I give the Other my word. At the same time that I give the other my word, I give myself a commandment to keep my word, and in so doing I testify to the infinite ("TDTT" 104). In sum, subjects speak truly because of their relation to the infinite in virtue of which they are summoned to an ethical responsibility for the Other. Truth in the subject is established in heteronomy.

The traditional reading of Descartes characterizes him as a thinker of autonomy. In identifying the idea of the infinite as a moment of heteronomy in Descartes' thought, Levinas shows Descartes' text to be more ambiguous and perhaps more interesting than the traditional reading allows. Although Levinas would concur that, in the end, Descartes' account of subjectivity is primarily focused on establishing its autonomy, he nonetheless sees in the idea of the infinite the possibility of an alternate path whose potential he seeks to develop and unfold in his own work and whose conclusions may ultimately undercut the Cartesian position. I have explored how Levinas employs this strategy in relation to the conception of truth. Reflection upon the concept of evidence and on the specific way it functions in the juridical imagery that Levinas employs leads to the observation that Levinas, like Descartes, has an account of truth with an objective and a subjective moment. For Descartes, the objective moment consists in the truth of judgment, which is grounded in the subjective moment, the truth of understanding. Both moments of truth are bound up with autonomy because the first is concerned with self-mastery of the will and the second with self-evidence in clear and distinct perception. For Levinas, the objective moment of truth as exemplified in propositions construed as utterances requires a relation to another to whom one speaks. The subjective moment—which grounds the objective—consists in the truthful speaking of the subject, and this in turn depends upon the subject's relation to the infinite in virtue of which she or he is ethical. Unlike in Descartes, however, these moments are constructed within heteronomy in relation to the other. This shift also seems to transform the sense of certainty that is typically linked with truth. Philosophy generally holds that truth is what is certain, which usually means what is objectively verifiable. This notion of truth is an epistemological one, and we see it employed in Descartes, for whom truth consists in certainty concerning what one perceives with the mind. If evidence is not something self-given but given by one person to another, then the kind of certainty a Cartesian would require for that evidence to be considered true is absent. A Cartesian would thus never accept the truth of what is said in evidence based on the witness's claim to sincerity. Although one might argue that Levinas distances certainty from truth, I think he may replace epistemological certainty with an ethical one. One must be certain or have the conviction that the speaker is sincere and tells the truth. Of course, one does not *know* that this is the case, but one is certain that honesty is ethically required, and so one must trust the Other.[16] If this seems to de-center the notion of truth, it should, for that is the effect of emphasizing heteronomy over autonomy.

In conclusion, a final word on the priority of heteronomy. Levinas tends to emphasize the heteronomy of the subjectivity with which he is concerned in contrast to the autonomy of the subjectivity thematized by the tradition, and the rhetorical force of his writing encourages one to view the tension between autonomy and heteronomy as a strict dichotomy. I think, however, that we should be cautious about fully embracing such a claim, for the ethical subject—in order to be responsible for the Other and to be able to act on that responsibility—must be capable of some kind of autonomous action beyond the passivity that Levinas describes and emphasizes when talking about heteronomy. Thus, his point cannot be that autonomy has no place in an account of subjectivity but rather that autonomy cannot be the whole story about subjectivity. Although it is beyond the scope of this essay to demonstrate this, I suspect that Levinas seeks to establish that subjectivity is grounded in heteronomy and that autonomy is possible only on the basis of this prior constitution. In that case, Levinas is no less unambiguously a thinker of heteronomy than Descartes is a thinker of autonomy. Thus, Descartes, who grounds autonomy in heteronomy without seeming to realize it, may be closer to Levinas than Levinas sometimes seems to acknowledge.

Notes

1. Cf. especially Jean-François Lavigne, "L'idée de l'infini: Descartes dans la pensée d'Emmanuel Levinas," *Revue de Métaphysique et de Morale* 92 (1987): 54–66; Robert Bernasconi, "The Silent Anarchic World of the Evil Genius," *Collegium Phaenomenologicum*, eds. J.C. Sallis, G. Moneta, and J. Taminiaux (Dordrecht: Kluwer, 1988), 257–272; Michel Dupuis, "Le cogito ébloui ou la noèse sans noème," *Revue Philosophique de Louvain* 94 (1996): 294–310; Dennis King Keenan, "Reading Levinas Reading Descartes' Meditations," *Journal of the British Society for Phenomenology* 28 (1998): 63–74.

2. Emmanuel Levinas, *Totalité et infini* (Hague: Martinus Nijhoff, 1961); *Totality and Infinity*, trans. Alphonso Lingis (Pittsburgh: Duquesne University Press, 1969). Page references refer to the English translation.

3. Emmanuel Levinas, "Philosophy and the Idea of Infinity," *Collected Philosophical Papers*, trans. Alphonso Lingis (Dordrecht: Martinus Nijhoff, 1987), 47–57; "La philosophie et l'idée de l'infini," *Revue de Métaphysique et de Morale* 62 (1957): 241–53; reprinted in Emmanuel Levinas, *En découvrant l'existence avec Husserl et Heidegger*, 2e éd. (Paris: Vrin, 1967).

4. Levinas's position on the priority of heteronomy over autonomy appears to evolve in his writings. The view elaborated in *TI* that there is another kind of "intentionality" which is more primordial than the traditional notion of intentionality seems to support the view that heteronomy has foundational priority over autonomy. In later works such as *Otherwise than Being or Beyond Essence* (*OTB*), the claim that there is an irrecuperable moment prior to subjectivity which is ambiguously active and passive suggests that what is anterior to autonomy may not be heteronomy but an ambiguity which can give rise to both possibilities. Cf. Emmanuel Levinas, *Autrement qu'être ou au-delà de l'essence* (Hague: Martinus Nijhoff, 1978); *Otherwise than Being or Beyond Essence*, trans. Alphonso Lingis (The Hague: Martinus Nijhoff, 1981).

5. That is, if ethics is to be first philosophy, or if ethics is to precede ontology, then accounts of epistemological subjectivity will need to be grounded on accounts of ethical subjectivity. If ethics lies in heteronomy, as Levinas's notion of responsibility requires, then accounts of epistemological subjectivity will have to take heteronomy as their point of departure.

6. "So I now seem to be able to lay it down as a general rule that whatever I perceive very clearly and distinctly is true" (24). René Descartes, *Philosophical Works of Descartes*, trans. Elizabeth S. Haldane and G.R.T. Ross (London: Cambridge University Press, 1984).

7. Edmund Husserl, *Gesammelte Schriften*, Band 8 (Hague: Martinus Nijhoff, 1984), 11; *Cartesian Meditations*, trans. Dorion Cairns (Dordrecht: Kluwer, 1991), 10.

8. See especially *Investigations* I and VI. Edmund Husserl, *Gesammelte Schriften*, Band 2–4 (Hague: Martinus Nijhoff, 1984); *Logical Investigations*, trans. J.N. Findlay (London: Routledge, 1970).

9. Furthermore, the experience of truth expressed in Husserl's notion of evidence is characterized as a truth experience in the subject, an experience of the fulfillment or adequation of an intention. The quality of the experience marks or indicates the truth of the object. Such a characterization is in tension with the view that there is an ideal or truth into relation with which we enter and in virtue of which the experience of truth occurs. This latter position is more consistent with Levinas's idea of heteronomy and the meaning he gives to the claim that "truth implies experience" ("PII" 47). Levinas resists the claim of classical phenomenology that objectivity and truth are phenomenal and thus he would think that Husserl's notion of self-evidence is still indicative of the tendency toward autonomy.

10. For Levinas the withdrawal or elusiveness of that which is exterior is primarily signaled in language, which implies that he is concerned mostly with people

here. The basic position concerning interiority and exteriority is, however, consistent with the idea that nonhuman objects may also withdraw. When I investigate an unknown object, the object does not "give itself" to me. Although I may be able to find out things about it, the object itself, it could be argued, always withdraws or withholds itself. The object as I thematize it is never the same as the object itself. Levinas perhaps would not agree with such an extrapolation of his position.

11. "Truth is sought in the other, but by him who lacks nothing. The distance is untraversible, and at the same time traversed. The separated being is satisfied, autonomous, and nonetheless searches after the other with a search that is not incited by the lack proper to need nor by the memory of a lost good. Such a situation is language. Truth arises where a being separated from the other is not engulfed in him, but speaks to him. Language, which does not touch the other, even tangentially, reaches the other by calling upon him or by commanding him or by obeying him with all the straightforwardness of these relations" (*TI* 62). Further, "this relation of truth, which at the same time spans and does not span the distance—does not form a totality with the 'other shore'—rests on language: a relation in which the terms *absolve* themselves from the relation, remain absolute within the relation" (*TI* 64).

12. "The objectivity of the object and its signification comes from language. This way the object is posited as a theme offered envelops the instance of signifying" (*TI* 96).

13. "*We call justice this face to face approach, in conversation.* If truth arises in the absolute *experience* in which being gleams with its own light, then truth is produced only in veritable conversation or in justice" (*TI* 70, original emphasis).

14. Levinas is very direct about this in *Ethics and Infinity*. In response to Nemo's question "But is not the Other also responsible in my regard?" Levinas replies, "Perhaps, but that is *his* affair. . . . In this sense, I am responsible for the Other without waiting for reciprocity, were I to die for it. Reciprocity is *his* affair" (98). Emmanuel Levinas, *Ethics and Infinity: Conversations with Philippe Nemo,* trans. Richard A. Cohen (Pittsburgh: Duquesne University Press, 1985).

15. Emmanuel Levinas, "The Truth of Disclosure and the Truth of Testimony," in *Basic Philosophical Writings,* ed. Adriaan T. Peperzak, Simon Critchley, and Robert Bernasconi (Bloomington: Indiana University Press, 1996), 98–107.

16. In thinking about the transformation of certainty, it might be helpful to think of the distinction Kierkegaard draws between objective certainty and subjective certainty in relation to faith in God and the infinite in *Concluding Unscientific Postscript.*

Le Doeuff and Irigaray on Descartes

Anthony David

For Michèle Le Doueff, Descartes' morality *par provision* consists of value-charged images, attitudes, and beliefs that are permanent, impossible to excise through systematic doubt. Such elements, including what Le Doeuff calls the "philosophical imaginary," are prior to and constitutive of reason itself. Consequently, the neutrality of reason, language, and subject in philosophy is illusory, expressive of masculine values that reject plurality or difference. Thus Descartes undermines his own project of securing certain grounds for science, grounds that are not already fertile with non-rational elements.

Luce Irigaray is equally critical of the Cartesian myth of philosophy as self-grounding rationality. But in Descartes' treatment of wonder Irigaray detects the potential for a radically different myth, one congenial to the feminine and to woman. Wonder celebrates sexual difference and in this way subverts the logic underlying the *cogito*. Sexual difference, not the *cogito*, becomes the touchstone of philosophy in the future: As irreducible difference, it banishes the neutrality of language and subject at the same time that it justifies the proliferation of discourse-types; and as embodiment, as lived experience, it rejects the split between body (change, history, existence) and mind (permanence, eternity, essence) in favor of reuniting them.

Descartes thus turns out to be essential not only for modernity but also for postmodernity. In the same way that reenacting the moves of Cartesian doubt initiates philosophy into the spirit of Enlightenment rationality and freedom, and thus into what Le Doeuff calls "the game of theoretical domination,"[1] taking pleasure in the morality *par provision* and in Cartesian wonder opens up an entirely different world—which is our world today. Le Doeuff and Irigaray appropriate aspects of Cartesian thought for feminism and so reveal Descartes' importance to contemporary debates over difference.

Morality Par Provision/Provisional Morality

In Part III of *Discourse on the Method,* Descartes compares the thorough-going renovation of a house to the trilogy of ends constituting his epistemo-logical project: clearing away his disordered and unreliable preconcep-tions, uncovering the indubitable status of the *cogito,* and then rebuilding knowledge in the form of universal science upon the foundation of the *cogito.* But just as the renovation of a house is not merely an affair of bricks and plumbing but upsets the entire human household, so the recon-struction of knowledge ushers in nontheoretical consequences and upsets the knower's *morale.* Systematic doubt is alienating, first of all; it is prima-rily *meditative* or solitary, a division of self from everything else. It is also traumatizing: The smooth circuit of habit together with opinion is broken; one no longer manages the simplest of exchanges with confidence but rather with a sense of dread, of not knowing what is around the corner. Acknowledging this, Descartes advises:

> before starting to rebuild your house, it is not enough simply to pull it
> down, to make provision for materials and architects (or else train your-
> self in architecture), and to have carefully drawn up the plans; you must
> also provide yourself with some other place where you can live comfort-
> ably while building is in progress. Likewise, lest I should remain indeci-
> sive in my actions while reason obliged me to be so in my judgments, and
> in order to live as happily as I could during this time, I formed for myself
> a provisional moral code consisting of just three or four maxims.[2]

Descartes suggests that if we plan to repeat the philosophical moves he lays down for us in his *Meditations on First Philosophy,* then we'll need, when the going gets rough, access to "some other place" where we can live "comfortably" or "happily." Defined by his "three or four maxims," it is a place in which one resolves to conserve the political and religious tra-ditions of one's upbringing; to practice one's convictions *as if* they were true; and, Stoic-like, to focus on improving oneself rather than the world (*DM* 122–24). As for the fourth maxim, it is unclear whether Descartes ac-tually meant it to be an action-guiding or character-building principle. In the first place, the way he numbers his maxims ("three or four") indicates hesitation; and in other places (as we shall see) he flatly states that his moral code consists of three, not four, items. At any rate, here theory and morality are seemingly incompatible; at the same time that Descartes in-tends to spark a scientific revolution, he prescribes political quietude and religious piety. But at least for him, the combination, paradoxical as it is, succeeds: It makes him happy and, most important, enables him to pursue decisively what is in his opinion the very best of professions.

Important as this "other place where you can live comfortably" is, the image of the dwelling in the *Discourse* appears to suggest that its status is merely temporary. As pleasure, the morality *par provision* is epistemologically impure and must be put aside so that, disinfected of possible error, a person might fully embrace the foundational cogito. Coupled with the image of the tree[3] in *Principles of Philosophy,* one might easily think that Descartes intends to replace his "three or four maxims" with a more complete ethics grounded not in pleasure but in metaphysics and physics.

The temporary quality of Descartes' morality *par provision* is also emphasized by standard histories of philosophy. For example, Frederick Copleston writes that "these maxims or resolutions constitute a rough-and-ready personal programme" whose imperfection is "obvious," and he ruefully concludes that a perfected Cartesian ethic "is missing from the system."[4] This is also Stephen Gaukroger's conclusion. However, their explanations differ. Copleston blames Descartes' inability to first establish a science of human nature, which would then serve as the foundation of morality; Gaukroger blames Descartes' fear of public censure in the wake of the hostile reaction of Church and Academy to Copernicanism:

> After all, the moral question at issue in the statement of a provisional morality is that of obedience. The provisional morality would then simply be the public commitment to social and religious mores and teachings, something to be abandoned when the truth of the matter can be established beyond question. Remember that Descartes' discussion takes place in the wake of his abandonment of *Le Monde.* This is a case where the question arose in a very striking way of whether one should follow one's own lights or follow the authorities, and the provisional morality in question is one that one follows until one has an indubitable demonstration of the truth of Copernicanism.[5]

Copleston and Gaukroger are not alone in their opinion that Descartes fails to offer a complete and satisfactory ethics. Even John Cottingham, a principle contributor to the standard English translation of Descartes' works, considers the Cartesian morality provisional or slated for replacement.[6]

This interpretation is a mistake, contends Le Doeuff. It focuses entirely on the implicit message of the *images* of the dwelling and the tree to the exclusion of Descartes' explicit claims. But why? In matters of interpretation, shouldn't we privilege a philosopher's explicit claims over mere imagery? Actually, for Le Doeuff the answer is not so simple—nor is her question. In *The Philosophical Imaginary*, her concern with Descartes is not merely the interpretation of the Cartesian ethic but, more generally, the status of rereadings—accounting for "misappropriation of meaning whose operation can be traced and located in the very textuality of the text."[7] This is our general direction as well, but not before we engage in what Le Doeuff calls a "philosophically blinkered reading": an examination of Descartes' explicit claims only, *sans* imagery (*PI* 62). Read in this manner, Descartes can reasonably be interpreted as viewing his "three or four maxims" as permanent, prior to reason, and constitutive of reason.

Le Doeuff begins by pointing out that the original phrasing in the *Discourse* is *not* "provisional moral code" but rather "morality *par provision*." She reminds us that in the seventeenth-century legal system in France, "*provision*" is a juridical term meaning "what a judgment awards in advance to a party." Thus a judge might award *par provision* a sum of money to a plaintiff suing for damages before hearing his or her case. Even if the judge ends up ruling in favor of the defendant, the judgment awarding money to the plaintiff remains unaffected. As Le Doeuff puts it, "The *provision* is not liable to be put in question by the final judgment; it is a first installment" (*PI* 62). The two expressions, "provisional" and "*provision*," are thus opposite in meaning. "Provisional" indicates something destined to be replaced, whereas "*provision*" indicates permanence, that which cannot be replaced or revoked no matter what the "final judgment" turns out to be. In his letter to Princess Elizabeth, dated 4 August 1645 (eight years after writing the *Discourse*), Descartes himself confirms this latter interpretation of his ethics by saying, "It seems to me that each person can make himself content by himself without any external assistance, provided he respects three conditions, which are related to the three rules of morality which I put forward in the *Discourse on the Method*."[8] Commenting on the significance of this letter, Le Doeuff says:

> Not only is the validity of the morality in the *Discourse* reaffirmed and generalized ('*each person*'), but Descartes does this without the least abashment. If the *Discourse* had contained a provisional morality, and so promised another, definitive and certain one, Descartes ought to have felt the need to excuse himself for finding nothing better after eight years of work. (*PI* 65)

Descartes, then, is content with his morality *par provision*; contrary to the standard interpretation, it is not merely the rough sketch for a more complete, more *certain*, ethics.

Le Doeuff points out that it does not even make sense to *talk* about an epistemologically certain morality, perfected (as one might expect) by applying the Cartesian Method. For Descartes himself claims that the realm of morality—the mind-body complex—is

> known only obscurely by the intellect alone or even by the intellect aided by the imagination. . . . Metaphysical thoughts, which exercise the pure intellect, help to familiarize us with the notion of the soul; and the study of mathematics, which exercises mainly the imagination in the consideration of shapes and motions, accustoms us to form very distinct notions of the body. But it is the ordinary course of life and conversation . . . that teaches us how to conceive the union of the soul and the body.[9]

Metaphysics, then, clearly and distinctly elucidates thought; physics clearly and distinctly enumerates extension. But morality is committed to investigating the "ordinary course of life and conversation" which is intrinsically unclear and confused, *blurred*. Descartes acknowledges this in distinguishing absolute certainty from what he calls *moral certainty:* "Moral certainty is certainty which is sufficient to regulate our behavior, or which measures up to the certainty we have on matters relating to the conduct of life which we never normally doubt, though we know that it is possible, absolutely speaking, that they may be false."[10] The point is that morality which achieves "more than moral" certainty would be a paradox (*PI* 68).

Morality *par provision* is permanent, then—incapable of being withdrawn by the "final judgment." It is the sort of pleasure which belongs not to the mind apart from the body but to "the whole human being"; as such, it escapes the control of thought.[11] Also, it is *prior* to rational thought. Consider again Le Doeuff's juridical conception of *provision*. In the same way that the judge awards a sum of money to the plaintiff even before the trial takes place, Descartes urges us to embrace a moral code before doing anything else:

> I would wish to explain here the order which I think we should follow when we aim to instruct ourselves. First of all, a man who still possesses only . . . ordinary and imperfect knowledge . . . should try before anything else to devise for himself a code of morals which is sufficient to regulate the actions of his life. For this is something which permits no delay since we should endeavor above all else to live well. (*PP* 185–86)

Next is the study of logic, the sort that helps us direct our reason toward the discovery of truth. In other words, the cultivation of passion and action should precede reason since moral excellence can't wait—even for certainty. The starting point for philosophy is not epistemological after all, but ethical.

In fact, given that the body's influence on the mind can be disruptive—"there are diseases which take away the power of reasoning and with it the power of enjoying the satisfaction proper to a rational mind"[12]—Descartes goes so far as to say that, if we must choose between speculative theory and medicine, we ought to choose the latter: "For the mind depends so much on the temperament and disposition of the bodily organs that if it is possible to find some means of making men in general wiser and more skillful than they have been up till now, I believe we must look for it in medicine."[13] Le Doeuff notes that by putting medicine ahead of speculative theory—and morality ahead of both—Descartes rejects the traditional concept of wisdom espoused, for example, by Plato. Plato, in the *Phaedo*, argues that we can become wise only by mortifying the flesh so as to perfect our focus on the intellect. Descartes, on the other hand, argues that the Platonic ascesis is impossible for us; constant negotiations with the flesh are unavoidable. Though our minds rise to rarified heights in the quest for epistemological certainty, our bodies and everything for which and in which thought stands—passions, *sex*, personal projects, histories, traditions, articles of faith, *texts*—nevertheless demand attention. This is what obliges him to offer his reader "some other place where [he or she] can live comfortably" while the reconstruction of knowledge takes place. Le Doeuff summarizes:

> The separation of soul and body produces the impossibility conditions of the classical concept of wisdom: in order for the practice of philosophy to be capable of totally regulating conduct and happiness, assuring by itself the good life, it is indeed necessary, as Montaigne puts it, for the sage not to be at the mercy of a maddening toothache. (*PI* 67)

If Descartes is right, then, contrary to Plato we cannot achieve knowledge at the expense of the body and all that it represents—nor can we attain virtue through knowledge. Truth is not coterminous with the Good. Swimming against a tide of venerable philosophical tradition, including the one that he himself sets down in the *Meditations*, Descartes says, "It is also not necessary that our reason should be free from error; it is sufficient if our conscience testifies that we have never lacked resolution and virtue to carry out whatever we have judged the best course. So virtue by itself is sufficient to make us content in this life."[14] Virtue, in its priority, is thus independent of knowledge; one can be virtuous without being error free or, more important, without being a possessor of the trademark

Cartesian certainty. It is indeed hard to read the above letter (the same one in which the validity of the morality *par provision* is reaffirmed and generalized) without imagining that Descartes is confessing a loss of confidence in the utter necessity of universal science.

But can science be value free? More specifically, is the Cartesian method even possible, never mind practicable, without the morality *par provision*? Descartes' answer is *no*. Recall how he offers "lodging" as a place of comfort and pleasure with which to offset the "indecision" and "unhappiness" caused by systematic doubt. But Descartes' instincts here are not merely those of a good host. For the morality *par provision* prevents systematic doubt from alienating and traumatizing the philosopher to such an extent that it becomes lethal. The systematic doubt of the mind threatens the life of the body and so undermines its own continuation in that body. But by insuring that one takes up a hobby, cultivates friendships, gets adequate sleep, and so on, the morality *par provision* both protects the body and enables systematic doubt to achieve fruition in the discovery of the *cogito:* "Once I had established these maxims and set them on one side together with the truths of faith. . . . I judged that I could freely undertake to rid myself of all the rest of my opinions" (*DM* 125). Descartes, then, would *not* feel free to reconstruct knowledge outside of a context of passion and praxis; he would be constrained from doing so.

Descartes ends up asserting, along with Le Doeuff, that "an element of non-knowledge unavoidably inhabits any undertaking, including a philosophical one" (*HC* 8). It goes without saying that this amounts to a radical reversal—deconstructive in nature—of the entire Cartesian scheme laid out in *Meditations*. Reason is not neutral but is constructed within a context of passion and praxis and in this way gains direction and fruition in pleasure. The direction of *Cartesian* reason toward discovering the *cogito* and then systematizing knowledge turns out not to have been inevitable at all, nor inscribed in the nature of things, but rather to have been determined all along by Descartes' "three or four maxims."

And what determines these maxims? Given that Western philosophy for the past 2,500 years has been a specifically *masculine* prerogative, practically undiluted by feminine contributions, it is reasonable to suspect, as feminists do, that its determining values belong to the masculine sex. But notice that Descartes (through the concept of morality *par provision*) allows for such an analysis even though he is otherwise committed to the notion of a "neutral" rationality and even though such commitment reflects the specifically masculine character of the Cartesian morality *par provision*. He is, in short, an unwitting feminist. I will pursue this notion more fully in connection with Irigaray.

The Site Outside Knowledge: Imagery

According to Le Doeuff, imagery as well as gender are prior to and constitutive of the rational enterprise. I turn to those ideas now to fill out the complexity of her reading of Descartes and to incorporate its wider implications about what was referred to earlier as "the status of rereadings" (and, by implication, of philosophy itself).

Images in philosophical texts, says Le Doeuff, are simply not considered a proper part of the philosophical enterprise (*PI* 7). Though philosophers might be incapable of giving "philosophy" positive definition, they certainly know what it is not: "not a story, not a pictorial description, not a work of pure literature. Philosophical discourse is inscribed and declares its status as philosophy through a break with myth, fable, the poetic, the domain of the image" (*PI* 1). Thales, then, is the first Western philosopher—not Homer or Hesiod.

Indeed, "good readers bypass such illustrations"; part of what it means to become a philosopher is to be trained out of attending to the role imagery plays in philosophical texts (*PI* 12). But unless we pay more attention to such imagery, certain puzzles of interpretation resist explanation. The puzzle, in Descartes' case, concerns the way in which his interpreters fail to use his own words to formulate a concept of his: "Thus where Descartes writes 'I formed for myself a morality *par provision*,' later tradition converts this into 'Descartes' provisional morality' (*morale provisoire*)" (*PI* 57). But how could Descartes' interpreters have misunderstood him so thoroughly? What accounts for what Le Doeuff calls "abduction or misappropriation of meaning" or "lexical mutation"? Possibly his readers are prejudiced; then again, perhaps they are simply uncovering what is hidden in the text, which the text itself conspires to hide (*PI* 58). Without discounting the possibility of prejudiced readings, Le Doeuff sides with the latter explanation: Descartes' discourse is "a double one, open to a double reading because traversed by indecision and slippage" (*PI* 58).

Consider again the image of the dwelling in the *Discourse* and that of the tree in the *Principles*. Le Doeuff contends that only these images lead to interpreting Descartes' morality as provisional, slated for abandonment in exchange for something better (*PI* 92). Both images, for example, respond to each other in so far as the image of the dwelling is designated as temporary and the image of the tree indicates that the conclusions of a proper morality are deduced from prior principles of metaphysics and physics. Furthermore, both images support the classical concept of wisdom in which reason is the basis of a perfected morality (*PI* 93).

But Le Doeuff asks us to consider that such imagery is not merely illustrative of Descartes' thinking on morality, as incidental to the substance of that thought as icing on cake. The hypothesis guiding her in the analysis of imagery in philosophical texts is this: "the image, far from being a more or less pedagogical 'illustration' of an abstract thesis contained elsewhere in the system, is always the mark of a tension, a signification incompatible with the rest of the system" (*PI* 93). Imagery indicates the possibility of the text's being a *palimpsest* in which the writer's earliest impulses are written over and, except for what imagery indicates, barely discernible. Furthermore, the writer's earliest impulses are embarrassing—"something which cannot be acknowledged, yet is keenly cherished" (*PI* 9). Thus the imagery betraying this inner conflict brings conflict to the text.

Imagery pieces together divergent textual impulses into what appears a united front and yet acts to subvert this artificial unity. Imagery *propagandizes* on behalf of repressed textual elements. The Cartesian images of the dwelling and the tree, for example, make their point tacitly and thus all the more powerfully: "The provisional character of the morality in question is given as self-evident and known to all; it is never formally established" (*PI* 93). Descartes thus bypasses his readers' intellects and is understood by them in the blink (wink) of an eye, so to speak. This, of course, is not unique to Descartes:

> Images are the means by which every philosophy can engage in straightforward dogmatization, and decree a 'that's the way it is' without fear of counter-argument, since it is understood that a good reader will bypass such 'illustrations'—a convention which enables the image to do its work all the more effectively. (*PI* 12)

The "straightforward dogmatization of images" is appropriate, given that what they attempt to voice is more prejudice than proposition. In Descartes' own case, the prejudice consists of simple nostalgia for the way philosophy has always been done: "The nostalgia for wisdom—that is, for a knowledge which makes possible the good" (*PI* 96). Though Descartes explicitly claims that it is impossible to integrate morality into his philosophical system, that morality is indeed extraphilosophical, he nevertheless wishes that it could be otherwise. Cartesian imagery, then, in attacking the morality *par provision*, "masks an irredeemable loss" (*PI* 96). Ironically, by relying on imagery to sustain the illusion of systematicity, Descartes ends up affirming the dependence of systematicity on imagery for its constitution (*PI* 93–94).

Cartesian nostalgia accounts not merely for the major "evasions" of his imagery but also for his minor ones—slips of tongue, as it were. For example, in the Prefatory Letter to *Principles*, just after Descartes presents his image of the tree, he says, "The first part of these essays was a *Discourse on the Method of rightly conducting one's reason and seeking the truth in the sciences,* where I summarized the principal rules of logic and of an imperfect moral code which we may follow provisionally while we do not yet know a better one" (*PP* 186–87). Here it appears that Descartes regards his *morality par provision* exactly as traditional interpretation makes it out to be—as a makeshift expedient slated for replacement when something better comes along. But Le Doeuff wonders, "What place should one give this late (1644) statement of depreciation, given that later still (1645) a letter to Elizabeth of Prussia will vaunt afresh the merits of this morality?" (*PI* 88). This is the same letter to Elizabeth which we examined earlier, in which Descartes proclaims the sufficiency of his moral code for everyone. Thus between him and his text exists "a complex negating relationship, which is a sign that something important and troubling is seeking utterance" (*PI* 8–9). That something, according to Le Doeuff, is both an admission of guilt (that he should be the one to point out that philosophy is powerless to determine the good) and the expression of a wish (that things should be otherwise—that philosophy should be all-powerful).

Descartes' imagery is a function of nostalgia, then. Le Doeuff's analysis, however, deepens into identifying how Cartesian imagery and its underlying nostalgia are uneasy or tense in a sense we have not yet explored: that of being self-contradictory or self-destructive. Imagery turns out not only to indicate repressed textual elements and to propagandize on their behalf but also to displace what is already repressed! Cartesian imagery sustains the dream of systematicity, but in self-destructive fashion it undercuts itself whenever the question of morality is raised. To illustrate, consider Le Doeuff's analysis of the image of the tree. The tree, she points out, retains coherence when referring to metaphysics, physics, mechanics, and medicine; but to raise the issue of morals is to disrupt the system:

> But morality introduces a total confusion into the design since it is simultaneously one of the branches among others, joined directly to the trunk, and *"presupposes an entire knowledge of the other sciences,"* in which sense it is no longer a branch among others but a result of all the branches—something which it is strictly impossible to represent within that image. (*PI* 96)

In other words, morality is simultaneously a subject set alongside medicine and mechanics and the result of all sciences put together; the tree of knowledge ends both by forking into three distinct branches *and* by joining the branches into one. Morality is the ultimate product of philosophy at the same time that it suggests that morality is not determinable within the system. The image, then, yokes together mutually exclusive claims and so works against the nostalgia for philosophical systematicity to which it gives rise in the first place.

As for the image of the dwelling: Le Doeuff points out, first of all, that associated notions of "loose" and "firm" foundations metaphorically govern Descartes' treatment of knowledge throughout the *Discourse*, but only when the issue of morality comes up does the image become distorted, self-undermining:

> on the level of vocabulary, the words "build" and "building," with their associations with the question of solidity, yield to those of "lodging" and "being lodged," associated rather with the question of commodity: the use value of the house, perhaps the affective value of the word "lodging," but above all the lexical juxtaposition of this morality with the body, for lodging is one of the modes of relation of the soul and body. (*PI* 95)

The image, which promises us a certain and perfected morality, actually undermines the very possibility of moral experience. Recall Descartes' claim that absolute certainty in morals is an impossibility: The mind-body complex, the condition of moral experience, is incapable of being known clearly and distinctly. Now "the mind-body complex" is the same thing as mind "lodged" in a body; "lodging," then, is a necessary condition for morality. If so, how can one vacate one's "provisional lodging" in exchange for something more solid and hope to continue moral experience?

In short, Le Doeuff argues that Cartesian imagery betrays the tension between contradictory commitments. Join this to the insight, stated earlier, that the morality *par provision* is not simply illuminated by Descartes' explicit claims but actually is demonstrated through his unspoken rejection of it through imagery, and we have a very interesting perspective on the nature of philosophy:

> Any form of rational discourse proceeds from, or originates in, things which can't be sustained or produced through reason, things such as beliefs, for example. In philosophy these beliefs are set forth in the form of myths, or "exempla," comparisons, images, or pictorial writing. But there is a contradiction here, since philosophy is also the assumption of a pure and total rationality: a philosophical discourse is supposed to appear as a self-grounded discourse. . . . This could be the origin of what you call a stratagem, namely the fact that no philosophical discourse can meet its own demands and standards. Daydream and myth fill the gap, as it were, by providing the basic grammar of the system, by taking over

from the conceptual work whenever there is a problem, and being sometimes ambiguous enough to support two opposing ideas at the same
time.[15]

Indeed, whenever the topic at hand is that of the power and rational
purity of philosophy, Le Doeuff warns that the discourse will never be free
of evasions of the Cartesian sort. The same holds for the interpreters of
such discourse (*PI* 97–98).

Psychoanalyzing the Cogito

Irigaray takes Le Doueff's warning one step further. Le Doeuff warns us
of the images, daydreams, and myths that ground Cartesian reason, but
Irigaray *psychoanalyzes* them.[16] What she discovers is an exclusively masculine logic that allows woman "no signs, no symbols or emblems, or methods of writing that could figure her instincts" (*Sp* 124), that indeed "violates" the feminine (*Sp* 231) by using it as a mere "interpretive modality":

> inverse, contrary, contradictory even, necessary if the male subject's pro-
> cess of specul(ariz)ation is to be raised and sublated. This is an interven-
> tion required of *those* effects of negation that result from or are set in
> motion through a censure of the feminine, though the feminine will be
> allowed and even obliged to return in such oppositions as: be/*become*,
> have/*not have* sex (organ), phallic/*nonphallic*, penis/*clitoris* or else
> penis/*vagina*, plus/*minus*, clearly representable/*dark continent*, logos/
> *silence*, or *idle chatter*, desire for the mother/*desire to be the mother*; etc. All
> these are interpretive modalities of the female function rigorously postu-
> lated by the pursuit of a certain game for which she will always find her-
> self signed up. (*Sp* 22)

The deep logic of the *cogito* is that of dialectical opposition. On top
is masculine desire which defines philosophical propriety and also defends it by repressing the feminine. Consequently Irigaray's program is
first to reclaim the feminine from philosophical oblivion, to "reopen the
figures of philosophical discourse" in order to "pry out of them what they
have borrowed from the feminine."[17] Doing so requires that we "assume
the feminine role deliberately" in *mimesis*, the process by which women
may "convert a form of subordination into an affirmation, and thus to begin to thwart it" (*TS* 76). Irigaray's tactic is thus, like Le Doeuff's, deconstructive. As Carolyn Burke describes it, "the 'inferior' terms of these

structural pairs are reinserted, but with a different status and, presumably, without placing the former devalued term in the position of its 'oppressor'."[18] It is to reveal a contradiction—that what constitutes systematicity is whatever systematicity rejects as nonphilosophical or lacking in philosophy—and to risk somehow reconciling the two.

Yet there is what Naomi Schor calls a "more essential mimesis": "a joyful appropriation of the attributes of the other that . . . does not signify a reversal of misogyny but an emergence of the feminine."[19] Schor suggests that in reclaiming the feminine from its bondage as the opposite—the inverse—of the masculine, Irigaray does not merely challenge masculine discourse to realize the hollowness of its pretension to be self-grounding. Rather, Irigaray also wants to identify positively what the feminine *is*. As Irigaray notes, "I search for myself, as if I had been assimilated into maleness. I ought to reconstitute myself on the basis of a disassimilation. . . . Rise again from the works already produced by the other. Searching through what is in them—for what is not there."[20] This "reconstitution" of the feminine is simultaneously the creation of a language appropriate to women's "instincts" or "desire" and of a genuine feminine subject.

And, unexpectedly, Descartes shows the way to achieve this goal. Through that "first of the passions," Cartesian wonder, women might, in fact, access a subjectivity and a language appropriate for them. They might also heal the split between mind and body, propriety and pleasure, which masculine philosophy creates and sustains. For Irigaray, then, as Schor points out, Descartes' role is dual. He is "the philosopher who irrevocably sunders body from soul and the one who most brilliantly reunites them."[21]

This is what must be kept in mind as we now turn to articulating Irigaray's psychoanalytic examination of the *cogito*. But why, to begin with, is her main orientation psychoanalytic? Why does she constantly refer to "instinct" and "desire"? Irigaray's response to such questions illustrates the extent to which Freud (Lacan) is the touchstone of her thought:

> Because in the process of elaborating a theory of sexuality, Freud brought to light something that had been operative all along though it remained implicit, hidden, unknown: *the sexual indifference that underlies the truth of every science, the logic of every discourse*. This is readily apparent in the way Freud defines female sexuality. In fact, this sexuality is never defined with respect to any sex but the masculine. Freud does not see two sexes. . . . The "feminine" is always described in terms of deficiency or atrophy, as the other side of the sex that alone holds a monopoly on value: the male sex. Hence the all too well-known "penis envy." (*TS* 69)

Freud's "sexual indifference," which Irigaray describes as "implicit, hidden, unknown," is nothing but masculine desire. As such, it is not a proper object of knowledge. Rather, as passion and as praxis it is prior to and constitutive of "the logic of every discourse." Here Irigaray acknowledges the definitive role of morality *par provision* (or, interchangeably, the imaginary or the unconscious) in the development of reason. Echoing Le Doeuff, she says, "We need to pay attention to the way the unconscious works in each philosophy, and perhaps in philosophy in general. We need to listen (psycho)analytically to its procedures of repression, to the structuration of language that shores up its representations, separating the true from the false, the meaningful from the meaningless, and so forth" (*TS* 75). But whereas Le Doeuff stresses imagery's role in determining the nature of reason, Irigaray stresses sexual desire. (This is not, of course, to imply that Le Doeuff's and Irigaray's foci are mutually exclusive.)

Freud also represents for Irigaray the exclusivity of masculine discourse. According to this logic, women are incapable of philosophy just because they lack a phallus together with its attendant instincts. Whereas for men, philosophical activity is stimulated by a lack of knowledge, women, lacking a phallus, lack a properly philosophical lack. Before she tries her hand at philosophy, then, a women ought to procure for herself a phallus, a man.[22] Le Doeuff in particular points out that this drama of procuring a phallus is instantiated often enough in the history of philosophy, as in the relationship between Descartes and Elizabeth. "Descartes was," says Le Doeuff, "the 'one who knows,' the one who is asked for knowledge (and not just any knowledge: you who know everything, tell me how to be happy despite all my troubles) and of whom one wants to be a favorable disciple, an intelligent reader, a 'good pupil'" (*PI* 104). Le Doeuff goes on to suggest that exclusivity affords masculine philosophy a way of repairing its current state of flaccidity: "By affirming that 'woman' is incapable of philosophical thought and that it is no task for her, philosophers strengthen and reassure themselves with the idea that philosophy can do something and has a task, no need to state exactly what" (*HC* 25).

The exclusivity of masculine discourse, in which only men are capable of independent thought, is furthermore locked in place by the mechanism of "penis envy." This mechanism reinforces the equation of "phallus" with "philosophy": the *desire to have it* would confirm man in the assurance that he has it" (*Sp* 51). Conversely, woman does *not* have *it* and this explains why "vagina-envy" or "uterus-envy" is unthinkable (*Sp* 52).

More generally, in Freud Irigaray detects the character of masculine desire (of which one manifestation is the exclusivity mentioned above). Irigaray's analysis in this regard centers on the constitution of the masculine subject in philosophy, the *cogito*. This happens, first of all, only by virtue of the feminine. "In order to touch himself," claims Irigaray, "man needs an instrument: his hand, a woman's body, language" (*TS* 24). He cannot produce his own pleasure, his own thought, unless it is mediated by something other than himself—and this other *is* the feminine. Nothing grows without her; she is the "[m]atrix—womb, earth, factory, bank— to which the seed capital is entrusted so that it may germinate, produce, grow fruitful" (*Sp* 18). Without her, nothing is imaged and valued: "if this ego is to be valuable, some 'mirror' is needed to reassure it and reinsure it of its value. Woman will be the foundation for this specular duplication, giving man back 'his' image and repeating it as the 'same'" (*Sp* 54).

But the debt the masculine subject owes to the feminine goes unpaid, unacknowledged: "What is now founding the subject's existence and reflection works like the backing of a mirror . . . and is thus beyond perception; it can barely be intuited because it has no reflections of its own" (*Sp* 181). The problem, then, is the masculine subject's *specularity:* Reality, its own as well, is self-reflected. So when he looks at himself in the mirror, all he sees is . . . himself. Thus, "in the wink of an eye," he mistakenly judges *himself* and not the feminine as the primal matrix and source of all.

This self-reflected reality effectively confirms the masculine subject in his characteristic "phallocentrism," his single-minded pursuit of mastery *in itself* and mastery *over.* Mastery in itself means being *best;* mastery *over* means being *better* and being *in control.* Starting with mastery *in itself,* what better way to achieve it than to create oneself from the ground up and then, god-like, create everything else? Referring to the Cartesian reconstruction of knowledge, Irigaray says, "The 'I' will confer existence upon itself. Being without any copulation? The 'I' therefore 'copulates' without copulation. . . . The 'I' therefore 'is', without any 'all' or 'if' or 'but'" (*Sp* 184). As is the pre-Hellenic Goddess Athene, knowledge is stripped of its genealogical origin and simply "springs from the head" of Olympian Zeus; reason becomes self-grounding and undefiled by fleshy ancestry. And then, the masculine subject "gives birth to the universe all over again" (*Sp* 182). It is a paradox of cosmic proportion in which the singular "has become necessary in reconstructing the whole, and lays down the general grounds whereby the *universal* may be reaffirmed" (*Sp* 180).

Of course, the "universal" is possible only through systematic doubt; and here we turn to the masculine subject's penchant for mastery *over* or for being better. The subject is self-grounding only if it can reject anything other than itself. Its power is proportional to its ability to say *no: "The basis for representation* must be purged of all *childish* phantoms or fantasies or belief or approximations. Anything picked up, accepted, and repeated without proof. About the other, the Other. Saying 'no' to everything is the crucial way to be assured that one is really (like) oneself" (*Sp* 181). Obsessively, compulsively, the feminine must be mastered, controlled; the masculine subject must again and again clean himself of her:

> he has brought himself back into the world in a way that avoids the precariousness of existence as it is usually understood. Once *the chain of relationships, the cord,* has been *severed,* together with ancestry and the mysteries of conception, then there is nothing left but the subject who can go back and sever them all over again whenever he likes. In a speculative act of denial and negation that serves to affirm his autonomy. (*Sp* 182)

To preserve his autonomy, he must always take care lest *she,* the feminine, endanger the clarity and distinctiveness of his thought with obscure matter: ancestry, history, earth, body. He must say *no* to her continually. He must "harden his heart to the glorious assault of her colors, to the fascination of her sheer size, to the seduction of her smells and sounds. Let him, above all, not want to smell, feel, or drink her" (*Sp* 185). And indeed, by this seduction he *feels assaulted.* Confronted by the vast Other to self-representation, Irigaray imagines Descartes living "in the middle of vortices, or an earthquake, full of unrest, racked and jerked around, going hither and thither without any rest, shaken from all sides" (*Sp* 189).

Most tellingly, the worst possible threat—which the masculine subject must therefore master all the more urgently—is the potential for woman's desire to outstrip its being the negative of man's and to actually achieve positive status. She is the mirror in which man knows and values himself, but should she herself be interpreted as positively *different,* should she attain her own voice, then all coherence would be lost: "Subjectivity denied to women: indisputably this provides the financial backing for every irreducible constitution as an object: of representation, of discourse, of desire. Once imagine that a woman imagines and the object loses its fixed, obsessional character" (*Sp* 133). In other words, imagine that the mirror of man's specularization can, by its own volition, *move*—shake, jerk around, go hither and thither—and this in itself is enough to *blur* his self-identity. It is to *castrate* him. Anxiety about this, contends Irigaray, is always there: "the ground threatens every minute to shake the present certainties of the subject" (*Sp* 181), a ground "lapsed within, disquieting in its shadow and its rage" (*Sp* 135). Nevertheless, this sadomasochism (which, as we saw, Irigaray links with the maternal) is an "essential rule of the game"—and as in any rivalry, one can achieve mastery over an opponent only to the degree that one is challenged (*Sp* 51).

Once defused through systematic doubt, however, the feminine becomes penetrable. The masculine subject can "*machine it into detached pieces* and then carefully analyse its mechanisms and principles of functioning, its cogs, its springs" (*Sp* 187). In this way, phallic logic is a logic of "solids" or of sharp boundaries, of number. The feminine becomes *pure extension,* stripped of seductive colors and smells. He will cut her up, mathematically or otherwise, into "any number of pieces, subject her to any number of visual angles, inscribe her in an even vaster space in order to draw a line around her: a map of the world" (*Sp* 185). His science is pornographic. Once she is "mapped" she becomes a commodity. She becomes a "use-value for man, an exchange among men" (*TS* 31) upon which the patriarchal order can be founded:

> Thus God is father; he begets a son, and for this purpose he uses a woman who is reduced to maternity. This has been the most abiding structure in our religious and civic traditions for centuries: a relation *between* men, or *in* man . . . through a woman. In such a culture the woman remains at home, and is the object of use and exchange between men. She is used for reproduction and for the material maintenance of life.[23]

Yet what woman is, her specificity, is nevertheless *there,* hidden underneath the masculine drama—not as the negative to his speculation merely, but different in its own right. This, in fact, is the defining intuition of feminism. To recover the feminine is to challenge the notion that the subject of philosophy is neutral or universal and thus to instigate revolution against the neutral subject's oppressiveness, to "*rack it with radical convulsions,*" to "*Overthrow syntax*" (*Sp* 142). The recovery of the feminine means reinterpreting *everything* "concerning the relations between the subject and discourse, the subject and the world, the subject and the cosmic, the microcosmic and the macrocosmic. Everything, beginning with the way in which the subject has always been written in the masculine form, as *man,* even when it is claimed to be universal or neutral" (*E* 6). Ultimately, in this recovery of the feminine and its consequent widespread recognition of "sexual difference," Irigaray sees the creation of utopia or a "new age of thought, art, poetry, and language: the creation of a new *poetics*" (*E* 5).

The First of the Passions

Irigaray answers the question of how such a creation is to be done succinctly: "We need to reread Descartes a little" (*E* 72). This might surprise us, considering how Irigaray claims that the deep logic of the *cogito* stands in the way of our recognizing sexual difference (*E* 14–15). Nevertheless, from Descartes we may learn how to develop values expressive of sexual difference. Irigaray maintains that "To arrive at the constitution of an ethics of sexual difference, we must at least return to what is for Descartes the first passion: *wonder*" (*E* 12).

No doubt, Irigaray's double move here would have surprised Descartes. After all, his *cogito* is impenetrable by any of the Evil Demon's deceits and is a fortress of clarity and distinctness amidst a world of potential illusion. According to Irigaray, such convictions are naïve, all clear and distinct ideas turn out to have false bottoms, and the *cogito* is exposed as merely a front for masculine desire.

Specifically, in Descartes Irigaray detects opposing logics: masculine logic, according to which systematic doubt neutralizes the human being into a thinking thing and leads to the regime of neutrality and universality in philosophy; and feminine logic, according to which wonder opens a person to the fullness of his or her being-in-the-world and leads to the unmasking of traditional philosophy as expressive of simply one set of values. Wonder turns out to be isometric to systematic doubt in its function of establishing a starting point for philosophy.

But what is wonder? Physiologically speaking, as a *passion* its condition is the "lodging" of mind in body, and it arises, Descartes observes, when the former is acted upon by the latter.[24] As such, the experience of it is *humane* as opposed to *merely thought* and affirms the mind-body unity. Given Descartes' nostalgia for clarity and distinctness in all things, however, we might reasonably expect Descartes to minimize the value of passions in general and wonder in particular. But on the value of the passions, as on the status of morality, Descartes is ambivalent. Passions must be mastered by reason, and yet "persons whom the passions can move most deeply [most spontaneously?] are capable of enjoying the sweetest pleasures of this life" (*PS* 404). To be open to such experiences is to feel the passion of wonder:

> When our first encounter with some object surprises us and we find it
> novel, or very different from what we formerly knew or from what we supposed it ought to be, this causes us to wonder and be astonished at it.
> Since all this may happen before we know whether or not the object is beneficial to us, I regard wonder as the first of all the passions. It has no oppo-

site, for, if the object before us has no characteristics that surprise us, we are not moved by it at all and we consider it without passion. (*PS* 350)

Calling wonder the first of the passions is in one sense *not* to privilege it over other passions but merely to indicate an order of occurrence: Wonder happens first. But in another sense Descartes does seem to privilege wonder. By acknowledging it as *first,* he tips his hat to Aristotle, for whom wonder was the characteristic passion of the philosopher. Most important, however, wonder "has no opposite": It is a thirst incapable of being sated, and thus the experience of wonder does not occur as some degree between mutually exclusive polarities. Rather, wonder liberates from the oppression of relative degrees of this or that at the same time it brings only increasing pleasure. This sort of thirst is risky, of course—"all this may happen before we know whether or not the object is beneficial to us"—but astonishment at some object is proportional to the risk taken.

It is not hard to understand why Irigaray regards wonder as the touchstone of sexual difference. For unlike systematic doubt, which denies the dynamics of woman's sexual organization or "economy" and is generally suspicious of pleasure of any sort, wonder is capable of shaping/ giving voice to the endless, polyvalent pleasure of the feminine. Though the "space" between man and woman is now glutted with "attraction, greed, possession, consummation, disgust, and so on" (*E* 13) and is thus painfully mundane, wonder can clear this space—make it a place of *jouissance*—as long as it "beholds what it sees always as if for the first time, never taking hold of the other as its object. It does not try to seize, possess, or reduce the object, but leaves it subjective, still free" (*E* 13). Wonder allows for difference in its own right and not simply as the dialectical opposition of something already known, already powerless to surprise. Indeed, Irigaray's wonder at the other is such that she can say, "Who or what the other is, I never know. But the other who is forever unknowable is the one who differs from me sexually" (*E* 13).

Charged with the passion of wonder, "man and woman, woman and man are always meeting as though for the first time because they cannot be substituted one for the other" (*E* 112–13). Their worlds are different and so is their writing. But the difference is not so radical that male and female lose contact with each other altogether. Rather, wonder ensures that male-female relationships are "fecund" because it preserves the tension inherent in sexual difference: "A separation without a wound, awaiting or remembering, without despair or closing in on the self. . . . Attracting me toward, wonder keeps me from taking and assimilating directly to myself" (*E* 75). Masculine logic, on the other hand, by denying that difference exists, creates an impassable gulf between the sexes: "Everything is constructed in such a way that these realities remain separate, even opposed to one another. So that they neither mix, marry, nor form an alliance" (*E* 15).

As Tina Chanter remarks, Irigaray (in keeping with Heidegger) objects to the Cartesian assumption that "the most basic relation between the 'I' and the world is one of knowledge" and instead affirms that "the foundational mode of experience is . . . one of existing in a context defined in terms of always already meaningful and significant relations."[25] Irigaray's unique contribution to this allusion to Descartes is her conviction that the foundational mode of experience is sexual difference and that it cannot be recognized as such without the passion of wonder. In counteracting the nihilism of masculine philosophy, in piecing together what masculine desire rends, philosophy based on sexual difference leads to healing. It would "constitute the horizon of worlds more fecund than any known to date" (*E* 5). The thinking here is clearly utopian—something we might not expect from a postmodern thinker (where "postmodern" is widely accepted to mean, as Lyotard puts it, "incredulity towards metanarratives"). As does Le Doeuff, Irigaray defends such forms of utopian thinking as long as they reject the Enlightenment metanarrative of being a "master discourse" and "referee for all other discourse types." However, this does not relieve postmodern strategies of their political responsibilities. As Le Doeuff writes:

> When feminists think that Simone de Beauvior's work mattered for the emancipation of at least a part of humankind, and that we must carry on, most of our up-to-date male colleagues at best smile, find us serious-minded, lacking a sense of playfulness, in short adopting an attitude which is neither up-to-date nor feminine. But we think we have to hold our heads above a stream of oppressive nonsense. Perhaps this is an eighteenth-century conception of philosophy—but he or she who will not live at all in the eighteenth century will never know what happiness is, as the saying goes.[26]

To live in the eighteenth century is to know happiness in the morality *par provision* and in wonder. By retrieving these features of Descartes' thought, Le Doeuff and Irigaray disclose the seeds of postmodernity already there but hidden underneath the obsessive need of modernity to dominate discourse via self-authorizing pronouncements. From now on, Descartes ought to be seen not only as contributing to the Enlightenment metanarrative but also as promoting and even embodying, in his divergent pronouncements, the difference at the heart of postmodernism.

Notes

An earlier version of this essay appeared in *Philosophy Today* 41 (1997): 367–82.

1. Michèle Le Doeuff, *Hipparchia's Choice: An Essay Concerning Women, Philosophy, Etc.,* trans. Trista Selous (Cambridge: Basil Blackwell, 1991), 27 (hereafter indicated as *HC*).

2. Rene Descartes, *Discourse on Method,* in *The Philosophical Writings [PW] of Descartes,* vol. 1, trans. J. G. Cottingham, R. Stoothoff, and D. Murdoch (New York: Cambridge University Press, 1985), 122; hereafter *DM*.

3. "Thus the whole of philosophy is like a tree. The roots are metaphysics, the trunk is physics, and the branches emerging from the trunk are all the other sciences, which may be reduced to three principal ones, namely medicine, mechanics, and morals. By 'morals' I understand the highest and most perfect moral system, which presupposes a complete knowledge of the other sciences and is the ultimate level of wisdom" (*DM,* 186).

4. Frederick Copleston, *A History of Philosophy,* vol. 4 (Westminster, MD: The Newman Press, 1959), 142, 146.

5. Stephen Gaukroger, *Descartes: An Intellectual Biography* (New York: Oxford University Press, 1995), 308.

6. John Cottingham, *A Descartes Dictionary* (Oxford: Blackwell Publishers, 1993), 129.

7. Michèle Le Doeuff, *The Philosophical Imaginary,* trans. Colin Gordon (Stanford: Stanford University Press, 1989), 57 (hereafter indicated as *PI*).

8. Descartes to Princess Elizabeth, 4 August 1645, in *The Philosophical Writings of Descartes,* vol. 3, trans. J. G. Cottingham, R. Stoothoff, D. Murdock, and A. Kenny (New York: Cambridge University Press, 1991), 257.

9. Descartes to Elizabeth, 28 June 1643, *ibid.,* 227.

10. Descartes, *Principles of Philosophy,* in *PW* 1: 289; hereafter *PP.*

11. Descartes to Elizabeth, 1 September 1645, in *PW* 3: 263.

12. *Ibid.,* 262.

13. *Rules for the Direction of the Mind,* in *PW* 1: 47.

14. Descartes to Elizabeth, 4 August 1645, in *PW* 3: 258.

15. Michèle Le Doeuff, "Michèle Le Doeuff," in Raoul Mortley, ed., *French Philosophers in Conversation* (New York: Routledge, 1991), 87.

16. See Luce Irigaray, *Speculum of the Other Woman,* trans. Gillian C. Gill (Ithaca: Cornell University Press, 1985), hereafter indicated as *Sp.*

17. Luce Irigaray, *This Sex Which Is Not One,* trans. Catherine Porter (Ithaca: Cornell University Press, 1985), 74 (hereafter indicated as *TS*).

18. Carolyn Burke, "Irigaray Through the Looking Glass," in Carolyn Burke, Naomi Schor, and Margaret Whitford, eds., *Engaging with Irigaray: Feminist Philosophy and Modern European Thought* (New York: Columbia University Press, 1994), 43.

19. Naomi Schor, "This Essentialism Which Is Not One: Coming to Grips with Irigaray," in *Engaging with Irigaray,* 67.

20. Luce Irigaray, *An Ethics of Sexual Difference,* trans. Carolyn Burke and Gillian C. Gill (Ithaca, New York: Cornell University Press, 1993), 9 (hereafter *E*).

21. Schor, "Essentialism," 71.

22. Cf. Toril Moi, Introduction to *French Feminist Thought* (New York: Basil Blackwell, 1987), 10.

23. Luce Irigaray, "Luce Irigaray," in *French Philosophers in Conversation,* 64.

24. Descartes, *Passions of the Soul,* in *PW,* 1: 337; hereafter *PS.*

25. Tina Chanter, *Ethics of Eros: Irigaray's Rewriting of the Philosophers* (New York: Routledge, 1995), 134. Cf. Irigaray, *Ethics,* 5.

26. Michèle Le Doeuff, "Ants and Women, or Philosophy without Borders," in A. Phillips Griffiths, ed., *Contemporary French Philosophy* (New York: Cambridge University Press, 1987), 48.

Between Pascal and Spinoza: The Vacuum

Pierre Macherey
Translated from the French by Stephen H. Daniel

Pascal and Spinoza are more or less contemporary: The first edition of the *Pensées* appeared in 1670, the same year as the *Tractatus Theologico-Politicus*. However, no direct communication passed between them; no real exchange occurred. It seems quite tenuous to argue that, because Spinoza's library contained the *Port Royal Logic,* his theory of definition recalls that of Pascal.[1] Then why draw these two thinkers closer when everything except their chronology seems to separate them? The explosive discourse of one, which gives free play to several possibilities or levels of readings, contrasts with the apparently closed system in which the other seems to envelop a homogeneous and univocal thought. But should we attribute the manifest (perhaps too obvious) characters that we are immediately tempted to give them, and should we think of them on the same scale of rationality, considering how Pascal seems to want to reduce the legitimate scope of reason's purview almost to the point of eliminating it, while Spinoza seeks on the contrary to extend it absolutely? Behind the proclaimed incoherence of Pascal's exasperated calls to disassemble the classic mechanisms of demonstration and bring them to where they turn against themselves, is there not a hidden order, a "veritable order" even more systematic than that which it subverts? Reciprocally, doesn't the irreversible sequence of propositions that constitutes the *Ethics* as an irreducible set of truths (to be taken or rejected as a whole) allow some room, if not for an alternative hermeneutic of interpretations, at least for the speculative tension of a demonstrative process that remains always open to later developments, and through such developments, to broadening or even questioning its own premises?[2] By juxtaposing the philosophical positions of Pascal and Spinoza and making them engage one another, we renovate our interpretations of them, deepen their significance, and at the same time give a new content to the concept of classical rationality.

L. Brunschwicq, who is interested in this juxtaposition, has used it to emphasize the difference that separates these two original modes of thought, and from this to map out the ideological or theoretical space to which they both belong and of which in a sense they occupy opposite sides: "Such a contrast is one of the most curious spectacles that the history of the thought can offer, and one of the most instructive as well. Its extent encompasses the entire intellectual horizon of the 17th Century, and it makes it possible both to illuminate its extremes and to fill in between them, while following, through the opposition of the two systems, the logical weaving that in their own ways and without gap or break joins mathematical principle and apologetic conclusion."[3] Far from being a superficial comparison seeking to isolate points of agreement and divergence, such a confrontation permits us then to highlight the intertext, "the intellectual horizon of the 17th century," on the grounds of which those points are detached and which they each designate in a distinctive manner. But is it even possible to retain this distinction between two types of exclusive argumentation, whose alternative would define the general problematic of classical rationalism? For two discourses to diverge, they also must engage or recoup one another and therefore share something in common—at least, for example, the same preoccupation with the difficulty of having to think along the lines laid out by Descartes, within the theoretical horizon he had opened and seemed in the same stroke to close again and that he had filled completely with his own concepts and procedures of arguing. In fact, Pascal and Spinoza start by recognizing the insufficiencies of a model of rationality that they will then try to transform by tackling precisely those questions that that model from its inception had pushed aside by refusing to allow reason any inroads, for example, into the domain of theology. From this point of view, it makes sense to read Pascal and Spinoza as if their difference or divergence belongs to the same discourse, not because they say the same thing but because the gap that separates them indicates a real contradiction, a historical contradiction proper to every intellectual conjuncture, which together they allow us to recognize in that they are themselves singular expressions of it.

In the limits of the exposition that follows, it will not be possible to examine this question as a whole: Rather than enumerate the points where Pascalian and Spinozistic discourse cross without joining or aligning with one another, it seems preferable to emphasize the stakes of this discussion by focusing on an analysis of only one clue (as long as it is a significant one). The problem of the vacuum (or void) is sufficiently symptomatic in this regard, in that it recalls Spinoza's and Pascal's relation to Cartesianism in the context of a well delimited and doubtlessly crucial question, the resolution of which involves the most fundamental notions of the philosophy.

On this question, the positions of Pascal and Spinoza seem to be extreme opposites of one another, and their encounter on this point has the appearance of an irreducible divergence. Indeed, on one hand, we find a declared partisan for the vacuum: From the *New Experiments on the Vacuum* of 1647 (the experiments in Rouen) to the *Treatises on the Equilibrium of Liquids and the Weight of the Mass of Air* (which must have been composed in 1651 but were published only in 1663), between which occurs the polemic with Father Noël and the "grand experiment of the equilibrium of liquids" (the experiment in Clermont-Ferrand in 1648), Pascal becomes known to the erudite public as a defender of the experimental point of view in questions of physics. It is this point of view that led him to dissociate himself from the "novels about nature" in which uncontrolled reason succumbs to traps of the imagination, as in the Aristotelian and Cartesian theories of nature, which have in common at least their rejection of the vacuum. On the other hand, Spinoza aligns himself no less expressly with the camp of the adversaries of the vacuum: not only in his *Principles of Cartesian Philosophy* of 1661 (II P3) but also in his correspondence of 1663 with Oldenburg about Boyle's experiments with nitre (Letters 6, 9, and 13). Even in the *Ethics* (I P15 schol.), he denounces as an "absurdity" the thesis of the existence of a vacuum, whose impossibility is accordingly established by strictly rational and theoretical (thus, a priori) procedures. The simple and perfectly explicit enumeration of texts, apart from raising any questions regarding interpretation, seems to lead us straight to this conclusion: Pascal's reflections and those of Spinoza inscribe themselves in incompatible contexts, revealing forms of reason that appear irreconcilable; nothing is left to do but admit to the difference that individualizes them in separating them. We can even confer by means of their opposition on this question of the vacuum an emblematic value, giving their respective works a specific stamp: Does not the dispersed structure of the *Pensées* reveal in an unstable and rarefied order of bodies the incomplete ideas at the heart of the apologetic void that digs into human existence the remoteness of a hidden God? By contrast, the dense and compact texture of the *Ethics* expresses continuously, without interruption or gap, the productivity of infinite substance, completely full of its power, to which nothing, thing or idea, can be lacking.

But is it possible to draw conclusions on this matter based on the simple consideration of the results and their avowed theses without taking into consideration the procedures of argument on which these theses depend as a whole? And can the basic opposition that has just been identified then be maintained, at least in these terms? We have to ask what, for

Pascal, a defense of the vacuum means exactly: Does it amount to the observation of an empirical fact, leading him unilaterally to take the side of experience against reason, and to what extent does this experience establish the effective or real existence of the vacuum apart from the presupposed rational whole? Alternatively, by discarding from the start the possibility of a vacuum, doesn't Spinoza extend Descartes' line of thinking by apparently borrowing his conception of *res extenso*, thus unifying absolutely the doctrines of physics and geometry? Or even more: Doesn't his strategy contribute to putting into place an original conception of nature that signifies, if not a complete renunciation of the theses of classical mechanism, at least a recasting of them in terms of a perspective that can no longer be considered Cartesian? In posing such questions, we engage in the enterprise of rereading the texts of Pascal and Spinoza to escape from the abusive simplification that isolates them from one another, and instead we think of them together, not by confounding their approaches but by specifying the different stakes at issue for each of them respectively.

Let's begin by looking at how Pascal poses the question of the vacuum. He does not confront it as a timeless and theoretical question, able to be considered by itself apart from any historical or practical determination. The writings he devotes to it must consequently be restored to the concrete context that gives them their meaning. But we should note how, when Pascal strikingly dissociates himself in 1647 from the then widespread denial of the vacuum, his rejection is expressed in terms of at least three fundamental positions that must carefully be distinguished. One, deriving from Aristotle, affirms that nature does not admit a vacuum and that it "abhors" it; this is, if you will, the thesis of absolute horror. Another position was defended by Galileo, for whom, even though nature abhors a vacuum, it is not impossible nevertheless that it admits a vacuum in some of its parts; this is the thesis of limited horror. Finally, Descartes maintained that nature, equated with pure extension whose matter and bodies are only determinations, has no place for a vacuum, but that does not mean that a vacuum is repugnant to nature in the sense that this would directly or indirectly imply any finality. Pascal himself will add to this list a new view, one whose content can be summarized this way: Nature does not abhor a vacuum; indeed, it must even admit it as one of its components.

What have we learned by enumerating these theses? That the discussion of the vacuum is complex insofar as it brings into play two questions that we should not confuse: One relates to the horror of the vacuum; the other to its effective existence. But the intervention of Pascal in this debate is remarkable initially because it carefully dissociates these two questions, to which it then successively applies completely different treatments.

The issue of the horror of the vacuum is for Pascal a simple question of physics, which as such can be decided using an experimental technique (viz., the one employed in Puy-de-Dôme). That technique simultaneously reveals and demonstrates how nature does not abhor a vacuum and how the effects traditionally attributed to this horror are explained perfectly by gravity of the mass of the air which constitutes its unique and true cause. This way of thinking, at the same time rational and experimental, as it appears in the reading of the *Treatises* of 1651, occurs in the context of the polemic against the qualitative physics of the Schoolmen. Furthermore, we know that despite claims that Pascal formulated this demonstration, Descartes had likewise confirmed these conclusions. It is not surprising, then, to see Spinoza, at least when he is treated as the interpreter of Descartes, adopting the same argument, even though he balances it with his own experimental confirmation and gives it a completely a priori form. As he comments, "Since the parts of matter are really distinct from one another (by *Principles* I, 61), one can exist without another (by IP7cor), and they do not depend on one another. So all those fictions about Sympathy and Antipathy are to be rejected as false. Moreover, since the cause of a certain effect must always be positive, we should never say that a body moves in order that there not be a vacuum, but that it is moved only from the impulse that it receives from another."[4] On this point the declarations of Pascal and Spinoza are therefore exactly convergent, which indicates that they both accept the insights of the scientific revolution acquired in the first half of the seventeenth century due to the efforts of Galileo and Descartes, who had completely discredited the traditional principles of the explanation of nature inspired fundamentally by Aristotle. But should we conclude that by that same step they ratify the new vision of the world that was part of the earlier view and is based on the project of a complete mathematization of nature? It is by examining the other aspect of the problem of the vacuum (viz., its effective existence)—on which Pascal and Spinoza differ from one another and Descartes—that it will be possible to answer such a question.

This problem initially arises for Pascal as a problem of physics, and he turns to an appropriate experimental technique to deal with it, namely, the experiments in Rouen a year prior to those in Clermont-Ferrand, "experiments so convincing that they were safe from all objections anyone could raise," according to the *Preface* devoted to them. Pascal's proposed interpretation of these experiments leads him to claim that "the empty space that appeared in these experiments is indeed empty of all material that is sensible and known in nature." This thesis is so different from the preceding one that it sounds as though, in his *Preface* of 1647, he still makes room for the horror of the vacuum that he will dismiss definitively only in 1648. But the distinction between these two theses relates not only to their contents but also to the form in which they are established and enunciated. Initially, the status of the experiments in Rouen is very different from that of the experiments in Puy-de-Dôme; despite Pascal's expressed declarations, we can question whether he actually conducted them and think of them as thought experiments. It is possible then to think of them, at least in spirit, as not that much different from the theoretical constructions of Aristotle or Descartes.[5] Here is what Pascal himself declares on this point in the conclusion of his *Preface* (the substitute for the anticipated *Treatise on the Vacuum*, which was never written or was lost): "After having shown that nothing sensible or known apparently fills this empty space, my view is that, unless someone shows the existence of the matter that fills it, it is truly empty and lacking all matter. This is why I will say of the real vacuum what I showed of the apparent vacuum." What does the experiment here "show," that the vacuum is real or fictitious? It shows that somewhere in the syringes, siphons, pipes, and tubes described by Pascal exists an apparent vacuum. When Pascal concludes from this apparent vacuum an effective (that is, real) vacuum, since this space is filled with no matter that is known or capable of being sensed, he well specifies that his move is based on a "feeling" (*sentiment*). This formula is rather important because it reappears in his correspondence with Father Noël: "Lastly, Father, consider, I pray you, that everyone knows how to show that no body seems to take the place of that which leaves an empty space, and that it is also not possible for anyone to show that, when water goes back up there, some body left that space. Wouldn't that be enough, on your principles, to prove that this space is empty? Nonetheless, I say simply that my feeling is that it is empty." Here the experiment establishes not the real existence of the vacuum, which is simply postulated, but the absence of any known matter where there is apparent vacuum; it is thus reason that passes from one of these assertions to the other, without reducing them to one another. Also, in his letter to Le Pailleur, Pascal defends himself vigorously against having confused them: "He (Father Noël) pretends that I have asserted in no uncertain terms the real existence of empty space; and based on this pretense which he takes for a constant truth, he works his pen to show the weakness of the assertion. But he could see that I put in my publication that I conclude simply that it will be my sentiment that this space is empty until someone shows me that some matter fills it, which is not a real assertion of the vacuum." Does this mean that Pascal definitely rules out such an assertion? If so, his position would not be far from Descartes' or the view defended by Spinoza, except that Pascal, in any case, eliminates the assumption of "subtle matter," which for him is still more a fantasy of the imagination than a rational construct.

It is here in his proceedings that Pascal takes into account the problem of definition: "He [always referring to Father Noël] believed that I affirmed the real existence of the vacuum in virtue of the very terms by which I defined it. I know that those who are not accustomed to seeing things treated in the correct order imagine that one cannot define a thing without asserting its being; but they should notice that we must always define things before looking to see whether they are possible or not." Pascal, though, attaches great importance to the distinction between "calling" and "asserting," a point that he rehearses in well-known passages of his small work, *The Spirit of Geometry.* By contrast, we should remember that Spinozistic discourse is based on definitions of words that are also indissociable from definitions of things since, according to the formula of his Letter 4 to Oldenburg, "any definition, being a clear and distinct idea, is true," that is, it necessarily agrees with its ideatum (the object of the idea). Is the vacuum therefore for Pascal only a name, an appellation, a conventional expression cut off from any relationship to reality, and thus only an object of a "sentiment," hardly distinct in that respect from a "nice idea" that cannot be proven and is open, by its very nature, to contradictory claims? Such an interpretation would obviously be unacceptable. It is necessary therefore that we ask what it means to define the concept of vacuum before discussing the reality to which it corresponds. Nonetheless, this preliminary definition has as its function precisely to rule out all arbitrariness from the concept by otherwise removing all its prerequisites. Again let us quote the letter to Le Pailleur: "When I wanted to oppose the conclusions of Father Noël that excluded the vacuum from nature, I thought that I could not enter into this research, nor even say a word about it, before having declared what I understand by the word *vacuum,* which seemed to me more required by certain remarks in his first letter, which made me realize that the concept he had did not conform to mine. I saw that he could not distinguish dimensions from matter, nor immateriality from nothing; and that this confusion made him conclude that, when I gave this space length, width, and depth, I was in effect saying that it was a body; and that once I made it immaterial, I had reduced it to nothing. To clear up all these ideas, I provided him with this definition, in which he can see that the thing that we conceive and that we refer to by the expression *empty space,* occupies a place between matter and nothing but does not participate in either; that it differs from nothing by its dimensions; and that its lack of resistance and immobility distinguish it from matter. In this way it remains tied to these two extremes without merging with either."

The work of definition to which Pascal attaches such methodological importance, and which is completely distinct from that of experimental demonstration, highlights what here constitutes the fundamental point of the discussion; that is, the possibility of thinking matter without space, extension without bodies, is what calls into question the synthesis between geometry and physics effected by Cartesianism. But the new investigation that arises from these presuppositions is no longer one of experimental physics; likewise, the existence of a vacuum as such is inaccessible to experiments, which can at most give only indirect and incomplete confirmations of it. This investigation concerns a theoretical speculation that has for its object nature in general. It is of the type that the ancients had devoted to Being and its kinds, but here, one will think more of Democritus and Epicurus than Aristotle. In his work on Gassendi's philosophy, O. Bloch has shown that, on this point, the views of Gassendi and Pascal are identical.[6] By portraying space as well as time as kinds of being that are not reducible to categories of substance and accident but have a different existence, both thinkers call into question the categories of Aristotelian ontology—it is no longer only about physics here—as well as the general interpretation of nature that follows from it. Conversely, we can ask whether Descartes and Spinoza themselves remain prisoners of this traditional ontology to the extent that they refuse to think of a reality that is of neither substance nor accident.

It is not possible to develop the details of this discussion, where physical and metaphysical speculation mix inextricably. So, let's go directly to its essence. Why don't Aristotle and his defenders admit the possibility of a vacuum, that is, a kind of existence that is not covered by the distinction of genus and accident? It stems from a principle invoked by Father Noël based on the following formula: "concerning that which is not, there are no differentiations" (*non entis not sunt differentiae*). Spinoza himself recalls this principle in the form of an axiom at the beginning of the second part of his *Principles of Cartesian Philosophy:* "Regarding nothing there are no properties (*nihili nullae is proprietates*)." But the argument developed by Pascal adopts a position exactly opposite to the reasoning that concludes with the absurdity of the vacuum (that is, a nothingness endowed with determinate characteristics). Pascal does not allot to nothingness necessarily imaginary properties, but he posits the need to think a reality apart from any determination, one that "occupies the middle ground between matter and nothingness." The meaning of this notion is well captured by the concept of a vacuum, or rather what Pascal calls a vacuum. The reality of an indeterminate space, which is thus incapable, whatever it is, of being identified with a body, would be its whole nature, comparable to an animated system, as Aristotle calls it, or even an abstract but still material extension, since as Descartes claims all corporeal reality can be recovered by thought. However, what is really at issue in this debate about the problem of the relation between the real and its limit is obviously the problem of infinity in the sense that it can adopt when applied to the study of nature and its limitlessness. To think the unlimited, which constitutes the crux of all Cartesianism, is also to think the reality of what is without limit, as with Gassendi's "imaginary space," which, as O. Bloch shows, is imaginary not because of its fictitious character but because it lacks any function and property. That is what makes it a negative reality, midway between being and nonbeing. The matter that composes all bodies of nature is distinguished from this empty space in that it by contrast is necessarily determined (that is, limited). What, then, according to Pascal, is nature? It is a mixture, composed of space and matter, which includes at the same time the unlimited and limited. Here we see a conception of the world sketched out that raises a problem for which classical rationalism does not have a ready solution: How to think together limitlessness and limit, the finite and the infinite, without reducing one to the other, without collapsing them into one another?

We see by this that the study of motion is completely renovated: Motion is a property of body, by which it expresses limitation in some manner; whereas space is itself motionless, which is the consequence of its infinity and by which it is eternally entire in oneself. Recalling his experiments in Rouen and anticipating those in Clermont-Ferrand, Pascal again specifies in his letter to Le Pailleur that "regardless of how it appears, the vacuum is not transported by a tube, and immobility is as natural to space as motion is to body. To make this truth obvious, we should note that space in general includes all bodies in nature, of which each in particular occupies a certain part. Nevertheless, all bodies are mobile, but not the space they fill, because when a body is moved from one place to another, it does nothing but change place, without carrying with it that which it occupied at the time of its rest." If space is motionless, it is not in the sense of having a property or being in a corporeal state, but it is in virtue of its limitlessness that in all its parts it is always the same space. This can be said of a vacuum as well to the extent that it is full only of itself, without requiring for its existence or nonexistence the addition of any determination. This also means that there cannot be gaps in its extension, just as Descartes and Spinoza also think. To say that nature is composed of space and body, as Pascal suggests, thus does not mean positing the existence of empty space along with bodies as separate entities, in terms of which it would consequently be necessary to think their combination by appeal to a third "kind" of being—but this is to portray bodies in space in such a way that, where there is body there is also space; in which case there cannot be a space without body, that is, an effective vacuum. We thus need to go all the way to these final consequences to understand what the thesis of the heterogeneity of extension and matter means.

We see then why barometric experiment, in all its forms, reveals only an apparent vacuum, not a real vacuum; it is that the reality of the vacuum, that is, unlimited space, cannot be enclosed in the limits of a tube where the movement of liquids, stopping at a given level that leaves the upper part vacant, to some extent casts a window of light on this infinite extension which, in any case, is everywhere present and the same, both where there is body and where there obviously is not. In the *Preface* of 1647, Pascal formulates a hypothesis whose content is evidently theoretical because seemingly no experimental device could exhaustively test it: "a tube so large that we would be able to empty it of all the known and sensible material things in nature." At its limit, the whole universe would thus, at least in thought, be "emptied" of all its corporeal substance without losing anything of its immense reality. The more developed fragment from the *Pensées*, "The Disproportion of Man," requires exactly such imaginative aids to provide content to this representation of the infinity of nature, a representation that encompasses, absorbs, and in a sense swallows all determinations that we can confer on it, without ever disappearing with them.

For Spinoza, such an infinite regress is the symptom of an inadequate and mutilated knowledge regulated not by reason but by imagination. The limitlessness that it deploys can be only that of the bad infinity, which is without effective content, applying as much to substance as to its modes, precisely because, being neither substance nor mode, the reality that it identifies is purely negative. If reason chooses the plenum rather than the vacuum, it does so to express by contrast the real meaning of infinity, which is absolutely positive. This same reasoning leads Spinoza to affirm in *Ethics* IP8 that "every substance is necessarily infinite." But this infinity means that it is impossible for substance to be divided; the traditional aporiae that oppose indivisibility and infinity have value only from the point of view of the imagination, which seeks to measure the infinite with the aid of number and thus misunderstands its true essence. According to Letter 12 to Louis Meyer, "they talk utter nonsense, perhaps even madness, who claim that extended substance is formed by an assembly of parts or bodies really distinct from one another. This would be as if someone were to try to form a square by adding or accumulating several circles, or to produce in the same way a triangle or anything else of a completely different essence." However, this error is in particular that of Descartes, who contrasts the divisibility of extension to the indivisibility of the thought; this contrast, expressed in particular in the sixth Meditation, is at the basis of his dualism. To resolve the difficulties resulting from this imaginary distinction, Descartes himself had to restore between the parts of extension a strict continuity, which reestablishes the unity of nature fictitiously. But the contiguous is not the continuous; the plenitude of nature, such as Spinoza conceives it adequately, completely reverses the traditional conception of material reality, which tends to separate it from the divine substance and relegates it to the rank of an appearance or a creature, thus breaking the unity of *Natura naturans* and *Natura naturata*. To understand extension as a substance is to give up opposing it to thought and to conclude that it forms with thought an indivisible whole to which nothing can be lacking that would limit its perfection. This is why "if only one part of matter were annihilated all extension would immediately vanish," according to Letter 4 to Oldenburg; and all extension is effectively present in one drop of water, exactly as all thought is also implied in the presence of one idea, whatever it is.

Come to think of it, if we look beyond the words to understand the sense that they communicate, does Pascal say anything other than this? In giving his "sentiment" on the vacuum, he well involves himself in postulating infinity, that is, the indivisibility of extension, which is irreducible as such to some corporeal part of the nature that it is, and which thus must be able to be thought in itself independently of the presence of all finite material reality. What we call this full or empty infinity is after all a question of designation, and that is matter of indifference regarding the content of the reasoning that it aids in formulating.

Does that mean that the conceptions of nature elaborated by Pascal and Spinoza are homogeneous or even convergent? Obviously not, as the simple following consideration indicates: If Pascal affirms the infinity of nature, it is to oppose it to that of God, of which it is only the apologetic inversion. The silence of infinite and empty spaces declares the absent presence of a hidden God, from whom our fallen nature separates us absolutely, even while binding us inextricably to that presence. "What is it, then, that this longing and this impotence proclaims to us, but that there was once in man a true happiness of which there now remains in him only the mark and empty trace, which he in vain tries to fill from all his surroundings, seeking from things absent the help he does not obtain from things present? But these present things are all inadequate, because the infinite abyss can only be filled by an infinite object, that is to say, only by God himself."[7] The exterior vacuum is only the sign of this interior vacuum that nothing can fill and is otherwise absolutely inaccessible: the infinite, that is, the void (or vacuum), is an abyss where all human hopes are absorbed, drawn by an irresistible movement that no reasoning can stop. It is here that the theme of the horror of the vacuum unexpectedly returns for Pascal, applied this time not to material nature but to human nature: "Nothing is so unbearable to man as to be completely at rest, without passions, without business, without diversion. He then feels his nothingness, his forlornness, his insufficiency, his dependence, his weakness, his emptiness. From the depth of his heart uncontrollably will arise weariness, gloom, sadness, fretfulness, spite, despair."[8] Spinozistic ethics condemns this negative passion precisely because it rules out thinking of the infinite negatively when it is tied to the return of transcendence. And it is finally this dilemma—should the infinite be thought positively or negatively— that conditions the alternatives of the plenum and the vacuum.

What should we conclude from this example whose presentation has been only sketched out? That it is undoubtedly impossible to reconcile Pascal and Spinoza because their philosophical positions are irreducibly divergent. But it is possible nevertheless to read them together and concurrently in order to reveal the true points of the conflict on which they differ and on which all classical thought differs as well.

Notes

"Entre Pascal et Spinoza: le vide" was originally presented at a colloquium organized in October 1982 by the University of Urbino to commemorate the 300th anniversary of Spinoza's birth. It was published in a collection of the colloquium presentations (*Proceedings of the First Italian Congress on Spinoza* [Naples: Bibliopolis, 1985], 71–87) and reprinted in Pierre Macherey, *Avec Spinoza* (Paris: Presses Universitaires de France, 1992), 152–67.

1. Stanislaus von Dunin-Borkowski, *Spinoza* (4 vols.; Münster: Aschendorff, 1933–36), 4: 187.

2. On this point, see Antonio Negri, *The Savage Anomaly: The Power of Spinoza's Metaphysics and Politics*, translated by Michael Hardt (Minneapolis: University of Minnesota Press, 1991).

3. L. Brunschwicg, *Spinoza et ses contemporains* (Paris: Presses Universitaires de France, 1951), 198.

4. *The Principles of Cartesian Philosophy*, part II, proposition 8, scholium.

5. This thesis is proposed by Alexandre Koyré in his study on "Pascal savant" (Colloque de Royaumont, 1954).

6. Olivier Bloch, *La philosophie de Gassendi* (The Hague: M. Nijhoff, 1971), 172 ff.

7. *Pensées. Texte de l'édition Brunschvicg*, ed. Charles Marc Des Granges (Paris: Garnier Frères, 1964), no. 425.

8. *Ibid.*, no. 131.

Potentia multitudinis, quae una veluti mente ducitur: Spinoza on the Body Politic

Etienne Balibar

Translated from the French by Stephen H. Daniel

In this essay I have a simple aim, but it is one that seems to raise fundamental questions in Spinozism: To try to explain the strange expression used by Spinoza notably at the beginning of the *Tractatus Politicus* III, section 2: "*potentia multitudinis, quae una veluti mente ducitur*" ("the power of the multitude guided, as it were, by one mind"). This expression (other instances of which I will mention shortly) occurs at a key moment in the argument of the *Treatise:* after equating "right" and "power" and before making a fundamental distinction between the two possible statutory conditions of an individual (dependence and independence: *esse alterius juris, esse sui juris*), Spinoza undertakes to define the nature of the power of the State and its relation to (1) the traditional concept of "sovereignty" and (2) the distribution of rights and duties among citizens. The remark has been a stumbling block for interpreters because of the restrictive qualification of the preposition *veluti* ("as it were") in that it seems to introduce a note of uncertainty into the reference to the *mens* (soul or mind) of political communities—and consequently also to their "body" or "corporeity" (*corpus*). Some commentators gloss over the passage quickly whereas others discuss it in detail, appealing to central themes in Spinoza's system; all recognize, however, that it presents a problem that needs to be addressed.

To try in my turn to determine what is concerned in this formulation, I will proceed by gradually expanding the scope of the enquiry. I initially propose to "read" Spinoza's sentence literally (using various translations as the occasion arises) to formulate what about it is or can seem to be paradoxical. I will then indicate how P. F. Moreau's critique of the interpretations of the Spinozistic formula developed by Matheron, Rice, and Negri tries to resolve their aporias in a way that is not yet fully satisfactory. To overcome this difficulty, I will place the Spinozistic formulation in a series of contexts that, for me, point to the principles on which rest a solution. Paradoxically, even though this approach aspires to be "literal" or "literalistic," it requires that I portray certain features of his system in a way that ultimately leads me (though this would really be the topic for another essay) to highlight even more general questions, first about the function of the concept of *mens* (mind) and second about the relation of "individuality," "causality," and "adequation" in the doctrines of the author of the *Ethics*. In a sense, then, the issues raised regarding this seemingly specific problem become a focus for understanding his system as a whole.

A Paradoxical Restriction?

Let's start by recalling the sentence of Spinoza in its entirety so that the syntactic articulations are made obvious:

> . . . patet imperii, seu summarum potestatum Jus nihil esse praeter ipsum naturae Jus, quod potentia, non quidem uniuscujusque, sed multitudinis, quae una veluti mente ducitur, determinatur, hoc est, quod [sicuti] unusquisque in statu naturali, sic etiam totius imperii corpus,[1] et mens tantum juris habet, quantum potentia valet.[2]

It is useful here to cite the translation of the passage in several languages to highlight the alternative interpretations that they imply. I have retrieved three notably authorized versions: in French, that of Pierre-François Moreau; in Italian, that of Paolo Cristofolini; in German, that of Wolfgang Bartuschat:

> . . . le droit de l'Etat, ou du pouvoir souverain n'est rien d'autre que le droit même de la nature. Il est déterminé par la puissance, non plus de chaque individu, mais de la multitude, qui est conduite comme par un seul esprit; autrement dit, comme c'est le cas à l'état naturel, pour chaque individu, le corps et l'esprit de l'Etat tout entier ont autant de droit que de puissance.[3]

> . . . il diritto dello stato, ossia del potere sovrano, non è altro se non il diritto stesso di natura, determinato dalla potenza non di un singolo, ma del popolo, come guidato da una sola mente; vale a dire che, come un singolo allo stato di natura, cosi pure il corpo e la mente dell'intero stato hanno tanto diritto quanta è la potenza che possono far valere.[4]

> . . . das Recht des Staates oder der höchsten Gewalten nichts anderes ist
> als eben das Recht der Natur, das durch die Macht, nun nicht mehr jedes
> einzelnen, sondern der wie von einem Geist geleiteten Menge bestimmt
> wird. Gerade so wie im Fall eines einzelnen im Naturzustand hat also
> auch der Körper und der Geist eines ganzen Staates so viel Recht, wie
> weit dessen Macht reicht.[5]

Several problems seem to arise in a close reading of the passage. The first concerns which type of modification, "explanatory" or "determinative," is introduced here by the *quae*. Should we think that the right/power of the State or the sovereign, considered as one sole individuality, is determined by the power of the *multitudo because* it "is guided as by only one mind" (or only one soul), or *when* (*to the extent that*) it "is guided as by only one mind"? Moreau, following the Latin, keeps both possibilities open. Without excluding the "explanatory" solution absolutely—it is of the essence of the multitude to be guided as by only one mind—Bartuschat suggests the second option: the *multitudo* or *Menge* that determines that the power of the State is not simply the "masses" but rather *that which* is guided as . . . and so on). By contrast, Cristofolini goes clearly in the first direction, in line with his translation-interpretation—by no means unlikely in a political context—of *multitudo* as *popolo*.[6] His translation suggests that the people are the masses or a multitude that acts "as guided by only one mind" and as such determines the power of the State (that is, is its foundation or substance). In the first case, we seek primarily to know the conditions under which a multitude can be unified by a direction that gives it a unique soul or mind. In the second—drawing on the principle that *omnia sunt animata*—we try to understand why Spinoza hesitates to name the *mens* that corresponds to this individualized "body" that is a people constituted in the State.

This first problem is complicated by a second: how to give due justice to the modality introduced by *veluti*. On which term or terms does its meaning depend? Taking into account the plasticity that the Latin syntax affords, there are at most three possibilities: *veluti* relates to the whole activity (it is as if the multitude were guided by only one mind or soul); *veluti* relates to the agent (it is as if the multitude were guided by a single soul, as if there were a soul to guide it); or *veluti* relates specifically to *una* (which is perhaps stylistically the most satisfactory), as if the soul or mind (even the thought, as in Appuhn's translation, to which I will return) which guides the multitude in the State were unique or unified. This third variation is interesting because it moves us from one extreme to the other regarding the question of *mens* in relation to the multitude, in the same way (as we will see shortly) as does raising the question of the relation of the *multitudo* to the *imperium*. It would seem, then, that the sentence taken in its entirety and qualified by a "hoc est" (*that is*) ought to remove our uncertainty on both points simultaneously: *hoc est, quod sicuti unusquisque in statu naturali, sic etiam totius imperii corpus, et mens tantum juris habet, quantum potentia valet.* But it is this explanation that actually puts us into the quandary.

Spinoza's claim is based on a comparison (*sicuti*) between the individuality of the singular human being ("in the state of nature," that is, in accord with nature) and the individuality of the *imperium* (which gives form, and thus body, to the *multitudo*). But one of two things can be said:

1. Spinoza introduces the restriction only to spare the reader who is not ready to consider the State or the body politic as an individual in the full sense, with all the consequences that follow in Spinozistic theory (in particular, the existence of a soul that as the "idea of the body" corresponds exactly to that "body"). But what is decisive here is the fact that, strictly applying the same law of composition to all individualities of various levels (or of different complexity, in which case some are "parts" of others), this establishes the correlative existence of one *corpus* and one *mens* in all individualities, and in particular (to generalize implicitly from *Ethics* IIP7S) *in the same sense* for the human individual and the political individual in which the *Civitas* is at the same time *imperium* and *multitudo*. This strict thesis raises all kinds of ambiguities and will serve as the basis for deductions that follow concerning the nature of the State and its various forms (in particular, all those that concern *conservation of its proper form*). But how can it happen that, in the many passages of the *TP* where Spinoza mentions the question of the unity and individuality of the "body politic" and the "mental reality" corresponding to it (to use one of the equivalent expressions suggested by Pierre Macherey), both *before* chapter 3, 2, and *afterward*, the expression *una veluti mente ducitur* can appear in an almost stereotypic way, sometimes in connection with *homines*, sometimes in connection with the *multitudo* itself, and all the while the polis or State is portrayed as an exception to the "absolute" use of the *corpus-mens* couple?

2. Or, by contrast, the restrictive modality contained in the *veluti*—however we take the first proposition of Spinoza (as reservation, approximation, analogy, or hypothetical assumption)—continues to apply to the second proposition and the comparison it highlights. The possibility of speaking of the *corpus* and *mens* of the State—acknowledging how the State is never anything other than the coming together or the expression of the power of the multitude—always ought to take account of the fact that here the *mens* that acts has only a metaphorical identity

(to use Lee C. Rice's term). What Spinoza would have meant, then, is that undoubtedly the constitution of a "body politic" illustrates general theorems that relate to individuation (which could be expressed ironically, recalling the celebrated formula of the Preface of part III of the *Ethics*, by saying that the *imperium* or the political State is not in nature *veluti imperium in imperio*, as "a State in the State") but that the comparison of several types of individuality immediately runs into an unavoidable dissymmetry. *In the proper sense* there would be no collective *mens*, but only an *effect* of mental or psychic unity which manifests itself in a "conduct" or "direction" of the State that would be confused in practice with the exercise of sovereignty. But if that is the case, embarrassing consequences seem to follow. Specifically, since there is some doubt about the reality of the collective unity or the ensemble of ideas (indicated here analogically by the term *mens*) which evokes the concept of the human soul revealed in the *Ethics* but which cannot correspond to it exactly, *is there any way to prevent such doubt from being extended as well to the possibility of characterizing the polis or the State as a body* in the strict sense of the term, that is, as a material individual that tends to preserve itself in virtue of its proper essence or law of composition?

Consider how the problem is closely linked to the question of interpretation posed by other formulations in both the *TP* and the *Ethics*. This is particularly the case in *Ethics* IVP18S, which is all the more interesting since it proposes an ideal genesis of collective individuality based on the junction (or composition) of forces of two or several simple individualities according to their natural "suitability" or reciprocal utility: "*nihil, inquam, homines praestantius ad suum esse conservandum, optare possunt, quam quod omnes in omnibus ita conveniant, ut omnium Mentes et Corpora unam quasi Mentem, unumque Corpus componant, et omnes simul, quantum possunt, suum esse conservare conentur.*"[7] One could obviously suppose that the *quasi* here (very much like our *veluti*) relates only to the unity of the soul, leaving untouched that of the body. But apart from the fact that such a reading contradicts the practice of the Latin rhetoric (which seeks a symmetry of meaning in the dissymmetry of the construction),[8] it would make unintelligible the explanatory position that the *Ethics* formulation occupies compared to the various formulations in the *TP*.

We should remember that in the latter work, besides the many occurrences of the expression *una veluti mente ducitur,* we also find a symmetrical formula about the body, which posits an element of approximation or analogy: *necesse ergo est, ut Patricii omnes legibus ita astringantur, ut unum veluti corpus, quod una regitur mente, componant* (*TP* VIII, section 19).[9] Here it is the supposed unity of the soul that determines on the side of the body the analogue of an autonomous individuality. *In any case, all this hap-*

pens as if the individuality perceived on one side (is it necessary to say "under one of the attributes"?) always proves to be problematic or deficient from the other side (as one would say, "under the other attribute"). This the text of the *Ethics* could explain clearly by indicating that, in the final analysis, the composition of the *conatus* of human individuals in a political collective realizes only *the analogue* of a higher individuality, not individuality in its proper sense. The designation of the polis as "individual," which stems both from Spinoza's desire to treat all ethical, political, and anthropological questions according to the principles of natural knowledge and from the need to explain the *transfer of right* that situates the formation of a polis between the sovereign and the particular subject (citizen), is thus permanently infected with an internal vacillation.

But we risk finding ourselves confronted with an even more embarrassing problem. Many of the formulas which I have cited[10] in effect rest on an analogy of the popular masses or institutions with the "body" of the State, whereas *mens* (sometimes *caput: TP* IX, section 14) retrieves the character of a command, decision, or legislation. This analogy is certainly traditional (since the fable of Menenius Agrippa at least). But it forces us to acknowledge that it contradicts the scheme of intelligibility commonly designated under the name of parallelism, which (according to the account given in *Ethics* II) would be better described as the *identity of difference* between the "orders" and "connections" of ideas (the whole ensemble of which forms *mens*) and things (the first heading of which is *corpora*).[11] It seems, then, that we find ourselves faced with a destructive dilemma. On one hand, the recognition of the individuality of political bodies or States is made possible only *in contrast* to the spirit of "parallelism." That is, individuality is or *is not* realized simultaneously as the material cohesion of parts and as an intellectual or (more generally) mental unity in the form of a collective thought or aim toward the collective. But on the other hand, insofar as the mechanism of unification ought to be described *politically* as a play of forces or powers and institutions, it can be depicted only as an effect of mental activity (deliberation, decision, representation) on suitably receptive bodies, which is to deprive it of ontological significance and thus to portray it in a way that otherwise is completely absurd from a Spinozistic point of view.

Some Problematic Attempts at a Solution

These difficulties have provided readers of the *TP* with a good bit to chew on. It is enough for me to invoke four justifiably well-known interpretations. I will call the first three "dogmatic," not to devalue them but because they all propose—although in opposing senses—that the solution lies immediately in a correct understanding of Spinozism that they aim to explicate. Moreau's interpretation, by contrast, can be called "critical" because, following on the others, it regards their opposition even as part of the problem and undertakes to construct a hypothetical solution that seeks in the texts the means to answer the questions that their confrontation poses.[12]

Dogmatic Solutions

Matheron

I would first like to note certain particularly interesting points made by Matheron, who returns on several occasions to the question we are considering. In *Individu et communité chez Spinoza* he opens his reconstruction of Spinozist political theory with an analysis of the relationship between the questions of individuation, complexity (or the nature of the relationship between wholes and parts), and adequation (and inadequation, regarding both their ideas and causes) based solely on the propositions of the *Ethics*. In that work he sees (following the leads of Spinoza himself) the foundations for understanding propositions relating to politics. He proposes to follow this route of explication rigorously, and so references to the *Tractatus Politicus* appear rather late in his discussion. On pp. 346–47 of his book, Matheron highlights the remarks of *TP* IV, §1: "*Jus summarum potestatum, quod earum potentia determinatur . . . in hoc potissimum consistere vidimus, nempe quod imperii veluti mens sit, qua omnes duci debent,*"[13] and uses this passage to turn to our proposition concerning the *potentia multitudinis*. He thus introduces a separation between the two terms that *TP* III, section 2 identifies by means of a *seu* ("or")—a term we know is always very significant for Spinoza), the *imperium* (the State) and the *summa potestas* (the Sovereign). In this way he extends the restriction that the *veluti* expresses from the first term to the second, suggesting that the State (or body politic) is likewise an "individual" endowed with a soul, of which the Sovereign represents only one part. The fundamental political as well as ontological question becomes, then, one of knowing under which conditions this "soul" of the Sovereign (that is, in Spinozistic terms, this ensemble of ideas which are those of the one Sovereign) can be made to coincide with the soul of the State itself. One would suspect that in general this correspondence is only partial or that it remains inadequate, except, perhaps, at the end of the evolution of political societies toward the maximum of rationality and power, in the case of the democratic *imperium*.

This reading, however, not only does violence to the letter of *TP* III, section 2 (dropping out, in particular, the *hoc est . . . etiam totius imperii corpus et mens*) but also refuses to confront the difficulty contained in Spinoza's *general* propositions concerning the power of the multitude and the "sovereign" way in which it incorporates (or combines) the powers of the citizens in the setting of *any* State whatsoever. On the other hand, it has the advantage of suggesting (I will return to this later) that the definitions and deductions of Spinoza can be read not merely as descriptions of *existing forms* or characteristics of a *given* essence of the State, but rather as the index of a *process* or *transition* always already at work in the life of States that would constitute the true object of politics. This transition would be directed toward the full realization of democratic "powers" inherent in any State without obviously being guaranteed to result in it.

It is striking that Matheron's remarks have given rise to rather different expansions among his most faithful disciples. I am thinking in particular of Laurent Bove, who simply eliminates Spinoza's precautionary language in favor of a "teleological structure" in the history of the State founded on the democratic essence of the collective *conatus*.[14] I also have in mind Christian Lazzeri, who sees in Spinoza's formulas that individualize the people or the State, with its "body" and "soul," a metaphor directed against Hobbes that shows that the multitude, "a natural ensemble of individuals," could be directed only by virtue of its own consent, whereby the convergence of the desires of all is expressed.[15] Undoubtedly most interesting is the way in which Matheron himself subsequently has clarified and transformed his idea. Thus, in a recent study,[16] he takes the question *negatively,* starting from the indignation of the multitude (who Spinoza says constitutes the very *limit* of sovereignty) and shows that it forms the basis not only for revolutions but also for States themselves, insofar as their power is organized precisely to thwart the passional mechanisms (*the imitation of affects*) according to which such indignation develops. But since the indignation which is a form of interhuman hatred is "necessarily bad," there is in the construction of the State a sort of *double bind* that clarifies the modality of *una veluti mente ducitur.* Struggling with the need for "conformism" in the multitude along with its own its fearful dangers—Matheron goes so far as to say that, for Spinoza, "the elementary form of democracy is lynching"—the State must simultaneously be based on a unanimity of the citizens and must constantly separate itself from it. The difficulty of holding such a position could furnish "one of the reasons for the incompleteness of the *Political Treatise.*" Apparently turning away from ontological considerations on individuality, Matheron here takes a distinctly sociological (quasi Tocquevillian) route, which succeeds in showing perfectly the emphasis Spinoza places on the *TP.* But from this perspective, the *TP* is limited to the problematic of consensus or the regulation of opinions and apparently leaves aside the question of decision, which, according to Spinoza's text, is inseparable from it.

Rice

Rice begins by opposing to what he perceives as "the organicism" of Matheron a version of a completely opposite reading, one situated on the side of "methodological individualism" (which at the same time attempts to recover it for a liberal politics from its monopolization by a Hegelian and Marxist tradition). For me the most interesting thing about his study[17] consists in the fact that, by pushing to their limit the examination of the problems raised by such a reading, he is led to reformulate the question of the logic of the modalities inherent in Spinozistic "naturalism."

Rice thinks that the organicist interpretation (which he also calls "literalistic" because it assumes that the term "individual" can be applied literally to political bodies) rests on a mistaken view that the *Ethics* discussion of simple and composite bodies (between IIP13 and IIP14) extends the naturalistic account to the social and cognitive functions of collectives when in fact it is limited solely to living organisms. Politics is thus replaced by ontology (summarized in the idea that the State possesses a *conatus*), and the intrinsic equivocation of the notion of individuation is ignored in favor of a general scheme that integrates all things into an increasing complexity.[18] Such a reading—open to different physicalist or vitalistic variations—would be at the heart of "holistic" interpretations of Spinoza's political thought that portray him as a precursor of Hegel and Marx.[19]

In contrast, Rice thinks of Spinoza as a fundamentally nominalist philosopher, a partisan of radical individualism in matters of morality and politics. For him, "communal unities" result primarily from the perception by individuals of the reciprocal utility that leads them to flee solitude and unite as circumstances dictate.[20] As McShea and Den Uyl claim as well, the formation of communities (which are always "historical" or "contingent") is not an act of individuation but a more or less complete harmonization (which expresses precisely the modality of the *veluti una mente*) that draws on the laws of psychology. There would then be two radically distinct types of causality, of which only the first relies on the formation of a *conatus*. As seen in the juxtaposition of the schema of integration revealed in Letter 32 and the political works, in one case, the activity of the parts can be *deduced* from the law of the composition of the whole; in another case (that is, regarding political communities), such determination is absolutely excluded. Indeed, Spinoza never maintained that citizens themselves act as a function of or with a view to the conservation of the State of which they are part. Whereas it is characteristic of individual organisms to represent a power *superior* to that of the parts that comprise it, such representation is excluded for political totalities, whose power is *less* than the sum of the powers of the constituent individuals. Hence Spinoza's emphasis on the fact that those within the society "retain their natural right" (*Letter 50*).

Having outlined this distinction, Rice forestalls an error in interpretation: Our task is not to ask whether socio-political collectives are less "real" than organic individuals but to note how for Spinoza they lack the same epistemological status. Consequently, Spinoza would never have defended the idea of a *science of politics,* not even in the sense of a "psychological science" that deduces laws of individual human behavior from the nature of the passions. The study of socio-historical phenomena (for example, the history of peoples or the more or less obvious stability of political regimes) is not considered a science (in the strong sense of highlighting the idea of nature and natural laws) but instead relies on empirical observation and generalization.

This way of arguing opens a very interesting alternative thesis that views the formation of "political individuals" as a *level of integration immediately above* the formation of human organisms. If this is not society, it must be thought of as a natural supra-individual level of integration, something between the laws of the composition of organisms and those of the *facies totius universi* that Spinoza identifies as the "ultimate" individual. Contemporary developments in physics and biology suggest a hypothetical (but not unlikely) right to introduce here a notion such as an *ecosystem,* that is, an integrated natural environment with its own laws of equilibrium. We might even be tempted to develop "Spinozistic epistemology" in the direction of Goodman's semantics,[21] in that the very notion of the individual is relative to a certain theoretical framework and the fundamental epistemological problem is one of the modality of necessary laws within a given theory when they are incorporated into a higher-order theory. According to Rice, even if we could doubt that Spinoza had been led to adopt the thesis of a "contingency of the necessity" of superimposed natural laws as the systems that render them accountable, we could not prove that this contradicts his principles.

As interesting as it is, this thesis seems me nevertheless to include two difficulties from its own point of view. The first is that Rice oscillates between two uses of the term "metaphor." Sometimes he refers to the metaphorical way in which commentators on Spinoza extend the signification of the term "individual." Other times he refers to the metaphorical way in which Spinoza himself occasionally treats "political bodies" as "pseudo individuals." In the latter case, the expression *una veluti mente duci* reverses its function (which proves not only that it "resists" Rice's reading but that it is capable of disrupting *both* organicist and individualistic strategies). The second difficulty is that Rice poses as self-evident a theoretical convergence between methodological individualism and socio-political individualism (that is, between nominalism in philosophy and liberalism in politics). This assimilation seems to me a prejudice, typical of a certain mainly Anglo-American tradition (but that tradition doesn't have a monopoly on it). The defect makes itself felt here by a specific discussion of the implications of the notion of *multitudo* at the heart of Spinoza's elaborations (particularly in the *TP*) and that can be understood in two registers: regarding the question of "power" and that of "right." This leads us straight to the proposals of Antonio Negri.

Negri

We find in Negri as well a systematic treatment of the problem posed by Spinoza's formula, with the double movement of introducing and withdrawing the trans-individual analogy that it comprises. There is nothing astonishing here if we recall that, for Negri, *potentia multitudinis* is almost a redundancy, because all "power" is that of a multiple or a multitude and all multiplicity is essentially a deployment of natural power. In his view *potentia multitudinis* is the key concept of Spinozistic thought, that which shows the absolute reversibility of metaphysical and political discourse. It is for the same reason that Negri sees in the *TP* the crowning achievement of Spinoza's metaphysics, despite its lack of completing the "constitution of the real." But we can even give this a positive spin: When he was interrupted before writing the corresponding chapter, Spinoza had completed all he wanted to say on democracy except for his discussion of specifically institutional developments (which in Negri's eyes mark a relapse into the ideologies of the time).

A close analysis reveals, however, a reversal between the readings proposed by two successive versions of the argument (in the course of which Negri takes into account a number of objections), although they ultimately end up with the same result. The chapter of *The Savage Anomaly* that he devotes to the commentary of the *TP*[22] has as its guiding thread the possibility of understanding all aspects of politics, including its apparent oppositions (the sovereign power of the State versus the freedom of the people or society, the absolute versus the internal limitation of power, and so forth), as developments of one principle alone: the expansiveness and capacity of the auto-organization of the "*multitudo.*" *Multitudo* is a term he doesn't usually translate, but it connotes for him the originally collective character of political force, which has its own *conatus* or desire, as opposed to the methodological individualism of contract theories. When he reaches the fundamental texts of chapters 3 and 4, where the "*potentia multitudinis*" is characterized by its being "guided as it were by one mind," Negri does not make the expression turn on the *veluti* but implicitly proposes an interpretation that retrieves the three following moments:

1. *Potentia multitudinis* (the "pure affirmation" of this power) must include the *antagonism of subjects* as an explanation of its productivity

(as opposed to the "juridical" representation of the unity of the State whose autonomization, in return, presumes noncontradiction).

2. However, the antagonistic structure of the *multitudo* finds its immediate corrective in the *fear of solitude* that originally gives life to the masses (*TP* VI, section 1) and their push to be united by seeking security: a seemingly negative passion, but one that is actually constructive, from which results the continuous growth of sociality without the necessary imposition of the mediation of an outside power.

3. The constitution is then, in the same movement, the emergence of a *subject*, which is precisely nothing other than the *multitudo*, or it is the multitude as such (and thus not representable in terms of power, moral persons, institutional sovereignty, and so on).

This interpretation is obviously diametrically opposed to the idea previously recounted by Matheron, but it does not endorse Rice's side of the argument. If the *una veluti mente* has a sense, it is not to mark a difference between the real individuality of the body politic and its approximation through the sovereign power. Rather, it is to indicate that real power *exceeds all representation of unity* and is presented as an essentially ontological multiplicity (simultaneously including and being nourished by antagonism rather than seeing it as a mortal danger).[23] In a later work,[24] in answer to "critiques that have attacked the concept of the *multitudo* as the subject and central metaphysical ascription of the Spinozistic doctrine of the State" and insisting on "the elusive character of the concept," Negri modifies the form of his argument. He tries more than ever to show that "for Spinoza the material elusiveness of the *multitudo*-subject does not prevent the effects of subjectivity from expressing themselves." However, it is necessary to acknowledge the tension, indeed the contradiction, running through the heart of the concept of the *multitudo*. For under these determinate conditions (a State construct whose conscious objective is the *limitation* of the autonomous power of the masses), it must be *represented as a unity* of decision and thought. The prototype of such a representation is Rousseau's "general will," the juridical fiction in which the contractualist tradition of the legitimation of the political state is fulfilled.

It is in short such a fiction ("idea of reason," "product of the imagination") that would aim in advance, in Spinoza's text, at the notion of a "quasi-mind," reinstating the formula *una veluti mente ducitur*. This is what makes the elusive intelligible. Nonetheless, the *multitudo* itself "remains an elusive ensemble of singularities." It is not a soul or a mind but a material historical power. For Negri, this idea remains dominant: "Reason or thought would prefer that the *multitudo* presents itself as a single soul: this demand of reason encompasses the natural domain of social life but it does not manage definitively to surmount the social life." Furthermore, the expansive (productive, creative) power of the *multitudo* appears precisely in its capacity to use the inadequate representations that reduce it to unity by means of passional mechanisms such as *pietas* or "the desire for the universal," the tendency toward the collective. Here, paradoxically, we are close to a concept of the "cunning of reason." That is, where reason is tending toward multiplicity and not the unity of the subject, its movement is posed as essentially incomplete and unachievable.

Even if we dispute his reading of the text, we need to acknowledge that the strength of Negri's interpretation lies in his pursuit of this idea to its end by making Spinoza's politics a philosophy of *praxis* and by placing in its service the idea of an intrinsic aporia, affecting not the theory but things themselves:

> In Spinoza's politics, real development has the power and the limit of the fact. . . . The non-solution of the problem of the political subject becomes the foundation of tolerance. . . . Every singularity is fundamental. . . . These conclusions relative to the concept of *multitudo* do not then suppress its aporetic nature, on the contrary they accentuate it. . . . Its conception cannot be concluded. . . . The political universe is a universe of action. The fact that democracy reveals itself as an objective aporia of the absolute and liberty, and that this aporia is posed as the dynamic condition of the political process, far from resolving the problem and the difficulties of the definition of democracy, actually aggravates it. . . . It is in virtue of knowing that the aporia is always inherent in action that we have to act: the aporia is thus transferred from objectivity to subjectivity. The subject must act while knowing the incompleteness of the universe in which she acts: she must act anyway. . . . My hypothesis is that the Spinozistic democracy, the *omnino absolutum democraticum imperium*, must be conceived as a social practice of singularities who intersect in a process of the masses, or rather, as the *pietas* that forms and constitutes the reciprocal individual relations established among the multiplicity of subjects that constitute the *multitudo*.

In short, for Negri the concept of the "subject" or "subjectivity" retrieves two antithetical meanings: on the one hand, the unity of a *representation* (including that of *mens* as an individual mind) and, on the other, the *power of acting* and ultimately *action* itself. According to Negri, Spinoza would clearly have chosen the latter, even at the cost of a sinuous elaboration of which his discourse retains the trace. I strongly doubt that such an alternative is Spinozistic. But it carries us to the heart of the difficulties of the text of the *TP,* which concern not only politics but also its "foundations," that is, metaphysics.

A Critical Solution: Moreau

With the analyses of Pierre-François Moreau, our method changes. Coming after a host of debates that proved the neuralgic nature of the question of the individuality of the body politic in Spinoza, Moreau devotes a section of his *Spinoza. L'expérience et l'éternité* to classify the various positions on the issue (leaving out Negri's, though) and to resituate the problem in the more general context of articulating the theory of the passions within a theory of history. This leads him to grant a privileged role to the complementarity of the *TP* and the *TTP* and to propose a strategy of original interpretation ("The Passional Root of the Symbolic and its Effects").[25] Without going into all the details here, I would like to highlight some of its salient points.

Before addressing the question of the individuality of a people, Moreau argues that the opposition between Hobbes and Spinoza on "natural right" rests on the fact that, for Spinoza, the effective reality of natural right consists in "the power of the passions." In the foundation or formation of the State, we never face a situation in which some passions play against others. Rather, we find in every man "a passional aspiration to the benefits of reason" that teaches the utility of social peace, an aspiration reinforced by experience and whose sovereignty prevails in instilling obedience to institutions. It should be possible, then, to extend this insight (which arises essentially from reading the *TTP*) to the *TP* as well. Furthermore, experience not only provides this auxiliary function but also, as result of its duration, seems to constitute the historical individuality that transforms "a people" into "this people." In these terms Moreau undertakes to resolve the question of the extension of political bodies (to societies that are also States with their own institutions) based on the model of individuality first forged with individual human beings.

On the one hand, his argument begins with a study of the way in which Spinoza applies the category of *ingenium* (which he translates as "make-up" [*complexion*]) to historic peoples (*nationes, gentes*). The *ingenium* of a people, made up by its mores and beliefs and acquired or constituted historically, forms the equivalent of a nature. It is absolutely singular (proper to each people), so a system of institutions is viable only if the system conforms to it. It defines, in short, the natural *limits* in which is developed the constitution of the State, the form of power. On the other hand, his argument leads to an analysis (based this time on the *Ethics*) of the mechanisms of adhesion that crystallize a "collective identity" of peoples and subjective conditions in which institutional forms (on which he projects in an anachronistic though illuminating way the modern concept of "symbolic order") assure (or prevent) perennial existence. Moreau's discussion of the form of individuality proper to the State occurs between these two extremes, and here is where we can identify the modality in which it is possible to say of the State that it is "as one soul."

The interpretation of *veluti* or *quasi* is at the heart of Moreau's rereading, which simultaneously concerns the set of Spinozistic texts and the set of interpretations to which they have given rise. (In a certain respect, this borrows from Claude Lefort's method of dealing with Machiavelli and highlights how thought cannot be dissociated from its writing.) On the analogy with the human make-up [*complexion*], each people has its own *ingenium*, so each "State" is *in a certain way* an individual. The problem would then be knowing if, in the "Spinozistic system," this individuality must be considered as real or metaphorical (that is, artificial). On one side is Matheron's thesis; on the other is that of Rice. The point of discrimination is the question of *conatus:* Can we say of the State that it tends to conserve itself in its being and therefore its form? The issue is thus about knowing whether the attachment of human individuals to the State determines the formation of a stable composite whose idea would constitute its "soul" in the sense of the second part of the *Ethics.*

While immediately relativizing some of the terms of the debate (since in a Spinozistic sense, there is no real artifice, or all artifice is itself natural), Moreau seeks to balance what he calls the "elements of the dossier." He juxtaposes the *naturalistic logic of Spinozism* projected directly onto the doctrine of *omnia sunt animata*[26] and the *counterarguments of the artificialists* focused essentially on the expression *una veluti mente.* Together, these two elements would connote the opposition of a logic of relations to that of whole and parts and would capture the continuity between the thesis of the *TTP* chapters 3 and 17 ("nature does not create peoples, but individuals") and that of *TP* V, section 2 ("men are not born citizens but must be made so"). But according to Moreau these two formulas do not have the same object or address the same domain: One refers to an ontological condition, the other to a problem of how institutions function. Thus he ultimately seems to grant the argument to the defenders of "naturalism" (Matheron), even as he transforms it in a completely new nonphysicalist but historicizing and historicist way. Implicitly, what he wants to say is that for Spinoza, *"nature" is history* (including philology, historical psychology, and so forth).[27]

What, then, are the guidelines for resolving the problem? For Moreau it is an involved process, one that involves a remarkable effort of taking the writing of Spinoza seriously and incorporating the set of his historico-political remarks into at least a probable synthesis. He begins by posing three preliminaries:

1. The use of the term *veluti* is not a sufficient basis to argue against the logic of the system, since Spinoza's text (*TP* III, section 2) indicates that the State (*imperium*) has both a *corpus* and a *mens*.[28] But the *corpus* would not be the focus of any restriction (see *TP* III, section 5). Indeed, the restriction contained in the word *veluti* would extend the assimilation of the soul of the State to the *sovereign* (and implicitly the sovereign's *person*).

2. As with all "things," there is even a *conatus* of the State, but this term, which is characteristic of the language of the *Ethics*, is replaced in the *TP* by the coupling of *jus* and *potentia*. The problem therefore is not one of knowing whether the State is an individual (since everything that tends to persevere in its being is an individual *to some degree*) but rather *what sort of individual* it is.

3. The relevance of this question is confirmed by how the thesis that "nature does not create peoples" is interpreted. According to Moreau, it means that since "the state of nature" is an abstraction, individuals are always already social, but we do not know, by virtue of this generic property, the norm by which they are "socialized." The characteristics of the State that reciprocally affect individuals cannot be derived from their fundamental individuality.

All this leads to a reformulation of the question about what would it mean to say that the State is a kind of individual and that there is a kind of *complexity* that characterizes State (that is, historic) individuality (a *nation*, to which I will return). Individuality and complexity (Spinoza speaks of the "very complex individual") are by definition *equivocal* (or at least plurivocal) categories. Moreau's thesis thus contrasts decidedly with the tradition (and Spinoza himself) that made the human organism as a complex of organs the *model* of political individuality.[29] However, it is necessarily quite different to say, on the one hand, that this talk of the State as a complex implicates *at the same time* both individuals *and the objective relations between them* (or "institutions") and, on the other (which seems to me to be fundamentally the same idea), that the *imperium* is not immediately identified with the people (or should we say *natio* or *gens* rather than *multitudo* or *populus?* Moreau sometimes benefits from the equivocity of the French word). There is a "superior complexity" that we should link to the cardinal thesis of the *TTP* and the *TP* (generalized from Tacitus): As far as State individuality is concerned, *the danger of death comes from within,* from internal conflicts. And a political individual never "dies" in the same way as a human body.

Here Moreau makes a strange leap. Drawing on the axiom in *Ethics* IV that posits external forces of destruction superior to all individuality, he turns it inside out like a glove to say: *This external superiority has the appearance of an internal cause* "because it proceeds by destroying the unity" of individuals or their bodies. The issue of the specificity of the political individual is then concerned with why, for these (generally imaginary) modalities, this type of natural individuality *appears to us as artificial.* That is, considering the fact that "we" are always citizens of a State, why would such individuality seem artificial to members of the State? In the context of this reformulation, Moreau's "solution" is brilliant. It proceeds by superimposing three mechanisms of socialization that he calls *association, integration,* and *adhesion,* allowing him to account for the kind of collective individuality that characterizes the *imperium* (the State) and other collective individuals (for example, religious sects).

From the idea of *association,* we must recognize how (in contrast to organisms) historico-social individuality is based not on the difference and complementarity of parts (corresponding in great measure to consciousness in the soul) but on the *similarity* of components united in a relation of *convenientia.* Here Moreau refers to *E* IVP18S. Using this he explains the fragility or weak character of the State-*mens* in which the *mentes* of citizens can still engage in conflict. The constitutive problem of the State is one of reinforcing its own *mens* while creating the *unanimity* (*animorum unio*) that would be designated precisely by *una veluti mente duci.* This is the primordial task of politics: to cover the organic imaginary of the State with its veil of illusion.

From the idea of *integration,* which he associates with the principle of reciprocal utility, Moreau draws the idea that the soul of the citizen ought to be identified with that of the State by different means. The most effective of those means are those that take on the *appearance of reason,* in particular the collectivization of hatreds and fears (*TP* VIII, section 6). This is the function of institutions: to support the satisfaction of common needs while concealing mutually irreconcilable desires.

Last is the idea of *adhesion,* the crowning touch of this construct which shows essentially how a State can create *in the imaginary* a simulacrum of rationality, even while producing tendentially the same effects as reason (that is, the practical recognition of common interest). Here Moreau retains the view that there must be *mechanisms of recognition* leading individuals to "represent themselves positively in their relationship to the totality" and to prefer subjection in the State to foreign slavery and reciprocal animosity. But in a bold move, he evokes the proximity of Spinoza and Machiavelli and gives it a Spinozistic twist. The means, he notes, to "reground a State on its originating principle" (with such means therefore being necessarily imaginary) consist in the *symbolic of identity* distinctive of each national tradition. That is, symbols and collective rituals (the braid of the Chinese, the circumcision of the Jews) are instituted as fetishes at the heart of a people's characteristic *ingenium* and thus individualize it. Moreover, this symbolic is at the heart of the correspondence between the *ingenium* of a people and that of the State (the "soul" of the people and "soul" of the State? or rather, in anachronistic but illuminating terms, the "unconscious" of a people and the State).

This resolution of the problem, which certainly borrows a number of elements from Moreau's predecessors, seems to me inescapable. The accent that it puts on the historico-anthropological dimension of Spinoza's thought also seems absolutely correct. But it doesn't fully satisfy me because I see four possible objections:

1. It seems to include an element of circularity. Moreau begins with the idea that, according to Spinoza, there is a *popular ingenium,* and at the end of the account he finds in this notion of *ingenium* and its modalities of expression the solution to the problem. The question of the theoretical (or systemic) consistency of the concept of *ingenium* (and notably of its articulation in the concepts of soul and body) remains obscure.

2. Moreau speaks rather loosely about the idea of the *ingenium* of the State, people, and nation. One initially has the feeling that these terms designate fundamentally the same thing: At the end of the account the issue focuses on establishing a more or less stable relationship or complementarity (a historical convergence) between the *ingenium* of a people and the *ingenium* of the State. But the former presupposes that the question of knowing what unites the *multitudo* is resolved, and the latter seems to me untraceable in Spinoza. More precisely, I don't see what the *ingenium* of the *imperium* could be other than that of a historically organized multitude. For the same reason I don't see how the "composition" of individualities and the intervention of "institutions" form two features that are different from the "complexity" being studied.

3. Moreau tends at the end of his account to fold back the entire question of knowing how a political body constitutes *an* individuality of a determined type to the question of knowing how it constitutes *such* singular individuality in history. But individuation and individualization are not the same thing, or at least we need to indicate how their identification is a problem. (Pushed to its extreme, we could have an absolute histori-

cal nominalism, in which there are no political "regimes" and every nation or people "invents" a political regime *sui generis* unless it is the
product of it, and here we see difficulties arising for reading the *TP*).
On this point let's note that, just as the question of *national identity* and
its relation to religious identity is central in the *TTP*, so it is marginal in
the *TP*, where it is *political* identity that counts. In fact, all this happens
as if, by contrasting Spinoza to Hobbes on the basis of current discussions, Moreau had differentiated their problematic as that of *sovereignty*
(Hobbes) and that of the relation between *citizenship and nationality*
(Spinoza). The *veluti una mente* would mark this transformation.

4. Between the two ways of "constituting the city" discussed in *Ethics* IV
(particularly in Proposition 37, with its double set of demonstrations
and scholia) and which form a kind of "intra-associative parallelism,"
Moreau completely privileges the *passional way*. For him the "rationality" of the State or the organization of the multitude is in fact the appearance produced by the activity or manipulation of the passions
(which he calls "symbolic"). This feature obviously carries the totality
of his efforts regarding the "sociological" dimensions of the problem of
the *animorum unio* and tends to eliminate or ignore any *ontological* dimension. I fear that, under these conditions, the properly "ethical"
point of view is lost from view.

In Favor of a "Literalistic" Solution

Retrieving for my account both the term "literalism" introduced in the
discussion of Lee C. Rice and some of the elements proposed up to this
point (but correcting what seems to me the momentum of the text), I
want to propose a solution based on the following principles:

1. We need to take into account *all* occurrences of the expression *una
veluti mente ducitur (ducuntur)*, regardless of the "topic" to which it applies.[30] In doing so we can see the equivocity that has stymied many
interpreters: Sometimes the "quasi-*mens*" is that of the entire State (to
which it confers the "power of the multitude") and sometimes it is that
of a particular State institution (which appropriates this power) and
which is expressed differently in different regimes, making itself part
of the problem.

2. We need to take into account all references to a social, political, or institutional *corpus*, but *only* such references.[31] In doing so we can see how
the expression *corpus imperii* is in fact as problematic as that of *mens civ-*

itatis, and so on. More precisely, we need to agree that the notion of the "body politic" that came from a tradition that was simultaneously legal, religious, and philosophical does not have for Spinoza a theoretical significance but rather an "ideological" significance. Placing the notion of *corporeal individuality* in relation to a theory (for example, in physics or ontology) is therefore the problem, not the solution or a manifest point of departure.

3. We need to juxtapose the expression *una veluti mente duci* systematically to other expressions that use *ducere* and *ductus* (in the *TP* first and later elsewhere), in particular *ratione duci, ex ratione ductu (convenire),* and so on. This reveals how *una veluti mente ducitur (ducuntur)* covers by definition no one univocal situation but an alternation (that is, an opposition of tendencies). On the one hand, the *animorum unio* (*TP* III, section 7) is realized through a purely passional mechanism (fear of the law, hatred of the foreign, hope for a common safety, to name a few); on the other hand, it is achieved with an aim to rational utility (and, by means of its representation that it does not exclude, as I will note later, a mobilization of the passions). We find here, in a certain way (and concerning which we also will have to return) the "double track" of constructing the concept of sociability presented in *Ethics* IV, in particular in the remarkable series constituted by P37 and its two demonstrations and two scholia.[32]

4. We need to juxtapose the expression to its manifest antithesis in the *TP, ex suo* (resp. *ipsius*) *ingenio vivere.*[33] In doing so we can see how one contradiction in Spinoza's terms covers in fact another more determinant contradiction: *There is a formal opposition* from the beginning between the unity of the *imperium* (unity of thought and thus of decision) and the "natural" independence of individual *ingenia.* More profoundly, though, there is a *substantial opposition* at the heart of the *multitudo* (including both *imperium* and human individuals with their own *ingenia*), between two regimes of autonomy, in which one is as paradoxical as the other. In the first regime, the "right" of each individual (*sui juris esse*) is based on an *ex suo ingenio vivere* that is in fact self-destructive and therefore practically "impossible." In the second, this "right" (which is formally identical, always *sui juris esse*) combines the possibility of *ex suo ingenio vivere* with communal right and thus with the common power achieved in a communal life, which seems to deprive it of all but a virtual content.

On the basis of these initial observations, we can draw a series of consequences that emerge when linked to other ideas. Considering the consequences of principles (3) and (4) together reveals how the constitution of a collective *mens* is for Spinoza essentially never anything other than the practical realization of an *animorum unio;* in other words, a reconciliation or combination of *ingenia.* This means:

1. That *all "degrees"* of union, from the dynamic of the passional opinion of a mob (for example, in an insurrection)[34] to the rational collective deliberation in the setting of stable institutions,[35] are included potentially in the idea of the *animorum unio.* In any case, a process of thought and its formation or transformation and subsequent ideas (here we see the slant of Appuhn's translation) is at work. This process, though, is by definition "trans-individual" and has as its precise object the way in which the more or less organized multitude "perceives" itself (its interests, its composition, its divisions, its situation in the world). In perceiving itself, it thus "organizes itself."

2. But this process of thought is not "ideal," purely "spiritual" (or even essentially "deliberate," even though it passes through moments of deliberation). On the contrary, what the insistent reference to *ingenia* connotes is the fact that this process of thought reflects and articulates the power of the bodies that comprise the multitude and its singularity, its particular "way of life" (what Cristofolini translates well as *a modo suo vivere*).[36]

3. The collective "*mens*" is, then, by definition a *quasi mens* (as *Ethics* IV P18S indicates), whose *unity-of-action* is thinkable only as an "as if." It is not that it is not "mental" (that is, ideal, a function of thinking), but that its orientation is unified (and therefore "definite") only tendentially (one could say "asymptotically") in terms of reason and communal utility. Thus *it* is unified only tendentially—one could say *precariously*—because for Spinoza a *mens* cannot be anything other than the organized ensemble of "its" ideas. In fact, it is its proper capacity to guide or direct (*ducere*) in a univocal way that gives it its unity, confers on it an internal "order" (the order of ideas in which it consists) and so makes it exist. Indeed, a disorganized *mens,* without any sort of unity, would hardly exist at all.[37]

All this, however, has an effect on the implications that we drew from principle (2) concerning the use and significance that Spinoza gives to the word "body." For here we are radically prohibited from thinking of a political "body" or the individuality of the body politic as something that both exists prior to the constitution of the quasi-*mens* (or the quasi-constitution of the *mens,* that is, the *animorum unio*) and that becomes an object of reflection after the fact. By reversing such a mechanistic representation, this approach treats the "body" politic as the effect of the unification of *mens,* as tendentious and precarious as that might be. (We might even have to think of its formation or coming to be as a *threshhold,* what I have elsewhere called, following Deleuze, an "incompressible minimum").[38] To repeat—and here we are at the heart of the critical engagement with Hobbes—the expression "body politic" prescribes nothing by itself. Or rather, it expresses the ambition of the State (of the *imperium* in its different forms) to integrate, unify, and incorporate the *potentia multitudinis* in its proper "life." This ambition is "in itself" rational and consistent with communal utility and interest but is realized more or less successfully according to the nature of the regime.

We could express this consequence thus: Without a *minimum* of communal thought and therefore a minimum of incorporation, there would be no State at all (or, if you prefer, only a contradictory and self-destructive *multitudo*). But the question then arises: Conversely, is there a *maximum?* One could be tempted to say that it would be the absolute unification of the thought of the masses, the "unique thought" in which individual differences which exist as many virtual contradictions would be completely reabsorbed or melt into what Matheron calls a *consensus,* a "conformism." But such is not the case. On the contrary, this hypothesis brings us back to the *minimum,* perhaps even on this side of the *minimum.* Here we need to complete the *TP* with the *TTP,* which is concerned with this very question. The attempt to standardize thoughts by abolishing their singularity (in the form of a *theologico-political creed* as perpetuated in absolute monarchy, or in a *myth of reason* as presented in the enlightened despotism of a certain "republican" tradition) is ultimately bound to fail. But as we know, before it does it is able—and Spinoza did not cease to be preoccupied by this thought—to generate extreme violence and the dissolution of the community.[39] Indeed, it does not provide a real synthesis or *universalization* of opinions and ways of life; it is rather the vain attempt of a particular ambition to appropriate all others unto itself. We need, then, to adopt the opposing position: There is *no maximum* of "communal thought," precisely because communal thought develops itself endlessly in the sense of the highest possible compatibility of the greatest possible number of singularities (which, in *Spinoza et la politique,* I called "being the most numerous possible thinking the most possible," referring to *Ethics* V, propositions 5–10).[40]

Finally, these interpretative hypotheses reflexively impact our first principle concerning the dispersion of uses of the expression *una mente ducitur.* What we have seen is the "subject" of the ascription of this action—or better, the dynamic process, where activity and passivity come together: "to be guided as by only one soul"—literally *fluctuates* between whole and part, between the *multitudo* and the *imperium,* between the *im-*

perium and the *summae potestates*. In one sense, all these terms are only one (that is, they express only modes of the same *conatus,* the same *res*); in another sense they do not cease dissociating themselves and even mutually opposing one another. As I see it, taking the preceding into account we should ignore Spinoza's hesitation on the question of knowing *where to localize* the unity of the body politic, social individuality. That question could arise only from an essentialist point of view, which is precisely what he renounced. Instead, we should note how the *limits of this individuality* themselves fluctuate: between "totalization" and "separation," in the double sense of the separation of the society (*civitas*) from the isolation of the sovereign. We could still say that it is the *potentia multitudinis* that is sometimes fully "interiorized" in terms of its totality, and sometimes in a sense "exteriorized" in terms of considering part of itself as exterior (including its core as a point of exception)—as in the power of a coercive State that aims to "represent" closely the masses whose unity it itself lacks.

But we know that this fluctuation is endless—even though it is traversed by an orientation, an ethical or ethico-political *effort* (to which also corresponds a "duty": see Spinoza's use of the verb *debere* in some of the passages cited). As Negri observes, this applies to the identity of the "political subject," but for very different reasons than his own "elusive," or more properly, *equivocal* ones. It is impossible to localize the political subject *either in whole or in part*, that is, either in "the people" or "the State." So if *multitudo* designates par excellence the popular authority on which depends the power of the State and its stability or instability, we cannot strictly say that the political subject *is the multitudo* without immediately specifying how such pronouncements raise prospects of insoluble contradictions in the form of an endless regress, and so forth. But suppose, conversely, that *multitudo* designates specifically a contradictory unity that varies among regimes and situations according to the model of the *fluctuatio animi* (perhaps we should even risk the expression *fluctuatio mentis*) of *imperium* and *populus* (or *dèmos*). Each alternate in its own way would then claim to embody or represent the political "subject," in which case we have to conclude that this subject is paradoxical as such or that it is a *nonsubject* in terms of classical conceptions.

Such a reversal of the classical treatment of the subject results in radically opposing both the Spinozistic concept of politics—Spinoza's metaphysics of politics—and that of Hobbes and Rousseau. This is not (as Negri suggests) because Hobbes and Rousseau share the same concept but rather because the two concepts illustrate contrasting possibilities for conferring on the "body politic" the unity of a classical subject, either as a transcendent unity or as an immanent unity. I agree with Negri that this reversal does not exclude certain forms or practices of *subjectivation*. Rather, it is a way to understand why politics (and history on the political stage) is never anything other than a field of subjective movements: activity and passivity, augmentation and diminution of the power of acting, composition or *convenientia* and decomposition of collective individualities or *seditio*. However, we have no reason—indeed, quite the contrary, in keeping with the complete Spinozistic analysis of the modes of *conatus*—to decide unilaterally that *one of these vectors* represents subjectivity "in itself."

Provisory Conclusion

I have tried to give a theoretical rule for understanding the idea of a "quasi *mens*" evoked in passing in the *Ethics* analysis of moving from individuality to trans-individuality. I have done this by suggesting that the *TP* develops this idea and that the insistence on the expression *una veluti mente duci* would provide us precisely with an indication of how this is done. For me, a "quasi *mens*"—if we can retain this expression—corresponds to the idea of a "trans-individual" *mens* or, more precisely, the mental identity of a composed trans-individual, as long as such a composed being is not identified as the limit-application of the concept of individuality or treated as a *quasi-individual* rather than as a given and complete "individuality." Using this hypothesis of a *limit-concept*, we would then still have to try to determine its extent for Spinozism as a whole by pursuing two strategies of generalization.

The first strategy would consist in returning to the general question of the *mens* and considering the following. On the whole, the concept of mind that is at the heart of demonstrations in the *Ethics* relates the passional and rational movements of the human soul (defined as the idea of multiplicity proper to the human body) to a general problematic of the attributes of substance and its expression through its attributes. Extending the concept beyond the limits of this primary use allows us to discern a doctrine of a quasi-psyche or better yet a doctrine of a quasi-individual psyche. This is because the concept concerns many of the same elements that enter into the formation of the individual human *mens*, namely, what Spinoza calls "ideas," which themselves correspond to movements or bodily encounters broadly understood. It is concerned with the transindividual regimen of the production and association of ideas that tends toward unity only to the extent that it is compatible with a degree of complexity and conflict greater than that of human individuality. It is what characterizes the political domain and coincides with its own uniqueness.

The guiding theme that I want to propose is thus simultaneously historical and philological. It begins with the axiomatic statement *omnia sunt animata*[41] and then, following in part a suggestion by Emilia Giancotti, explores its transformation. Giancotti notes that as Spinoza's thought matured, references to *anima* and the idea of the *animatio* of the body were tendentially eliminated in favor of what one can consider a radicalization of Cartesianism, that is, a reframing of the analysis of the passions based on the logic of idea-complexes designated specifically by the word *mens*.[42] In this way all affects obviously are radically intellectualized, and all ideas, including the most adequate, become inseparable from affective modalities or realizations of desire. But we need to adopt Moreau's suggestion as well: Even though the objects of *ingenium* are only of "practical use" (as Althusser would say), the term "*ingenium*" contains the key to the problem of the *identity of individuals*. This can be said of collective quasi-individuals as well. What seems to me to play a decisive role in the most elaborate version of Spinozistic thought on this issue is not the identification of the *ingenium* of peoples or nations (which I am not reluctant to consider also as a "quasi *ingenium*," at least if we need to understand it as a "natural" thing persevering in history).[43] Rather, what is decisive is the relationship between the formation of trans-individual ideas (whose socio-political content, we know, is the unification of the opinions and common notions of the masses, the enacted formation of the multitude's thought) and the *ingenium* of each.

I am tempted, then, to retranslate this term, not only by "make-up," "natural thing," or "personality,"[44] but by *resistance to assimilation:* a resistance proper to a doctrine of an individual psyche, deeply rooted in the psycho-physical complex. And my (provisory) hypothesis is that the Spinozistic identification of emotional processes with intellectual (or ideal) processes in the concept of the *mens* includes to some extent a "remainder" designated precisely by the term "*ingenium*." *In addition to* the concept of *mens*, we still need the concept or quasi-concept of *ingenium* in order to analyze that which corresponds to both the movements of bodies in the attribute "thought" and especially the kinds of attraction and repulsion between the individualities thus produced. Even though the concept emerges in its irreducible function when the question of ethics is applied to the trans-individual collectivities of the political domain, it undoubtedly encompasses a broad range. Or perhaps we should rather say that its persistence captures the insight that *all* mental processes, "individualized" as they are, always already have a trans-individual dimension.

This raises the issue of the second strategy according to which I organize the preceding questions. I believe that the discussions that have been addressed or examined thus far raise a double difficulty. On the one hand they continue to confront us with a transgression of the rules of correspondence between the attributes (commonly designated under the name "parallelism" or whatever we believe is included under the name). Following the *TP* literally, this strategy starts from the surprising logical "weakness" of Spinoza's evoking not an identity in difference between the corporeal individuality and mental individuality of the State but rather— at least in the case of monarchy—an action of the *imperium* (identified as one "soul") on the *multitudo* or the *civitas* (identified with a "body"). It continues by means of the hypothesis to which I myself was led about how the constitution of the State as a "quasi *corpus*" results from its constitution as a "quasi *mens.*" What should we make of these paradoxes? Do we here see proof of the incompatibility of Spinozism with its own premises, in that this inconsistency goes to the very foundation of politics? Or on the other hand, does this simply put Spinozism itself to the test and necessarily transform our understanding of the parallelism-of-attributes axiom and the causality of substance by supposing that the *Ethics* had not yet explored, not yet elucidated, all aspects of Spinoza's thought?

In my view these questions are inseparable from the problem posed profoundly by Moreau[45] and that I have tried to rephrase by means of the category of the "trans-individual." Undoubtedly there is a general concept of individuality and individuation in Spinoza. It is tied to that of the production of the effects of substance, for in the final analysis these effects are indeed *individualities,* singular things, causes and effects, that produce and are produced. But it is deeply wrong-headed to represent *all* the processes of individuation on the model of *human* individuation (that of the individual human body and soul). Therein lies precisely the anthropomorphic illusion, the fundamental structure of the imaginary, of which the representation of political phenomena occupies a privileged place—on occasion even becoming a theological anthropomorphism, as one sees with Hobbes' *Mortall God.* But in response, the analysis of political phenomena is the crowning path of a critique of this illusion. It puts us in mind of a limit-individuality (a quasi- or trans-individuality) that concerns bodies and souls, physical movements and the associations of ideas but that functions according to a totally different model. Moreover, if this trans-individual dimension turned out to be also *always already* embedded in the life of human individuality, particularly in the movement of the passions, and to be always *overdetermined,* as *Ethics* III and IV more than suggest, we would then have— via politics—a fundamental indication of the fact that, for Spinoza, the great philosophical project *is to think the human outside of any anthropomorphism,* freed as theoretician (should we say "sage"?) of all the *models* that human beings (that is, the multitude) incessantly assign to themselves.

ETIENNE BALIBAR

Notes

Presented at the International Congress of the Spinoza-Gesellschaft, October 2000; subsequently published in *Ethik, Recht und Politik bei Spinoza,* ed. Marcel Senn and Manfred Walther (Zürich: Schulthess, 2001), 105–37.

1. The comma inserted by Gebhardt between *corpus* and *et mens* has been removed in Bartuschat's edition. Cristofolini indicates that the word *sicuti,* missing in the *Opera Posthuma,* is a correction added by editors.

2. "It is clear that the right of the supreme authorities is nothing else than simple natural right, limited, indeed, by the power, not of every individual but of the multitude, which is guided, as it were, by one mind—that is, as each individual in the state of nature, so the body and mind of a dominion have as much right as they have power" (R. M. H. Elwes, trans. 1883).

3. Pierre-François Moreau, in Baruch Spinoza, *Tractatus politicus. Traité politique* (Paris: Editions Réplique, 1979), 33–35.

4. Baruch Spinoza, *Trattato Politico.* Testo e traduzione a cura di Paolo Cristofolini (Pisa: Edizioni ETS, 1999), 55.

5. Baruch de Spinoza, *Politischer Traktat. Lateinisch-Deutsch,* Neuübersetzt, herausgegeben mit Einleitung und Anmerkungen versehen von Wolfgang Bartuschat (Hamburg: Felix Meiner Verlag, 1994), 35.

6. See Cristofolini's note, *Trattato Politico,* 245.

7. "Man, I say, can wish for nothing more helpful to the preservation of his being than that everyone should so agree in all things that their minds and bodies would compose, as it were, one mind and body; that all should strive together, as far as they can, to preserve their being; and that all together should seek for themselves the common advantage of all."

8. Noting this very point, the majority of translators have restored the *quasi* as a "common factor." Thus Bernard Pautrat: "en sorte que les Esprits et les Corps de tous composent pour ansi dire un seul Esprit et un seul Corps"; Emilia Giancotti: "in modo che le Menti e i Corpi di tutti compongano quasi una sola Mente e un solo Corpo"; Bartuschat: "nichts Geeigneteres . . . als dass alle in allem so übereinstimmten, dass die Geister und die Körper von allen zusammen gleichsam einen einzigen Geist und einen einzigen Körper bilden."

9. "It is therefore necessary that all the patricians be so bound by the laws as to form, as it were, one body governed by one mind."

10. To which we should here add *TP* VI, section 19, in connection with monarchy: "et absolute Rex censendus est veluti Civitatis mens, hoc autem Consilium mentis sensus externi, seu Civitate corpus, per quod mens Civitatis statum concipit, et per quod mens id acts, quod sibi optimum esse decernit."

11. Matheron (*Individu et communité chez Spinoza* [Paris: Editions de Minuit, 1969]) gets rid of this embarrassing formula, portraying it as an "unwelcome guest," but he includes it in an argument intended to distinguish Hobbesian and Spinozistic uses of the concept of individuality or political "body": see 347, note 152.

12. In fact, Moreau is worried primarily about the first two and does not attach particular importance to Negri's ideas.

13. "The right of the supreme authorities is limited by their power. . . . Surely the most important part of that right, as we have seen, is that they constitute, as it were, the mind of the State, whereby all ought to be guided."

14. Laurent Bove, *La stratégie du conatus. Affirmation et résistance chez Spinoza* (Paris: Vrin, 1996), 241–54.

15. Christian Lazzeri, *Droit, pouvoir et liberté. Spinoza critique de Hobbes.* (Paris: Presses Universitaires de France, 1998), 280–84.

16. A. Matheron, "L'indignation et le conatus de l'Etat spinoziste," in *Spinoza: puissance et ontologie*, sous la direction de M. Revault d'Allonnes et de H. Rizk (Paris: Editions Kimé, 1994), 153–65.

17. Lee C. Rice, "Individual and Community in Spinoza's Social Psychology," in *Spinoza: Issues and Directions*, Proceedings of the Chicago Spinoza Conference, ed. Edwin Curley and Pierre-François Moreau (Leiden: E. J. Brill, 1990), 271–85.

18. Rice incorporates this critique of intriguing remarks in a way that should interest anyone who has struggled either to interpret Spinozistic "physics" in terms of the history of science or to understand the role of these remarks (which appear like a parenthetical without any explicit final application) in the rational arrangement of the *Ethics*. On one front, his treatment rails against a corpuscular account of the "oscillating" or "undulatory" interpretation developed by Jonathan Bennett ("field metaphysics"). On another, it goes so far as to suggest that by isolating this discussion Spinoza fails to exhibit the "correspondence" between thought processes and body processes that his "psychophysical parallelism" postulates.

19. Naturally, as Rice understands them, as critics of the tradition of liberal individualism.

20. It is undoubtedly significant that proponents of the "organicist" interpretation tend to emphasize the *passional genesis* of the Spinozistic polis (Matheron speaks of a "theory of passions of the body politic," though he by no means ignores the duality of perspectives in the *Ethics*), whereas those who endorse the "individualistic" interpretation tend to emphasize its *rational genesis*, in particular in the sense of the logic of utility. I will come back to this problem when I discuss Moreau, who on this point inclines clearly toward the first view. As for Negri, he pulls off a tour de force by maintaining that, for Spinoza, the true name of reason is "imagination" (in a way that is close to Deleuze's interpretation of "active affects").

21. See Nelson Goodman, *Of Mind and Other Matters* (Cambridge: Harvard University Press, 1984).

22. A. Negri, *L'anomalie sauvage. Puissance et pouvoir chez Spinoza* (Paris: Presses Universitaires de France, 1982), chapter 8, "La constitution du réel," particularly 293–318.

23. This is also why in his reconstruction of the movement that (for him) impels Spinoza's work toward its proper clarification, Negri privileges the *TP* (at least its first part) over the *Ethics:* He sees in the *TP* the definitive reversal of orientation toward unity in favor of an orientation toward multiplicity (including an emphasis on "modes" over "substance" in their constitutive relation).

24. *Reliqua desiderantur.* Conjecture pour une définition du concept de démoc-

ratie chez le dernier Spinoza," reedited in *Spinoza subversif. Variations (in)actuelles* (Paris: Kimé, 1994), 39–84.

25. P.-F. Moreau, *Spinoza. L'expérience et l'éternité* (Paris: PUF, 1994, chap. III, section 3: "L'*ingenium* du peuple et l'âme de l'Etat," 427–465.

26. But without thematizing the issue of the *anima-mens* relation, which we will see is in fact directly linked to the status of the words *quasi* and *veluti*.

27. This dissymetrical tendency of Moreau's "critical solution" has an interesting result: The form under which it tends to retrieve some of the suggestions of the "artificialists" consists in a reinterpretation within "naturalism." For example, what Rice calls "relations" and whose "contingency" he always emphasizes becomes, for Moreau, "institutions," for which it is necessary to account in the composition of political bodies *in addition to* individuals, and of which he emphasizes their "historical" character.

28. Amazingly, even though Moreau is interested alternately in both parts of the neuralgic sentence (*TP* III, section 2), he never really discusses the syntax and rhetoric of their linkage, as I have tried to show above.

29. In his commentary on Part II of the *Ethics,* P. Macherey defends a similar position based on a "minimalist" rereading of the "treatise on bodies" inserted after P13.

30. Without error or omission: *TP* II, sections 16 and 17; II, section 21; III, sections 1 and 2; III, section 5; III, section 7; IV, sections 1 and 2; VI, section 1; VI, section 19; VIII, section 6; VIII, section 19. To which can be added IX, section 14 (*veluti corpus*) and X, section 1 (*sicuti humano corpori*).

31. Influenced by the terminology of "political bodies" or the "body politic" among classical authors, Moreau adds some references in his translation of the *TP* (e.g., in translating *Civitas*).

32. I have shown elsewhere (*Spinoza et la politique* [Paris: Presses Universitaires de France, 1985], 93–105) how this dual-facing proposition organizes the whole of *Ethics* IV.

33. "To live based on one's own natural disposition."

34. Or even the "democratic lynching" of which Matheron speaks.

35. Here we should pay particular attention to the importance that Spinoza places on an idea from Aristotle and Machiavelli: Expanding the number of different opinions expressed in collective deliberation that leads to a majority resolution of conflicts is a guarantee of rationality and wisdom (*TP* IV, section 4; VII, sections 4–7; and so on). On this point, see my *Spinoza et la politique,* 88–89; and "Spinoza, l'anti-Orwell: la crainte des masses," in *La crainte des masses. Politique et philosophie avant et après Marx* (Paris: Galilée, 1997), 81–82.

36. See also the notable expansions on this point in Warren Montag's recent book *Bodies, Masses, Power: Spinoza and his Contemporaries* (New York: Verso, 1999), especially 62 ff, "The Body of the Multitude."

37. To go to the other extreme, one can wonder whether it would not be a limit hypothesis, as paradoxical as that of *corpora simplicissima* (simplest bodies), as Cristofolini suggests and with which I agree.

38. "Spinoza, l'anti-Orwell," see 95 ff.

39. Does this mean that in fact—as the classical tradition has maintained since Plato and Aristotle—anarchy and tyranny are not two different conditions?

40. *Spinoza et la politique*, 118.

41. To be precise: *Individua . . . omnia, quamvis diversis gradibus animata tamen sunt*, E2P13S.

42. Cf. Emilia Giancotti Boscherini: "Sul concetto spinoziano di *Mens*," in Giovanni Crapulli and Emilia Giancotti Boscherini, ed., *Ricerche lessicali su opere di Descartes e Spinoza*, Lessico Intellettuale Europeo III (Rome: Edizioni dell'Ateneo, Roma 1969), 119–69.

43. Apart from this, we have very few means, on the descriptive level at least, for distinguishing Spinoza from a representative of the "psychology of peoples" and their "character" or proper "mind."

44. In German, Manfred Walther proposes *Eigensinn*, which seems to me also to introduce a very interesting problematic; in any event, it concerns an extraordinarily polysemic notion, which does not contradict (far from it) the function of the "remainder" or "supplement" of which I speak here.

45. See also Pierre Macherey's remarks in his *Ethics* II commentary on the role of the little treatise on the "physics of bodies," to which we need to return in detail. In addition, this comes in for particular analysis in François Zourabichvili, *Spinoza: une physique de la pensée* (Paris: Presses Universitaires de France, 2002).

Spinoza and Materialism

Susan James

Chameleons have survived as long as they have because they can flourish in different environments—changes in their color enable them to coexist with other kinds of creature among lush vegetation, on sandy banks, or on grey rock faces. Some philosophers—those we tend to regard as the greatest of all—are similarly adaptive. Their work speaks to people living at different times, in different places, with different cultural and intellectual interests. These philosophers are like chameleons; they can live unnoticed for long periods, and the characteristics that enable them to stay alive are constituted by their relation to their environment. In this essay I focus on Spinoza, who is, it seems to me, a notable chameleon. His work has survived in hostile surroundings—has sat for days motionless on a rock. Its character has altered from one environment to another and has been atheist, pantheist, deist, idealist, and materialist by turns. Furthermore, it has sometimes managed to take on more than one guise at one time. For example, in France during the last thirty years or so it has been simultaneously perceived as a pinnacle of rationalist metaphysics and as an antecedent of historical materialism.

The view that Spinoza's work provides insights that are in some sense continuous with those of Marx has recently been elaborated by Louis Althusser in France and Antonio Negri in Italy. For these writers, Spinoza is a materialist, and it is this particular reading that I discuss. I begin by saying a bit about the positioning of Spinoza in the materialist tradition. I then focus on a particular aspect of Althusser's reading and show how he appeals to Spinoza's analyses of imagination and knowledge to resolve some questions about Marx's account of ideology. Althusser's doing so, I argue, brings him upon a series of problems which take him beyond Marx and indeed beyond ideology. My overall aim, then, is to show how a materialist reading of Spinoza has played a part in the great epic of the ending of ideology. I end by saying a little about the way that the aspects of Spinoza which carried Althusser almost beyond ideology have been taken up by English-speaking philosophers interested in the imaginary, who have created for him yet another character. I hope to persuade you that this strand of interpretation is one of the most fascinating in recent studies of Spinoza, as well as one that speaks to the rich theme of this volume.

Spinoza and the Materialist Tradition

It is important to Althusser and Negri that Spinoza belongs to a materialist *tradition,* to a canon of names culminating in that of Marx. The figures in this canon are heroes, first because they anticipated Marx's insights but also because they were radicals, authors who wrote against the grain of the philosophical mainstream and questioned its deepest and dearest presuppositions. For one reason or another, their work combined a resistance to established positions and research programs, with qualities that enabled it to survive against the odds. What philosophers figure in the materialist tradition, and what do they have in common? The answers to these questions are not simple. In *The Holy Family* Marx provides a rollicking story of two strands of materialism, one stemming from Descartes' physics, the other from opposition to Cartesian metaphysics. The first strand issued in mechanistic, reductionist scientific accounts of both matter and mind. The second, more philosophical strand combined criticism of Cartesian dualism with a nominalism first developed by Duns Scotus, and a vitalist theory of matter to be found in Francis Bacon. In England, it ran through Hobbes, who systematized Bacon without explaining how the senses can be the source of ideas, to Locke, who addressed this problem to such eighteenth-century writers as Hartley and Priestley. In France, Locke's contribution was taken up by Condillac, and English materialism was progressively civilized by Helvetius, La Mettrie, Holbach, and Diderot. These *philosophes* shared an interest in the effect of social conditions on manners and paved the way for socialism. In France their legacy can be seen in the work of Fourier. In England, via the influence of Helvetius, it issues in Bentham and Owen.

Spinoza does not figure in Marx's story, nor does he appear in the history of materialism sketched by Engels in the Introduction to the English edition of *Socialism: Utopian and Scientific,* which sticks fairly closely to the lines laid down by Marx. However, in *Ludwig Feuerbach and the End of Classical German Philosophy,* Engels set out, as he explains in the "Foreword," to acknowledge the influence that Feuerbach had had on him and on Marx during the 1840s. In this work, Engels singles out Feuerbach as the post-Hegelian philosopher who reinstated materialism. True, he did not fully appreciate the difference between eighteenth-century and modern materialism; true, he did not entirely emancipate himself from idealism.[1] Nevertheless, he paved the way. This welcoming of Feuerbach into the fold is significant, because it creates a kind of retrospective space for Spinoza within the materialist tradition. According to Feuerbach, Spinoza had espoused something like the "sensualist" form of materialism that he himself defended, and this relationship was reaffirmed in subsequent histories of materialism. We find it, for example, in Plekhanov who, commenting on Engels on Feuerbach, remarks that "Spinoza is an indisputable materialist although historians of philosophy refuse to recognize him as such."[2]

For Marx and Engels, materialism is set over against what they classify as traditional metaphysics. The latter includes both dualism and idealism, each of which is initially defined by its view of the relation between thought and being. Whereas dualists hold that mind and matter, thought and being, are separate, and whereas idealists assimilate being to thought, the materialist tradition gives priority to matter as the ground or precondition of thought. At the same time, materialism opposes the theological tendency of metaphysics—its appeals to God, or to comparable transcendental principles which supply a nonhistorical point of origin—and aims to provide broadly naturalistic explanations of all phenomena. Within this matrix, Spinoza can readily be cast as a metaphysician if one focuses on his interpretation of God, who remains the source of existence, causation, and power. At the same time, aspects of his philosophy can be interpreted as leaning toward materialism. Spinoza advocates naturalistic explanation of mental as well as material phenomena; his theory of parallel attributes can be seen as providing a nonreductionist account of the identity of matter and mind; he holds that all existing things are part of nature. These are the aspects of his philosophy that impress Feuerbach, and subsequently Plekhanov, and through which Spinoza is first eased into the materialist tradition. Moreover, they set the scene for the expansive interpretations of the materialist canon offered by Negri and Althusser.

Writing in 1968, Althusser rails against academic French philosophers who are convinced that they have nothing to learn from politicians or politics, and have only recently even begun to study "the great theoreticians of political philosophy, Machiavelli, Spinoza, Hobbes, Grotius, Locke and even Rousseau, 'our' Rousseau."[3] Among the French academic philosophers who had recently embarked upon this study was Althusser himself. As he explains elsewhere, he turned to these writers because he wanted to unite his lives as philosopher and as Marxist, and because he wanted to understand how philosophy and politics are related. Perhaps it is hardly surprising, then, that Althusser enlarges the materialist canon to include some of "the great theoreticians of political philosophy," Machiavelli, Hobbes, Spinoza, Rousseau and, of course, Marx. Negri, likewise, identifies a materialist tradition running from Machiavelli through Spinoza to Marx, but he opposes it to a mainstream, bourgeois tradition from Hobbes, through Rousseau to Hegel.

What licenses these expansions? In part, a shift of attention from metaphysics to politics, a desire to situate Marx as a political philosopher, and in part an associated and more wide-ranging conception of materialism itself. As did their predecessors, Negri and Althusser hold that materialism eschews transcendental principles and gives explanatory priority to whatever is counted as matter; they also emphasize, however, a number of corollaries. Materialism is not concerned with origins—for example, with the origins of human activity or political society. Instead, it offers a metaphysics of self-producing being (this is how Negri expresses it) which focuses on existing states of affairs, events, and occasions (which is how Althusser puts the point). Equally, materialism has no truck with teleology, no more interest in ends than in origins. Furthermore, its opposition to all dualisms has a number of implications; it means that materialism views the self as embodied; and it means, according to Negri, that it opposes those political theories which distinguish state from people and elevate the former above the latter.

Since it is hard to see that all the figures included in the expanded materialist canon satisfy all these criteria, it is most fruitful to take the latter as a list of family resemblances. It then has to be acknowledged that Spinoza possesses more family features than most. He is arguably less concerned with political origins than are many other seventeenth-century political theorists, and his interpretation of the social contract reflects this fact. He is opposed to, though interested in, teleological explanation. He agrees that the self is embodied; and his ontological analysis of individuals leads him to emphasize the interdependence of state and people. So when the problem is set up this way, it is not difficult to argue that he qualifies as a materialist philosopher.

Nevertheless, this method of canon-construction, so long favored by both European and Anglophone philosophers, sits uneasily with a materialist approach. It is mildly ironic that materialists who eschew teleological explanation should employ such a flagrantly teleological method. The properties that Althusser or Negri make central to materialism are more or less overtly selected to produce progressions culminating in Marxism, so that the history of philosophy is made to answer to their hopes and aspirations. This comes very close to what Spinoza called superstition—our disposition to interpret the world as answering to our hopes and fears—and in Althusser's case, at least, there is evidence that his passions were in fact energetically engaged in his defense of Spinoza as a materialist.

One of the striking things about Althusser's own account of his interest in Spinoza is the extent to which he identifies with him. Let me give two examples. First, Althusser was fascinated, he explains, by the rhetorical boldness with which Spinoza occupied the positions and adopted the language of his opponents while giving them novel and subversive meanings. The features of Spinoza's work which so struck Althusser would, I imagine, have included the fact that he endorses the Jewish and Christian belief that God is all powerful, the source of all existence, and all knowing, while at the same time identifying God with Nature. Or to take another case, Spinoza takes over the New Testament doctrine that divine law enjoins us to love God and our neighbors; it is just that the divine law is completely naturalized and obliges us only as long as it is enforced by a temporal power. This audacious way of subverting Judeo-Christian philosophy from within inspired Althusser and provided a model, he candidly admits, for his own attempt to subvert the French Communist Party. (Both attempts were, of course, unsuccessful.) Moving to a second example, Althusser asks himself how a work such as the *Ethics*, couched in dogmatic geometrical order, could have opened up a space for novel ideas which challenged philosophical orthodoxy. This apparent paradox in Spinoza's writing, so Althusser argues, reveals to us that the significance of a philosophy lies not in its form but in the effects of freedom that it produces. To be accused of dogmatism, of employing apparently constraining and conventional philosophical tools, as Spinoza was, and as Althusser himself had been, is not necessarily a bad thing. What matters are the effects that one's philosophy produces. Once again, it seems, Spinoza's example is a source of comfort to an embattled Althusser. It gives him hope that the critics who accuse him of dogmatism have misconstrued his philosophy and underestimated its power.

While Althusser's commentaries on his own intellectual journey were written after the fact and are not without their own intended rhetorical effects, they suggest, I think, that his engagement was not with Spinoza's materialism as such but rather with particular themes in Spinoza's work that he found suggestive and useful. Althusser needed Spinoza to be a materialist, perhaps because this facilitated identification, perhaps because it kept criticism at bay. But the materialist tradition was, for him, a useful receptacle. Placing Spinoza in it (which was not after all a novel gesture) legitimated a fascination with the work of this particular philosopher, a fascination that focused above all on Spinoza's theory of knowledge as a model for a Marxist account of ideology. "Spinoza," Althusser writes was the first man ever to have posed the problem of *reading*. . . . and he was also the first man in the world to have proposed both a theory of history and a philosophy of the opacity of the immediate. With him, for the first time ever, a man linked together in this way the essence of reading and the essence of history in a theory of the difference between the imaginary and the true. This explains to us why Marx could not possibly have become Marx except by founding a theory of history and a philosophy of the historical distinction between ideology and science.[4]

Spinoza as a Theorist of Ideology

For much of his career, Althusser was preoccupied by three related questions: How should we distinguish ideology from science? What account should we give of the process by which we move from an ideological to a scientific understanding of the world and ourselves? And finally, how can we arrive at a *theory* of ideology? Althusser responds to this set of problems by trying to map an aspect of Spinoza's philosophy on to Marxism, more specifically by relating Spinoza's account of three kinds of knowledge to Marx's account of the transformation of raw material into product by way of instruments of production. By superimposing these disparate elements, he aims to arrive at a satisfying account of the acquisition of knowledge as a kind of production, and as a process in which ideology gives way to science. Althusser's first move is to equate ideology, the raw material of the knowledge process, with what Spinoza calls imagination. Imagination is Spinoza's term for our everyday, pretheoretical way of thinking. It is shaped by our passions (the affective responses that chart our relationship with objects external to us), which are themselves the outcome of our past experiences and the patterns of association we have acquired. For example, the fear I feel when confronted by a snake is a manifestation of the interaction between the body of the snake and my own body—this is one sense in which imagination is material—but is also determined by my previous encounters with snakes and similar objects, and the passions these evoked. This much is part of my individual psychology, and each of us has a unique constellation of passionate dispositions, the accretion of our own experience. However, some of a person's associations and passions are also social in the sense that they are shared by other members of her community and are the result of collective experience. This claim prompts Althusser to describe the grasp of the world that we get from imagination as the *Lebenswelt*, or "the material world as men live it."[5] Ideology, as he sees it, exists in the *Lebenswelt*, in the shared resources of imagination.

Among the distinctive features of imagination is the fact that it is organized around the subject. When we imagine, we concentrate on the way the world affects *us,* and tend to explain events in the light of our own, or human, purposes. This orientation inclines us to project our concerns and ends on to the world, even to the extent of creating objects for our hopes and fears, whether gods, demons, extraterrestrial forces, or "the government." This teleological mode of understanding cuts us off from knowledge of the efficient causes of events (including our own passions) so that, as Althusser puts it, "imagination lives in the effects of invisible causes."[6] Imagination yields feelings and beliefs about the world around us, our social relations, and our own passions, which are limited by our ignorance of their causes. As Althusser expresses the point, our imaginary or ideological thinking contains imaginary relations between people and their conditions of existence.[7]

What is the epistemological status of imagination? Spinoza argues that it provides us with what he calls knowledge of the first kind, the knowledge that we gain either from singular things that have been represented through our senses, or from signs—for example, things we have heard or read (*Ethics* IIP40, scholium 2). Such knowledge is, in his phrase, mutilated and confused, in that it gives us only a partial, patchy understanding of things, and in this sense it can be described as inadequate. Nevertheless, it is often good enough for getting around in the world, and we are bound to rely on it. For Althusser, this account of imagination offers two particular insights. It offers a way to explain the illusory nature of ideology as an incomplete sort of knowledge. And it offers a way to open a space between the illusory and the false, a way to think of ideology as misleading in the sense of being incomplete but not wholly mistaken.

Turning to his second question, Althusser goes on to make use of Spinoza to articulate an initial distinction between ideology and science which focuses on the type of explanation that each employs. Ideology relies, at least to some extent, on teleological explanation, whereas science trades only in efficient causes. As we acquire scientific or more broadly theoretical understanding, we move from imagination to what Spinoza calls the second kind of knowledge, or reason, by coming to understand the efficient causes of our own ideological beliefs and attitudes. According to Spinoza, we possess knowledge of the second kind, or reason, when we have adequate or complete ideas of things (that is to say, when we have filled in the gaps characteristic of imagination) and are no longer ignorant of their causes. As we acquire this knowledge, we progressively shift to an understanding of the world of which we are no longer the center, and instead see ourselves as part of a much larger causal nexus. The key claim here for Althusser's purposes is that science provides us with the means to perceive the limitations of the ideologies through which we live and thus to distance ourselves from them. Through science, we replace our imaginary grasp of the world with a more adequate one.

There still remains Althusser's third question about the character and status of a theory of ideology, and he deals with this issue by appropriating Spinoza's third kind of knowledge, intuition. Intuition proceeds, as Spinoza says, "from an adequate idea of the formal essence of certain attributes of God to the adequate knowledge of the essence of things." His elucidation of this definition suggests that, whereas reasoning is a step-by-step process, intuition is the capacity to reach the conclusion of an argument without demonstrating it by working through the intervening steps. For instance, Spinoza mentions the ability of mathematicians to see the answer to a problem at a glance, and also gives the example of Christ, the last of the prophets, who was able to intuit the content and universal status of the moral law without having to depend on a demonstration or proof. Intuition thus has something in common with imagination; both kinds of knowledge enable us to arrive at conclusions without laboriously traversing the path by which we reached them. But whereas imaginary judgments are distorted and only morally certain, intuition is the supreme manifestation of the intellect and yields absolutely certain conclusions.

How, though, does intuition bear on the construction of a theory of ideology? To make the connection, Althusser concentrates on the idea that intuitions are not arrived at inductively, by sifting data and comparing cases. Instead, intuitive thinkers are able to grasp general truths by seizing on the salient features of a particular case. For example, he says, Spinoza discovered a constant about religion by reasoning about the history of the Jewish people. He first came to understand the causes of the Jews' religious beliefs, thus acquiring knowledge of the second kind, and then leapt intuitively to a general account of religion as such. Similarly, it ought to be possible to arrive at a general understanding of ideology from a rational investigation of a particular case. This would be the culmination of a process of production in which raw material (ideology) had been transformed by reasoning (instruments of production) into a knowledge product (a general theory).

Although Althusser does not explicitly say so, he is presumably alluding here to the theory of ideology that he himself outlines. In *Ideology and Ideological State Apparatuses* he begins by discussing the way that, in Christian ideology, God is represented as speaking to individuals and as setting out norms of behavior and guarantees of reward which are then internalized. Althusser's account operates first at the level of imagination by describing the projections that constitute people's pretheoretical understanding of Christianity, before moving to the level of reasoning insofar

SUSAN JAMES

as it gestures toward the causal processes that create this imaginary understanding. Then comes the intuitive leap. Althusser sees that what is really going on in this case, as in other ideologies, is the creation of individuals as subjects. As he puts it, the subject is the constitutive category of all ideology, whatever its determination and whatever its historical date. Thus, as St. Paul explained, "it is in the 'Logos', meaning ideology, that we live, move and have our being."[8] Imagination not only enables us to invest the world with individual and collective meaning but also creates us as subjects who stand in a certain relation to this interpreted world and its practices. At the same time, however, imagination also conceals this last fact from us, thereby leaving us exposed to a patchy and distorted form of knowledge.

At this point we need to keep at least three considerations in play: Spinoza's account of intuition; Althusser's account of theoretical innovation; and materialism. Apropos the relation between the first two, it is perhaps worth bearing in mind that intuition, for Spinoza, is the capacity to intuit connections of a particular kind, namely deductive ones, and that this is what guarantees the certainty of its conclusions. One might therefore want to ask how this ability relates to Althusser's analysis of theoretical innovation, which sounds in some ways more akin to a Kuhnian paradigm shift. Apropos the relation between the first and third, it is worth remembering that intuition, or the third kind of knowledge, is for Spinoza knowledge of God (*Ethics* V P15) and that this intellectual love of God constitutes our blessedness and salvation (*Ethics* V P36). Spinoza uses intuition as a bridge between our everyday existence and a form of eternal existence which Althusser and Negri would, I think, classify as transcendental and which has little to do with materialism as they understand it. However, putting these points aside, let us turn our attention back to the relation between Althusser's reading of Spinoza and materialism.

Althusser picks out four aspects of Spinoza's account of knowledge that qualify it, in his view, as materialist. The first two involve an implicit contrast with nonmaterialist approaches to epistemology which, according to Althusser, are preoccupied with the origin of knowledge and the need to lay down criteria for what is to count as knowledge. Spinoza is held to acquire materialist credentials by virtue of the fact that he eschews both aspects of this nonmaterialist approach: He does not ask how anyone ever got knowledge in the first place but begins instead from the assumption that we do possess some knowledge; also, he never offers a definition of knowledge, or criteria for distinguishing it from other epistemological states.[9] For at least two reasons, both these claims strike me as debatable. First, it is true that Spinoza is not interested in skeptical questions about the origin of knowledge, but this by itself doesn't tell us much. After all, a good many early-modern philosophers simply assume that the senses and imagination provide us with at least some knowledge, and this by itself hardly qualifies them as materialists. Second, it is not clear that Spinoza refrains from providing definitions of the three kinds of knowledge—it would depend what one meant by a definition. Moreover, he does provide criteria for identifying one form of knowledge of the first kind when, in the *Tractatus Theologico-Politicus,* he specifies three conditions that distinguish true from false prophecy. I don't want to be fruitlessly pedantic here. Althusser is emphasizing that Spinoza does not work with an entirely a priori account of knowledge, and to this extent he is right. As often, however, he posits an unduly sharp divide between materialists and nonmaterialists, and it is difficult to place Spinoza unequivocally on either side of the line.

That's as much as I shall say about the first pair of grounds on which Althusser identifies Spinoza's theory of knowledge as a materialist one. The last two strike me as more important to Althusser's argument. Althusser begins by emphasizing that knowledge of the second and third kinds is a historical achievement only in some material circumstances. A people whose life has been deeply insecure and whose members are as a result prey to hopes and fears which make them changeable and superstitious, are too much in the grip of imagination to acquire much knowledge of the second kind and are thus blocked from gaining knowledge of the third kind. To take one of Spinoza's examples, this was true of the Jews when they came out of Egypt. Only after the Jews had lived for a while in the security of their theocracy were they able to internalize the habits of thought that enabled them to understand the causes of their own passions, thereby extending their knowledge of the second kind. The inhabitants of the Dutch Republic, by contrast, having lived for many years in a prosperous, secure, and tolerant state, are better placed to acquire a more adequate understanding of human nature and the ends of political society, and to order their lives accordingly. This historical conception of knowledge does indeed stand out in the context of early-modern philosophy, and it is easy to see why Althusser, and for that matter Negri, claim it as an antecedent of Marx's materialism.

The point on which Althusser lays greatest emphasis, however, has to do with a puzzle he finds in Marx. In the Introduction to *A Contribution to the Critique of Political Economy,* Marx had argued that knowledge proceeds from the abstract to the concrete. In acquiring knowledge, one does not begin in an empiricist vein with concrete perceptions and images but rather with perceptions and images viewed as abstractions, and from there one proceeds to concepts. But how can perceptions and images be abstract? Here, Althusser suggests, Spinoza can help us to understand what Marx is getting at. The everyday perceptions and images on which the labor of knowledge production gets to work are abstract in the sense that they are incomplete and distorted and are thus knowledge of the first kind. Our senses are not, in Bacon's phrase, a plane mirror which faithfully reflects the world. Instead, our understanding of the world and ourselves is shaped by our imagination, so that the acquisition of adequate knowledge—knowledge of the second kind—is a matter of filling in gaps and correcting biases. As we do this, our knowledge becomes more concrete—that's to say less distorted and more critical. In place of a viewpoint enmeshed in imagination, we gain one that takes account of the material causal nexus of which we are a part. In this way, we arrive at knowledge which is scientific.

Where does this leave us? We have seen that Althusser draws on aspects of Spinoza's philosophy in order to develop his own interpretation of Marx's distinction between ideology and science. Spinoza functions as a source of inspiration, and in order for him to do so it is helpful to read him as a materialist, as the possessor of an honorable lineage and thus as a philosopher with whom it is respectable to ally oneself. However, looking back at this episode (and from here to the French Marxism of the 1960s and 1970s is a long way), we may glimpse an element of resistance. If, as Deleuze argues, great philosophers coin new terms through which to ask new questions, is Althusser perhaps clinging with a submerged sense of desperation to the Marxist vocabulary of ideology, materialism, and science? As he appeals to Spinoza to confirm and sustain his Marxist philosophy, is Spinoza carrying him to the edge of Marxism, and even beyond the categories of science and ideology which are so central to his own intellectual concerns?

Why might this suspicion even occur to one? First, as Althusser himself acknowledges, Spinoza offers an escape from the division between true science and false ideology, at least insofar as he allows that imagination or ideology is true. The inadequacy of the conceptions of the world that we derive from imagination does not lie in the fact that they are false but only in the fact that they are incomplete. It is as though we have been gazing at a few scattered dots on the page of a newspaper, struggling to construct the photograph of which they are fragments. We might agree upon an interpretation and yet be amazed to find, when the dots are filled in, that the photograph is not at all as we expected. Yet the dots are not in themselves misleading. Similarly, a claim does not become ideological by virtue of being false in itself but by virtue of belonging to a set of ideas and practices which provide us with only a patchy grasp of the world and ourselves. When we arrive at a fuller understanding, we may be in for a surprise.

In addition to carrying us beyond the distinction between true science and false ideology, Spinoza's philosophy puts pressure on the idea of the transition from ideology to science as one that is undergone by an enduring subject who initially suffers from illusion but then comes to appreciate the truth. As well as upholding the argument we've just rehearsed to the effect that knowledge of the first kind is not illusory in any straightforward sense, Spinoza encourages us to think of subjects as constituted by their relations with the world. Human beings are bodies interacting with other bodies, and our minds—our ideas of these interactions—change as our interactions do. Equally, social groups are constituted by their relations with the world, which helps to determine what they can do and what they can think. So although there are continuities between subjects whose thinking is mainly imaginary and those subjects after they have learned to reflect more critically on their imaginary experience, the two are not exactly the same.

Third, the condition of blessedness that Spinoza discusses at the end of the *Ethics* is in tension with his conviction that neither individuals nor social groups can completely free themselves from imagination. This is partly because we need the everyday, imaginary ideas that contribute to our individual and collective identities. It is partly because we are incapable of reflecting critically on all our experience. And it is partly because critical reflection does not always do away with imagination. In the first place, some imaginary ideas are unaffected by knowledge of their causes, as when the knowledge that the sun is far away does not prevent it from looking as though it's quite close to the earth. In the second place, some imaginary ideas are hard to shift, even when knowledge of their causes ought by rights to undermine them. For example, my belief that Saddam Hussein was a demonic character may linger on, even though I recognize that it's the fruit of collective projection. So if knowledge of the first kind is, as Althusser claims, ideology, then Spinoza seems to be saying that ideology will never go away completely.

These three points about the implications of Spinoza's philosophy would not surprise Althusser, and I do not mean to suggest that he would have repudiated them outright. On the contrary, they are all to be found, more or less explicitly, in Althusser's work. Nevertheless, they are among the problems that prompted some of his contemporaries, such as Michel Foucault, to abandon all talk of ideology, together with the idea that we can transcend an ideological understanding of ourselves and arrive at a science of society. So while Althusser in fact relied on Spinoza in his attempt to produce a satisfying account of ideology and thus a strengthened form of Marxism, it seems that he might equally have appealed to Spinoza's work in order to depart from ideology. This is what I meant when I said that there is a sense in which Spinoza carries Althusser beyond the Marxist categories which preoccupied him for most of his life.

This alternative reading of Spinoza as a philosopher who carries us beyond ideology has recently become prominent, notably in the work of Moira Gatens and Genevieve Lloyd. Lloyd and Gatens emphasize many of the features of Spinoza's philosophy that endeared it to the materialists discussed in this essay. They stress Spinoza's nonreductive identification of body and mind, the embodied character of his individuals, and the historicity of his conception of self-understanding. Above all, they stress the central role of imagination in his work—an imagination which is both resilient and pervasive. However, rather than construe imagination as ideology, Gatens and Lloyd stress its constructive aspects. Drawing on recent discussion of the imaginary (particularly, perhaps, on the work of Castoriadis) they dwell on its productive character. The stock of symbols, images, and significations which make up the imaginary help to constitute our identities, and we cannot do without them. Furthermore, if we remember with Spinoza that the imagination is historical, the fruit of diverse experiences and circumstances, we shall be better placed to understand the diversity of our own identities and the way they come to be organized around dimensions of race, gender, nationality, ethnicity, religion, and so forth. Finally, although the imaginary is always with us, it is not something we simply have to put up with. Our ability to reflect on its causes can enable us, as Spinoza saw, to distance ourselves from some images, redescribe others, and invent new ones.

Although Gatens' and Lloyd's project is in some ways a continuation of Althusser's, they do not describe Spinoza as a materialist or relate his philosophy to that of Marx. Rather, they are constructing a new Spinoza, this time a theorist of identity who may be able to steer a course between the shoals of liberalism and communitarianism toward a fuller understanding of individual and collective identity, and a richer knowledge of how to modify both. Once again, Spinoza the chameleon is taking on a new color.

Notes

1. Friedrich Engels, *Ludwig Feuerbach and the End of Classical German Philosophy*, 373–76.

2. Georgi Plekhanov, "Notes to Engel's *Ludwig Feuerbach and the End of Classical German Philosophy*," in Georgi Plekhanov, *Selected Philosophical Works*, 3rd ed. (5 vols.; Moscow: Progress Publishers, 1977), 1: 467.

3. Louis Althusser, *Lenin and Philosophy, and Other Essays*, trans. Ben Brewster (London: New Left Books, 1971), 34.

4. Louis Althusser and Etienne Balibar, *Reading Capital,* trans. Ben Brewster (London: New Left Books, 1970), 17.

5. Cf. Althusser, *Lenin and Philosophy,* 163.

6. Althusser, *Reading Capital,* 159.

7. *Ibid.,* 154–55.

8. *Ibid.,* 161.

9. Louis Althusser, *Essays in Self-Criticism,* trans. Grahame Lock (London: New Left Books, 1976), 188 ff.

Deleuze's Spinoza: Thinker of Difference, or Deleuze against the Valley Girls

Todd May

Of all the pre-nineteenth-century philosophers who have exerted a fascination on both philosophers and nonphilosophers alike, probably none has exerted more fascination than Spinoza. Certainly, there have been pre-nineteenth–century philosophers, such as Descartes or Hume, who have proven more influential than Spinoza. And no doubt many have been more often cited than Spinoza. But for sheer fascination, it's hard to beat the excommunicated Jew from Amsterdam.

What is it, we might want to ask, that pulls so many people in Spinoza's direction? What is the source of his lingering allure? Why does reading him—or even reading about him, which has its advantages— tingle our skin and kindle our minds (or, as Spinoza might have it, our mind)? Whatever it is that moves us, we know that it doesn't have anything to do with his philosophical style: the propositions, the proofs, the scholia, the lemma. A student of mine once said of Spinoza's style that it was like reading Proust minus the action. I don't think it would be too harsh to say that in a prose competition between the *Ethics* and *Pilgrim's Progress,* it's pretty much a wash.

What is it, then, that remains always enticing in Spinoza's thought? I suggest that it's the same thing that moves us in much of Eastern thought and Taoism in particular: Spinoza's core idea that we are all part of something larger than ourselves, and that we belong to it not contingently or indirectly but rather immediately and intimately. The idea that in some way, we are all one, or all part of some kind of One, exerts a continuing appeal that keeps Spinoza's thought, and his *Ethics* in particular, fresh and alive in a way that's hard to match.

What I would like to talk about with you today is precisely that One of Spinoza's, and to offer a Deleuzian way of understanding the One that may well differ from certain received views. But first, in order to see what those received views are, I would like to offer a portrait of one of them. Granted, this portrait draws upon resources outside the immediate circle of philosophy, but it is central to the culture at large, and I trust that you will find it not entirely marginal to the role philosophy might play in our larger cultural milieu.

The received view I use as a contrast case might be thought of as a certain form of Taoism. It is summed up in a word that is at the same time a phrase that is, in turn, at once both an explanation and a permissive prescription. You have already guessed, no doubt, what that word is: whatever. Even a cursory examination of the use of the word "whatever" reveals salient characteristics of its philosophical bent. As an explanation, "whatever" signifies that it is all the same, so it doesn't matter what happens. As a permissive prescription, it indicates that the choice of future action is up to the listener, since nothing of larger consequence can possibly flow from the listener's action. Of course, the reason that nothing of consequence can possibly flow from the choice of future action is that it's all the same anyway, so, whatever.

For those who are less conversant with recent cultural history, there is a temptation to think of this form of Taoism as something we might call "GenX Taoism," the Taoism associated with a group of young adults who are so lazy, self-indulgent, and unmotivated that now, a decade or so after the coining of the term, they're all on the Internet making ten times the salary that we'll ever pull in. In fact, however, the term "GenX Taoism" ignores the proper roots of this philosophical viewpoint, as any astute Heideggerian will attest. If we trace "whatever," a term which is at once an entire philosophy, back to its primordial roots, we discover it in Southern California, where, as Heidegger would no doubt remind us, it is pronounced entirely differently from the way it has come down to us through the distortions of history. What we have come to pronounce "whatever" and associate with Generation X is, in fact, a product of the Valley Girls and is pronounced "what-EVER." Thus, the view with which I shall contrast Deleuze's own appropriation of Spinoza is a view that is properly labelled Valley Girl Taoism.

As an aside, I should mention that Valley Girl Taoism instantiates one of the less discussed ontological categories in Heideggerian thought, *Im-Nebel-Sein*, or, in English, "Being-in-a-fog."

The animating thought behind Valley Girl Taoism is that, however things go, it's all pretty much the same anyway, so what's the point. Now my particular focus in this essay is not on the "what's the point" part but on the "pretty much the same anyway" part, which, as I take it, you can immediately recognize as a possible heir to Spinoza's One. I argue here that, if we follow Deleuze's reading of Spinoza, then we will read Spinoza's One not as a matter of sameness or identity but of difference, and reading it that way furnishes us with a take on Spinoza that is, to paraphrase another common locution, dynamic as you wanna be.

Let me start, however, not with difference and sameness or identity but with a concept closer to the One, the concept of immanence. For Deleuze, immanence, as opposed to transcendence, is among the most important structural elements of any adequate philosophy. In *What is Philosophy?*—written with Félix Guattari—Deleuze discusses the great illusions that have stalked the history of philosophy, saying, "We must draw up a list of these illusions and take their measure, just as Nietzsche, following Spinoza, listed the 'four great errors'. . . . First of all, there is the *illusion* of transcendence, which, perhaps, comes before all the others."[1]

Why is immanence so important a concept for Deleuze? Why does his entire philosophical corpus from beginning to end seek to eliminate any form of transcendence? The motivation, in fact, is Nietzschean. Recall Nietzsche's "History of an Error" in *Twilight of the Idols,* in which he describes how the true world, the world divorced from our world but next to which our world looks merely apparent, even meretricious, eventually distances itself so much from our world that it disappears altogether, and the distinction between the true world and the apparent 'world is lost. For Nietzsche, this disappearance of the true world is a good thing because it is always in the name of the true world, the name of some world other than our own, that our world is criticized, diminished, derided. And, concommitantly, it is in the name of the true world (recall Christianity here as Nietzsche's prime example) that we are asked to hate our lives, to hate life itself, and thus to abandon the creative possibilities that our lives might sustain. It is, finally, the illusion of transcendence that renders people reactive rather than active and affirmative.

Deleuze adopts this Nietzschean theme in his own philosophical work. The problem transcendence brings to any philosophical approach is twofold: It both criticizes and constrains the possibilities for living. By turning against our world, it compels us to look outside that world for meaningful ways of living. Any adequate philosophy, any philosophy that is to be of use in attempting to live in interesting and creative ways, then, must be a philosophy of immanence. And here Spinoza provides the model. As Deleuze and Guattari write in *What is Philosophy?*:

> Spinoza is the Christ of philosophers, and the greatest philosophers are hardly more than apostles who distance themselves from or draw near to this mystery. Spinoza, the infinite becoming-philosopher: he showed, drew up, and thought the 'best' plane of immanence—that is, the purest, the one that does not hand itself over to the transcendent or

restore any transcendent, the one that inspires the fewest illusions, bad feelings, and erroneous perceptions.[2]

Spinoza's One, his one substance, then, provides for Deleuze the model of a philosophical approach. But note that, at this point, we have not yet gone a step beyond Valley Girl Taoism. What Valley Girl worth her chewing gum would deny that there is no transcendent value or truth from which to criticize the immanence of our existence? In fact, I take it that when Valley Girl Taoists invoke the phrase "gag me with a spoon," it is precisely as a culinary indication that someone has attempted to introduce a transcendent value, to force one down her throat as it were, in an attempt to alter a current mode of existence. There is, of course, no justification for the recourse to such an illusion; however, if the critic himself or herself wants to act in accordance with that illusion, well, whatever.

Spinoza, however, unlike the Valley Girl Taoist, does not stop with this indifferent One. Substance is not static, not closed in upon itself. In terms Deleuze uses in another context to describe Leibniz's thought, Spinozist substance is constantly folding and unfolding. Specifically, it folds and unfolds in the way of attributes and modes. By turning to attributes and modes, then, we will begin to see the dynamism Deleuze discovers in Spinoza.

According to Deleuze, "Attributes are for Spinoza dynamic and active forms. And here we have what seems essential: attributes are no longer attributed, but are in some sense attributive. . . . As soon as we posit the attribute as 'attributive' we conceive it as attributing its essence to something that remains identical for all attributes, that is, to necessarily existing substance."[3] Now what might Deleuze mean by the concept "attributive," which he distinguishes from the more passive concept "attributed"? We get a clue a few lines down when he writes, "what do they attribute, what do they express? Each attribute attributes an infinite essence, that is, an unlimited quality."

The idea of attributes as unlimited qualities is, of course, straightahead Spinoza. But in this passage Deleuze uses another term as coequal with attributive: the term "expressive." Attributes express substance, or better, each attribute expresses an infinite essence of substance. We can see the same idea in the *Ethics,* Proposition 11, in which Spinoza writes, "God, or substance consisting of infinite attributes, each of which expresses eternal and infinite essence, necessarily exists."[4] The question then is, what is meant by the idea of expression?

Deleuze contrasts expression with emanation as two types of causality. Expression is immanent causality; what is expressed in expression remains within the source of that expression. "What is expressed has no existence outside its expression, but is expressed as the essence of what expresses itself."[5] Emanation, by contrast, is transcendent causality. In emanation, what is emanated becomes distinct in any one of a number of ways from the source of that emanation. *"While an emanative cause remains in itself, the effect it produces is not in it, and does not remain in it."*[6] Thus, the difference between expression and emanation (or creation, another form of causality Deleuze discusses) is that expression is the only form of causality which resists transcendence. Deleuze summarizes this difference when he writes that "the themes of creation or emanation cannot do without a minimal transcendence, which bars 'expressionism' from proceeding all the way to the immanence it implies. Immanence is the very vertigo of philosophy, and is inseparable from the concept of expression (from the double immanence of expression in what expresses itself, and of what is expressed in its expression)."[7]

Although we have not yet gone all the way to the idea of difference, by introducing the concept of expression in the discussion of attributes, Deleuze moves beyond the static immanence of Valley Girl Taoism toward the beginnings of a more dynamic immanence. The discussion of modes will deepen that dynamism and, like all deepenings, complicate matters in a way that leads Deleuze to introduce difference, a concept that does not appear, at least explicitly, in the *Ethics.*

If attributes express substance, then what do modes do, and how do they, in turn, resist transcendence? Modes, let's recall, are usually considered to be the objects that we encounter in the world. You and I are modes, as are all other things in the universe. We will see further on that the idea of modes as things or objects, although Deleuze uses that terminology, is in fact a bit misleading. But for the moment let's hold onto it as an initial approach.

Modes, according to Deleuze, express attributes just as attributes express substance. "[A]ttributes in their turn express themselves in modes. This expression is the production of the modes themselves: God produces as he understands; he cannot understand himself without producing an infinity of things, and without also understanding all that he produces."[8] Now this passage may, at first, seem at variance with what we've been saying so far. In it, Deleuze uses the term "producing," which rings more of the idea of emanation or causation than it does of expression as we just saw it. This, in fact, is a false ring. Producing, in the sense this passage uses it, is the same thing as what Deleuze elsewhere calls "explicating." Explication is a form of evolution, an unfolding, rather than a creation. If the modes express their attributes, they do so by way of evolving them, by way of the attributes unfolding into different modal arrangements.

The contrast between the way we usually think of production and evolution as Deleuze uses the term is parallel to the distinction between emanation or creation and expression. Evolution is like origami, the traditional Japanese art of folding paper into different figures. In origami, one does not cut the paper or introduce any outside elements into it; only the paper itself is folded and unfolded into new arrangements, with those arrangements being the modes of the paper which is the origami's substance. If the paper could fold and unfold itself, we would, I think, be very close to the idea of evolution as Deleuze conceives it. It would be as though, to use the terms in the quote above, the paper were capable of "producing an infinity of things," and in order to "understand" itself, it would have to produce those things as its own possibilities.

At this point in the discussion, however, the Valley Girl Taoist returns with a vengeance. If evolution produces a variety of things, then we seem to be on the threshold of saying, not that it is all one, but that it is all lots of things, and the tension between the one that produces and the many that is produced comes to the fore. In his classic essay "Uncomfortable Strains in Deleuzian Spinozism: The Parmenidean Return to the Heart of Postmodernism," a work with which I'm sure you're all familiar, Valley Girl Taoist Saul Wontomee argues, "It's like, you know, if you have the One, you know, the one that isn't, like, supposed to be more than one, and you have the many, just like lots of things, well then come on, I mean what is it really already? I mean, are we like stupid, or what?"

Oddly, Deleuze himself seems to presage this critique in *Difference and Repetition,* a work that appeared at the same time as *Expressionism in Philosophy,* his most extended treatment of Spinoza. In *Difference and Repetition,* Deleuze writes, "there still remains a difference between substance and the modes: Spinoza's substance appears independent of the modes, while the modes are dependent on substance, but as though on something other than themselves."[9] You can see the problem that is emerging here. If substance is One and the modes are many and varied, then how are we to conceive the relation between them, otherwise than on the model of transcendence? It's not that we can't conceive the relation between the One of substance and the many of the modes at all. We can. But we seem to need to do so on the basis of separating substance from its modes, of making it something so divorced from them that it is, in Deleuze's terms, "independent" of them. But where you have independence, don't you also have transcendence, at least the minimal transcendence that he ascribed to emanation and creation and from which he was trying to distance Spinoza? Don't you have something so other to the modes that are produced that it cannot be conceived as having an internal relation to them?

That depends on how you conceive substance. In offering this critique, the Valley Girl Taoist and the early Deleuze seem to identify the oneness of Spinoza's substance with the idea of sameness or identity. The oneness of substance implies identity, and since it does, there seems to be no route from the One to the many without some kind of transcendence. But what if we did not conceive the One, conceive substance, as some sort of identity? What if we conceived it in terms of difference, as some sort of multiplicity? Then the route from the One to the many could remain expressive in the way Deleuze seeks and could retain the immanence that he wants to preserve for it.

In fact, in the passage from *Difference and Repetition* just cited, Deleuze suggests just this sort of move, identifying it with Nietzsche. Immediately after the words just cited, he writes:

> Substance must be said *of* the modes and only *of* the modes. Such a condition can be satisfied only at the price of a more general categorical reversal according to which being is said of becoming, identity of that which is different, the one of the multiple, etc. That identity is not the first, that it exists as a principle but as a second principle, as a principle *become;* that it revolve around the Different: such would be the nature of the Copernican revolution which opens up the possibility of difference having its own concept, rather than being maintained under the domination of a concept in general already understood as identical. Nietzsche meant nothing more than this by the eternal return.[10]

Those familiar with Deleuze's thought will recognize this as the move by which Deleuze articulates what he calls the "univocity of Being" as difference itself. "Being is said in a single and same sense of everything of which it is said, but that of which it is said differs: it is said of difference itself."[11]

Later, Deleuze, writing with Guattari, ascribes the same idea, the positing of difference as the substance from which all identities flow, directly to Spinoza. In *A Thousand Plateaus,* discussing Spinoza, they write, "It is a problem not of the One and the Multiple but of a fusional multiplicity that effectively goes beyond the one and the multiple. A formal multiplicity that, as such, constitutes the ontological unity of substance."[12] Thus Spinoza, the Christ of philosophers, becomes the first thinker to identify Being with difference. Substance, the One, is not a Oneness of identity or sameness, as the Valley Girl Taoists would have it, but a Oneness of difference.

Looking back over where we have been so far, we can identify three entwined concepts that form the core of Deleuze's Spinoza. This is, I guess, as it should be. After all, the Christ of philosophers must have his Trinity. In this case, the Trinity is that of immanance, expression, and difference (or what Deleuze sometimes calls "multiplicity"). Immanence requires expression if it is not to lapse into the transcendence of emanation or creation. And the expression of immanence requires that its source be an immanence of difference if the expressed are not to become too removed, too different in kind, too "independent" from the source. Thus, the three concepts operate as a single whole in determining the nature and operation of Spinoza's substance. Substance, that substance which expresses itself in attributes and then again in modes, is a substance of difference that is immanent to the attributes and modes in which it expresses itself.

The last move I want to make with you will involve a further articulation of the relation of substance to attributes and especially to modes, but before doing so let's pause a moment over the contrast that is emerging between Deleuze's Spinoza and Valley Girl Taoism. What I hope you are seeing is the dynamism of the philosophical view that Deleuze associates with Spinozist Oneness, in contrast to the more static Oneness of the Valley Girl Taoist. In the latter case, since it is all the same anyway, and since therefore nothing of consequence can distinguish itself from this sameness, then the only appropriate response to any proposed theoretical or practical proposal is the bland indifference of "whatever." As the Hegelian faction of Valley Girl Taoism has put it, it is the all-nighter in which all freaks wear black. By contrast, Deleuze's Spinoza is a dynamic unfolding of difference into attributes and modes, and in which the modes are not separate creations from that unfolding, neither Platonic inferior copies nor Christian degraded mortals tainted with the stain of original sin, but immanent expressions of the substance that produces them. Thus, rather than stasis, we have the unfolding movement of expression; rather than impotence, we have the unlimited possibility of what substance is capable of (or, as Deleuze puts it with respect to modes, what a body can do); rather than indifference, we have joy.

To see more clearly how this immanent unfolding may be conceived, I want to introduce a bit more of the Deleuzian framework into our reading of Spinoza. This framework will help articulate the temporal aspects of the relation of substance to modes. When we speak of Spinoza's dynamism and use terms such as "expression" and "unfolding" to describe substance's production, we are implying that there is a temporal dimension to Spinoza's thought. In fact, Deleuze embraces that temporal dimension, and although he does not discuss it specifically with respect to Spinoza, he does introduce concepts that are readily applicable to Spinoza's thought. If we follow the trajectory of those concepts for a moment, we can begin to see in a little more depth the richness of thought that Deleuze finds in Spinoza's ontology.

The Deleuzian concepts I introduce here are that of the virtual and the actual. Deleuze often invokes these concepts and in doing so is always at pains to distinguish them from the concepts of the possible and the real. In Deleuze's take on these concepts, the possible is exactly like the real; it is a copy of the real, except that, unlike the real, it does not exist. What is possible is the real minus its character of existing. It is like a mirror image of the real, an image that remains in the mirror unless by some chance it is realized, in which case it becomes the real and is no longer the possible.

The virtual contrasts with the possible in two ways. First, it is already real. It does not have to be realized since it is already there. It is not real in the same way as the actual, a difference that Deleuze sometimes marks by saying that while the actual "exists," the virtual "subsists" or "insists," but virtuality is no less real for all that. When Deleuze says that the virtual is "actualized" by the actual, we should not equate actualization with realization, a point I'll return to in just a moment.

Second, the virtual does not mirror the actual in the way that the possible mirrors the real. The virtual is different in kind from the actual. It is not the actual minus its character of being real. Rather, it is real in a way that is different from the actual.

But if this is so, then what is the relationship between the virtual and the actual? The actual, Deleuze says, actualizes the virtual. To actualize is not to add on a character of being real but rather to unfold the virtual into a specific existing arrangement. To get an initial grasp on this idea, I borrow an example that Constantin Boundas once offered me. A specific person actualizes information in his or her genes. This actualization is not a bringing forth into the real of that which is possible. The genetic information, which is real in the gene, is already there. And the person who is brought forth does not resemble the information in the way that the possible resembles the real. After all, nobody looks like his or her genetic code. Instead, a person actualizes that information; a person is an unfolding of his or her genetic code into a specific existing arrangement.

Now there are limits to the analogy with genetics. For one, a person is more than his or her genetic code; a person is also an actualization of specific environmental conditions. However, I think the analogy gets us some way toward understanding the relation of the virtual to the actual. The next step is to use the concept of the virtual more precisely in Deleuze's reading of the French philosopher Henri Bergson and then use that to see more clearly the temporal aspect of Spinoza's thought.

For Bergson, the way we usually think about time, as a succession of instants that pass from the unreality of the future to the unreality of the past by means of the instantaneous reality of the present, is mistaken. The idea of time as a succession of independently existing presents is, he thinks, a spatialized concept of time. Just as space presents us with distinct objects, so we think of time as presenting us with distinct instants. Bergson's proposal is that we think of time temporally rather than spatially. How might we do that? In his view, time, especially the past and the present, is a whole, a "pure duration." The present does not cease as it passes. Rather, it becomes part of a past that exists (or, to use Deleuzian terms, subsists or insists) just as the present does. What's more, the past is not distinct from the present; it does not subsist apart from the present but rather in the present. The present, in Bergson, is an actualization of the past rather than a moment that exists apart from the past and then joins it as it passes. Thus, for Bergson the whole of time—past and present—is there, is real, at every moment. As Deleuze puts it, "Not only does the past coexist with the present that has been, but, as it preserves itself in itself (while the present passes), it is the whole, integral past; it is *all* our past, which coexists with each present."[13]

The model of this coexistence, of pure duration, that Bergson uses is that of a cone, with the present at the apex and the past trailing out all the way to the base. In this model, the whole of the past exists (or subsists, or insists) at every moment of the present but in different degrees of what Bergson calls "relaxation" or "contraction." Closer to the present, the past is more contracted. Further from the present, it is more relaxed. Now in considering this image, we should not think of each cross-section of the cone as containing a single moment of the past. Rather, each cross-section contains all of the past, just as the present moment at the tip of the cone does. However, the further back one goes from the apex of the cone to its base, the more relaxed the whole of the past is. But the cone, the whole of the cone, is always there, and it is always there at every moment: actualized in its apex as the present, virtual in the rest of the cone.

Now what might Bergson's cone of pure duration have to do with Spinoza? We can begin to see the relevance with Deleuze's own summation of pure duration in his book on Bergson, when he contrasts the static multiplicity of space with the dynamic multiplicity of time. Referring to time, he writes, "The other type of multiplicity appears in pure duration: It is an internal multiplicity of succession, of fusion, of organization, of heterogeneity, of qualitative discrimination, or of *difference in kind;* it is a *virtual* and *continuous* multiplicity that cannot be reduced to numbers."[14] Recalling Deleuze and Guattari's idea of "a formal multiplicity of substantial attributes," and Deleuze's ascription of difference itself first to Nietzsche and later to Spinoza, we can begin to see the continuity of Deleuze's reading of Bergson and his reading of Spinoza.

I don't want to say that, for Deleuze, Spinoza collapses into Bergson or Bergson into Spinoza. For one thing, Bergson works largely with a contrast of two concepts, the past and the present, whereas Spinoza has a tri-partite conception of substance, attributes, and modes. Rather, we read Deleuze's Spinoza as being concerned, as is Bergson, with a virtual unity of difference that unfolds in time. Substance and its attributes, the "for-mal multiplicity," are best seen not on the model of things that give rise to other things—an idea that will likely return us to ideas of emanation or creation and thus to transcendence—but as temporal virtualities that un-fold or actualize into modes which, when they perish, refold into sub-stance.

If we approach matters this way, then Spinoza's modes, which initially looked like things or objects, begin to seem more like temporal matters than spatial ones. This reading is, I think, more in keeping with Deleuze's Spinoza. In *Expressionism in Philosophy,* Deleuze writes, "A given mode 'comes to exist,' comes into existence, when an infinity of extensive parts enter into a *given* relation: it continues to exist as long as this relation holds."[15] This relation of parts is, as both Deleuze and Spinoza note, one of motion and rest. As Spinoza writes in the *Ethics* (II.P13, lem. 3 def), "When a number of bodies of the same or different magnitude form close contact with one another through the pressure of other bodies upon them, or if they are moving at the same or different rates of speed so as to preserve an unvarying relation of movement among themselves, these bod-ies are said to be united with one another and all together to form one body or individual thing, which is distinguished from other things through this union of bodies."[16]

Here, of course, Spinoza is writing about the formation of single bodies, not the formation of modes themselves. However, when he thinks of the formation of bodies as matters of motion and rest, of varying rates of speed, he is giving a temporal interpretation of bodily existence rather than a spatial one. And that, it seems to me, is the crucial point. Modes and the bodies that comprise their extensive parts are temporal matters, unfoldings and refoldings of the attributes they express and the substance expressed in turn by those attributes.

Before closing, let me respond briefly to an objection that one may be tempted to raise but that does not appear, at least to my knowledge, in the Valley Girl literature. The objection is the inverse of Wontomee's ob-jection cited earlier. There he argued that the tension between the one of substance and the many of the modes seemed to force transcendence back upon substance. As you recall, I tried to counter that objection by claiming that for Deleuze, at least for the later—and shall we say, ma-ture—Deleuze, substance, as difference, could well be continuous with the modes. But if substance is immanent to its modes by way of difference, what keeps substance from collapsing entirely into its modes? By introducing difference into the nature of substance, haven't we saved the continuity of substance with its modes at the price of being unable to distinguish them? Just as we might ask of Bergson what keeps the past distinct as past in its subsistence in the present, what keeps substance and its attributes, as virtual, distinct from the modes that express them?

There are, of course, those who would prefer just such a collapse. For instance, the Material Girl School of Valley Girl Taoism, which argues that the reason it is all the same anyway is that we are in the end all just bodies in shopping, embraces just such a perspective. Rather than defend the preservation of the distinction in a wholesale way, however, I confine myself to the more narrow theoretical point that it is possible to keep substance and its modes conceptually distinct.

In Deleuze's view, substance is not a specific differentiated arrangement like a mode; rather, it is difference itself, difference conceived as prior to any identity. Recall the earlier passage from *Difference and Repetition* on Spinoza and Nietzsche when Deleuze writes that "being is said of becoming, identity of that which is different, the one of the multiple, etc." Difference, difference itself, is first; all identities and specific differences flow from that. Virtual difference, which is substance, is what gives rise, by way of expression, to the specific differences which are modes. In *Difference and Repetition*, Deleuze distinguishes the difference which is virtual difference itself and that which is actual by distinguishing "differentiation" with a "t" from "differenciation" with a "c." He writes, "Whereas differentiation determines the virtual content of the Idea as problem, differenciation expresses the actualisation of this virtual and the constitution of solutions."[17] In Spinoza's case, the Idea is substance and the solutions are the modes.

Thus substance, while immanent to the modes that express it, does not collapse into modes. The latter are specific arrangements of difference, the former difference itself. As Deleuze puts it in *Expressionism and Philosophy*, "The production of modes, it is true, does take place through differentiation [not distinguished here from differenciation—my note]. But differentiation is in this case purely quantitative. If real distinction is never numerical, numerical distinction is, conversely, essentially modal."[18]

To conclude, what I have attempted to do in this paper is to wrestle the Spinozan legacy away from what is probably its most influential descendent in contemporary culture: Valley Girl Taoism. I have tried to do so by contrasting a dynamic Spinoza whose substance is difference from the Valley Girl's static Spinoza whose substance is sameness, to rescue a Spinoza in motion from the clutches of a Spinoza on a couch. Whether such an attempt will, in the end, prove successful seems to me to depend on two things. First, it will depend on the scholarly question of whether, ultimately, Deleuze's reading of Spinoza turns out to be a defensible one. Second, and surely of more moment, it will depend on whether the dynamic Spinoza whom Deleuze has put before us can take the pride of place now accorded to the static Spinoza at the heart of contemporary culture. I for one find it harder to imagine a more urgent task facing philosophers. If there is another culture war on the intellectual horizon, let me suggest that its name be Spinoza and its clarion call be that of difference.

Notes

1. *What is Philosophy?* trans. Graham Burchell and Hugh Tomlinson (New York: Columbia University Press, 1994), 49.
2. *Ibid.*, 60.
3. Gilles Deleuze, *Expressionism in Philosophy: Spinoza,* trans. Martin Joughin (New York: Zone Books, 1990), 45.
4. Baruch Spinoza, *The Ethics and Selected Letters,* trans. Samuel Shirley (Indianapolis: Hackett, 1982), 37.
5. *Expressionism,* 43.
6. *Ibid.*, 171.
7. *Ibid.*, 180.
8. *Ibid.*, 185.
9. *Difference and Repetition,* trans. Paul Patton (New York: Columbia University Press, 1994), 40.
10. *Ibid.*, 40–41.
11. *Ibid.*, 36.
12. *A Thousand Plateaus,* vol. 2 of *Capitalism and Schizophrenia,* trans. Brian Massumi (Minneapolis: University of Minnesota Press, 1987), 154.
13. *Bergsonism,* trans. Hugh Tomlinson and Barbara Habberjam (New York: Zone Books, 1988), 59.
14. *Ibid.*, 38.
15. *Expressionism,* 208.
16. *Ethics,* 74.
17. *Difference and Repetition,* 209.
18. *Expressionism,* 182–83.

Deleuze on Leibniz: Difference, Continuity, and the Calculus

Daniel W. Smith

Gilles Deleuze once characterized himself as a "classical" philosopher, a statement that no doubt was meant to signal his indebtedness to (and affinities with) the great philosophers of the classic period, notably Spinoza and Leibniz. Spinoza provided Deleuze with a model for a purely immanent ontology, while Leibniz offered him a way of thinking through the problems of individuation and the theory of Ideas. In both cases, however, Deleuze would take up and modify Spinoza's and Leibniz's thought in his own manner, such that it is impossible to say that Deleuze is a "Spinozist" or a "Leibnizian" without carefully delineating the use to which he puts each of these thinkers.

In this essay, I examine at least the initial outlines of Deleuze's reading of Leibniz. Although Deleuze published a book-length study of Leibniz late in his career, *The Fold: Leibniz and the Baroque* (1984),[1] his more profound (and, I believe, more important) engagement with Leibniz had already occurred in *Difference and Repetition* (1968) and *Logic of Sense* (1969).[2] In these earlier works, Deleuze approached Leibniz from a resolutely post-Kantian point of view, returning to Leibniz in his attempt to redefine the nature of the transcendental field. Following Salomon Maimon, Deleuze had argued that, in order for Kant's critical philosophy to achieve its own aims, a viewpoint of *internal genesis* needed to be substituted for Kant's principle of *external conditioning*.[3] "Doing this means returning to Leibniz," Deleuze would later explain, "but on bases other than Leibniz's. All the elements to create a genesis such as the post-Kantians demand it, all the elements are virtually in Leibniz."[4] One of these other "bases" was the formulation of a pure principle of *difference*, which alone would be capable of freeing thought from "representation" (whether finite or infinite), and its concomitant subordination to the principle of identity. As Maimon had shown, whereas identity is the condition of possibility of

DANIEL W. SMITH

thought in general, it is difference that constitutes the genetic condition of *real* thought. In what follows, then, I show how Deleuze uses Leibniz to "deduce" the necessity of a principle of difference by making his way through the four fundamental principles of Leibniz's philosophy: identity, sufficient reason, indiscernibility, and the law of continuity (see figure 1). What emerges from Deleuze's reading of Leibniz is, as he himself puts it, "a Leibnizian transcendental philosophy that bears on the event rather than the phenomenon, and replaces the Kantian conditioning."[5]

The Principle of Identity

We begin with the simplest statement of the principle of identity. The classical formula of the identity principle is "A is A": "blue is blue," "a triangle is a triangle," "God is God." But such formulae, says Leibniz, "seem to do nothing but repeat the same thing without telling us anything."[6] They are certain but empty. A more popular formulation of the principle of identity would be "A thing is what it is." This formula goes further than the formula "A is A" because it shows us the ontological region governed by the principle of identity: Identity consists in manifesting the identity between the thing and what the thing *is,* what classical philosophy termed the "essence" of a thing. In Leibniz, every principle is a *ratio,* a "reason," and the principle of identity can be said to be the *ratio* or rule of essences, the *ratio essendi.* It corresponds to the question, "Why is there something rather than nothing?" If there were no identity (an identity conceived as the identity of the thing and what the thing *is*), then there would be nothing. But Leibniz also provides us with a more technical formulation of the principle of identity, derived from logic: "every analytic proposition is true." What is an analytic proposition? It is a proposition in which the subject and the predicate are identical. "A is A" is an analytical proposition: The predicate A is contained in the subject A, and therefore "A is A" is true. But to complete the detail of Leibniz's formula, we would have to distinguish between two types of identical propositions: An analytic proposition is true either by reciprocity or by inclusion. An example of a proposition of *reciprocity* is "a triangle has three angles." This is an identical proposition because the predicate ("three angles") is the same as the subject ("triangle") and reciprocates with the subject. The second case, a proposition of *inclusion,* is slightly more complex. In the proposition "a triangle has three sides" there is no identity between the subject and the predicate, yet there is a supposed logical necessity: One cannot conceptualize a single figure having three angles without this figure also having three sides. There is no reciprocity here, but there is a demonstrable inclusion or inherence of the predicate in the subject. One could say that analytic propositions of reciprocity are objects of *intuition,* whereas analytic propositions of inclusion are the objects of a *demonstration.* What Leibniz calls *analysis* is the operation that discovers a predicate in a notion taken as a subject. If I show that a given predicate is contained in a notion, then I have done an analysis. All this is basic logic; up to this point, the Leibniz's greatness as a thinker has not yet appeared.

Principle of Sufficient Reason

Leibniz's originality, Deleuze suggests, first emerges with his second great principle, the principle of sufficient reason, which no longer refers to the

---

Four Principles in Leibniz

Principle of Identity
Reason: *ratio essendi* ("reason for being") ("Why something rather than nothing?")
Popular Formulation: "A thing is what it is."
Technical Formulation: "Every analytic proposition is true."

Principle of Sufficient Reason
Reason: *ratio existendi* ("reason for existing") ("Why this rather than that?")
Popular Formulation: "Everything has a reason."
Technical Formulation: "Every true proposition is analytic."

Principle of Indiscernibles
Reason: *ratio cognoscendi* ("reason for knowing")
Popular Formulation: "No two things are the same."
Technical Formulation: "For every concept, there is one and only one thing."

Law of Continuity
Reason: *ratio fiendi* ("reason for becoming")
Popular Formulation: "Nature never makes leaps."
Technical Formulation: "A singularity is extended over a series of ordinary points until it reaches the neighborhood of another singularity, etc."

FIGURE 1

domain of essences but the domain of things that actually exist, the domain of existences. The corresponding *ratio* is no longer the *ratio essendi* but the *ratio existendi,* the reason for existing. The corresponding question is no longer, "Why something rather than nothing?" but rather "Why this rather than that?" The popular expression of this principle would be "Everything has a reason." This is the great cry of rationalism, which Leibniz will attempt to push to its limit. Why does Leibniz need this second principle? Because existing things appear to be completely outside the principle of identity. The principle of identity concerns the identity of the thing and what the thing is, even if the thing itself does not exist. I know that unicorns do not exist, but I can still say what a unicorn is. So Leibniz needs a second principle to make us think in terms of existing beings. Yet how can a principle as seemingly vague as "everything has a reason" make us think of existing beings?

Leibniz explains how in his technical formulation of the principle of sufficient reason, which reads, "all predication has a foundation in the nature of things." What this means is that everything that is truly predicated of a thing is necessarily included or contained in the concept of the thing. What is said or predicated of a thing? First of all, its essence, and at this level there is no difference between the principle of identity and the principle of sufficient reason, which takes up and presumes everything acquired with the principle of identity. But Leibniz then adds something no philosopher before him had said: What is said or predicated of a thing is not only the essence of the thing but also the totality of the affections and events that happen to or are related to or belong to the thing. For example: Caesar crossed the Rubicon. Since this is a true proposition, Leibniz will say that the predicate "crossed the Rubicon" must be contained in the concept of Caesar (not in Caesar himself, but in the concept of Caesar). "Everything has a reason" means that everything that happens to something—all its "differences"—must be contained or *included* for all eternity in the individual notion of a thing. "If we call an 'event' what happens to a thing, whether it submits to it or undertakes it, we will say that sufficient reason is what comprehends the event as one of its predicates: the concept of the thing, or its notion. 'Predicates or events,' says Leibniz."[7]

How does Leibniz arrive at this remarkable claim? He does so, Deleuze suggests, following Couturat, by reconsidering *reciprocity.* The principle of identity gives us a model of truth that is certain and absolute—an analytical proposition is necessarily a true proposition—but it does not make us *think* anything. So Leibniz reverses the formulation of the principle of identity using the principle of reciprocity: A true proposition is necessarily an analytic proposition. The principle of sufficient reason is the reciprocal of the principle of identity, and it allows Leibniz to conquer a radically new domain, the domain of existing things.[8] By means of this reversal, the principle of identity forces us to *think* something. The formal formula of the principle of identity ("A is A") is true because the predicate *reciprocates* with the subject, and Leibniz therefore applies this principle of reciprocity to the principle of identity itself. In its first formulation, however, the reciprocal of "A is A" is simply "A is A," and in this sense, the *formal* formulation prevents the reversal of the identity principle. The principle of sufficient reason is produced only through a reversal of the *logical* formulation of the principle of identity, but this latter reversal is clearly of a different order: It does not go without saying. Justifying this reversal is the task Leibniz pursues as a philosopher, and it launches him into an infinite and perhaps impossible undertaking. The principle of sufficient reason says not only that the notion of a subject contains everything that happens to the subject—that is, everything that is truly predicated of the subject—but also that we should be able to *demonstrate* that this is the case.

After Leibniz launches himself into the domain of the concept in this way, however, he cannot stop. At one point in the *Metaphysics,* Aristotle—who exerted an extremely strong influence on Leibniz—proposes an exquisite formula: at a certain point in the analysis of concepts, it is necessary to *stop* (*anankstenai*).[9] This is because, for Aristotle, concepts are *general,* not individual. Classical logic distinguishes between the order of the concept, which refers to a generality, and the order of the individual, which refers to a singularity. By nature, a concept was seen to be something that comprehends a *plurality* of individuals; it went without saying that the individual as such was not comprehensible by concepts. Put differently, philosophers have always considered that *proper names* are not concepts. At a certain point, then, the process of conceptual specification must stop: One reaches the final species, which groups a plurality of individuals. Leibniz, however, does not heed Aristotle's warning: he does not stop. Instead, he attempts to push the concept all the way to the level of the individual itself; in Leibniz, "Adam" and "Caesar" are concepts and not simply proper names. The cry of sufficient reason—"everything *must* have a reason"—is the problem that will propel Leibniz into an almost hallucinatory conceptual creation. As Deleuze puts it, "Leibniz pushes the presuppositions of classical philosophy as far as he can, down the paths of genius and delirium."[10] It is never much use to raise objections, to argue against Leibniz, says Deleuze; one has to let oneself go and follow Leibniz in his production of concepts. What then is the delirious chasm into which Leibniz plunges?

If everything I attribute with truth to a subject must be contained in the concept of the subject, then I am forced to include in the notion of the subject not only the thing I attribute to it with truth, but also *the totality of the world*. Why is this the case? By virtue of a principle that is very different from the principle of sufficient reason, namely, the principle of *causality*. The principle of sufficient reason ("everything has a reason") is not the same thing as the principle of causality ("everything has a cause"). "Everything has a cause" means that A is caused by B, B is caused by C, and so on—a series of causes and effects that stretches to infinity. "Everything has a reason," by contrast, means that one has to give a reason for causality itself, namely, that the relation A maintains with B must in some manner be included or comprised in the concept of A.[11] This is how the principle of sufficient reason goes beyond the principle of causality: The principle of causality states the *necessary cause* of a thing but not its *sufficient reason*. Sufficient reason expresses the relation of the thing with its own notion, whereas causality simply expresses the relations of the thing with something else. Sufficient reason can be stated in the following manner: For every thing, there is a concept that gives an account both of the thing and of its relations with other things, including its causes and its effects. Thus, after Leibniz says that the predicate "crossing the Rubicon" is included in the notion of Caesar, he cannot stop himself: He is forced to include the totality of the world in Caesar's concept. This is because "crossing the Rubicon" has multiple causes and multiple effects, such as the establishment of the Roman empire; it stretches to infinity backward and forward by the double play of causes and effects. We therefore cannot say that "crossing the Rubicon" is included in the notion of Caesar without saying that the causes and effects of this event are *also* included in the notion of Caesar. This is no longer the concept of inherence or inclusion but rather the fantastic Leibnizian concept of *expression:* The notion of the subject expresses the totality of the world. Each of us—you, me— in our concept expresses or contains the entirety of the world. This is the first hallucinatory Leibnizian concept that follows from the principle of sufficient reason.

A second concept follows immediately. For there is a danger lurking here for Leibniz: If each notion of the subject expresses the totality of the world, that could seem to indicate that there is only a single subject and that individuals are mere appearances of this universal subject (a single substance à la Spinoza, or absolute Spirit à la Hegel). But Leibniz cannot follow such a path without repudiating himself since his entire philosophy remains fixed on the individual and the reconciliation of the concept with the individual. To avoid this danger, Leibniz creates another new concept: Each individual notion comprehends or includes the totality of the world, he says, but from a certain *point of view*. This marks the beginning of "perspectivist" philosophy, which would be taken up by later philosophers such as Nietzsche (who nonetheless understood perspectivism in a very different manner than did Leibniz). Point of view, however, is such a common notion that one easily risks trivializing Leibniz's conception of perspectivism. Leibniz does *not* say that everything is "relative" to the viewpoint of the subject; this is what Deleuze calls an "idiotic" or "banal" notion of perspectivism. It would imply that the subject is prior to the point of view, whereas in Leibniz it is precisely the opposite: In Leibniz, the point of view is not constituted by the subject; the subject is constituted by the point of view. Points of view, in other words, are the sufficient reason of subjects. The individual notion is the point of view through which the individual expresses the totality of the world.

But here again, Leibniz cannot stop. For what is it, then, that determines this point of view? Each of us may express the totality of the world, Leibniz tells us, but we express most of the world in an obscure and confused manner, as if it were a mere clamor, a background noise, which we perceive in the form of *infinitely small perceptions.* These minute perceptions are like the "differentials" of consciousness, which are not given as such to conscious perception (apperception). However, there is indeed a small, reduced, finite portion of the world that I express clearly and distinctly, and this is precisely that portion of the world that affects my *body.* Leibniz in this manner provides a deduction of the necessity of the body as that which occupies the point of view. I do not express clearly and distinctly the crossing of the Rubicon, since that concerns Caesar's body; but there are other things that concern my body—a certain relation to this room, this computer, this glass of water—which I express clearly. This is how Leibniz defines a point of view: It is the portion or the region of the world expressed clearly by an individual in relation to the totality of the world, which it expresses obscurely in the form of minute perceptions. No two individual substances occupy the same point of view on the world because none have the same clear or distinct zone of expression on the world.

The problem posed by the principle of sufficient reason thus leads Leibniz to create an entire sequence of concepts: expression, point of view, minute perceptions. . . . "In the majority of great philosophers," writes Deleuze, "the concepts they create are inseparable, and are taken in veritable sequences. And if you don't understand the sequence of which a concept is a part, you cannot understand the concept."[12] But the notion of point of view will lead Leibniz into a final set of problems. For the world, Leibniz continues, has no existence outside the points of view that express it. The world is the "expressed" thing common to all individual substances, but what is expressed (the world) has no existence apart from what expresses it (individuals). In other words, there is no world in itself. The difficulty Leibniz faces here is this: Each of these individual notions must nonetheless express the *same* world. Why is this a problem? The principle of identity allows us to determine what is contradictory, that is, what is *impossible*. A square circle is a circle that is not a circle; it contravenes the principle of identity. But at the level of sufficient reason, things are more complicated. In themselves, Caesar's not crossing the Rubicon and Adam's not sinning are neither contradictory nor impossible. Caesar could have not crossed the Rubicon, and Adam could have not sinned, whereas a circle cannot be square. The truths governed by the principle of sufficient reason are thus not of the same type as the truths governed by the principle of identity. But how, then, can Leibniz at the same time hold that everything Adam did is contained for all time in his individual concept, and that Adam the nonsinner was nonetheless possible? Leibniz's famous response to this problem is this: Adam the nonsinner was possible in itself, but it was *incompossible* with rest of the actualized world. Leibniz here creates an entirely new logical relation of incompossibility, a concept that is unique to Leibniz's philosophy and which is irreducible to impossibility or contradiction. At the level of existing things, it is not enough to say that a thing is possible in order to exist; it is also necessary to know with what it is compossible. The conclusion Leibniz draws from this notion is perhaps his most famous doctrine, one which was ridiculed by Voltaire in *Candide* and by the eighteenth century in general: Among the infinity of incompossible worlds, God makes a calculation and chooses the "best" of all possible worlds to pass into existence, a world governed by a harmony that is "preestablished" by God. But this rational optimism implies an infinite cruelty: The best world is not necessarily the world in which suffering is the least.

Principle of Indiscernibles

This sets us on the path of the third principle, the principle of indiscernibles, which is the reciprocal of the principle of sufficient reason. The principle of sufficient reason says: For every thing, there is a concept that includes everything that will happen to the thing. The principle of indiscernibles says: For every concept, there is one and only one thing. The principle of indiscernibles is thus the reciprocal of the principle of sufficient reason. Unlike Leibniz's first act of reciprocity, this reciprocation is absolutely necessary. (The move from the principle of identity to the principle of sufficient reason, by contrast, was Leibniz's *coup de force* as a philosopher; he could undertake it only because he created the philosophical means to do so.) Banally, this means that there are no two things that are absolutely identical: no two drops of water, no two leaves of a tree, no two people. But more profoundly, it also means—and this is what interests Deleuze—that in the final analysis *every difference is a conceptual difference.* If you have two things, there must be two concepts; if not, there are not two things. In other words, if you assign a difference to two things, there is necessarily a difference in their concepts. The principle of indiscernibles consists in saying that we have *knowledge* only by means of concepts, and this can be said to correspond to a third reason, a third *ratio: ratio cognoscendi,* or reason as the reason of knowing.

This principle of indiscernibles has two important consequences for Deleuze. First, as we have seen, Leibniz is the first philosopher to say that concepts are proper names, that is, that concepts are *individual* notions. In classical logic, by contrast, concepts are *generalities* which, by their very nature, cannot comprehend the singularity of the individual. But can we not say that the concept "human," for instance, is a generality that applies to all individual humans, including both Caesar and Adam? Of course you can say that, Leibniz retorts, but only if you have *blocked* the analysis of the concept at a certain point, at a finite moment. But if you push the analysis, if you push the analysis of the concept to infinity, there will be a point at which the concepts of Caesar and Adam are no longer the same. According to Leibniz, this is why a mother sheep can recognize its little lamb: It knows the lamb's concept, which is individual. This is also why Leibniz cannot have recourse to a universal mind: He has to remain fixed on the singularity, on the individual as such. This is Leibniz's great originality, the formula of his perpetual refrain: Substance is individual.

Second, in positing the principle of indiscernibles ("every difference is conceptual"), Leibniz is asking us to accept an enormous consequence. For there are other types of difference, apart from conceptual difference, that might allow us to distinguish between individual things. For example, numerical difference: I can fix the concept of water and then distinguish between different drops numerically: one drop, two drops, three drops; I distinguish the drops by number only, disregarding their individuality. A second type of difference is spatio-temporal difference. I have the concept of water but I can distinguish between different drops by their spatio-temporal location ("not *this* drop; *that* drop over there"). A third type is differences of extension and movement. I can have the concept of water and distinguish between drops by their extension and figure (shape and size), or by their movement (fast or slow). These are all nonconceptual differences because they allow us to distinguish between two things that nonetheless have the same concept. Once again, however, Leibniz plunges on; he appears on the scene and calmly tells us, no, these differences are pure appearances, provisional means of expressing a difference of another nature, and this difference is always conceptual. If there are two drops of water, they do not have the same concept. Non-conceptual differences only serve to translate, in an imperfect manner, a deeper difference that is always conceptual.

It is here that we reach the crux of the matter in Deleuze's reading of Leibniz. Although no one goes further than Leibniz in the exploration of sufficient reason, Leibniz nonetheless subordinates sufficient reason to the requirements of "representation": In reducing all differences to conceptual differences, Leibniz defines sufficient reason by the ability of differences to be represented or mediated in a *concept*. As Deleuze notes, "According to the principle of sufficient reason, there is always one concept per particular thing. According to the reciprocal principle of the identity of indiscernibles, there is one and only one thing per concept. Together, these principles expound a theory of difference as conceptual difference, or develop the account of representation as mediation."[13] In Aristotle, what "blocks" the specification of the concept beyond the smallest species is the individual itself. Leibniz is able to reconcile the concept and the individual only because he gives the identity of the concept an *infinite* comprehension: Every individual substance, or monad, envelops the infinity of predicates that constitutes the state of the world. Where the extension of the concept = 1, the comprehension of the concept = ñ. It is one and the same thing to say that the concept goes to infinity (sufficient reason) and that the concept is individual (indiscernibility). In pushing the concept to the level of the individual, however, Leibniz simply renders representation (or the concept) infinite while still maintaining the subordination of difference to the principle of identity in the concept.

For Deleuze, this subordination of difference to identity is illegitimate and ungrounded. We have seen that, in Leibniz, the principle of sufficient reason is the reciprocal of the principle of identity and that the principle of indiscernibles is in turn the reciprocal of the principle of sufficient reason. But would not the reciprocal of the reciprocal simply lead us back to the identity principle?[14] The fact that it does *not*, even in Leibniz, points to the irreducibility of the principle of difference to the principle of identity. Deleuze's thesis is that, behind or beneath the functioning of the identical concept, there lies the movement of difference and multiplicity within an *Idea*. "What blocks the concept," writes Deleuze in *Difference and Repetition*, "is always the excess of the Idea, which constitutes the superior positivity that arrests the concept or overturns the requirements of representation."[15] Indeed, *Difference and Repetition* reveals how the roots of sufficient reason can be formulated in terms of a theory of nonrepresentational Ideas. As Deleuze explains there, "the immediate, defined as the 'sub-representative,' is not attained by multiplying representations and points of view. On the contrary, each composing representation must be distorted, diverted, and torn from its center"—in order to reveal not the immediacy of the Given but rather the differential mechanisms of the Idea that themselves function as the genetic conditions of the given.[16] Deleuze understands the term "Idea" largely in its Kantian sense, except that Kantian Ideas are totalizing, unifying, and transcendent, whereas Deleuzian Ideas are of necessity differential, genetic, and immanent. It is on the basis of his post-Kantian return to Leibniz that Deleuze develops his revised theory of Ideas in *Difference and Repetition*.

The Law of Continuity

This brings us to the law of continuity. What is the difference between truths of essence (principle of identity) and truths of existence (principles of sufficient reason and indiscernibility)? With truths of essence, says Leibniz, the analysis is *finite*, such that inclusion of the predicate in the subject can be demonstrated by a finite series of determinate operations (such that one can say, "q.e.d.").[17] The analysis of truths of existence, by contrast, is necessarily *infinite:* The domain of existences is the domain of *infinite analysis*. Why is this the case? Because if the predicate "sinner" is contained in the concept of Adam, then if we follow the causes back and track down the effects, the entire world must be contained in the notion of Adam. When I perform the analysis, I pass from Adam the sinner to Eve the temptress, and from Eve the temptress to the evil serpent, and from the evil serpent to the forbidden fruit, and so on. Moving forward, I show that there is a direct connection between Adam's sin and the Incarnation and Redemption by Christ. There are *series* that are going to begin to fit into each other across the differences of time and space. (This is the aim of Leibniz's *Theodicy:* to justify God's choice of *this* world, with its interlocking series.) Such an analysis is *infinite* because it has to pass through the entire series of elements that constitute the world, which is actually infinite; it is an *analysis* because it demonstrates the inclusion of the predicate "sinner" in the individual notion "Adam." "In the domain of existences, we cannot stop ourselves, because the series are prolongable and must be prolonged, because the inclusion is not localizable."[18] This is the Leibnizian move that matters to Deleuze: At the level of truths of existence, an infinite analysis that demonstrates the inclusion of the predicate ("sinner") in the subject ("Adam") does *not* proceed by the demonstration of an identity. What matters at the level of truths of existence is not the *identity* of the predicate and the subject but rather that one passes from one predicate to another, from the second to a third, from the third to a fourth, and so on. Put succinctly: *If truths of essence are governed by identity, truths of existence, by contrast, are governed by continuity.* What is a world? A world is defined by its continuity. What separates two incompossible worlds? The fact that there is a discontinuity between the two worlds. What defines the best of all possible worlds, the world that God will cause to pass into existence? The fact that it realizes *the maximum of continuity for a maximum of difference.*

Now this notion of an *infinite analysis* is absolutely original with Leibniz; he invented it. It seems to go without saying, though, that we, as finite beings, are incapable of undertaking an infinite analysis; in order to situate ourselves in the domain of truths of existence, we have to wait for experience: We know through experience that Caesar crossed the Rubicon or that Adam sinned. Infinite analysis is possible for God, to be sure, whose divine understanding is without limits and infinite. But this is hardly a satisfactory answer. God may indeed be able to undertake an infinite analysis, and we're happy for God, but then we would wonder why Leibniz went to such trouble to present this whole story about analytical truths and infinite analysis if it were only to say that such an analysis is inaccessible to us as finite beings.

It's here that we begin to approach the originality of Deleuze's interpretation of Leibniz; for according to Deleuze, Leibniz indeed attempts to provide us finite humans with an artifice that is capable of undertaking a well-founded approximation of what happens in God's understanding, and this artifice is precisely the technique of the infinitesimal calculus or differential analysis. We as humans can undertake an infinite analysis thanks to the symbolism of the *differential calculus.* Now the calculus brings us into a complex domain, having to do not only with the relation of Leibniz to Newton but also the debates on the mathematical foundations of the calculus, which were not resolved until the development of the limit-concept by Cauchy and Weierstrass in the late nineteenth and early twentieth century—debates that lie beyond the scope of this paper.[19] In what follows, I focus on two aspects of Leibniz's work on the metaphysics of the calculus that come to the fore in Deleuze's own reading of Leibniz: the differential relation and the theory of singularities. These are two theories that allow us to think the presence of the infinite within the finite.

The Differential Relation

Let us turn first to the differential relation. At stake in an infinite analysis is not so much the fact that there is an actually existing set of infinite elements in the world, for if there are two elements—for example, Adam the sinner and Eve the temptress—then there is still a *difference* between these two elements. What then does it mean to say that there is a continuity between the seduction of Eve and Adam's sin (and not simply an identity)? It means that the relation between the two elements is an infinitely small relation, or rather, that *the difference between the two is a difference that tends to disappear.* This is the definition of the continuum: Continuity is defined as the act of a difference insofar as the difference tends to disappear. Continuity, in short, is a *disappearing* or *vanishing difference.* Between sinner and Adam I will never be able to demonstrate a logical identity, but I will be able to demonstrate (and here the word "demonstration" obviously changes meaning) a continuity, that is, one or more vanishing differences.

What, then, is a vanishing difference? In 1701, Leibniz wrote a three-page text entitled "Justification of the Infinitesimal Calculus by that of Ordinary Algebra," in which he tries to explain that, in a certain manner, the differential calculus was already functioning before it was discovered, even at the level of the most ordinary algebra.[20] Leibniz presents us with a fairly simple geometrical figure (see figure 2).

Two right triangles—ZEF and ZHI—meet at their apex, point Z. Since the two triangles ZEF and ZHI are similar, it follows that the ratio of straight lines y/x is equal to $(Y - y)/X$. Now if the straight line EI increasingly approaches point F, always preserving the same angle at the variable point Z, the length of the lines x and y will obviously diminish steadily, yet the ratio of x to y will remain constant. What happens when the straight

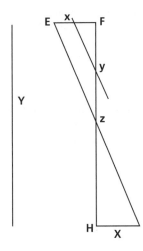

FIGURE 2

line EI passes through F itself? It is obvious that the points Z and E will fall directly on F and that the straight lines x and y will vanish; they will become equal to zero. And yet, Leibniz says, even though x and y are equal to zero, they still maintain an *algebraic* relation to each other, which is expressed in the relation of X to Y. In other words, when the line EI passes through Z, it is not the case that the triangle ZEF has "disappeared" in the common sense of that word. The triangle ZEF is still "there," but only virtually, since the relation x/y continues to exist even when the terms have vanished. Rather than say that the triangle ZEF has disappeared, Leibniz says, we should say that it has become unassignable and yet is perfectly determined, since in this case although $x = 0$ and $y = 0$, the relation x/y is not equal to zero, since it is a perfectly determinable relation equal to X/Y. Unassignable, yet perfectly determined—this is what the term "vanishing difference" means: the relation continues even when the terms of the relation have disappeared. The relation x/y continues when Z and E have disappeared. This is why the differential relation is such a great mathematical discovery; the miracle is that the differential relation dx/dy is not equal to zero but rather has a perfectly expressible *finite* quantity, which is the differential derived from the relation of X to Y.

The differential relation is thus not only a relation that is *external* to its terms but also in a certain sense *constitutes* its terms. It provides Deleuze with a mathematical model for thinking "difference-in-itself" (the title of the second chapter of *Difference and Repetition*). The differential relation signifies nothing concrete in relation to what it is derived from, that is, in relation to x and y, but it signifies something else concrete, namely a z, which is something *new*, and this is how it assures the passage to limits. Thus, to consider several famous examples, Leibniz can comprehend rest as an infinitely small movement, coincidence as an infinitely small distance, equality as the limit of inequalities, and the circle as the limit of a polygon the sides of which increase to infinity. The reason of the law of continuity is thus the *ratio fiendi*, the reason of becoming. Things *become* through continuity: Movement becomes rest; the polygon, by multiplying its sides, becomes a circle. This is the source of the popular formulation of the law of continuity in Leibniz: Nature never makes leaps (there is no discontinuity in nature). What, then, is an infinite analysis? An infinite analysis fills the following condition: there is an infinite analysis, and a material for infinite analysis, when I find myself before a domain that is no longer directly ruled by identity but by continuity and vanishing differences.

Now to understand what this theory of the differential relation means in concrete terms, consider the corresponding theory of perception that Leibniz develops in relation to it.[21] Leibniz observes that we often perceive things of which we are not consciously aware. We recall a familiar scene and become aware of a detail we did not notice at the time; the background noise of a dripping faucet suddenly enters our consciousness at night. Leibniz therefore draws a distinction between conscious perceptions ("apperceptions," or molar perceptions) and unconscious perceptions ("minute" or molecular perceptions), and argues that our conscious perceptions must be related not simply to recognizable objects in space and time but rather to the minute and unconscious perceptions of which they are composed. I apprehend the noise of the sea or the murmur of a group of people, for instance, but not the sound of each wave or the voice of each person that composes them. These unconscious minute perceptions are related to conscious "molar" perceptions, not as parts to a whole but as what is ordinary to what is noticeable or remarkable: A conscious perception is produced when at least two of these minute and "virtual" perceptions enter into a differential relation that determines a singularity, that is, a conscious perception. Consider the noise of the sea. At least two waves must be minutely perceived as nascent and "virtual" in order to enter into a differential relation capable of determining a third, which excels over the others and becomes conscious. Or, consider the color green. Yellow and blue can be perceived, but if the difference between them vanishes by approaching zero, then they enter into a differential relation $(db/dy = G)$ that determines the color green; in turn, yellow or blue, each on its own account, may be determined by the differential relation of two colors we cannot detect $(dy/dx = Y)$. The calculus thus functions in Leibniz as the psychic mechanism of perception, a kind of automatism that determines my finite zone of clarity on the world, my point of view. Every conscious perception constitutes a threshold, and the minute or virtual perceptions (infinitely small perceptions) constitute the obscure dust of the world, its background noise. They are not "parts" of conscious perception but rather the "ideal genetic elements" of perception, or what Maimon called the "differentials of consciousness." The virtual multiplicity of genetic elements, and the system of connections or differential relations that are established between them, is what Deleuze terms the "Idea" of sensibility. The differential relations between these infinitely small perceptions are what draw them into clarity; they "actualize" a clear perception (such as green) out of certain obscure, evanescent perceptions (such as yellow and blue). "The Idea of the world or the Idea of the sea are *systems of differential equations,* of which each monad only actualizes a partial solution."[22]

In Leibniz, the differential calculus refers to a domain that is both mathematical and psychological, a psycho-mathematical domain: There are differentials of consciousness just as there are differentials of a curve. Several important consequences follow. Space and time here cease to be pure a priori givens (as in Kant) but are determined *genetically* by the ensemble or nexus of these differential relations in the subject. Similarly, objects themselves cease to be empirical givens and become the product of these relations in conscious perception. Moreover, Descartes' principle of the "clear and distinct" ideas is broken down into two irreducible values, which can never be reunited to constitute a "natural light": Conscious perceptions are necessarily clear but confused (not distinct), whereas unconscious perceptions (Ideas) are distinct but necessarily obscure (not clear). Kant had already objected that Maimon, by returning to Leibniz, thereby reintroduced the duality between finite understanding (consciousness) and infinite understanding (the divine) that the entire Kantian critique had attempted to eliminate.[23] Against Kant, however, Deleuze argues that

> the infinite here is only the presence of an *unconscious* in the finite understanding, an unthought in finite thought, a non-self in the finite self (whose presence Kant himself was forced to discover when he hollowed out the difference between a determining ego and a determinable ego). For Maimon as for Leibniz, the reciprocal determination of differentials does not refer to a divine understanding, but to minute perceptions as the representatives of the world in the finite self.[24]

Indeed, Leibniz can be said to have developed one of the first theories of the unconscious, a theory that is very different from the one developed by Freud. The difference is that Freud conceived of unconscious in a *conflictual* or *oppositional* relationship to consciousness, and not a *differential* relationship. In this sense, Freud was dependent on Kant, Hegel, and their successors, who explicitly oriented the unconscious in the direction of a conflict of will and no longer a differential of perception. The theory of the unconscious proposed by Deleuze and Guattari in *Anti-Oedipus* is a differential and genetic unconscious and thus thoroughly inspired by Leibniz.[25]

The Theory of Singularities

There is a final problem that Deleuze points to in Leibniz's thought. On the surface, there would appear to be a contradiction between the principle of indiscernibles and the law of continuity. On the one hand, the principle of indiscernibles tells us that every difference is conceptual, that no two things have the same concept. To every thing there corresponds a determinate difference, which is not only determinate but also assignable in the concept. On the other hand, the principle of continuity tells us that things proceed via vanishing differences, infinitely small differences, that is, unassignable differences. Thus, Leibniz seems to be saying, at one and the same time, that everything proceeds by an unassignable difference and that every difference is assignable and must be assigned in the concept. So the question is: Is it possible to reconcile the principle of indiscernibles with the law of continuity?

Deleuze's thesis is that the solution to this problem has to be posed in terms of a theory of *singularities,* which naturally extends the theory of differential equations. In logic, the notion of the "singular" has long been understood in relation to the "universal"; in mathematics, however, the singular is related to a very different set of notions. The singular is distinguished from or opposed to the regular; the singular is what escapes the regularity of the rule. More important, mathematics distinguishes between points that are singular or remarkable and those that are ordinary. Geometrical figures can be classified by the types of singular points that determine them. A square, for instance, has four singular points, its four corners, and an infinity of ordinary points that compose each side of the square (the calculus of *extremum*). Simple curves, such as the arc of circle, are determined by a single singularity, which is either a maximum or minimum or both simultaneously (the calculus of *maxima* and *minima*).[26] The differential calculus deals with the more difficult case of complex curves: The singularities of a complex curve are the points in the neighborhood of which the differential relation changes sign (focal points, saddle points, knots, and so on): The curve increases; the curve decreases. These points of increase or decrease are the singular points of the curve; the ordinary points are what constitute the series between the two singularities. The theory of singularites provides Deleuze with his final, more technical definition of the law of continuity: The continuum is the prolongation of a singularity over an ordinary series of points until it reaches the neighborhood of the following singularity, at which point the differential relation changes sign and either diverges from or converges with the next singularity. The continuum is thus inseparable from a theory or an activity of prolongation; there is a composition of the continuum because the continuum is a product.

In this way, the theory of singularities also provides Deleuze with a model of individuation or determination; one can say of any determination in general (any "thing") that it is *a combination of the singular and the ordinary,* that is, a "multiplicity" constituted by its singular and ordinary points. Just as mathematical curves are determined by their points of inflection (extrema, minima and maxima, and so on), so physical states of affairs can be said to be determined by singularities that mark a change of phase (boiling points, points of condensation, fusion, coagulation, crystallization, and so forth) and psychological persons by their "sensitive" points (points of tears and joy, sickness and health, fatigue and vitality, hope and anxiety, and so on). But such singularites, Deleuze insists, can be considered *apart from* their actualization in a physical state of affairs or a psychological person.[27] Deleuze here reaches a domain that is distinct from, and logically prior to, the three domains that Kant would later denounce as transcendental illusions or Ideas: the Self, the World, and God. Each of these Ideas has a determinate place in Leibniz's philosophy: God is the Being who, faced with the infinity of possible worlds, chose to actualize this World, a world that exists only in its individual monads or Selves, which express the world from their own point of view. But what this Leibnizian schema presupposes, Deleuze argues, is the determination of a "transcendental field" that is prior to God, World, and Self, a field populated by singularities that are atheological, acosmic, and preindividual. It implies a transcendental logic of singularities that is irreducible to the formal logic of predication. Here, for example, are three singularities of the individual "Adam," expressed in logical form: "to be the first man," "to live in a garden of pleasure," "to have a woman come out of one's rib." And then a fourth singularity: "to sin." We can prolong each of these four singular points over a series of ordinary points such that they all have common values in both directions: A continuity is established between them. But then add a fifth singularity: "to resist the temptation." The lines of prolongation between this fifth singularity and the first three are no longer convergent, that is, they do not pass through common values; there is a bifurcation in the series at this singularity, a *discontinuity* is introduced. Adam the nonsinner is thus incompossible with this world because Adam's being a nonsinner implies a singularity that diverges with this world.

The theory of singularities thus plays a double role in Deleuze's work on Leibniz. On the one hand, it allows Deleuze to solve the riddle posed by the relation between indiscernibility and continuity within Leibniz's own philosophy. The world "in itself" is indeed governed by the law of continuity since continuity is nothing other than the composition of singularities insofar as they are prolonged over the series of ordinaries that depend on them. But the world does not exist "in itself"; it exists only in the individuals who express it. And the real definition of the individual is: *the accumulation or coincidence of a certain number of preindividual singularities* that are extracted from the curve of the world, each of them being discontinuous and unique and hence governed by the principle of indiscernibles. Individuation, in other words, "does not move from a genus to smaller and smaller species, in accordance with a rule of differentiation; it goes from singularity to singularity, in accordance with the rule of convergence or prolongation that links the individual to such and such a world."[28] On the other hand, Deleuze is not content simply to provide a reading of Leibniz. "These impersonal and preindividual nomadic singularities," Deleuze writes, speaking in his own name, "are what constitute the *real* transcendental field."[29] *Difference and Repetition* and *Logic of Sense* are Deleuze's attempt to define the nature of this transcendental field, freed from the limitations of Leibniz's theological presuppositions and using his own conceptual vocabulary (multiplicity, singularity, virtuality, problematic, event, and so on). In Deleuze, the Ideas of God, World, and Self take on completely different demeanors. God is no longer a Being who chooses the richest compossible world but is now a pure Process that makes *all* virtualities pass into existence, forming an infinite web of divergent and convergent series; the World is no longer a continuous curve defined by its preestablished harmony but is a chaotic universe in which divergent series trace endlessly bifurcating paths, giving rise to violent discords; and the Self, rather than beclosed on the compossible world it expresses from within, is now torn open by the divergent series and incompossible ensembles that continually pull it outside itself (the monadic subject, as Deleuze puts it, becomes the nomadic subject).[30] It is at this point that Deleuze's reading of Leibniz would end and one's own reading of Deleuze's philosophy would have to begin.

Classical reason, says Deleuze, collapsed under the blow of divergences, discordances, and incompossibilities, and Leibniz's philosophy was one of the last attempts to reconstitute a classical reason. It did so by *multiplying its principles*, relegating divergences to so many possible worlds, making incompossibilities so many frontiers between worlds, and resolving the discords that appear in this world into the melodic lines of the preestablished harmony. But Leibniz's Baroque reconstitution could be only temporary, and with the collapse of classical reason, the task of philosophy would be to think without principles, to start *neither* with the identity of God, the Self, or the World but rather with a transcendental field of differences and singularities that conditions the construction of empirical selves and the actual world. This is the task that Deleuze adopts as his own: "We seek to determine an impersonal and preindividual transcendental field that does not resemble the corresponding empirical fields."[31] It is a thoroughly contemporary project, but one that allows Deleuze to dip back into the history of philosophy and make *use* of Leibniz's philosophy and Leibniz's concepts in the pursuit of his own philosophical aims.

Notes

1. Gilles Deleuze, *The Fold: Leibniz and the Baroque*, trans. Tom Conley (Minneapolis: University of Minnesota Press, 1993). References to the original French edition, *Le Pli: Leibniz et le Baroque* (Paris: Minuit, 1988) are also included.

2. Gilles Deleuze, *Difference and Repetition*, trans. Paul Patton (New York: Columbia University Press, 1994); *Logic of Sense*, trans. Mark Lester with Charles Stivale; ed. Constantin Boundas (New York: Columbia University Press, 1990).

3. For a discussion of Deleuze's relation to Maimon and the post-Kantian tradition, see my "Deleuze, Hegel, and the Post-Kantian Tradition," in *Philosophy Today* (Supplement 2001), 126–38.

4. Deleuze, seminar of 20 May 1980. Deleuze's seminars on Leibniz can be found online at http://www.webdeleuze.fr, transcribed by Richard Pinhas and translated into English by Charles Stivale. I follow closely the conceptual deduction Deleuze presents in his 1980 seminars.

5. Deleuze, *Fold*, 122; *Pli*, 163.

6. Gottfried Wilhelm Leibniz, *New Essays on Human Understanding*, 2d ed., ed. Peter Remnant and Jonathan Bennett (Cambridge: Cambridge University Press, 1997), 361.

7. Deleuze, *Fold*, 41; *Pli*, 55, translation modified.

8. See Louis Couturat, "On Leibniz's Metaphysics," in *Leibniz: A Collection of Critical Essays*, ed. Harry G. Frankfurt (Garden City, N.Y.: Anchor Books, 1972), 19–45. "The principle of identity states: every identity (analytic) proposition is true. The principle of reason affirms, on the contrary: every true proposition is an identity (analytic)" (22).

9. See Aristotle, *Metaphysics*, book 2, chapter 2, 994b24, in *The Basic Works of Aristotle*, ed. Richard McKeon (New York: Random House, 1941), 714.

10. Deleuze, seminar of 20 May 1980.

11. See Benson Mates, *The Philosophy of Leibniz: Metaphysics and Language* (Oxford: Oxford University Press, 1986), 157: "To discover the reason for the truth of the essential proposition 'A is B' is to analyze the concept A far enough to reveal the concept B as contained in it." Deleuze, however, would disagree with Mates' statement that Leibniz "appears to use the terms 'reason' and 'cause' interchangeably" (158).

12. Deleuze, seminar of 26 November 1980.

13. Deleuze, *Difference and Repetition*, 12. On the relation of difference and repetition in the classical theory of the concept, see *Difference and Repetition*, 288: difference is always inscribed within the identity of the concept in general, and repetition is defined as a difference *without* a concept, that is, in terms of the numerically distinct exemplars or individuals that are subsumed under the generality of the concept (x1, x2, x3, . . . xn), and which block further conceptual specification.

14. Deleuze, seminar of 6 May 1980.

15. Deleuze, *Difference and Repetition*, 289.

16. *Ibid.*, 56. See also 222: "Difference is not diversity. Diversity is given, but difference is that by which the given is given as diverse."

17. However, Deleuze will argue, against Leibniz himself, that the analysis of essences must itself be infinite since it is inseparable from the infinity of God. See *Fold*, 42; *Pli*, 56–57.

18. Deleuze, *Fold*, 51; *Pli*, 69, translation modified.

19. For an analysis of Deleuze's relation to the history of the calculus, see my "Mathematics and the Theory of Multiplicities: Badiou and Deleuze Revisited," *Southern Journal of Philosophy* 41 (2003), pp. 411–49.

20. Gottfried Wilhelm Leibniz, "Justification of the Infinitesimal Calculus by that of Ordinary Algebra," in *Philosophical Papers and Letters*, 2nd ed., ed. Leroy E. Loemker (Dordrecht: D. Reidel, 1956), 545–46.

21. Deleuze analyzes this theory in an important chapter entitled "Perception in the Folds," in *Fold*, 85–99; *Pli*, 113–32.

22. Alberto Gualandi, *Deleuze* (Paris: Les Belles Lettres, 1998), 49.

23. Immanuel Kant, letter to Marcus Herz, 26 May 1789, in *Immanuel Kant: Philosophical Correspondence, 1759–99*, ed. Arnulf Zweig (Chicago: University of Chicago Press, 1967), 150–56.

24. *Fold*, 89; *Pli*, 118–19, translation modified. See also *Difference and Repetition*, 192–93.

25. Gilles Deleuze and Félix Guattari, *Anti-Oedipus*, trans. Robert Hurley, Mark Seem, and Helen R. Lane (New York: Viking, 1977). See also *Difference and Repetition*, 106–8, for Deleuze's most explicit advocation of a differential unconscious (Leibniz, Fechner) over a conflictual unconscious (Freud).

26. See Leibniz's analysis of simple curves in "*Tentamen Anagogicum*: An Anagogical Essay in the Investigation of Causes," in *Philosophical Papers and Letters*, 477–85.

27. See Deleuze, *Logic of Sense*, 52.

28. Deleuze, *Fold*, 64; *Pli*, 86, translation modified.

29. Deleuze, *Logic of Sense*, 109, translation modified.

30. *Ibid.*, 174: "Instead of a certain number of predicates being excluded by a thing by virtue of the identity of its concept, each 'thing' is open to the infinity of predicates through which it passes, and at the same time it loses its center, that is to say, its identity as a concept and as a self."

31. *Ibid.*, 102.

On the Function of the Concept of Origin: Althusser's Reading of Locke

Warren Montag

It would be difficult to think of a philosopher apparently less likely to capture the interest of Althusser than John Locke. Indeed, one might easily make the case that Locke's philosophy in its entirety (the metaphysical and epistemological propositions expressed in the *Essay Concerning Human Understanding* and the political arguments of the *Two Treatises of Government*) exemplifies that "theoretical denial of its own practice and the gigantic efforts to register this denial in coherent discourse"[1] that Althusser declared dominated the history of philosophy.

First, Locke's epistemology: the under-laborer who sought to remove some of the "rubbish that lies in the way to knowledge,"[2] a phrase that in certain ways might appear to anticipate certain of Althusser's formulations concerning the activity of philosophy, cleared the way not so much forward for knowledge as backward to the absolute simplicity of a mind supposed to be "the white paper void of all characters, without any ideas,"[3] the only adequate beginning for rigorous knowledge. Does not Locke posit experience (whether of external objects or of internal operations) as an origin, an absolute starting point for knowledge? Althusser regarded the concept of the origin as perhaps the most common strategy by which a philosophy could conceal from itself the historical and political realities of its own practice, taking as a starting point that it discovers what in fact is a product of its own labor (heavy with political and ideological consequences) and as such a result rather than a beginning: "The function of the concept of origin, as in original sin, is to summarize in one word what has not to be thought in order to be able to think what one wants to think."[4]

Second, the relation of Locke's political doctrines to Althusser's Marxism would appear to be, if anything, even more antagonistic than that of his epistemology. What could be said about the philosopher who proposes not only that "government has no other end than the preservation of property"[5] but also seeks to prove beyond any shadow of a doubt that the "disproportionate and unequal possession of the earth" that characterized his own time rested on a foundation of right: "men have agreed" to this unequal distribution of wealth "by a tacit and voluntary consent"?[6] Locke's notion of consent (another origin) would appear to be precisely that theoretical sleight of hand which Althusser identified as the ideological interpellation of individuals as subjects: Individuals are addressed as the authors of their own servitude, which, however rigorous it may be by virtue of originating in the free will of individuals, must be regarded as legitimate and morally and legally binding. Indeed, it would be possible, from the perspective of Althusser's philosophy, to write an entire history of liberalism through an extended mediation on the paradoxes contained in the phrase "tacit and voluntary," not the least of which is the use of the conjunction "and" to tie tacit to voluntary consent. The phrase speaks of the fleeting and evanescent nature of consent in Locke's world; as with Pascal's God, we must often seek the signs of its absence; the empty spaces where it was but can be found no longer. Such difficulties clearly require the services of a philosopher; who else might explain that consent is present precisely where it appears to be absent, or rather present in its very absence in the slave who had freely engaged in war, the vagabond who chooses a life of debauchery instead of the sober virtue of wage labor, the voluntary criminal, the hostile savage who resists the Godly appropriation of wild waste? It might thus appear that the very coherence of Locke's positions on knowledge and politics, which coincided almost totally with the dominant world-view of the ruling class in capitalist society, would deprive them of a genuinely philosophical, as opposed to historical, significance.

Such was not the case, however, for Althusser. He read Locke very carefully, lectured on him with some frequency at the École Normale Supérieure, and even wrote some intriguing and dense pages on the seventeenth-century philosopher.[7] While it is true that Althusser did not regard Locke as an authority and predecessor as he did Locke's contemporary Spinoza, nor even accorded Locke the importance he did Hobbes, he nevertheless considered him a powerful thinker. For Althusser, the complexity and richness of Locke's work lay concealed under an "ideological myth" fabricated by the liberal tradition in France. By becoming "the element in which an entire century," the eighteenth, "thought its problems,"[8] Locke shared the fate of his moment and passed into history. In the early Fall of 1960, Althusser wrote a review of Raymond Polin's *La politique morale de John Locke* (published earlier that same year)[9] in which he played the under-laborer himself, removing some of the obstacles that composed the generally accepted and sanctified reading of Locke in order to make it possible to say something new about them. He credits

WARREN MONTAG

Polin's work with producing something of an alienation effect that distances the reader from the ideological myth. Althusser, however, in no way limits himself to a review of Polin's arguments; he takes the opportunity to propose the outline of an entirely new reading of Locke.

According to Althusser, Locke had in fact been subjected to a double condemnation in France: On the one hand, he was an "empiricist philosopher" whose arguments had been refuted by Leibniz in his *New Essays on Human Understanding,* and even worse, he belonged to a precritical tradition rendered obsolete by Kant. On the other hand, Locke's political writing was judged historically important but not truly philosophical, given its failure to account for its own conditions of possibility. The merit of Polin's work, for Althusser, was that it

> constituted in fact a (sometimes direct) critique of the prejudices that deterred the French philosophical tradition from the study of 'political' philosophers. Not only has M. Polin acquainted us with that unknown figure that is Locke, but he has revealed to us the *philosophical* interest of his political philosophy and the fundamental role it has played in the elaboration of the concepts that constitute the very matter of the great philosophical systems of German idealism and through it of modern thought.[10]

Althusser departs from Polin, although in doing so, he believes that he has not "betrayed Polin's purpose by saying that Locke's political theory has a *double philosophical importance.*"[11]

Althusser begins by specifying the discrepancy that, according to the dominant French interpretation, haunts Locke's work, depriving it of the rigor and coherence expected of a philosophical work:

> what is striking in reading Locke is the apparent contradiction between what might be called his gnoseological empiricism and his political idealism. The gnoseological empiricism is illustrated by the famous formula of the tabula rasa against which Leibniz directed his critique. The human mind would only be a blank page on which would be written the lessons of pure "experience." But the same human mind is, in politics and morality, that morality that is humanity's fundamental object, subjected to a *natural law* which has all the appearances, or, better, all the attributes of a transcendental obligation.[12]

To begin to address this problem, Althusser turns to Polin's discussion of the concept of natural law in Locke, in which the latter identifies a link between the *Essays on the Law of Nature,*[13] a text of a series of lectures Locke delivered at Christ Church, Oxford, in 1663–64 (but which were published only posthumously) and the *Two Treatises of Government,* written during the Exclusion crisis of 1678–82. Polin, attentive to the historical specificity of these texts, argues that although written in very different contexts and against very different adversaries, they exhibit profound continuities.

The *Essays* were directed primarily against the views of Hobbes as expressed in *Leviathan,* then very much in vogue in the court of Charles II. Locke argues, against Hobbes, that there is morally binding law and thus right and wrong (and, he will later add, property), outside of and prior to the social state, and that this law is independent of and therefore potentially opposed to individual self-interest. Above all, however, the question that concerns Althusser, following Polin, is how this law of nature comes to be known (a question discussed at great length in the *Essays* whose position, according to Polin, is presupposed without discussion in the *Two Treatises*). True to the arguments of the *Essay Concerning Human Understanding,* Locke argues that the law of nature, although eternal and universal, is not "inscribed in the minds of men."[14] It is knowable but not necessarily known, and Locke's description of the means by which we arrive at a knowledge of the law of nature considerably complicates the empiricism that is both imputed to him and claimed by him. Our knowledge of natural law, Locke argues, is derived from sense-experience and reason, the latter working upon the material furnished by the former. But certain ideas must precede the work of sense-experience and reason for them to arrive at a knowledge of any law of nature: "in order that anyone may understand that he is bound by a law, he must first know *beforehand* (emphasis added) that there is a lawmaker, i.e., some superior power to which he is rightly subject."[15] The idea of God, which must be known before we can identify through sense-experience the laws He has decreed, cannot itself be derived from sense-experience. On the contrary, while sense-experience can identify the "order, array and motion" of the things and even the "wonderful art and regularity" of the visible world these things compose, it cannot pass beyond this world to the power that created and maintains it. Even (or perhaps especially) our knowledge of human nature, which cannot merely consist of a knowledge of the body and the mind and the functions proper to them but must consist of the knowledge of what human beings are supposed to be, the end for which they were created (their "essence," a concept that Althusser insists is present in Locke), cannot be derived from mere sense-experience. Reason, although initially guided by the senses, must take its leave of them and postulate a God that transcends the sensible world as the principle necessary to the intelligibility of the laws of which the senses furnish evidence. From this Althusser concludes

> the refutation of innate ideas, so forcefully contested by Leibniz, in no way diminishes the transcendence of mathematical or moral truth: it merely arrives at what in Cartesian philosophy is presented as the particular psychology of this transcendence: the total presence, from the origin, of the truth in man and substituting another psychology of the access to knowledge (*connaissance*). In this way Locke can say that natural law is not literally and clearly inscribed in every human mind from the origin, but that it must be discovered and stated through an effort of reflection and reasoning. But because this discovery is, however, only the discovery of a preexisting law that expresses the essence of human nature, this knowledge (*connaissance*) is nothing more than recognition (*reconnaissance*).[16]

Althusser thus follows Polin in reading Locke as an unrecognized predecessor of Kant who offers his own critique of practical reason in order to demonstrate that true freedom lies in obedience to law rather than lawlessness. When Locke writes in chapter 2 of the Second Treatise that "all men are naturally in . . . a state of perfect freedom to order their actions and dispose of their possessions and persons as they see fit,"[17] he does not mean that an individual has the natural right to live according to his desires which are in turn "the manifestation of his instincts and power as the expression of his conatus."[18] On the contrary, as Locke explains, the perfect freedom that someone enjoys in the state of nature must be distinguished from "a state of licence. . . . The state of nature has a law to govern it, which obliges every one: and reason, which is that law, teaches all mankind who will but consult it, that being all equal and independent, no one ought to harm another in his life, health, liberty or possessions."[19] Here as in the earlier text on natural law, Locke's concern is to demarcate himself from Hobbes, in whose state of nature as described in chapter 13 of *Leviathan* "the notions of Right and Wrong, Justice and Injustice have there no place" and where there can be "no propriety, no Dominion, no mine and thine distinct; but only that to be every mans that he can get and for so long as he can keep it."[20] But there is more than the critique of Hobbes: Althusser argues that for Locke, freedom is "conceived as obedience to the law . . . and law far from being an order emanating from a transcendent power is identified with reason."[21] The law of nature cannot be discovered through sense-experience, whose most important discovery from the point of view of morality and politics is its own limits, the point beyond which it cannot legitimately proceed. When Locke says, in the passage cited above, that the law of nature is reason, he means that it is from itself that reason derives the idea of the necessity of a universal and eternal lawmaker in accordance with whose will is ordered all visible and terrestrial things, in the same way that it can "describe" (that is, produce) ideal mathematical objects that have never been present to sense-experience.

The notion of natural law identified with reason and therefore with the very notion of the human, given that it is reason that, for Locke, distinguishes human beings from beasts, becomes essential to any understanding of Locke's political thought. If, for Althusser, Locke remains a liberal, the specificity of his liberalism must be established. Unlike Montesquieu, to whom Althusser had recently devoted a full-length study,[22] Locke was not concerned with setting up a "balance of powers" which would insure that no one group could dominate others, as if "groups" were all in some sense equivalent (for example, the people, the nobility, and the monarchy). Such schemes served to justify, despite appearances, the subordination of certain groups to others. Locke's doctrine, in contrast, represents, in Althusser's words, a "popular and revolutionary liberalism"[23] insofar as he subordinated all powers to the legislative, which was itself nothing more than the expression of the body of the people. The latter, according to Locke, may on the occasion of the legislative's violating the law of the commonwealth or of nature withdraw their obedience from it, declare it dissolved and constitute a new one in its place: "and thus the community perpetually retains a supreme power of saving themselves from the attempts and designs of anybody, even of their legislators, whenever they shall be so foolish, or so wicked, as to lay and carry on designs against the liberties and properties of the subject."[24]

In describing Locke's "popular and revolutionary liberalism," however, Althusser sets aside the two alternatives that continue to dominate the interpretation of Locke's politics (and often seemed to be posed in terms of being for or against Locke). To name only the most well-known works associated with these positions: C.B. Macpherson's *The Theory of Possessive Individualism*[25] (often read by its critics as a condemnation of Locke) and Richard Ashcraft's *Revolutionary Politics and Locke's Two Treatises of Government*[26] (which struck a number of readers as a suspiciously sympathetic account of Locke as a radical—and perhaps not only in terms of seventeenth-century politics). While Althusser probably read Macpherson's work only after the publication of *Possessive Individualism* in 1962 (and it should be noted that Macpherson was very important to Althusser and influenced his work in ways that remain to be explored), the views expressed in the review of Polin coincide with Macpherson's to the extent that, for Althusser, Locke describes a land in which the rights of possessors of absolute property have not yet been fully recognized.[27] For Althusser the key to Locke's position lay again in the theory of natural law, the sense in which natural law is the "hidden essence of every political body" and "the transcendent truth of political society":

> The visible proof of this transcendence is its reign in the state of nature. It is not an exaggeration to say that for the theoreticians of natural law, the *structure* (and therefore the essence of which the structure is merely the manifestation) of *the state of nature* expresses their fundamental ideas, even their hidden motives. It does not matter that once the reign of natural law in the state of nature is asserted, the transition to the civil state poses a problem: this reign, prior to any political organization is nothing more than the incarnation, in the form of the myth of the origin, of Locke's fundamental conviction: that natural law is the very essence of man, and that this essence is already triumphant even before the struggles of human political history.[28]

Property is "an original law of nature" according to Locke, perhaps, the original law of nature insofar as one's property of oneself is the beginning of morality and politics. Let us therefore recall Althusser's thesis on the function of origins in philosophy: "to summarize in one word what has not to be thought in order to be able to think what one wants to think." What does Property, as defined by Locke, enjoin us not to think? The state of nature, as we have seen, is ruled by laws which are themselves instituted by the Divine Lawmaker, and certain of these laws remain in force even in the midst of the civil state. People do not have the right to destroy or permanently cede ownership of themselves to another but have the right to govern themselves and to consent to always limited government of others over them in exchange for protection and convenience. Their right to their persons also entitles them to the proceeds of their labor. The one follows from the other: "every man has a property in his own person: this no body has any right to but himself. The labor of his body and the work of his hands, we may say, are properly his. Whatsoever then he removes out of that state that nature hath provided, and left it in, he hath mixed his labor with, and joined it to something that is his own and thereby makes it his property."[29] This is a crucial passage in several respects. Locke, in direct opposition to Hobbes, here places property and the distinction between mine and yours in the presocial state of nature so as to place it out of reach of any civil authority: "whenever the legislators endeavor to take away and destroy the property of the people . . . they put themselves into a state of war with the people."[30] Of course, it might be objected that with the majority of the people being mere laborers who have no property, Locke appears here to have reduced the people to landowners, as Macpherson has argued. Such a view, however, misses a fundamental point: All individuals, according to Locke, own property, the property of their own person. Indeed it is this self-ownership alone that serves as the foundation of absolute property for Locke. Because we own ourselves, we own by extension all that we mix our labor with. But self-ownership has another function here: It consolidates the alliance between the laboring classes and agrarian capitalists by asserting that any attack on even the largest productive estate simultaneously calls into question the humblest laborers' ownership of their very persons. It is therefore not only natural law, and therefore eternal and universal justice, that enjoins to fight any threat to landed property; it is, Locke demonstrates, a matter of self-interest.

But the notion of property as the consequence of an individual's labor on the external world (or at least that part of it that does not belong to another) serves other functions as well. In the state of nature as Locke imagines it, individuals are so separate that their labor and its fruits are immediately and clearly distinguishable from those of others.[31] Locke has thus declared absolute property to be, if not the only form of property, the original form in relation to which all others are secondary and derivative. Indeed, the only other form he mentions, the commons established by contract, is projected to wither away through enclosure by agreement of the commoners. Locke's reduction of all the extraordinarily complex forms of land ownership and tenure in the England of his time to absolute property or commons by compact does more than suppress the competing legal claims attached to the different conceptions of land tenure; even more important, it renders invisible the often undefined and constantly changing customary, that is, extralegal claims made by those with no property except their own person on those who have appropriated land and enclosed it for productive purposes. The success of the operation can be judged by its effects: In the texts of Locke's most historically minded commentators (again, to cite only the authors whose works have become nodal points of controversy, that is, Macpherson, Ashcraft, and James Tully), the specific forms of resistance to the establishment of absolute property are rendered invisible. Indeed, to allude to such struggles at all is to risk being dismissed as anachronistic, attempting to import into the seventeenth century ideas and practices from a later time. We might well wonder, however, whether for both the landed and the landless the relatively simple concept of "property" (either precapitalist or capitalist) might not itself be yet another anachronism. Although it is true that we will not find such a contestation of the emerging concept (and its legal, practical, and institutional incarnations) in the works of such natural law theorists as Grotius or Suarez, nor in the parliamentary debates during the Exclusion crisis, the historical scholarship of the last decade has provided ample evidence of such struggles, their aims, and the philosophical positions immanent in them.[32]

To illustrate the point, we might examine the conflicting commentaries on what has become a well-known passage from chapter 5 of the *Second Treatise*. For Locke, as we have noted, because "every man has a property in his own person," whatever he mixes his labor with and thereby "removes out of that state that nature hath provided, and left it in"[33] becomes his property. In that original state prior to the emergence of property in land (which can be the consequence only of a compact), labor alone transforms what is common into private property.

After the wild Indian picks the fruit from the vine which belongs to no one, it becomes his and his alone. Even in England, where the commons "remain so by compact,"[34] the removal of plants or minerals does not require the "express consent of all the commoners" ("express" presumably because having expressly agreed to leave a certain area in common, commoners have agreed to allow each other free access to the resources present in the commons and may thus be said tacitly to have approved every specific appropriation by a fellow commoner). It is at this point that an apparent gap arises in the text, an absence that renders the argument inconsistent, requiring, as in the case of Holy Scripture, numerous interpretations designed to restore to Locke's text the coherence expected of it. Such interpretations explain away without explaining the silence of the text at this point by attempting to supply what is lacking: what Locke meant to say (and thus could have said) but, for unexplained and apparently uninteresting reasons, did not.

> Thus the grass my horse has bit; the turfs my servant has cut; and the ore I have digged in any place, where I have a right to them in common with others, become my property, without assignation or consent of anybody.[35]

The gap is as clear as day. What is missing is an explanation of how "the turfs my servant have cut . . . become my property without the consent or assignation of anybody" if indeed he is the owner of his own person and "the labor of his body, and the work of his hands, we may say, are properly his." Macpherson argues that the passage in fact exhibits no discontinuity whatever; Locke simply assumes that because the individual is the owner of his person,[36] he can sell himself (according to Macpherson, his labor-power) as did some among the ancient Jews,[37] not absolutely, of course (that is, into slavery), giving another absolute power over him, but for a specific period of time and to a limited extent. Tully, who believes that capitalism did not become the dominant mode of production in England until the end of the eighteenth century,[38] rejects Macpherson's view, of course, but similarly asserts the consistency of Locke's argument. For Tully, the laborer cannot alienate his labor but has agreed to exchange the fruits of his labor for money.

Both explanations restore coherence to the text by referring to the set of capitalist or precapitalist social relations and the ideology (a word neither uses but which perfectly characterizes their analysis) that corresponds to it and which Locke's text expresses. Both reject the objectively determined confusion engendered by Locke's text as epiphenomenal, something to be resolved by reducing the text to the historical moment from which it emanates. To approach this passage from Althusser's perspective is to regard it as irreducible and to ask of what it is the symptom.

To explain Locke's lapsus we must indeed turn to the historical situation of the text. Tully, whose choice of authorities on property relations in seventeenth-century England is, to say the least, whimsical,[39] is certainly incorrect in his assertion that capitalist wage labor did not become dominant until the end of the eighteenth century. Robert Brenner, one of the leading historians of the transition from feudalism to capitalism, declares that

> by the end of the seventeenth-century, English landlords controlled an overwhelming proportion of the cultivable land—perhaps seventy to seventy-five percent—and capitalist class relations were developing as nowhere else, with momentous consequences for economic development. In my view, it was the emergence of the "classic" landlord/ capitalist tenant/wage-laborer structure that made possible the transformation of agricultural production in England, and this in turn was the key to England's uniquely successful overall economic development.[40]

This, however, does not compel us to accept Macpherson's assertion that the difficulties of the passage vanish when we impute to Locke the assumption of capitalist wage labor. For if landlords struggled to secure absolute property rights (in land as well as in the labor-power they purchased), their struggle was not, as Locke insinuates, a struggle solely or even primarily against the threat of absolute government. They simultaneously waged a struggle against their laborers who in practice refused to accept these newly asserted rights. This refusal did not simply take the form of resistance to enclosure (including enclosure by agreement—and by the end of the seventeenth century nearly all enclosures were "by agreement," a phrase that raises all the problems associated with the notion of consent as constructed by Locke),[41] it also took the form of resistance to the employer's absolute right to the product of wage-labor against what were regarded as irrational local customs, such as the right to glean the leftover at harvest time and the right to "lops and tops" of trees cut on the landlord's property.[42] These "precapitalist" practices even extended into manufactures and mines: Peter Linebaugh has described in detail the way in which "employers aggressively and systematically attacked and, in the end, successfully expropriated rights and usages that employees had customarily practiced,"[43] the rights, never legally sanctioned, of workers to the sweepings, overflows, and remnants of production which they might sell or make domestic use of. It is here that the unity of Locke's project, the attempt to forge an alliance of property owners (a category that includes the laborers, whose property in their own persons is irreducible, as well as the largest landholders) against a threat from above, founders against the historical reality of their irreconcilable differences. Locke has revealed in a moment of excess and infelicity the contradiction that haunts his notion of property. It is the moment at which the right of the laborer served as the foundation for labor discipline and the criminalization of custom, now made to appear in the light of Locke's argument as nothing more than the theft of the employer's rightful property. For the briefest of moments, then, but in an unmistakably jarring way that has, as we have noted, attracted the attention of numerous commentators, Locke's focus shifts from abstract rights to the very concrete and material processes of labor and labor discipline, in short to the inescapable struggle between the employer and wage-laborer.

Althusser's lecture notes on Locke from a course given in the Fall of 1971 reveal a vivid interest in the idea that a crime against property is for Locke not simply a violation of civil law but also and more important a violation of natural law, itself coextensive with reason. And consequences of such a violation are clear. Althusser writes, "every criminal (and a man can only be a criminal because he violates the natural law of the human species) places himself through his act outside the human species: he descends into a non-human species: an animal species."[44] The natural laws that govern the presocial state, then, produce a distinction within the human species as it actually exists between the human and the inhuman; by violating natural law, especially the law of property, "a man so far becomes degenerate and declares himself to quit the principles of human nature and to be a noxious creature."[45] Thus he may kill the thief "when he sets on me to rob me but of my horse or coat" as he would "a lion or a tyger, one of the savage wild beasts, with whom men can have no society nor security."[46]

Althusser's lecture notes conclude with a handwritten citation from Macpherson, who in turn simply cited what was to become, thanks to his insistence on reading Locke's texts to the letter, another celebrated and much debated passage. It would appear to offer, however, none of the ambiguity associated with the labor of Locke's servant. Rather, amid the sober considerations of interest rates and the value of money, and, more generally, amid the exaltation of man's natural rights and liberty, it blazes at the reader like a flash of lightning in a tranquil sky, illuminating everything for a moment only then to give way to darkness. Behind the image of the cultivated field and the prosperous farmer, behind the portrait of august assemblies of men multiplying "positive laws to determine property, this original law of nature,"[47] a scene of irrationality, animality, and violence is revealed, which perhaps is nothing more than the "legitimate" violence of property owners (as well as the more subtle violence of capital), contemplating itself and its inhumanity in inverted form, the imagined revenge of all those it sweeps away like a deluge. It is all that must not be thought for Locke to think property as origin:

> the laborers share, being seldom more than a bare subsistence, never allows that body of men time or opportunity to raise their thoughts above that or struggle with the richer for theirs (as one common interest) unless when some common and great distress, uniting them in one universal ferment, makes them forget respect and emboldens them to carve their wants with armed force; and then sometimes they break in upon the rich and sweep all like a deluge.[48]

Notes

1. Louis Althusser, *Reading Capital* (London: New Left Books, 1970), 132.

2. John Locke, *Essay Concerning Human Understanding*, 2 vols. (New York: Dover, 1959), 1:14.

3. Locke, *Essay*, 1:121.

4. Althusser, *Reading Capital*, 63.

5. John Locke, *Second Treatise of Government*, ed. C. B. Macpherson (Indianapolis: Hackett, 1980), 51.

6. Locke, *Second Treatise*, 29.

7. Louis Althusser, "Sur Raymond Polin, *La politique morale de John Locke*," in *Solitude de Machiavel*, ed. Yves Sintomer (Paris: Presses Universitaires de France, 1998); first published in the *Revue d'histoire moderne et contemporaine* 9 (avril–juin 1962). Also, "Cours sur Locke" (1971), unpublished ms., Fonds Althusser, Institut Mémoire de l'Édition Contemporaine.

8. Althusser, "Sur Raymond Polin," 34.

9. Raymond Polin, *La politique morale de John Locke* (Paris: Presses Universitaires de France, 1960).

10. *Ibid.*, 35.

11. *Ibid.*

12. *Ibid.*

13. John Locke, *Essays on the Law of Nature,* ed. W. von Leyden (Oxford: Clarendon Press, 1954).

14. *Ibid.*, 137.

15. *Ibid.*, 151.

16. Althusser, "Polin," 36.

17. Locke, *Second Treatise,* 8.

18. Althusser, "Polin," 37.

19. Locke, *Second Treatise,* 9.

20. Thomas Hobbes, *Leviathan,* ed. C. B. Macpherson (London: Penguin, 1968), 188.

21. Althusser, "Polin," 37.

22. Louis Althusser, *Montesquieu: la politique et l'histoire* (Paris: Presses Universitaires de France, 1959).

23. Althusser, "Polin," 38.

24. Locke, *Second Treatise,* 78.

25. C. B. Macpherson, *The Theory of Possessive Individualism* (Oxford: Oxford University Press, 1962). A sort of neo-Macphersonian reading of Locke emerged in the 1980s and 90s, based on the argument that capitalism had its origins in agrarian class relations and class struggle, especially in the ability of the English landowning class to secure absolute ownership of its property. See Neal Wood, *John Locke and Agrarian Capitalism* (Berkeley: University of California Press, 1984); David McNally, "Locke, Levellers and Liberty: Property and Democracy in the Thought of John Locke," *History of Political Thought* 10 (1989), 17–40; and Ellen Meiksins Wood, "Locke Against Democracy: Consent, Representation and Suffrage in the *Two Treatises,*" *History of Political Thought* 13 (1992), 657–89.

26. Richard Ashcraft, *Revolutionary Politics and Locke's Two Treatises of Government* (Princeton: Princeton University Press, 1986). Ashcraft's work represented perhaps the high point of a wave of scholarship in the late 1970s and 1980s that, very much in the spirit of the time, sought to recover the radicalism of Locke and of the liberal tradition in general. Another essential text of this movement is James Tully, *A Discourse on Property: John Locke and his Adversaries* (Cambridge: Cambridge University Press, 1980).

27. Althusser, "Polin," 38.

28. *Ibid.*, 39.

29. John Locke, *Two Treatises of Government,* ed. Peter Laslett (New York: Cambridge University Press, 1988), 18.

30. Locke, *Two Treatises,* 111.

31. I discuss this matter at greater length in "Spartacus as Tyrant: Locke's Fear of the Masses" in *Bodies, Masses, Power: Spinoza and His Contemporaries* (London: Verso, 1999).

32. Some of the most notable works include Peter Linebaugh and Marcus Rediker, *The Many-Headed Hydra: Sailors, Slaves, Commoners and the Hidden History of the Revolutionary Atlantic* (Boston: Beacon Press, 2000); Christopher Hill, *Liberty*

Against the Law (London: Penguin, 1996); E. P. Thompson, *Customs in Common: Studies in Tradition Popular Culture* (New York: The New Press, 1993); J. M. Neeson: *Commoners: Common Right, Enclosure and Social Change in England, 1700–1820* (Cambridge: Cambridge University Press, 1993); Peter Linebaugh, *The London Hanged: Crime and Civil Society in the Eighteenth Century* (Cambridge: Cambridge University Press, 1992); Roger B. Manning, *Village Revolts: Social Protest and Popular Disturbance in England 1509–1640* (Cambridge: Clarendon Press, 1988); David Underdown, *Revel, Riot and Rebellion: Popular Politics and Culture in England 1603–1660* (Oxford: Oxford University Press, 1987); Buchanan Sharp, *In Contempt of All Authority: Rural Artisans and Riot in the West of England, 1586–1660* (Berkeley: University of California Press, 1980).

33. Locke, *Two Treatises*, 19.

34. *Ibid.*

35. *Ibid.*, 19–20.

36. Macpherson, *Individualism*, 215–20.

37. *Ibid.*, 18.

38. Tully, *Property*, 140.

39. Harry Braverman's *Labor and Monopoly Capital* (New York: Monthly Review Press, 1974), an extraordinarily interesting examination of labor discipline in twentieth-century capitalist industry, is not a serious source of information on the emergence of capitalist property relations in England.

40. Robert Brenner, "Agrarian Class Structure and Economic Development in Pre-Industrial Europe" in *The Brenner Debate*, ed. T. H. Ashton and C. H. E. Philpin (Cambridge: Cambridge University Press, 1985), 48–49. Brenner's work has strongly influenced the Neo-Macphersonian current of Locke commentary described above.

41. See Manning, "Resistance to 'Enclosure by Agreement'" in *Village Revolts*, 108–31.

42. See particularly Thompson, *Customs*, and Hill, *Liberty*.

43. Linebaugh, *The London Hanged*, 404. On the struggle against wage labor in the mining industry in the seventeenth and eighteenth centuries, see George Randall Lewis, *The Stannaries: A Study of the English Tin Miner* (Cambridge: Harvard University Press, 1924), 176–226. In his "Essay on the Poor Law" (1697), Locke warns that the poor who are set to work in wool and other manufactures must be watched very closely and that an "exact account" of all materials advanced them must be made to prevent embezzlement of materials. See John Locke, *Political Essays*, ed. Mark Goldie (Cambridge University Press, 1997), 194.

44. Althusser, "Cours sur Locke."

45. Locke, *Two Treatises*, 11.

46. *Ibid.*

47. *Ibid.*, 20.

48. Locke, "Some Considerations of the Consequences of Lowering the Interest, and Raising the Value of Money: In a Letter Sent to a Member of Parliament, 1691," in *Works*, 9 vols. (London: Rivington, 1824), 71.

Locke and the Event of Appropriation: A Heideggerian Reading of "Of Property"

Robert Bernasconi

In "The Origin of the Work of Art" Heidegger describes how a Greek temple "first fits together and at the same time gathers round itself the unity of those paths and relations in which birth and death, disaster and blessing, victory and disgrace, endurance and decline shape the paths of human essencing."[1] He explains that this is the way in which the world of a historical people is opened so that it can return to itself for the fulfillment of its vocation: "The temple first gives to things their look and to men their outlook on themselves" (*H* 32; *PLT* 43). The thesis of "The Origin of the Work of Art" is that the work of art is an origin, that is to say, a way in which truth becomes historical for a people as it transports that people into its task on the basis of its endowment (*H* 64; *PLT* 77). Heidegger does not restrict such happenings to works of art. He includes also, among other things, the founding of political states, the essential sacrifice, and the thinker's questioning (*H* 50; *PLT* 62). These are ways in which epochal change happens. One might call them changes of world rather than merely changes to the world. Heidegger's interest in changes of world was certainly enhanced by his conviction that he believed that such an epochal change was possible in the 1930s. He had already called this "another beginning," a phrase designed to show that this beginning, as does any beginning, always takes place in some way as a transformation but also as an excess over what preceded it. It cannot be reduced to what went before, but it is not altogether new.

When John Locke wrote the *Second Treatise*, he did so to justify a revolution, a change of monarch. Furthermore, it was, as it happened, a change from the Catholic James II to the Protestant William and Mary. However, Locke's justifications of the revolution were such that it could take place without a change in the ownership of property. This might make the change seem relatively minor. However, I shall suggest that there was a more significant change taking place in the *Second Treatise* that was also a change of world in Heidegger's sense, and that this change can be elucidated in ways that Heidegger illuminates in his account of the worlding of the world. I begin by briefly recalling Heidegger's account of world.

One can identify at least three different conceptions of the world in Heidegger. The first belongs to the period of *Being and Time*. There Heidegger introduces the idea of the world as "that 'wherein' a factical Dasein as such can be said to 'live'."[2] This conception is introduced in direct contrast to the idea of the totality of entities, the whole of what exists. Both are prephilosophical concepts of the world, but in Heidegger's concept the world is not "nature," either as organic or inorganic. It is rather existing human beings in their manner of existing.[3] Corresponding to this conception is an ontological-existential concept of the world, which Heidegger calls "the worldhood of the world" (*SZ* 65).

In 1936 in "The Origin of the Work of Art," Heidegger introduces a second concept of the world. Here the focus is not on the world as that wherein Dasein dwells but on the world as the space opened by the work of art. A work has its own world or realm that it uniquely opens, although the work can be torn from its world, for example, if it is displaced (*H* 30; *PLT* 40–41). Heidegger alters the concept of world from *Being and Time* even more radically by introducing at this time a counterconcept, that of the earth. The initial example is that of a Greek temple standing in a rock-cleft valley. The temple not only opens a world that first gives to things their look and to men their outlook on themselves but also simultaneously sets this world back again on earth, which emerges as native ground (*H* 31–32; *PLT* 42–43).[4] Heidegger's account points to a strife between world and earth as it takes place in the work of art. In this strife, the opposition between world and earth raises each into the self-assertion of their natures (*H* 37–38; *PLT* 49).

Soon after "The Origin of the Work of Art," Heidegger begins to explore in his private manuscripts what he later called the fourfold. Initially this took the form of world and earth, gods and mortals.[5] Subsequently, the fourfold becomes earth and sky, gods and mortals, and their mutual appropriation is called by Heidegger "the worlding of the world."[6] Let us recall briefly the account from "Building Dwelling Thinking," a lecture delivered in 1951. Heidegger explains that mortals save the earth by setting it free into its own presencing and not by exploiting it, wearing it out, mastering it, or subjugating it, which, as Heidegger insists, is "merely one step from unbridled spoliation" (*VA* 150; *PLT* 150, trans. modified). Furthermore, mortals dwell in that they receive the sky as sky and do not turn night into day, nor day into a harassed unrest. Mortals also dwell in that they await the gods as gods: "they do not make their gods for themselves and do not worship idols" (*VA* 151; *PLT* 150). Finally, mortals dwell in being capable of death as death, which does not mean making it the goal (*VA* 151; *PLT* 151). This takes place as a staying with things. None of the four insists on its own separate particularity, but each is expropriated within their mutual appropriation. Appropriation, *Ereignis,* is the key word of Heidegger's later thinking.

There is no doubt that Heidegger draws much of his initial inspiration both for his account of world and earth and, subsequently, for the introduction of the fourfold from Hölderlin, but apart from some discussions of art and poetry and some readings of Heraclitus, these conceptual innovations have not worked their way into the philosophical discourse of the last fifty years. The strangeness of this vocabulary serves in the remainder of this essay to make Locke's use of similar terms also seem stranger than they have hitherto and thus open them to a different kind of reading. However, this reading of Locke must be judged on its intrinsic merits. In this effort, faithfulness to the letter of Heidegger's framework will be entirely subordinated to an attempt to illuminate Locke's text and the issues that it raises.

In the chapter on property in the *Two Treatises of Government,*[7] Locke attempts to derive unequal distribution of land and wealth from a world given to "mankind in common." This is what Locke sought to establish in the chapter of property: not the justification of property as such, but the justification of unequal shares starting from the same Biblical assertion about the original community of property which some of the Church Fathers had used to condemn private property (*1T,* section 16, p. 152). Filmer, Locke's immediate target, dealt with the Biblical text by reinterpreting it. Locke contested this reading but did not offer an alternative reading of Scripture. In Locke it is the movement of thought which does the work. Isolated quotations can be particularly misleading and so it is necessary to rehearse Locke's narrative argument in some detail.

It is sometimes overlooked that the first form of property described in the *Second Treatise* is not man's common ownership of the world but God's ownership of man: "they are his Property" (*2T,* section 6, p. 271). This is not only the first use of the word "property" in the *Second Treatise.* It provides the fundamental theological premise which determines everything that follows.[8] Because men are "the servants of one Sovereign Master," all the forms of property which are subsequently ascribed to man are in fact only forms of stewardship. This includes the property that someone has "in his own Person" (*2T,* section 27, p. 287). Indeed, it is preeminently true in that case. Self-ownership of one's own person is not absolute and so any attempt to interfere with the title of that property is excluded. This is reflected in Locke's condemnation of suicide as well as in the limitations he imposes on the institution of slavery (*2T*, section 23, p. 284). As I shall attempt to show, property in one's own person also provides the framework in terms of which the limitations placed on the other forms of property ownership subsequently described by Locke are to be regarded. Locke says in the *First Treatise* that God is "sole Lord and Proprietor of the whole World," and so Man's "propriety" is only that of "Liberty to use" it (*1T*, section 39, p. 168). It is, one might say, leasehold rather than freehold. Or, as Locke himself puts it, the dominion "which a Shepherd may have" rather than "full Property as an Owner." Furthermore, and this too will prove important for what follows, God's property in man is explicitly understood in terms of work:

> For Men being all the Workmanship of one Omnipotent, and infinitely wise Maker; All the Servants of one Sovereign Master, sent into the World by his order and about his business, they are his Property, whose Workmanship they are, made to last during his, not one anothers Pleasure. (*2T*, section 6, p. 271)

In a reconstruction of Locke's argument it is as unwise to overlook the designation of God's activity as *work* as it is to neglect the sense in which man is and remains the property of God. Insofar as work can be ascribed to God, the need to work cannot be construed as a punishment. The passage from property in one's own person to other forms of property is accomplished by working in imitation of God. Locke does not dwell on the difference between work, which employs materials, and creation, which since the Church Fathers has been understood as *ex nihilo*.

The major part of the fifth chapter of the *Second Treatise* is devoted to a narrative set in the state of nature. The questions raised by this notion illustrate the difficulties which arise when Locke's text is read with an exclusive focus on, for example, political or religious concerns at the expense of philosophical considerations.[9] The widespread uncertainty about how Locke's state of nature functions is compounded by one-sided readings. Does Locke's state of nature have a historical reference, as a number of Locke's references to it seem to assume? Does it have a normative role, as is suggested by the relation between the state of nature and the natural law "which obliges every one" (*2T*, section 6, p. 271)? Or is the overriding consideration that a return to the state of nature could always remain an open possibility on Locke's account, both for individuals and for societies?[10] Or is it in the manner of a hypothesis which, as Rousseau put it with regard to his own account of the state of nature, is "a state which no longer exists, which perhaps never did exist, which probably never will exist, and about which it is nevertheless necessary to have exact Notions in order to accurately judge of our present state?"[11] It would seem that all these considerations are in play and that none can be excluded.

Locke's narrative describes at least three stages in the development of property.[12] Even though these stages are well enough known in outline, I will rehearse them here because they are the markers that establish the dynamic of Locke's account. The stages can be characterized according to their different determinations of God, man, and the earth. These are the basic elements of Locke's account. "God" always means to Locke the Christian God. In the first stage or condition, Locke introduces God as a Creator working from a design. Furthermore, God is marked by his generosity as well as his workmanship. The world is a gift. The earth in this first condition is understood as the support: "The earth, and all that is therein, is given to Men for the Support and Comfort of their being" (2T, section 26, p. 286). Man is the sole beneficiary of this gift. When God gave the earth to mankind in common, the gift included not only the fruits of the earth but the animals, too. Locke gives the example of a deer belonging to the one who has killed it (2T, section 30, p. 289). God also gave man reason and revelation. It is revelation which instructs man both about the gift and the giver. It is reason which instructs man on how to use the gift. But man is also mortal and his mortality is also a gift. It is in terms of death that man confronts his particularity.[13]

Reason, which Locke identifies with the law of nature (2T, section 6, p. 271), instructs each man to take possession of God's gift of the fruits of nature in order to stave off the threat of mortality. This is accomplished by labor. But because God, man, and earth are different in the three stages, so is labor. In this the first stage, man appropriates by gathering (2T, section 28, p. 288; section 31, p. 290; section 46, p. 300). Gathering is not without restrictions. Reason wills the "Preservation of all Mankind" (2T, section 7, p. 312). That is why it is clear to Locke without any further argument that the right is restricted to the case "where there is enough, and as good left in common for others" (2T, section 27, p. 288). Furthermore, it is because the fruits of the earth are a *gift* that no man has a right to destroy or spoil them. They are there to be enjoyed (2T, section 31, p. 290). This has given rise to what in the secondary literature is called "the spoilage limitation." But the very phrase is indicative of the incomplete way it has been understood. Locke writes, "As much as any one can make use of any advantage of life before it spoils; so much he may by his labor fix a Property in." Positively the issue is one of use, and this is what Locke will focus on subsequently.

The second stage of property ownership in the state of nature is that wherein an individual can take ownership of a parcel of land. Here Locke emphasizes that his God is a God who commands obedience (2T, section

32, p. 291). He stresses this characteristic because not everyone responds to the command which is communicated through reason. It is heard only by the industrious. Property in the earth itself, as opposed to its fruits, is given to those who respond to this command. Hence "man" no longer means all men but only "the Industrious and Rational" (*2T,* section 34, p. 291). So when Locke repeats the phrase "God gave the world to Men in Common," it no longer means the same. It no longer means that the fruits of the earth are given to every man for his preservation but that a property in the land is given to those who work the earth. That is to say, the land is given to those who make best use of the gifts that God has given them as men: the gifts in question are the capacity to reason and to labor.

What of those who do not use these gifts? The world was given "to the use of the Industrious and Rational . . . not to the Fancy or Covetousness of the Quarrelsom and Contentious" (*2T,* section 34, p. 291). This does not mean that the covetous were excluded from sharing in the fruits of the earth. But it does mean that if they failed to employ their capacity to reason and to labor and so did not work the land, then they were not rewarded by the gift of land. The earth is no longer the support which gives its fruits. The earth is to be subdued: "God and his Reason commanded him to subdue the Earth, i.e. improve it for the benefit of Life, and therein lay out something upon it that was his own, his labor" (*2T,* section 32, p. 291).

In keeping with the changes in the fundamental determinations of God, Man, and the earth, labor is no longer understood as gathering but as cultivation in the form of tilling and sowing. Cultivation is a form of production which multiplies the fruits that the earth produces. The transformation of man's relation to the earth, the transformation of laboring into cultivation, brings a greater return from the earth. There is no permanent transformation of the earth, for Locke believes that the field which has been cultivated will soon return to its previous state if it is no longer farmed. Nevertheless, until the field is returned to the state of nature the use of it is exclusive: "He that in Obedience to this Command of God, subdued, tilled and sowed any part of it [the earth], thereby annexed to it something that was his *Property,* which another had no Title to, nor could without injury take from him" (*2T,* section 32, p. 291).

The second stage has seen a redetermination of God's gift of the world. This redetermination is not a departure from God's original design but a closer approximation to it. Locke writes, "it cannot be supposed he [God] meant it [the earth] should always remain common and uncultivated" (*2T,* section 34, p. 291). This is where the positive side of the so-called spoilage limitation comes into play. It enjoins men to make the best *use* of God's gift of the world. Furthermore, the existence of America guarantees that there is "enough and as good left in common for others," so that taking a property in land does not *in principle* harm the interests of anyone else, although it might *in fact*, if they do not have the means and the opportunity to travel. Locke is clear that the land left in common in England cannot be appropriated, as it can be in Spain, for example. This is because in England its status as common land is established by compact (*2T*, section 35, p. 292). Passage to America amounts to a return to the state of nature, so that in such a case the state of nature represents a possibility, not just a historical fiction.

The third of the three stages is inaugurated by the invention of money. God seems to play a less prominent role in the discussion of this condition. No doubt this has encouraged all those who have cast Locke as a secular thinker. But before accepting this reading, it is necessary to examine the text more closely. Let us begin with its more familiar features. Money allows value to be accumulated. Apples which are hoarded deteriorate. Before the invention of money, nature set the limits on property simply through the threat of wastage. Collecting more than was needed would be irrational. It would also be a misappropriation of God's generosity. By contrast, money can be stored. It does not spoil. Through it one can own more than one has immediate use for.

What underlies the legitimacy of money is the recognition that waste is wrong because it amounts to a misuse of God's gift. Money diminishes wastage because it allows more of the earth to be cultivated or put to use. Excess in property continues to be measured by Locke not in terms of size or differentials but by wastage (*2T*, section 46, p. 300). When Locke says that "larger Possessions" had been introduced by consent, he means that, insofar as money made it possible to hoard without wastage, a way had been found of bypassing the practical limitation of spoilage which had hitherto governed accumulation. But there is more to it than that. Locke's argument can be clarified further by referring to a difficult sentence which needs to be read carefully, establishing first what it is *not* about.

When Locke says that the "Rule of Propriety . . . that every Man should have as much as he could make use of, would hold still in the World, without straitning any body," were it not for the invention of money, he does not *mean* to concede what he later tries to deny, that poverty can be blamed on the introduction of money (*2T*, section 36, p. 293). Locke will argue vehemently that those who are counted poor can be shown to have benefited from the invention of money insofar as it has led to an increase in "the common stock of mankind" (*2T*, section 37, p. 294). Even so, what is important to Locke is that by accepting the invention of money, men tacitly agreed to "disproportionate and unequal Possession of the Earth" (*2T*, section 50, p. 302). Furthermore, Locke makes reference to the fact that "there is Land enough in the World to suffice double the inhabitants" in order to show that the opportunities that the rich benefited from are still available to those who are sufficiently industrious and rational to take advantage of them. America is Locke's answer to the question of whether "enough and as good" is left "in common for others." The invention of money does not address this limitation which was never lifted. It is assumed that nature will remain abundant in its *opportunities*. And there is no reason why it should not, Locke seems to think, as long as the world's population does not double. It would appear that Locke simply does not conceive of population growth on this scale as a possibility. That is to say, he does not suppose that the limitation on accumulation would ever have applied. The fact that Locke's predictions have proved grossly mistaken and threaten catastrophic results, notwithstanding the changes brought about through the applications of modern technology, means that the assumptions on which Locke based his argument no longer hold and that to this extent the question of unequal shares is thrown open.

However, at the same time that the limitation of leaving "enough and as good . . . for others" remains intact, another safeguard for the poor seems to disappear, even though one must read carefully to see how this happens in Locke's text. In the *First Treatise* Locke is clear that anyone in need has a right to another's surplus in order to secure his preservation. "Charity gives every Man a Title to so much out of another's Plenty, as will keep him from extreme want, where he has no means to subsist otherwise" (*1T*, section 42, p. 170). Tully, in his somewhat idiosyncratic interpretation, was among the first commentators to recognize the importance of the passage on charity, but his discussion is compromised by his failure to establish its context.[14] This enabled Wood to include it in a list of passages which, with some justice, he accused Tully of misunderstanding.[15] It needs to be recognized that in presenting this view, Locke is not advocating a new form of political radicalism so much as rehearsing a position which had already been held by, for example, Thomas Aquinas, and, more recently, Hugo Grotius.[16] But there is little trace of this idea in the *Second Treatise* except for the passage, early in the text, in which Locke denies that charity is to be conceived as a noble action on the part of a benefactor, or even, as he finds it in Hooker, "a natural duty" (*2T*, section 5, p. 270). What one finds is that Locke explicitly denies this right later in the *Second Treatise* because he recognizes that it contradicts his conception of property: "For I have truly no *Property* in that, which another can by right take from me, when he pleases, against my consent" (*2T*, section 138, pp. 360–361). Although this passage occurs in the context of a discussion of the extent of the Legislative power of government and is primarily directed against it, the fact that the argument is presented as a conceptual argument suggests that it has wider application. It also serves as an answer to those commentators who have tried to present Locke as extending this right to charity into civil society.[17] Indeed, the fact that entry into society through compact impacted the right to charity was already hinted at in the *First Treatise* when he wrote that one can become a *servant* through need: "The Authority of the Rich Proprietor, and the Subjection of the Needy Beggar began not from the Possession of the Lord, but the Consent of the poor Man, who preferr'd being his Subject to starving" (*1T,* section 43, p. 171).

It seems that just as the claim that God gave the world to mankind in common is introduced by Locke in order to transform it radically so as to further God's design, so similar considerations of rewarding industry and increasing wealth impact the right to charity. It is introduced only to be subverted, and this takes place when the "Rule of Propriety" that "every Man should have as much as he could make use of" is overturned. It happens when the notion of surplus is transformed, because Locke presented the right to charity as a right of a "needy Brother" to "the Surplusage" of another's goods when "his pressing Wants call for it" (*1T,* section 42, p. 170). Once money is introduced a surplus is not always simply a surplus; it need not go to waste. The ambiguity marks the transition between two conceptions of charity.

The passage on the subversion of the "Rule of Propriety" in chapter 5 is presented by Locke as not primarily about the "straitning" of the *poor* or about leaving "enough and as good" for everyone. Locke's point is that the limitation whereby everyone has only "as much as he could make use of" would—were it not for the invention of money—be a restriction or "straitning" of the industrious. It is Locke's contention that maintaining the "Rule of Propriety" would amount to a misunderstanding of God's design. That is why the invention of money is not only not contrary to God's design but also required by it. To restrict the industrious simply to what they can use straightaway or in the immediate future both damages the less industrious and interferes with God's plan that we should increase and multiply the world as stock. The best stewardship men can exercise over God's gift is to see it prosper, and that means to allow the accumulation of value. It means to conceive a future and live for it. In a world without money one is, by the terms of Locke's narrative, limited to what one can enjoy in the present.

But even if the invention of money can retrospectively be seen to have been justified (in the sense of legitimated in terms of God's law), how did it come to be invented? Does Locke require that everyone should have spontaneously become capable of foreseeing the benefits which would result in the adoption of money? Locke does not say this and commentators do not propose it. The question is simply not asked. It is as if we are at the agreed limits of Locke's narrative structure. But there is something mysterious about this story. Locke presents the invention of money as having been brought about by tacit consent. It is crucial to his argument that the consent should be tacit, because express consent would require men to come together to agree upon it. Locke wants to explain society in terms of the property which money makes possible and not the other way around; otherwise, money would be conventional and so the institution of unequal shares would be open to renewed debate. Are we to suppose that this point around which Locke's whole theory of government hinges is beyond the limits of his narrative? Is Locke as silent about this question as are his commentators? Does he provide no hint of an explanation of how money was introduced?

I would maintain that, even though there must always be a point at which the narrative breaks down, Locke's account does go further than is usually acknowledged. It is not that Locke lacks an explanation so much as that his explanation has not been recognized. It can be found in the following sentence, which answers the question of why those things selected to serve as the instruments of money have been given a value beyond their use: "Gold, Silver, Diamonds, are things, that Fancy or Agreement hath put the Value on, more than real Use, and the necessary Support of Life" (*2T*, section 46, p. 300). The sentence is ambiguous: "Fancy or Agreement." Fancy might mean the same as agreement. This is how the sentence has been read. The value accorded to money is a convention, and the problem of its origin remains. To that extent there would be a contingency at the heart of the narrative structure interrupting its otherwise remorseless sequentiality. But fancy might mean desire. In that case what makes agreement—tacit agreement—possible is the fact that gold, silver, and diamonds are themselves inherently desirable. And if the point was not already clear, Locke explains further in the very same paragraph, that a man gives nuts for a piece of metal "pleased with its color," just as he would exchange sheep for shells, or wool "for a sparkling Pebble or a Diamond." Gold, shells, and diamonds may not be desired for their "intrinsick value" in the sense of their utility. Furthermore, their qualities are not limited to the merely functional ones required of money that they be "both lasting and scarce, and so valuable to be hoarded up" (*2T*, section 48, p. 301). Many other things meet that criteria, but gold and silver have a value beyond mere convention, and that value is rooted in a desire for them arising out of their inherent attractiveness. In this sense their value is situated in the nature of man. The desire for gold is not simply conventional but forms a natural bond between men, a bond which expresses itself in the invention of money. The invention of money would appear to be situated at the point of transition from nature to culture. It both is and is not natural. Locke says that in the only way open to him—in an ambiguous sentence.

The transformation that Locke's narrative effects emerges only when it is seen that this double sense of fancy is in play. It will be recalled that in an earlier passage fancy had been opposed to industry and reason in the phrase "the Fancy or Covetousness of the Quarrelsom and Contentious" (*2T*, section 34, p. 291). Fancy in this sense, the sense of covetousness, is condemned and continues to be condemned in political society. Later in the *Second Treatise*, during a discussion of political society, Locke identifies the golden age as that "before vain Ambition, and *amor sceleratus habendi*, evil Concupiscence, had corrupted Mens minds into a Mistake of true Power and Honour" (*2T*, section 111, p. 341). What Locke objects to is presumable not unlike what Rousseau would subsequently call *amour propre*. By contrast, that "fancy agreement" that introduces money is praiseworthy because it unwittingly cooperates with God's design. This latter sense of fancy is neither covetous nor, insofar as it is blind—as it must be—strictly rational. Hence the role of fancy in the invention of money marks a shift, an acceptance of desire that breaks the otherwise exclusive hold of immediate utility. The "larger possessions" which are introduced following the inauguration of a money economy are legitimated not by need but obedience; they are, however, motivated by fancy in the sense of desire.

The thrust of Locke's chapter is the legitimation of a certain desire, a desire which surpasses utility but that is not that of the vain or ambitious. As Locke puts it, "the desire of having more than Men needed . . . altered the intrinsick value of things, which depends only on their usefulness to the Life of Man" (*2T*, section 37, p. 294). That is to say, and it is already remarkable, what Locke calls the "intrinsick value of things" is only the value which use places on them. It answers only to one side of man. Whereas labor simply adds to the value of Nature (*2T*, section 28, p. 288), desire alters the character of that value so that it is no longer confined to needs. The time of need and of the conveniences of life are dominated by the present. After fancy was legitimated following the invention of money, the future came to dominate. Locke describes this as no more than a tendency, but it is a crucial one nevertheless.[18] The paragraph which clarifies how fancy puts the value on gold opens with the statement, "The greatest part of things really useful to the life of Men . . . are generally things of short duration" (*2T*, section 46, pp. 299–300). Concern with need and use focuses on the present. By contrast, money is both durable and desirable.

The consequences of this change can be reformulated in terms of Hannah Arendt's distinction between labor and work.[19] Labor is repetitive, leaves no lasting residue, and belongs to an unending cycle imposed by the necessity of consumption. Work, which imposes a design on the materials at its disposal, results in a lasting product. In this way man imprints his design on things irrevocably. In terms of Locke's account it is with the invention of money that the cycle of labor gives way to the world of work. In terms of Locke's narrative, gold and the fancy it introduces makes work possible. It is the condition of possibility of work. It opens the way to a world that is not only in a sense man-made but also has a certain permanence, such that the earth does not immediately revert to its original condition. Man is able to leave a certain legacy, his mark, beyond his mortality. However, there is also a suspicion that man in this way moves toward the center, and this is emphasized in the way that Locke emphasizes that gold and silver have "*value* only from the consent of Men" (*2T*, section 50, p. 302).

Locke's argument about desire must be seen in the light of the history of political discussions of property. The Fathers of the Christian Church had maintained the same starting point that Locke adopted—the idea that God had given the world to mankind in common. But for them the condition of common ownership remained the most perfect way of life. Private property was the consequence of the Fall and reflected human greed.[20] By contrast, Locke attempted to show that within a certain framework, the operation of desire produced a society which better responded to God's design for man. This transformation of a longstanding tradition was momentous, and all the more so for using the resources of the very tradition which was at issue. In so doing, Locke was in step with the current of his time. In his classic work, *The Protestant Ethic and the Spirit of Capitalism,* Max Weber had referred to the new use to which St. Paul's dictum, "He who will not work shall not eat," was put. Weber contrasted the limited sense Aquinas gave to the phrase and its much stronger reinterpretation at the hands of the Puritan Richard Baxter.[21] Locke made even more of it by taking it as the basis for private property. What, so far as I am aware, was new was the justification given to industrious laboring, or rather productive work, such that waste on the part of nature was to be condemned as heartily as was idleness in man. Indeed, on the Lockean model, man's calling was to avoid waste in nature (see *2T*, section 31, p. 290) and to "increase and multiply" (*1T*, section 41, p. 170) —both with reference to population and the use to which nature was put (*1T*, section 33, p. 164).

It is now possible to summarize the third condition of property described by Locke, as I have done for the previous stages, in terms of the characterization of God, man, and earth. God is not displaced by the invention of money but finds his design followed by man in his work. Man is not simply someone who works in accord with reason to satisfy his needs but for the first time becomes a unity of reason and desire. Man plays the dominant role in the creation of value. He places the value on gold and silver, and this makes it possible to enhance the value of the earth. The initial gift of the earth is now devalued in the narrative. The earth as it had been "given to Men for the Support and Comfort of their being" (*2T*, section 26, p. 286) is now regarded as waste: "Land that is left wholly to Nature, that hath no improvement of Pasturage, Tillage, or Planting, is called, as indeed it is, *waste*" (*2T*, section 42, p. 297). Land left as waste now serves as the paradigm case of all wastage, so that until it is appropriated, land is "almost worthless." Of course, this is in part because it is not scarce but it is also because the world has been transformed into one where "*labor makes the far greatest part of the value* of things" (*2T*, section 42, p. 297. Locke's italics.).[22] "*'Tis Labor then which puts the greatest part of Value upon Land, without which it would scarcely be worth any thing*" (*2T*, section 43, p. 298. Locke's italics.). That the earth is reduced to "Materials to work on" (*2T*, section 35, p. 292), of themselves "almost worthless" (*2T*, section 43, p. 298), shows how far the model of production or work has taken over and determined the nature of the thing.

Historians of political thought have tended to question Locke's originality by emphasizing his dependence on certain longstanding theological assumptions and by referring his language to that of the economic and political debates of his day. By focusing on the role of fancy, and to a lesser extent that of charity, in his justification of property, I have attempted to suggest that the novelty of Locke's recasting of the religious framework has been overlooked. Locke confronts the distrust in which desire was held by showing how amongst the industrious it could serve God's design, although as we have seen, Locke's argument depended on further assumptions about limited population growth and the continued existence of surplus land that can no longer be sustained.

Nevertheless, we cannot stop with the fact that Locke in this way legitimates a certain transformation of the place of desire. Not all desires are legitimated. Not even all desires for those things that are most striking, most apparent. What Locke describes is the opening of a world that is measured in terms of gold. In a sense he puts the world on the gold standard. However, it is not that Locke treats money as an origin in the same way that the temple was an origin for Heidegger in his account of the Greeks. It is true that money on Locke's account gathers the unity of the paths and relations that certain industrious and rational peoples now follow. It gives to things their look and to men their outlook on themselves. But the transformation is taking place in and through Locke's text. Gold is not the work. Locke's text is. It is in this work of philosophy, functioning as it does in a manner well described by Heidegger as he offers his account of the work of art, that the modern epoch achieves one of its founding formulations. I am leaving open here the question of the extent to which Locke is truly an origin or whether, in Heideggerian terms, he is the preserver of an origin that takes place elsewhere, in part because of the complexity of such decisions.

In this essay I have tried to suggest some ways in which we might approach this text in a Heideggerian register in order to help open what might be taking place there. My doing so does not depend on the fact that Locke talks about world, earth, God, and mortality, although the fact that he did helped me, undoubtedly, to articulate the connection. I have tried to show that Locke's argument, as we often still like to think of it, relies on a host of historical presuppositions that radically exceed the structure of logical argumentation and any effort it might make to detail the assumptions necessary to make the argument valid. Of course, all arguments rely on more assumptions than can possibly be stated. They assume a common discourse and starting point. But what happens here where Locke, whatever he is trying to do, marks a shift between historical epochs? To the extent to which men and women of the Middle Ages acknowledged that God gave the world to mankind in common, they were well aware of their obligations to the poor and the sinfulness of wealth. No amount of argumentation could have persuaded them that this idea was compatible with limitless inequality of wealth, let alone the idea that God might have favored such inequality. This is true even though they lived in a world of great inequality of wealth and station. Did Locke think he could have persuaded such people? Or was his argument nothing less than a cynical exercise in sophistry which subsequent generations have gullibly taken at face value? It seems to me that we do better not to think of Locke as someone who knew what he was doing. He was trying to justify a change in monarch while property relations remained intact, thereby avoiding the upheavals of the Norman Conquest and preparing the way for William and Mary to replace James II with the support of the landowners. Hence property rights were established outside the social contract. He also was aware that his argument had implications in its details for the introduction of what has become known as agrarian capitalism, just as he almost certainly knew that his account opened the way to colonial conquest. Hence his references to America. But it is unlikely that he was fully conscious of the enormity of the transformation in the way human beings related to God, to the earth, and to each other that he was articulating through his idolization of the pursuit of money. Furthermore, I suspect that most of the time when we read him neither are we. It is in part to emphasize that shift that I have written this paper.

My suggestion is that Locke's text marks the passing of one epoch into another where charity and especially desire appear differently. To read epochal changes in a text is a difficult task, and they disappear altogether when the text is reduced to an argument judged simply on those terms. Arguments may go astray in equivocity, but that does not mean that equivocity is simply the occasion of illegitimate inferences or sophistry. It is perhaps also the case that that is where the originary work of philosophy takes place. Or, as a Heideggerian might say, the happening of truth occurs.

Notes

1. Martin Heidegger, *Holzwege* (Frankfurt: Klostermann, 1950), 31; trans. Albert Hofstadter, *Poetry, Language, Thought* (New York: Harper and Row, 1971), 42, translation modified. Henceforth abbreviated *H* and *PLT* respectively.

2. Martin Heidegger, *Sein und Zeit* (Tübingen: Niemeyer, 1953), 65. Henceforth *SZ*.

3. Martin Heidegger, *Metaphysische Anfangsgrunde der Logik im Ausgang von Leibniz*, Gesamtausgabe 26 (Frankfurt: Klostermann, 1978), 231–32; trans. Michael Heim, *The Metaphysical Foundations of Logic* (Bloomington: Indiana University Press, 1984), 180–81.

4. For a fuller account of Heidegger's conception of earth, see Michel Haar, *Le chant de la terre* (Paris: Herne, 1987), 122–33; trans. Reginald Lilly, *The Song of the Earth* (Bloomington: Indiana University Press, 1993), 57–63. Haar lists but problematizes the idea of native ground.

5. Martin Heidegger, *Die Geschichte des Seyns*, Gesamtausgabe 69 (Frankfurt: Klostermann, 1998), 124.

6. Martin Heidegger, *Vorträge und Aufsätze* (Pfullingen: Günther Neske, 1954), 178. Henceforth *VA*. Trans. in *Poetry, Language, Thought*, 179.

7. John Locke, *Two Treatises of Government* with introduction and notes by Peter Laslett (Cambridge: Cambridge University Press, 1988). References are to this edition. I have retained the spelling but not the use of italics and have given the section numbers to help readers using a different edition. *1T* and *2T* refer to the two treatises respectively.

8. There have been some extraordinary instances of the exclusion of this aspect of Locke's discussion. Perhaps the most alarming is that where Laslett describes the proposition that men are the workmanship of God as "an existentialist proposition," "a common-sense starting-point," which "relies . . . upon the possibility of taking what might be called a synoptic view of the world, more vulgarly, a God's eye view of what happens among man here on earth. If you admit that it is possible to look down on men from above, then you may be said to grant to Locke this initial position" (*Two Treatises of Government*, 93). Remarkable in its own way, because it does not reinterpret the proposition but excludes it altogether, is the in-

terpretation offered by J. P. Day, who finds the idea that men are God's property "clearly incompatible" with the proposition that "every man has a right to own his person" and so simply disregards it. See Day, "Locke on Property," *Philosophical Quarterly* 16 (1966): 215.

9. See Richard Ashcraft, "Locke's State of Nature: Historical Fact or Moral Fiction?" *American Political Science Review* 62 (1968): 898–915.

10. Jean-Jacques Rousseau, *Oeuvre complètes*, vol. III (Paris: Pléiade, 1964), 123; trans. Victor Gourevitch, *The First and Second Discourses and Essay on the Origin of Languages* (New York: Harper and Row, 1986), 130.

11. A civil society is returned to the state of nature in the case of foreign conquest (*2T*, section 211, p. 406). This and other cases of the dissolution of government are discussed by Locke in the final chapter of the *Second Treatise*. A contextual reading of the *Two Treatises* quite properly stresses the importance of this chapter, although I cannot take it up here.

12. It is possible to introduce a fourth stage by identifying section 38 as a pastoral period following food gathering and hunting but prior to agriculture and commerce. See Neal Wood, *John Locke and Agrarian Capitalism* (Berkeley: University of California, 1984), 51.

13. Following the usage of his day, Locke often employs the term "man" to refer to human beings in general, but he also often uses it in a sense that we today would unhesitatingly recognize as sexist. Because this essay is largely expository, I shall follow Locke's usage in the hope and expectation that the reader finds that usage grating, if not offensive. To correct it would, in this instance, only serve to confuse the issues at stake.

14. James Tully, *A Discourse on Property* (Cambridge: Cambridge University Press, 1980), 131–32.

15. Wood, *Locke and Agrarian Capitalism,* 78–79, 89–90.

16. Aquinas, *Summa Theol.* II, qu. 66.2 and Hugo Grotius, *De Jure Belli Acc Pacis,* 2.2.6. The position of Grotius is particularly significant because he explicitly insists that this right survives the social contract. For the larger context which is essential for understanding Locke's place in the history of the transformation of the conception of charity, see Robert Bernasconi, "The Poor Box and the Changing Face of Charity in Early Modern Europe," *Acta Institutionis Philosophiae et Aestheticae* 10 (1992): 33–54.

17. See, for example, P. P. Cvek, "John Locke, Social Welfare, and the U.S. Constitution," *Synthesis Philosophica* 10 (1990): 633–42; Bruno Rea, "John Locke: Between Charity and Welfare Power," *Journal of Social Welfare* 18 (1987): 13–26; and Kristin Shrader-Frechette, "Locke and Limits on Land Ownership," *Journal of the History of Ideas* 54 (1993): 201–219. Locke is clear in a paper written for the Board of Trade in 1697 that the community is obliged to attend to the poor, so that a parish should be fined if a person were to die there for want of relief. See H. R. Fox Bourne, *The Life of John Locke* (Bristol: Thoemmes Press, 1991), 1: 390. This is because by agreeing to the invention of money, nobody can be understood to have agreed to the possibility of exchanging nature's plenty for starving to death, whatever the other possible benefits, because that would have put at risk what nobody has the right to dispose of: God's property in their person (*2T*, sec-

ROBERT BERNASCONI

tion 27, p. 287). Nevertheless, the focus of Locke's proposals is on reducing the burden that falls on the industrious for maintaining the poor by making them work (p. 378). It should also be noted that even though the *right* of the poor to charity disappears, it might still "always be a Sinn in any Man of Estate, to let his Brother perish for want of affording him Relief out of his Plenty" (*1T,* section 41, p. 170).

18. It is true that to cultivate a field is already to exhibit a concern for the future, but it is a concern still contained by the cycle of nature rather than a future in which something permanent can be established. Locke's account of desire is actually more complex than it has been presented here. One would need to take account of the transformation of the notion of desire between the two editions of the *Essay Concerning Human Understanding.* See Jonathan Brody Kramnick, "Locke's Desire," *Yale Journal of Criticism* 12, # 2 (1999): 189–208. As far as the *Two Treatises* is concerned, only C. B. Macpherson saw the importance of desire for Locke's argument. However, he posed it as an unresolved problem in Locke's text, whereas I have presented it as governing the text's dynamics. See C. B. Macpherson, *The Political Theory of Possessive Individualism* (Oxford: Oxford University Press, 1979), 204–235.

19. Arendt refers to Locke in drawing the distinction. She cites Locke's phrase "the labor of his Body and the Work of his Hands" (*2T,* section 27, pp. 287–88) in *The Human Condition* (Chicago: University of Chicago Press, 1958), 79. Although I do not think that at that point Locke believes he is making an important distinction, I do believe that the distinction, as Arendt understands it, is helpful for illuminating the change which is introduced with the invention of money.

20. For a summary of the position adopted by Church Fathers, see Rev. A. J. Carlyle, "The Theory of Property in Mediaeval Theology," in *Property, Its Duties and Rights,* ed. Charles Gore (London: Macmillan, 1913), 118–32.

21. Max Weber, *The Protestant Ethic and the Spirit of Capitalism,* trans. Talcott Parsons (London: Unwin, 1930), 159.

22. The use of these terms should not leave the impression that Locke holds a labor theory of value. See Karen Iverson Vaughn, *John Locke: Economist and Social Scientist* (London: Athlone Press, 1980). It should be added that value for Locke was always in relation to man—intrinsic value was not natural but use value. That value became integrated into a system of exchange.

From Kristeva to Deleuze: The Encyclopedists and the Philosophical Imaginary

Katherine Arens

This essay ties the work of Julia Kristeva on linguistics into the general postwar critique of the Enlightenment, but not in the form of the Enlightenment project so familiar to the Anglo-American world. Instead, it addresses a more technical, disciplinary critique of the Enlightenment most familiar from Michel Foucault but also shared by Gilles Deleuze, Félix Guattari, Michèle Le Doeuff, and others. Together, they critique the rationalism of Enlightenment disciplinary practices that have been naturalized in today's academy as truth-producing narratives.

To make this case, I take Kristeva's account of the Encyclopedists' linguistics from *Language, The Unknown: An Initiation to Linguistics*[1] as a paradigmatic critique of a rationalist system realized as an emergent discipline. There she argues how the alignment of that (and much current) linguistics with philosophy naturalizes a discipline constructed as if it were a natural science, a choice with very specific epistemological gains and losses. Against this background, Kristeva's own linguistics, aligned with psychoanalysis rather than the natural sciences, emerges as a critical philosophy challenging Enlightenment disciplines to produce knowledge as historical and critical sciences of self rather than as master disciplines of abstract systems. In this way Kristeva's work on linguistics challenges the rationalization of academic disciplines that the Enlightenment has naturalized as the norm for production of truth and knowledge.

This redefinition of linguistics exemplifies the critique of technologies of reason that also emerges in Gilles Deleuze and Félix Guattari's *What is Philosophy?* As does Kristeva, Deleuze and Guattari reject the naturalized legacy of Enlightenment disciplines, in this case philosophy. Where Kristeva argues for a linguistics of embodiment and social ideology rather than logic, Deleuze and Guattari reject the disciplinary habit of philosophy that separates epistemology, ontology, and ethics. These two critiques

KATHERINE ARENS

of Enlightenment disciplines lead beyond simple institutional or disciplinary analyses more familiar from Foucault's work into the heart of the critical project espoused by the so-called poststructuralist generation of French theorists and philosophers, including Barthes, Lacan, and French feminism. They thus share methodological premises and the goal of renovating the human sciences as systematic disciplines which no longer exclude humanity itself.

The Enlightenment and Its Science

Kristeva's putative textbook, *Language, The Unknown,* "initiates" her readers not just into the sciences of language but also, and more important, into the strategic critique of disciplines that Kristeva shares with her contemporaries. Outwardly a history of linguistics as a discipline that has had various theory bases over history, her book reappropriates various aspects of that science and its assumed (post-Enlightenment) relation to human society and subjectivity in order to offer a new theoretical basis for contemporary linguistics.

Kristeva claims that Encyclopedist linguistics is based on the limiting ideological and theoretical configurations favored by Enlightenment rationalism and is thus an epistemological system privileging formal knowledge of systems rather than, for example, social uses of language. Consequently, Kristeva uses a critique of linguistics to question the purportedly value-neutral methodology of the natural sciences as "modern" disciplines. This assumption of value neutrality, she argues, has been naturalized by long practice but obscures the historicity of each discipline's practice of knowledge production and thus our ability to critique each as ideological social practices. Assuming that "scientific" disciplinary formations are neutral circumscribes, if not proscribes, our ability to trace the specific ideological relationships between the discipline's subject of knowledge and the more general social field in which it operates. *Language, the Unknown* addresses not only the formalisms of science as epistemological constructs but also the ideology of the human sciences since the Enlightenment in order to exemplify the institutional analyses of social and disciplinary power developed, for example, by Foucault. Her "initiation into linguistics" thus offers a genealogy of power relations hidden behind a discipline's appeal to science.

In *Language, the Unknown* Kristeva addresses the grammar of Port Royal as the exemplar of the early modern era's rule-bound grammars. The grammarians of Port Royal sought to have French, a vernacular, compete with the perfection of the Latin language—in essence, to describe French with a terminology that grants it social and intellectual parity with Latin (*LU* 159). In creating this system, they relied on Descartes, who had divorced things from ideas and thus made language subservient to ideas (*LU* 160). The solution proposed by the Port Royal thinkers and expressed in their *Grammar* and *Logic* retained a strong bias toward ideas:

> they reintroduced the medieval theory of the sign that the humanists-formalists had forgotten, or at least silenced. *La langue* was indeed a system, as Sanctius had demonstrated, but a system of signs. Words and linguistic expressions clothed ideas that referred back to objects. The logical or natural relation, which revealed the truth about things, was at work at the level of ideas: the logical level. Grammar would deal with an object, *la langue,* that was only the sign of this logical and/or natural dimension. In this way, *la langue* would depend upon logic, while having its own autonomy. This was the methodological *coup de force* that allowed a common and necessary ratio to be posited as the core of *la langue.* On this ratio, in relation to it but also at a distance from it, the interplay of specifically linguistic signs—forms—would operate, and the laws of a new linguistic construction would be specified. (*LU* 161)

The first lines of the *Grammar* designate speaking as the main component of language; grammar studied the reason (*ratio*) behind the system of spoken signs of language, with the spoken word (*logos*) as its revealed form.

In the following chapter, "The *Éncyclopédie: La Langue* and Nature," Kristeva traces how this first systematic grammar, one that equated language with logic (a *langue*), was adapted in a very specific ideological context to accommodate new models of human nature: "Language was seen as a variety of idioms based on the same logical rules, which constituted a kind of constant, human nature. . . . [The Encyclopedists sought to free language] from the impact of Latin . . . and from its dependency on logic" (*LU* 172). That is, construed as part of a spoken logic, language now claimed more than a tie to abstract logical form; it acquired a "natural" foundation, anchored in the materiality of creation and human nature. Not surprisingly, the origin of language also emerged as a new theoretical requirement: "The variety of language had to be taken back to a common, natural source where linguistic universals were articulated. In order to establish the relation between natural language, real objects, and sensation, a theory of the sign was proposed" (*LU* 172). Thus the eighteenth century made its own linguistics a parallel to philosophy, but not its interchangeable equivalent:

> On the grammatical level, which was, by the way, inseparable from the philosophical one, since every philosopher in the eighteenth century tackled language and every grammarian was a philosopher, the particularity of specifically linguistic relations, differentiated from the (logical) laws of thinking, was brought to light, and led to a syntactic description of sentence and inter-sentence relations. (*LU* 172–73)

At this point Kristeva acknowledges the emergence of a new focus in the development of theory-formation relationships in linguistics. She finds the genesis of this paradigm in Vico and his assumption that speech is mental (and thus divine) language that emerges in different historical forms, such as the hieroglyphs, "poetic," or "heroic" language (*LU* 173). The Encyclopedists, however, found this historicist account to be lacking in scientific rigor and so they subjected Vico's analysis of language to "the spirit of classification and systematization that invaded the sciences of that century" (*LU* 174). They drew in other sources, such as Leibniz's discussion of Adamic language (a sensationalist approach), which hoped to recreate the purity of the origin of language in an artificial language; and James Harris's theories in England, which extended Berkeley's philosophy to outline the roots of a general grammar. The result was a theory of language (represented in works by De Brosses, Abbot Pluche, and Nicolas Beauzée) that stressed structure: "Language appeared to be an operational system, a mechanics whose rules could be studied like those of any physical object" (*LU* 175).

At the same time, the Encyclopedists also tried to accommodate a sensationalist, more constructivist, account of mind and knowledge, in addition to the earlier a priorist ones. As they saw it, Locke had taken words as marks of ideas, but they noted that the signs also had apparent relations to history. Leibniz followed in this vein, keeping language attached to ideas. But the new French accounts transformed these impulses into a special language for talking about language, creating a new discipline. This new linguistic terminology conceives universals as "natural" variations of underlying logical forms, emerging due to concrete influence of social conditions and history: "Condillac maintained that the original language named what was directly given to the senses: first things, then operations; first "fruit," then "to want," and lastly "Peter" (*LU* 180). Nonetheless, the new disciplinary metalanguage would still present logical relations as the "natural" ground of all linguistic expression, one

> that began sentences with the subject and ended them with what one wanted to say about his subject. Evolution and change were likely with both these categories of language for two reasons: climate and govern-

ment. The idea that social conditions influenced the character of a language seems to be creeping in here, but Condillac exalted the role of the inspired individual much more than that of the social organism. His theory was, nonetheless, materialistic. (*LU* 180)

This new scientific empiricism of linguistics drew on another source as well: Destutt de Tracy and his study of ideologies. In this frame, language is seen as a system of signs, each "dressed" according to real experience, and with meaning affected by syntax (its position in an utterance). Here, the inheritance of Port Royal decisively joins that of the Ideologues.

Not surprisingly, the "rational and deterministic sensationalism" that resulted did not satisfy all new materialists. For instance, Rousseau tried to tie language more closely to the user when he stressed not discourse but passions as the true seat of language. In Kristeva's account, it took Diderot to complete a "materialistic conception of language" that posited language as a logic and as a sensationalist system:

> Diderot took up the major themes developed by the Sensationalists and Ideologues: the sign and its relation to the idea and perceptible reality; the types of language in history; the development of language; alphabetism and hieroglyphy; types of signifying systems that were like languages (the arts: poetry, painting, music), etc. He definitely and resolutely placed the rough drafts of the Ideologues and Sensationalists on a rigorously material base, by proposing one of the first modern materialist syntheses dealing with the theory of knowledge, and consequently, of linguistic operation. (*LU* 182)

This is the linguistic thought that comes to fruition in the *Éncyclopédie* in articles by Turgot and Voltaire. The formalist grammars of the older generation yielded to a new technical terminology and analysis strategy "that still goes on in traditional grammar teaching," where the "natural order" of a sentence becomes its anatomy (*LU* 186). Thus, for example, the genitive "marks the relation of one thing that belongs to another by production, or by use/possession, or by any other manner" (*LU* 185–86). Such theories defined the clause, defined syntactically as a system of complementation, as the discipline's unit of analysis. The science that dealt with it had two levels of analysis—one grammatical and the other logical-situational (*LU* 188).

In the era's critical grammatical works, such as those of the Abbot Girard (1747) and Du Marais, declensions on the Latin model disappeared, and syntactical elements such as prepositions became important evidence of language's logic. It was Beauzée, however, who provided the final methodological innovations in his articles on government and binding ("Régime" and "Gouverner") for the *Encyclopedia*. These exemplified the methodological center of the new science, later formalized in his *Grammaire generale* (1767):

> The descriptions wandered from logicism to semanticism or went back to Aristotelian categories, but the framework of the syntactic study was fixed and has remained so for scholastic grammarians up to the present. The bourgeoisie had succeeded in forging a sure ideological weapon for itself: it surrounded language with the logical framework classicism had bequeathed it, while granting it suppleness and relative autonomy when it turned the analysis slightly toward linguistic "facts." Universalism and empiricism, interpenetrating one another, modeled this conception of sentence construction that the grammar of the eighteenth century had been able to elaborate on the foundation of a "natural" conception of language. (*LU* 189)

The later nineteenth century would move away from describing "mechanism" and "systematization" toward a more explicit historicism:

> While the grammarians of Port Royal had demonstrated that language obeyed the principles of the logic of judgment, and while the Encyclopedists wanted to see in it the logic of perceptible nature and the confirmation of the influence of material circumstances (climate, government), the nineteenth century wanted to demonstrate that language itself also had an evolution, so that on this evolution they could base the principle of the evolution of the idea and society. (*LU* 194–95)

No matter how empiricist this shift may seem to today's historians of linguistics, Kristeva still classifies this science of language as abstract, stressing methods to organize reproducible data into systems. In one sense, Kristeva's account of this linguistic theory-formation starts as a Foucauldian archaeology, outlining how a linguistics based on logic yields to one based on natural attributes, privileging different images of mind and linguistic meaning. Yet where Foucault was interested in "technologies of the self"—the ways in which individuals are themselves rationalized into the framework of a state apparatus (to borrow a term from Althusser) —Kristeva is interested in more than a historical archeology. She wishes instead to move beyond the Enlightenment's legacy and refound linguistics as a human science (*Geisteswissenschaft, science humaine*), as a systematic study of language as communication (not as a syntax system, whether logical or natural).

Kristeva is thus interested in remapping the formal science of linguistics, a science that has not moved appreciably beyond its Enlightenment roots. Her goal is to produce a new science, a semanalysis (*sémanalyse*), as a decisively interdisciplinary and humanistic critical discourse analysis, resisting the trends of analysis of knowledge and power in place since the Enlightenment.[2] Her semanalysis represents a new disciplinary paradigm apart from the traditional orthodoxies of linguistics; it thus redefines the discipline's subjects and objects of knowledge alike.

Language, the Unknown

Where Enlightenment linguistics purported to be a science of communication (based on the spoken language rather than on logic), a *sémanalyse* has a broader theoretical claim. Kristeva hopes to force linguistics to "refound itself in a general theory of signification" (*LU* 328) and thus transcend its very clear contemporary limits. A semanalysis is more than a science of logic and communication; it is a science of human signifying practices.

The act of "signification" (*signifiance*) becomes the key to this new science because it highlights the user of language rather than language's structure (as in formalist linguistics). "Signification" refers to the set of practices used by individuals in the act of communication, some of which are language based, some more social, physical, traditional, or semiotic in nature. Her new analysis thus does not start with postulates from logic (pure or communicative) but rather with the social stratification of signifying practices in concrete historical space, a study of ideology-marked acts in social-historical context. Semanalysis privileges not the language system but rather the subject who uses language and other signifying system (acts or signs). It outlines how an individual acquires (occupies, defines) a "subject position" or social identity within the field of signifying practices through which a group articulates its values, identities, and goals. That is, Kristeva's post-Enlightenment linguistics becomes the science not of language structure but of how a subject is established as a "speaking subject,"[3] as a social subject of knowledge who possesses agency within the communication community.

Crucially, the *sémanalyse* of a speaking subject is much more than a sociolinguistic analysis, which would focus more straightforwardly on how available language *structures* allow individuals to mark their belonging to specific sociological groups. Kristeva's new science of signification is much more radical and of greater scope, since she will not discuss "users" of

"forms" but rather how usages (speech acts, acts of constructing knowledge, acts of self-assertion) are configured and occupied by speakers and
writers within the group. She will study not only how linguistic forms cor-
relate with users' intended results but also the users' (subjects) social and
psychological identities as correlated with group ideology and agency.[4]

Her analysis of the Encyclopedists' linguistics grounds Kristeva's
entire remapping of the theoretical paradigm for her linguistics as *sémanalyse*. For example, her textbook begins by borrowing terms from Saus-
sure, noting that the study of *langage* (the complex phenomenon of language in theory and practice, competence and performance) has been
reduced to the study of *la langue* (the formal properties of language). The
user of a language, the speaker and her actual expressions (*parole*), have
traditionally been elided in the history of linguistics, in which language
"was made the privileged object of thought, science, and philosophy" (*LU*
3). That is, the Enlightenment's science of language followed the empiricism of the new pure sciences, which led them to study human language
as a system divorced from spirit. In a real sense, then, the Encyclopedists
described *la langue* as an artifact system and granted it primacy and
authority over individual uses of language, *paroles*. Kristeva describes her
analysis in contrasting terms:

> it hopes to find the general principles and elements [of that system],
> which one can call the linguistic universals. *La langue* therefore appears
> to be not an evolution, a family tree, or a history, but a structure with
> laws and operational rules that must be described. The separation
> *langue*/speech (*parole*), paradigm/syntagm, synchrony/diachrony . . .
> indicates very well this orientation of linguistics toward *la langue*, para-
> digm, and synchrony rather than toward speech, syntagm, and
> diachrony. (*LU* 218)

This formal paradigm for linguistics as a science is exhausted, she
believes, because, perhaps unwittingly, it has reduced the social world to
an abstract system, even while claiming attention to the empiricism. Today's psychoanalysis and semiotics highlight that reduction by accounting
for other dimensions of language in use, beyond formalist paradigms.
Just as important, the exhausted linguistics is ideologically intertwined
with modern technocratic society and its focus on rationalized, abstract
structures. In contrast, a *sémanalyse* ties affect, power, and status into the
knowledge and communication potential conveyed in language.

Kristeva's semanalysis veers away from the study of abstract systems:
"it will take into account the subject, the diversity of modes of signification, and the historical transformation of these modes in order to refound

itself in a general theory of signification" (*LU* 328). This new linguistics will thus interpret language systems as part of human activity, as part of a greater set of social signifying practices supporting communication:

> Whoever says language says demarcation, signification, and communication. In this sense, all human practices are kinds of language because they have as their function to demarcate, to signify, to communicate. To exchange goods and women in the social network, to produce objects of art or explanatory discourses such as religions or myths, etc. is to form a sort of secondary linguistic system with respect to language, and on the basis of this system to install a communications circuit with subjects, meaning, and signification. (*LU* 4)

Kristeva thus retains the scientific dimension of *sémanalyse* (its systematicity) while correcting linguistics' privileging of logical systems over the users of language, which has divorced language forms from their realizations in media (speech, writing systems, sign systems) that all serve the purpose of communication.

Defining a new approach to science also redefines an object of study. Whereas linguistics studies language systems, semanalysis studies discourses in use in individuals' acts within a communication or speech community:

> Discourse implies first the participation of the subject in his language through his speech, as an individual. Using the anonymous structure of *la langue,* the subject forms and transforms himself in the discourse he communicates to the other. *La langue,* common to all, becomes in discourse the vehicle of a unique message. Without being aware of it, the subject thus makes his mark on *la langue.* . . . The term "discourse," on the other hand, designates any enunciation that integrates in its structure the locutor and the listener, with the desire of the former to influence the latter. (*LU* 11)

In this sense, Kristeva is accounting for the "materiality" of language (the title of her chapter 3): the "concrete matter and the objective laws of its organization. . . . laws that organize the different subsets of the linguistic whole, and that constitute phonetics, grammar, stylistics, semantics, etc." (*LU* 18), along with the materiality of the communication situation (the historical setting, the users involved, and the like).

This redefined object of study thus immediately signals the emergence of a new science, one of greater scope than any formal linguistics. Thus Kristeva incorporates into the traditional subfields of formal linguistics (logic, lexicography, grammar, syntax) other ways of studying language phenomena, especially studies of writing and speech as communication. Thus Kristeva includes as part of semanalysis disciplines such as rhetoric and stylistics that have not traditionally been part of linguistics but are necessary to descriptions of how individual subjects are produced in and produce discourse. From these viewpoints, language is more than *langue* and *parole;* it includes social-signifying "practices" in many forms, permeating human lives and subject to discrete investigation. Such forms of "language" are still largely alien to formalist linguistics, but they need not be since they are available to study as an archive of material data in documents of social functions and subjects' social identities.

Kristeva's theoretical move changes not only the objects and methods of linguistics but also the ideological and truth-producing functions that it serves within the domain of science. To use a term from Jean-François Lyotard,[5] she has changed the regime of truth produced by the sciences' practices and signifiers. Semanalysis becomes a science of historically attested forms of human subjectivity at play in communication—a science of discourse. Its goal is to study historical forms of discourse as they answer to particular needs of its speech community:

> A discourse bears and imposes an ideology, and every ideology finds its discourse. One can then understand why every dominant class pays particular attention to the practice of language and controls its forms and the means of its distribution: the news, the press, literature. One can understand why a dominant class has its favorite languages, its literature, its press, its orators, and why it tends to censor any other language. . . . Literature is no doubt the privileged realm in which language is exercised, clarified, and modified. (*LU* 287)

The study of language thus becomes the study of social ideology in play in communication, and the study of its material forms as they condition individual identities within a community as epistemes of practice and knowledge.

This redefinition of linguistics from a formalist tradition into a *sémanalyse* in a more humanist-critical mode enacts a double move within a history of the human sciences.

First and foremost, it works within the tradition of linguistics to renovate what Kristeva considers an antiquated science model inherited from the Enlightenment. What up through Noam Chomsky and the transformational-generativist schools of linguistics has been a linguistics in the mode of natural science is remapped in Kristeva's work as a *science humaine*. More than an abstract *Geisteswissenschaft*, it models a systematic approach to analyzing communication within social groups. That new "human science" uses as its data set the materially attested acts of communication through which individuals enter into the group as subjects of knowledge and achieve psycho-social identities constructed in response to the ideologies embedded in that group's communication and knowledge systems. Kristeva thus redefines the scope of the linguistic sciences to make what has been a range of relatively discrete disciplines, each claiming aspects of value-neutral natural sciences, into a more comprehensive and coherent discipline that takes as central to its charge the analysis of forms that produce and reproduce ideologies, identity, and power each time they emerge in acts of communication.

Kristeva's second important theoretical move in defining a *sémanalyse* thus points beyond linguistics itself to reclaim a new approach to epistemology in historical context. Her redefinition of the *speaking subject* also redefines the *knowing subject,* what Lacan calls the *sujet supposé savoir*—the subject not only authorized as a producer and purveyor of knowledge but also instantiated and interpolated into a material form within a system of knowledge that creates that subject as its author/authority.[6] In this model, the analyst does not consider the subject of knowledge as creator but rather as an *authorized subject/producer of knowledge within a communication community.*

Kristeva is alone in the poststructural generation in taking on linguistics (and, by extension, the linguistic turn in philosophy) in the context of critiques of disciplinary power since the Enlightenment. However, the link between the social-psychological and critical linguistics posited as a semanalysis connects her work with that generational project no matter how it is labeled. "Pure science" emerges as implicated in epistemologies and social formations of power that may be considered the material forms of ideology in historical contexts. Her work on the history of formalist linguistics clearly parallels now-familiar critiques of power, disciplinary knowledge, and their subjects or agents by Derrida, Le Doeuff, and Deleuze and Guattari.[7]

If Deleuze and Guattari's model of how a discipline's preferred meaning units create a world peopled by particular agents of knowledge is compared to Kristeva's model of how Enlightenment linguistics needs to move into a semanalysis, an additional dimension of her program emerges that illuminates the strength of Deleuze's analysis as well. What Deleuze defines as a conceptual persona Kristeva has called the "speaking subject" of a system, reflecting her preferred focus on the sense of empowerment or lack thereof which an agent of knowledge experiences in transacting meanings within the system. Deleuze and Guattari take this pattern somewhat further. Enlightenment linguistics' privileged logic is revealed in its distinct meaning units, which are distinctly different from the concepts of philosophy or the percepts and affects of art. Linguistics deals in meaning units such as *morphemes* (structural forms of words), *phonemes* (sound units), and *syntagmemes* (structural units within sentences or other complete utterances). These indeed are units of meaning that intend a world of logical structure and relations, with "language" as the name given to that world's horizon of expectations, its plane of meanings. The linguist emerges as a conceptual persona interested in formal relations and is closer to a scientist than to a philosopher because a *morpheme* has, in the world of linguistics, in many ways a less concrete, less multiple referent on the plane of meaning than does a *concept* in linguistics.

In contrast, the semanalysis as Kristeva drew it in *Language, the Unknown,* focuses on *semes,* units of signification, each which functions as a reference point for understandings which necessarily extract different kinds of knowledge and expressions from the plane of the discipline's practice. A *seme* necessarily materializes an understanding in a form that encompasses social relations as well as logical ones, personal-psychological intentions as well as meanings, their forms, and the logical relationships among those forms (more traditional semantics, morphology, or syntax, respectively). Kristeva's semanalysis thus is a science producing understandings that necessarily account for speakers and signifiers, signs and their agents, meanings and the power relations effecting their transfers. Semanalysis thus includes agents in a way that linguistics does not.

Deleuze and Guattari sketch philosophy as producing professionals, the particular actors inhabiting its plane. The concepts on that plane also point toward or intend the acts or events that can occur or which actors can initiate or experience in that meaning world of philosophy:[8]

> Concepts are concrete assemblages, like the configurations of a machine, but the plane is the abstract machine of which these assemblages are the working parts. Concepts are events, but the plane is the horizon of events, the reservoir or reserve of purely conceptual events: not the relative horizon that functions as a limit, which changes with an observer and encloses observable states of affairs, but the absolute horizon, independent of any observer, which makes the event as concept independent of a visible state of affairs in which it is brought about. Concepts pave, occupy, or populate the plane bit by bit, whereas the plane itself is the indivisible milieu in which concepts are distributed without breaking up its continuity or integrity. (*WP* 36)

Each plane thus ultimately becomes populated by "tribes," communities of conceptual personae—in this case, "professionals"—who produce and reproduce linkages among various concepts and bring the philosophy to life by "populating" that plane as its conceptual personae.[9]

This interaction between meaning-producing units of reference (here: concepts) and the plane on which they assemble themselves into a world shows how an abstract plane of reality acquires a concrete dimension:

> The conceptual persona is not the philosopher's representative but, rather, the reverse: the philosopher is only the envelope of his principal conceptual persona and of all the other personae who are the intercessors [*intercesseurs*], the real subjects of his philosophy. Conceptual personae are the philosopher's "heteronyms," and the philosopher's name is the simple pseudonym of his personae. . . . The conceptual persona is the becoming or the subject of a philosophy. (*WP* 64)

In other words, a philosophy creates its appropriate subject, the person who is master of its discourse, who benefits from its symbolic power (to borrow the term from Pierre Bourdieu).[10] Philosophy is under the management of professionals, stressing an authority of knowledge.

By fulfilling the identity potential of a plane's conceptual persona, a philosopher-subject also helps to give a discipline of philosophy its aesthetic form, its style of interacting with and enacting the philosophical plane's affects and percepts (what might be termed its autopoesis). The system thus creates its users:

> The difference between conceptual personae and aesthetic figures consists first of all in this: the former are the powers of concepts, and the latter are the powers of affects and percepts. The former take effect on a plane of immanence that is an image of Thought-Being (*noumenon*), and the latter take effect on a plane of composition as the image of a Universe (*phenomenon*). (*WP* 65)

Thus the discipline of philosophy not only has a distinct plane on which meanings come into existence through the mediation of concepts but also populates its plane with particular conceptual personae (professionals). The assemblage that results also has its own autopoesis, its own aesthetics of "affects and percepts" that results in a distinctive style.

The new philosophy that Deleuze and Guattari point to as the answer to "What is Philosophy?" is not, then, the traditional discipline of logic, systems, and truths. Instead it is a discipline that sponsors a "logo-drama" or "figurality." In this sense, Kierkegaard's work, where he tests truths against the experience of figureal types, is paradigmatic, joining affects to thoughts to stage enactments of his philosophy's concepts on a plane of immanence, in a determinate here and now (*WP* 66):

> The role of conceptual personae is to show thought's territories, its absolute deterritorializations and reterritorializations. Conceptual per-

> sonae are thinkers, solely thinkers, and their personalized features are
> closely linked to the diagrammatic features of thought and the intensive
> features of concepts. (*WP* 69)

The conceptual personae of philosophy—its authorized, "native speaker" cast of characters—thus make overt the covert sets of features in the concepts as related on the plane of philosophy: relational, dynamic, juridical, and existential features (*WP* 70, 72). For Deleuze and Guattari, then, philosophy is not simply a system of ideas or truths, or a system of ideas that creates a profession administered by an institution.

Yet this *model* of what philosophy could be by no means corresponds with an existing philosophy. The philosophy which Deleuze and Guattari know from the present has claimed its existence only on a single plane, as a region of consistency of knowledge and action—a largely formalist system. A different vision of philosophy is possible: a discipline that could also demonstrate how concepts condition a particular lived historical reality as its conceptual personae turn their intentionality into the extensionality of lived experience.

In its new incarnation, philosophy would not be defined as prior to or anterior to the world of society, meaning, and ideologies, since it creates that world and the individuals in it, just as they create it. Similarly, defining philosophy as having intensive and extensive appearances means that it will have a different form in each historical epoch. That is, it will *territorialize* its plane of immanence differently (as the term is used in *A Thousand Plateaus*) and so its concepts will create different personae within the type. This move is crucial in opening a science of knowledge to an ideological critique and to a kind of relativity, since each philosophy will privilege different styles and assemblages, different alignments of concepts, and hence different conceptual personae within the general framework of philosophical knowledge.

At this point, Deleuze and Guattari tie their disciplinary critique to an explicit historical and social one, very parallel to Kristeva's remapping of linguistics into a more modern form. In the case of philosophy, a very distinct style and truth claim has emerged: modernity's plane of knowledge has been territorialized, split, between the discourses of philosophy, art, logic, and science. Philosophy analyzes and relates concepts; science traces functions; logic traces the forms of prospects or predictions (section 6); and art deals with systems of affects and percepts (below the level of concepts). Thus the "philosophical imaginary" of modern philosophy includes an unusually disembodied vision of the discipline's practices, paying little attention to the professionals and their contribution to its knowledge (let alone to the jurisdiction or administration of that knowledge). Contemporary philosophy, then, has generated knowledge that underplays the significance of the actors who instantiate knowledge's concepts and thus tends to overlook the historicity of the system's manipulation of concepts on a material plane of immanence.

This points to a potentially devastating critique of modern philosophy, since Deleuze and Guattari argue for a philosophy that combines considerations of value and intention in conjunction with knowledge and truth, as well as with human motivation (in the form of conceptual personae acting with particular styles). To accept a philosophy of any lesser scope is to settle for a discipline of knowledge that impoverishes the field of the known and knowing, just as Kristeva showed that a formalist linguistics did to the truth of language.

In the critique shared by Kristeva, Le Doeuff, Deleuze, and Guattari, a discipline should no longer be defined by its objects or by the systems of knowledge it produced—that is the legacy of the Enlightenment that has proved itself persistent but inadequate for the modern epistemology of disciplines. Instead, all knowledge production must be evaluated in full acknowledgment of the ideology inherent in a discipline's particular scheme or organization of knowledge, its own style and language. Each discipline, like each dialect of a language, is thus more than a system or assemblage of signifiers (words, concepts). Each is also instantiated in a unique historical form; each has equivalent (not identical) elements that embody both knowledge and ideology in historical space.[11]

Conclusion

Seemingly disparate accounts of the modern era's characteristic linguistics and philosophy therefore not only share a description of the origin and forms of the human sciences but also critique their potential for power and for creating agency or passivity in the subjects who engage in them. In particular, Kristeva's example aims at questioning modern science's ability to naturalize relative concept formations as being value free. *Language, the Unknown* argues how one of those sciences, linguistics, can attain a new, more humanist, and more critical form if it becomes a semanalysis, a more truly human science rather than a mechanistic one. As her example of the Encyclopedist linguists demonstrates, post-Enlightenment disciplines have become systematic and form driven—driven by abstracts rather than accounting for the ideologies and conceptual personae that are formed simultaneously with the preferred theory-formation patterns.

Deleuze and Guattari (reflected also in Le Doeuff) tell an even

KATHERINE ARENS

more complex story. Up through the Enlightenment, philosophy had been closer to other fields, virtually an incubator for other fields of study and professional activities, as Kant argues in his way in *Conflict of Faculties* (1798). Philosophy, for example, was the university study which included the natural sciences (under the term "natural philosophy") until the eighteenth century and which formed the umbrella for many of the social sciences in nineteenth-century Germany. Yet the form that philosophy assumed after the Enlightenment—its plane of immanence and territorialization vis-à-vis other human sciences—has remained very constant in a single dominant form, as the discipline of philosophers mastering concepts, a formalistic-logocentric discipline.

If one sought to remap philosophy to overcome these limits, in the way Kristeva did for linguistics, then Deleuze's long-term program in the history of philosophy takes on a different face—and his work moves considerably closer to that of Kristeva, Lyotard, and Foucault than many have assumed. As do they, he argues that disciplinary knowledge does not exist apart from the ideology of its plane of immanence because it posits its own professionals as agents of its distinctive style of knowledge production. Deleuze has made this point earlier, in studies of earlier disciplinary formations from the history of philosophy, from Leibniz and Kant through Nietzsche. These philosophers enter into knowledge production in ways unlike that of today's philosophers: They are agents of different kinds of knowledge than we know today as the purview of philosophy.

Thus Deleuze presents our contemporary map of philosophy just as Kristeva discussed linguistics: as a historical legacy of the Enlightenment that needs to be questioned, especially as it maintains as "natural" a formalist split among its subdisciplines within a formalist concept of knowledge production. Ontology, epistemology, and ethics can no more represent the dynamics of knowledge production and reproduction than syntax, morphology, and phonology can the dynamics of language. Yet by asserting these subdisciplines as producers of valid knowledge, the Enlightenment has taught us to ignore philosophy's engagement with the plane of immanence, its historical contexts, and the ideologies enacted by the personae acting within its network of concepts.

By identifying these strategic exclusions as part of the Enlightenment's legacy of discipline formation and knowledge, contemporary French theorists call into question the formalist master narratives of knowledge that characterize modernity. They thus retrieve the subject of knowledge and the communication community in which that subject is implicated and produced, focusing on ideology as central (and hence in need of critique) to any act of knowledge production. In this way they indicate how the philosophical imaginary of modernity, comprising as it does concepts of knowledge apart from values and removed from its agents, can be reconceived—as Deleuze and Guattari do particularly in *A Thousand Plateaus*—to highlight subjectivity, institution, agent, and values within community in a renewed effort to valorize humanity rather than the empty formalism of modernity.

Notes

1. Julia Kristeva, *Le Langage: cet inconnu* (Paris: Éditions du Seuil, 1981); *Language, The Unknown: An Initiation into Linguistics*, trans. Anne M. Menke (New York: Columbia University Press, 1989); hereafter *LU*.

2. For more detailed discussions of this point, see Katherine Arens, "The Linguistics of French Feminism: Sémanalyse as Critical Discourse Practice," *Intertexts* 2 (1998): 171–184; and "Discourse Analysis as Critical Historiography: A *Sémanalyse* of Mystic Speech," *Rethinking History* 2 (1998): 23–50.

3. The term is featured most prominently in Kristeva's essay "The System and the Speaking Subject," in *The Tell-Tale Sign: A Survey of Semiotics*, ed. Thomas A. Sebeok (Lisse: Peter De Ridder, 1975), 47–55; rpt. *The Kristeva Reader*, ed. Toril Moi (New York: Columbia University Press, 1986), 24–33.

4. An aside: Kristeva's semanalysis also differs from the functionalist approach associated with the Prague School in that she draws from Emile Benveniste the link between the functions of language and the empowerment of the subject/ speaker. The Prague School linguists, including Jan Mukarovsky and Roman Jakobsen, still studied language as a logical system, albeit much more in tune with users than in today's transformational-generative grammar. Kristeva (and her contemporary Tzvetan Todorov) clearly knows the work of the Prague School and draws on their descriptions of interactions between language systems and readers, yet she develops her semanalysis around the subject/speaker in a way that moves far beyond their work.

5. See Jean-François Lyotard, *The Differend: Phrases in Dispute*, trans. Georges Van Den Abbeele (Minneapolis: University of Minnesota Press, 1988), xii, for a discussion of phrase regimes.

6. This discussion is explicated in Jacques Lacan, *Four Fundamental Concepts of Psychoanalysis*, ed. Jacques-Alain Miller; trans. Alan Sheridan (New York: W.W. Norton, 1998).

7. See, for example, Jacques Derrida, "Mochlos; or, The Conflict of the Faculties," in *Logomachia: The Conflict of the Faculties*, ed. Richard Rand (Lincoln: University of Nebraska Press, 1992), 1–32, especially 20–21; Michèle Le Doeuff, *Hipparchia's Choice: An Essay Concerning Women, Philosophy, etc.*, trans. Trista Selous (Oxford: Blackwell, 1991), 135; Michèle Le Doeuff, *The Philosophical Imaginary*, trans. Colin Gordon (Stanford: Stanford University Press, 1989), 1–4, 20, 99, 124–

25; and Gilles Deleuze and Félix Guattari, *What is Philosophy?* trans. Hugh Tomlinson and Graham Burchell (New York: Columbia University Press, 1994) (hereafter *WP*).

8. Deleuze and Guattari emphasize how this is also an intensive spatial mapping: "But in reality, elements of the plane are diagrammatic features, whereas concepts are intensive features. The former are movements of the infinite, whereas the latter are intensive ordinates of these movements, like original sections or differential positions: finite movements in which the infinite is now only speed and each of which constitutes a surface of a volume, an irregular contour marking a halt in the degree of proliferation. The former are directions that are fractal in nature, whereas the latter are absolute dimensions, intensively defined, always fragmentary surfaces or volumes. The former are intuitions, and the latter intensions" (*WP* 93–4).

9. This reference to "planes" is likely a reference to Michel Foucault's *Archaeology of Knowledge,* trans. A. M. Sheridan Smith (New York: Pantheon Books, 1972), which uses this metaphor to investigate the episteme of an era (the set of planes of consistency available).

10. See Pierre Bourdieu, *Language and Symbolic Power,* trans. Gino Raymond and Matthew Adamson (Cambridge: Basil Blackwell, 1991).

11. In *The Philosophical Imaginary,* Le Doeuff picks up this notion of different territorializations in her idea of philosophical imaginaries. When she speaks of Kant, for example (9–11), she specifies that he speaks from a world in which science takes part of the role of philosophy as an "island of reason."

Deleuze's Hume and Creative History of Philosophy

Jay Conway

> Blue-eyed boy: a boy, some blue, and eyes—an assemblage.
> AND . . . AND . . . AND, stammering. Empiricism is nothing
> other than this.
> > Gilles Deleuze and Claire Parnet, *Dialogues,* trans. Hugh
> > Tomlinson and Barbara Habberjam

Gilles Deleuze's remarkable encounter with Hume's empiricism is composed of commentaries and unpredictable applications, moments of silence and scattered allusions. As for the question "What did Deleuze discover in Hume's philosophy?" or better yet "What did he do with Hume's philosophy?" there are no straightforward, which is to say convenient, answers. At the beginning of 1952's *David Hume: Sa vie, son ouevre,* Deleuze and André Cresson remark that one can discern in the life and work of any great philosopher an implicit philosophy, an art of living that relates biography to *ouevre* albeit in complex, indirect ways.[1] This emphasis on what is unspoken but constitutive suggests that Hume's philosophy, but also Deleuze's decision to study and put to use the words of Hume, cannot be understood entirely in terms of method and doctrine. Deleuze did find in Hume's work a set of theoretical positions (a critique of representation, a principle of difference, an account of subjectivity). But it should be acknowledged at the outset that he found a style or orientation as much as a content. This style is a mistrust of abstraction, a suspicion of organicism, and an interest in novelty. This style is a display of humor and irreverence—qualities Deleuze's own writings came to exemplify.

Identifying the historical significance of Deleuze's involvement with Hume is complicated by the extent to which it falls outside established narratives of French intellectual life in the fifties and sixties. This is not to say that a book such as 1953's *Empiricism and Subjectivity*—Deleuze's most sustained treatment of Hume's empiricism—seems to come out of nowhere. Rather, it is a way of acknowledging the manner in which Deleuze within the same text changes location, shifts registers, and participates in diverse conversations. In Deleuzian terms, *Empiricism and Subjectivity* is a machine supporting different tasks and permitting different readings. We can regard the book as traditional exegesis, as a critique of phenomenology, as an extension of Jean Wahl's research on Anglo-American philosophy, as an intervention in the methodological debate between historians of philosophy Ferdinand Alquié and Martial Guéroult, as a philosophical response to nascent structuralism, and as a forerunner to poststructuralist theories of difference. *Empiricism and Subjectivity* traverses each of these contexts, and Deleuze's meeting with Hume is more than the sum of these intersections. Therefore, in the following pages I do not elucidate Deleuze's Hume by referring to these general trends. Instead, I delineate those aspects of Hume's philosophy that were important to Deleuze and that represent a bridge connecting a chapter of eighteenth-century philosophy to what is beginning to be known as Deleuzism.

The following presentation is divided into three sections. In the first, I sketch and clarify Deleuze's reading of Hume's work, his reconstruction of Hume's system, by contrasting it with popular views of the philosopher's thought and the significance of empiricism. For Deleuze these views are levels of distortion generated by the history of philosophy, a discipline he associates with assumptions of commensurability and the suppression of historical difference. Through a recovery of the positive, constructive dimension of Hume's thought, Deleuze fashions an image of empiricism as a practical philosophy. In such a philosophy, knowledge is not the identification of first principles or the possession of flawless representations; it is the construction of fictions the value of which lies in their ability to help us get around in the world. In the second section, I indicate the problem or question that Deleuze contends is the essence of empiricism: What are the conditions required for the formation of the speaking subject (for the formation of a being that believes, judges, and says "I")? Given Hume's definition of the mind and his conception of the subject, the question is that of how distinct, separable ideas are related. As such it represents a way of thinking difference nonorganically—a way of thinking with AND rather than IS. In the final section, I make a few general remarks concerning the attitude toward, and way of performing, the history of philosophy that Deleuze expresses in sundry reflections on the topic and exhibits in his work on Hume.

A Theory of Practice

Empiricism, Hume's in particular, is often defined as a simple, point-by-point rejection of Cartesianism.[2] If Cartesianism promotes the doctrine of innate ideas, classical empiricism deems it suspect. If Cartesianism argues for the existence of mental and corporeal substances, empiricism comes to contest the very idea of substance. If the rationalist invokes the idea of moral principles transcending human needs and interests, Hume considers such values illusory. Elucidated thus, as a series of cancellations, empiricism appears to be a largely skeptical enterprise. A closely related approach is that of defining empiricism in terms of sense-experience. On this account, the empiricist, preoccupied with the destruction of reason's palace, chooses as his weapon the thesis that knowledge and meaning are derived from sensation, and leaves as his legacy the bifurcation of discourse into regions of sense and nonsense, science and pseudo-science.

All too often, Hume's writing is described as the culmination of these interrelated moves and strategies. More tenets of rationalism are challenged in his *Treatise* than in other empiricist texts, and these challenges can be perceived as empiricism realizing its potential in conclusions of an extremely skeptical nature. Additionally, many interpretations concentrate on Hume's account of the understanding to the exclusion of his ethics and his theory of the passions. As a result, Hume is largely associated with issues belonging to epistemology or the philosophy of science (the problem of induction, the nature of causation, the distinction between analytic and synthetic propositions, and so forth).

Hume's empiricism is in part a negative response to Cartesianism, but this response is intended only to set the stage for more positive undertakings.[3] For Deleuze, inflating its importance reinforces and is symptomatic of a tacit image of philosophy's history. The assumption is that the history of ideas is a perennial dialogue, or at the very least a number of conversations. Deleuze challenges this assumption, though his remarks do not have to be read as an outright denial of continuity and conversation within philosophical discourse. In *Coldness and Cruelty*, Deleuze shows how the histories of literature and the history of perversion similarly suppress difference.[4] Therefore, we can speak of a general logic of concealment, one infecting the practices of history and interpretation. This logic—the dialectic—does not operate by denying difference altogether. Rather, it proceeds by forcing what is different onto a common plane: Hume's philosophy becomes the inverse of Descartes', masochism becomes the complement of sadism, Sacher-Masoch's *Venus in Furs* becomes Sade's *120 Days* turned upside down. Throughout Deleuze's writings we find him combating this logic of assimilation and doing so through the application of a principal of incommensurability: "In place of a dialectic which all too readily perceives the link between opposites, we should aim for a critical and clinical appraisal able to reveal the truly differential mechanisms as well as the artistic originalities."[5]

Masoch's specificity is recovered when his *ouevre* and that of Sade's are delineated as self-contained, noncommunicating vessels.[6] As for Hume's empiricism, Deleuze's recovery efforts are accomplished through the articulation of a metatheory. By defining theoretical activity as the creation of questions, he jettisons one of the fundamental principles of unity governing the interpretation of philosophical texts.[7] That is, he challenges the penchant for representing disparate theories as different answers to the same question. Applying this metatheory to Hume's philosophy throws light on a series of precise substitutions. New questions and concepts replace familiar ones; a unique image of thought is set in motion.

According to Deleuze, the importance of the empiricist critique of innate ideas has been inflated and misunderstood.[8] At least in Hume's case this cancellation has more to do with assigning philosophy new tasks than with determining the origin of ideas. Hume contends that ideas represent not things but impressions, and designates impressions as being original occurrences (which is to say that he brackets the whole question of origin and representation). Philosophy is thus steered away from representational theories of knowledge and from the picture of the mind as a mirror of nature.

Hume conceives of knowledge in a way that conflicts both with rationalist epistemology and with the popular view of empiricist epistemology. With rationalism, knowledge is a matter of reason discovering the modalities of necessity and universality within particular ideas or representations. As is well known, Hume considers impressions of sensation the origin of ideas, and he holds that necessity cannot be found in any sequence of such impressions. Deleuze, though, emphasizes the way in which Hume neither claims knowledge to be impossible nor denies that knowledge is in some sense conveyed by expressions such as "always," "necessarily," and "everywhere."

For traditional, foundationalist conceptions of knowledge, Hume substitutes the notion of belief.[9] Beliefs are regular, habitual connections arising from but irreducible to sensation. These connections are unrepresentable because they transcend or go beyond sense experience and because all mental representations can be analyzed down to impressions of sensation. As such, beliefs are not so much possessed as performed. For example, one mode of understanding is the use of general terms: particulars are grouped together by being subsumed under a single concept. This form of belief is elucidated, not by identifying a mental representation but by describing a practice. While a particular idea may serve as the representative of a host of others, there are no ideas of essences. There are no ideas of internal connection between particulars, thus no traditional foundation for our classificatory schemes exists.[10]

In response to the experience of a sensible pattern, the principles of association connect ideas (connect them in the sense that, in the future, the mind will, with considerable regularity, travel from one specific idea to another). The mind goes from an impression of bread to the idea of nourishment; we observe smoke and infer fire; we expect the sun to appear tomorrow morning. Similarly, despite the absence of rational or experiential justification for either the notion of personal identity or external existence, the principles of association link together impressions and ideas of sensation in such a way that the fictions of identity and an external world are born.

This way of interpreting Hume's theory of knowledge brings into sharp focus what Hume refers to as his skeptical solutions to doubts raised by the critique of rationalism.[11] Hume does not say that, because they cannot be derived from sense-experience, the notions of necessity, causality, and identity are unwarranted or meaningless. Instead, for traditional conceptions of knowledge he substitutes the concept of belief (where beliefs are now assemblages rather than representations). When belief replaces knowledge, phrases such as "necessary" or "always" cease to mean metaphysical necessity, signifying instead observed conjunctions or habits of thought.

One reason that Deleuze highlights this redefinition of knowledge is his desire to show how Hume's empiricism calls into question the traditional distinction between theory and practice. In other words, he wants to demonstrate that above all else, Hume's philosophy is a practical philosophy.[12] There are two parts to Deleuze's demonstration. The first is his description of Hume's theory of knowledge as a theory of practice. The second is his argument that in Hume's system, the investigation of the passions and values is prior to epistemology. In each of his three essays on Hume's work Deleuze proclaims Hume to be, first and foremost, a moral theorist and provides the following, nonlinear rationale: Hume affirms that association is always performed for the sake of some end, contends that only passions can establish ends, and regards the passions as the basis for morality. For present purposes, though, the symmetry Deleuze uncovers between Hume's epistemology and his ethics is more significant than their order of priority.

As with the understanding, Hume begins his discussion of morality by challenging rationalist approaches, and once again critique is a preparation for the invention of new problems and concepts. With rationalism, moral distinctions are universal rules that can be discovered through reason, justified through argumentation. Moral character is achieved through conformity to these principles, and this is possible only because reason is able to regulate the passions. In contrast, Hume defines reason in a way that prevents it from serving as the ground for moral distinctions.[13] The faculty of reason is no more than the capacity to examine relations of ideas or matters of fact. Since passions are not in and of themselves relations, the notion of an irrational passion is contradictory. Furthermore, reason can influence action through the analysis of certain matters of fact (those connecting actions to consequences) but only passions have the power to set ends and initiate action.

After removing this traditional foundation for morality Hume does not conclude that moral discourse is simply a cloak donned by individual interests and preferences. Once again he produces a skeptical solution by way of a fundamental substitution. The question is no longer that of the possibility of genuine morality but of the conditions responsible for the practice of morality. Hume subscribes to the view that morality entails universal distinctions, but he judges universality to be a predicate of certain sentiments, not of principles outside human reality. Real moral distinctions are feelings of approval and disapproval reflecting an impartial concern for others. One reason for these feelings is the fact that human beings naturally sympathize with others. They are motivated by more than self-interest. Neither selfishness nor a paucity of rationality is the main problem as far as community and moral evaluation are concerned. The problem is that our concern for others is naturally partial. By nature people sympathize with and display generosity toward only those related to them by the principles of association. Contiguity, causality, and resemblance connect the idea they have of themselves to the ideas they have of their family and friends, their neighbors and fellow citizens, and these connections are responsible for the conversion at the heart of sympathy. Unless they have been associated with a person, the ideas they have of that person's feelings remain ideas rather than become feelings in their own right.[14] The incongruity of the various partialities means the persistent threat of violence and the impossibility of satisfying natural passions by natural means.

As Deleuze puts it, the challenge becomes that of constructing an artificial whole capable of harmonizing naturally incompatible parts.[15] By artificial whole is meant a body of institutions or conventions. Institutions are rules of conduct that emerge when several individuals recognize that it is in their own self-interest, and in the interests of those they naturally sympathize with, to behave in certain ways while presuming others do the same. Therefore, a sense of common interest develops prior to any law or contract. Though this notion of public interest is reinforced through conversation and instruction, a problem still remains. How, in specific situations, are individuals able to overcome their natural passions and adopt the disinterested perspective that is a prerequisite to morality?

One salient distinction in Deleuze's reconstruction of Hume's system is a distinction between two kinds of sentiments. On the one hand, there are feelings of approval and disapproval, pleasure and displeasure, indicative of partiality. On the other hand, there are feelings of approval and disapproval that reflect a disinterested perspective, a sympathy extended through artifice. Hume seems to equivocate when it comes to describing the interplay of these sentiments and their relation to moral evaluation. At times, a disinterested perspective and concomitant feelings seem to be a necessary condition for moral judgments. Elsewhere, all that appears to be required is the recognition that we would have these feelings were our situation different—were we or those we care about among those affected by a person's conduct.

Unfortunately, Deleuze's reading removes neither this ambiguity nor the overall obscurity of Hume's discussion of moral sentiment. Nevertheless, he does make us aware of the nuances of Hume's attempt to explain the production of real (that is, universal) moral distinctions. Through reflection the natural passions can, at least in principle, be corrected. A person's awareness of his or her own partiality can, at least in certain instances, elicit new sentiments. Though weak, even ineffectual, the existence of these sentiments are the basis for Hume's claim that real moral distinctions exist.[16]

More important is Deleuze's demonstration that Hume substitutes for the problems of traditional ethics an entirely new set of problems. Instead of the conflict between reason and passion, we have the conflict between limited and extended sympathy, partial and impartial sentiments. Similarly, differentiating authentic from counterfeit judgments has nothing to do with conformity to principles transcending human needs and interests. At issue is whether the feeling of approval or disapproval reflects the interests of an insular group or those of an open community.

Having examined Deleuze's reconstruction of Hume's system, it now makes sense to consider its relationship to Deleuze's own philosophical commitments. When we look at the language of Deleuze's interpretation, when we compare it to the language of his other writings, the difficulty of discerning this relationship is clear. On the one hand, his interpretive style results in texts that are nearly devoid of negativity. In other words, in the essays on Hume, or for that matter any of his monographs, you rarely find Deleuze in explicit disagreement with his subject. On the other hand, when we peruse Deleuze's other writings, we do not find him invoking the principles of association, positing human nature as an explanatory foundation, or speaking of the need to integrate partial sympathies. Consequently, if a connection between Hume's empiricism and Deleuzism is to be found, it will be found someplace other than in Hume's lexicon, specific explanations, and overt methodology.

True, Deleuze does not inherit the notion of associative principles, but he does declare relations to be inventions, not representations or discoveries. Deleuze does not appropriate Hume's notion of sympathy, or reinforce the problematic notion of general interest. He does, though, invoke Hume's distinction between institution and contract. In fact, this distinction is the central theme of his book *Instincts and Institutions,* and in *Coldness and Cruelty,* the masochistic contract is contrasted with the sadistic institution.

Just as Hume introduces the notion of competing sympathies as an alternative to psychological egoism, so he introduces the concept of the institution as an alternative to the notions of social contract and natural law. The institution is a system of means—a circuitous way of gratifying natural passions; the aim of the social contract is the suppression of natural instincts. For Deleuze the notion of institutions and juridical concepts such as law or contract represent two very different ways of understanding the social. In the case of the law, social practices are explained entirely in terms of the natural instincts they repress. When it comes to the notion of institution the situation is quite different. For Hume, the tension between natural sympathies explains the need for institutions but not the actual form institutions take. This gap between the necessity and form of an institution makes the institution a genuine display of inventiveness.

This emphasis on creation links Hume's ethics to his theory of knowledge. Just as institutions are irreducible to natural desires, so relations are irreducible to the ideas they relate. Moreover, as Deleuze's reading shows, this emphasis on creation can be found not just in Hume's specific theories but in his overall theoretical style. Hume's theoretical production cannot be explained as a response to Cartesianism, captured as a moment within any conversation. Likewise, in Deleuze's philosophy knowledge and ethics are creative affairs—the production of new forms of thinking and living; his metaphilosophy defines theoretical activity as the production of new questions, and his own theoretical style is one in which original concepts proliferate and borrowed concepts find a home on new planes.

The Meaning of Empiricism

Deleuze first advanced the idea that philosophies are implicit questions in the course of interpreting Hume's work. When his metatheory operates thus, as a method of interpretation, the effects are immediate. Hume's myriad texts, and different passages of the same text, are represented as a theory, moments of a single question. Additionally, a distinction Deleuze employs when he criticizes established interpretations—the distinction between a question and its implications, a problem and its enunciation— organizes these moments hierarchically around a purported center. In the conclusion, I address this apparent assumption of internal textual unity. Before doing this, though, I want to locate what Deleuze calls the essence or true meaning of empiricism.

Hume's critique of the doctrine of substance implies his definition of the mind as a theater of ideas or bundle of perceptions. According to Deleuze, the importance of this definition is that with it the mind and subject are distinguished.[17] As evidenced by ideas of mythological creatures, the mind has the ability to fuse or connect any two ideas. However, these fanciful, arbitrary connections are very different from relations.[18] In the case of belief, a specific idea regularly follows from another specific idea because the two have been connected by the principles of association. The subject is defined by this constancy and by related discursive habits: the habit of using general terms, the habit of saying "always" and "every," and the habit of employing the pronoun "I": "Isn't this the answer to the question 'what are we?' We are habits, nothing but habits—the habit of saying 'I'. Perhaps, there is no more striking answer to the problem of the Self."[19]

The fact that none of these activities is a product of the mind alone suggests the question which, according to Deleuze, is the essence of empiricism: How does the mind become a subject? How is a subject transcending the given constituted in the given?[20] As has been shown, Hume's answer to the question is that the subject is constituted through the activity of forces extrinsic to the mind (the principles of association and the natural passions). These principles of nature are responsible for the mind, in and of itself nothing more than a sequence of unrelated perceptions, being a system of habits.

Because the distinction between mind and subject corresponds to the distinction between ideas and relations, the problem of the subject's constitution can be recast as the problem of constituting relations between disparate ideas. Frequently, then, Deleuze defines empiricism as a theory of difference and unity. Empiricism is the belief that relations are external to what they relate. Consequently, unity is fabricated, something fashioned alongside of other parts. For example, in his essay on Walt Whitman's *Specimen Days*, Deleuze argues that this nonorganic conception of difference is the most important contribution of Anglo-American philosophy and literature:

> a kind of whole must be constructed, a whole that is all the more para-
> doxical in that it only comes *after* the fragments and leaves them intact,

making no attempt to totalize them. This complex idea depends on a principle dear to English philosophy, to which the Americans would give a new meaning and new developments: *relations are external to their terms.* Relations will consequently be posited as something that can and must be instituted or invented.[21]

Whitman's style of composition consists of fashioning assemblages out of heterogeneous scenes. The empiricist view of part and whole can likewise be regarded as a style of thought, as a way of thinking with AND rather than IS. The standard philosophical question assumes the form "what is x?" And in philosophy, questions of this kind are often symptomatic of a belief in essences and a faith in the possibility and desirability of explanatory closure. Thinking with AND means regarding parts as articles of genuine difference, not as parts of some antecedent or future whole. Thinking with AND means adopting an attitude of suspicion toward abstract principles of unity (for example, substance, species-essence, origin, and final-cause) and toward the foundationalist belief in final, exhaustive explanations. This suspicion, though, is not the same thing as a denial of unity. Because unity is not found, it is waiting to be practiced.

Two obvious objections could be raised against Deleuze's identification of empiricism with the notion of external relations. The first is that this position can hardly be the defining feature of empiricism because it is found outside empiricism. For Descartes, the current existence of a finite substance is not internally related to its past existence. For Malebranche, no two events are internally related; the occurrence of one is never sufficient to explain the occurrence of the other. The second objection is that Hume himself rejects the view that every relation is an external one. In the *Treatise,* Hume claims that some relations depend entirely on the terms related.[22] This distinction between different kinds of relation is often read as anticipating the analytic/synthetic distinction. If so, he is a proponent of the view that while some relations are external, others, namely those whose predicate is contained within their subject, are internal.

The first objection is useful, for responding to it requires foregrounding the specific character of Hume's thesis of externality. By criticizing the notion of substance, Hume carries the thesis further than Descartes (further than Locke and Berkeley, for that matter). Moreover, for Descartes, Malebranche, and Berkeley, God is the external principle of connection. In Hume's philosophy the principles of human nature are responsible for relations between ideas. While Hume allows God to be considered the cause of the principles of nature, this thought, concerning as it does first causes, is placed outside philosophy.

Deleuze anticipates the second objection and defends his interpretation by emphasizing how for Hume "relation" signifies the act of relating. The terms of a relation may resemble one another or accompany one another in experience, but this resemblance or pattern does not, independently of the principles of association, explain why the idea of one gives rise to the other. As Hume writes, even if the relation is one of mathematical equivalence, the relation is not "a property in the figures themselves, but arises merely from comparison, which the mind makes betwixt them."[23] Consequently, while Hume does say there are relations whose truth can be known with complete certainty (some of which are even empirical), there are no analytic judgments. One term of a relation is never sufficient to explain the appearance of the other.

Deleuze and the History of Philosophy

Deleuze's reconstruction of Hume's philosophical project is one that effectively throws into relief the positive strands of empiricism and assembles them into a theory of practice, difference, and subjectivity. How, though, should we reconcile this careful interpretation, this contribution to the history of philosophy, with the disparaging remarks Deleuze makes elsewhere concerning the history of philosophy? How should we reconcile his decision to engage in interpretation with his critique of representation and his promotion of philosophical creativity?

Speaking of his own efforts in the area of historical commentary, Deleuze once remarked that he imagined himself taking the great philosophers from behind, forcing them to give birth to children they would want to disown but would have to acknowledge.[24] We should avoid attaching too much weight to this scene, for it suggests that while Deleuze's relationship to philosophy's past is hermeneutically faithful, it is largely adversarial. But if Deleuze takes Hume from behind he does so with affection as well as fidelity. Perhaps, then, the best way of reconciling Deleuze's interpretation of Hume with his critique of the history of philosophy is by taking a closer look at what he means by "the history of philosophy." What practices are being criticized when the phrase "history of philosophy" is used as a pejorative? For Deleuze "the history of philosophy" means the penchant for treating philosophy's past as a series of conversations. In addition, "the history of philosophy" signifies the stifling way in which philosopher's names and philosophical concepts circulate in university settings.[25] The history of philosophy is "philosophy's own version of the Oedipus complex," repressing thought through the imposition of prerequisites and parameters.

What should be clear is that the above meanings of "history of philosophy" should be distinguished from philosophy's past. The former are ways the latter is interpreted and used. In his essays on Hume, we see Deleuze himself working with the philosophical tradition, and his language is not primarily one of objection. In fact, Deleuze's method of practicing the history of philosophy differs greatly from those in which that history is represented as a series of variations on an unfortunate but tenacious theme such as logocentrism, phallogocentrism, or the metaphysics of presence. As he remarks, "Philosophy is always a matter of inventing concepts. I've never been worried about going beyond metaphysics or any death of philosophy. Philosophy feels small and lonely . . . but the only way it's going to die is by choking with laughter."[26]

This is not to say that Deleuze does not think there are tendencies within the history of ideas needing to be subjected to criticism. The identification and rejection of such tendencies is central to his discussion of "images of thought." Nevertheless, when it comes to his interpretation of Hume, his strategy is comparable to Hume's strategy with regard to rationalism. Refutation takes a back seat to the creation of concepts, questions, and problems—to the creation of alternative, minor images of philosophical thought. Moreover, Deleuze's work shows how philosophy's creative function and the history of philosophy are not mutually exclusive. He offers us a vision of interpretation as both recovery and invention. The interpretation of another philosopher's work should bear some clear, nonarbitrary relation to that work, but at the same time the relation should not be one of identity. As with portraiture, if the image is made in the likeness of its subject, it is fashioned out of different materials and expresses a specific agenda.[27] Such a practice continually demonstrates that the texts that make up philosophy's past are anything but stable, frozen units. They are composed of multiple strands, and these strands are always lying in wait for a passion to take them up again creatively—to resurrect them for the present.

Notes

I wish to thank Stephen Daniel, Constantin Boundas, Katherine Arens, and Todd May for their questions on an earlier version of this paper, as well as Richard Delli-Fraine and Catherine Newman for their helpful comments and fierce support.

1. Gilles Deleuze and André Cresson, *David Hume: Sa vie, son oeuvre* (Paris: Presses Universitaires de France, 1952), 1.

2. Gilles Deleuze, "David Hume," in *La philosophie*, ed. Francois Châtelet (Paris: Librairie Hachette, 1972), 226.

3. *Ibid.*, 226.

4. Gilles Deleuze, *Coldness and Cruelty,* trans. Jean McNeil (New York: Zone Books, 1991), 13.

5. *Ibid.*, 14.

6. *Ibid.*, 45, 67.

7. Gilles Deleuze, *Empiricism and Subjectivity,* trans. Constantin Boundas (New York: Columbia University Press, 1991), 106: "In fact, a philosophical theory is an elaborately developed question, and nothing else; by itself and in itself, it is not the resolution to a problem, but the elaboration, *to the very end* of the necessary implications of a formulated question." See also Todd May, *Reconsidering Difference* (Philadelphia: University of Pennsylvania Press, 1997), 168.

8. Deleuze, "Hume," 226; *Empiricism,* 31, 88.

9. David Hume, *A Treatise of Human Nature,* ed. L. A. Selby-Bigge (New York: Oxford University Press, 1978), 17–19; and Deleuze, *Empiricism,* 28–29.

10. David Hume, *An Enquiry concerning Human Understanding* and *An Enquiry concerning the Principles of Morals,* ed. L. A. Selby-Bigge (New York: Oxford University Press, 1975), 40–55.

11. Deleuze and Cresson, *David Hume,* 50; Deleuze, *Empiricism,* 32.

12. Hume, *Treatise,* 458–59.

13. *Ibid.*, 320.

14. Deleuze and Cresson 1952, 50–54; Deleuze, *Empiricism,* 35–36.

16. Hume, *Enquiry concerning Human Understanding,* 229; Hume, *Treatise,* 581–86.

18. Hume, *Enquiry concerning Human Understanding,* 18–19.

19. Deleuze, *Empiricism,* x; see also 101. Cf. Gilles Deleuze and Félix Guattari, *What Is Philosophy?* trans. Hugh Tomlinson and Graham Burchell (New York: Columbia University Press, 1994), 48.

20. Deleuze, *Empiricism,* 22–23, 99.

21. Gilles Deleuze, *Essays Critical and Clinical,* trans. Daniel Smith and Michael Greco (Minneapolis: University of Minnesota Press, 1997), 58.

22. Hume, *Treatise,* 69.

23. *Ibid.*, 46.

24. Gilles Deleuze, *Negotiations,* trans. Martin Joughin (New York: Columbia University Press, 1995), 6.

25. Deleuze, *Negotiations,* 5.

26. *Ibid.*, 136.

27. *Ibid.*, 135.

Althusser and Hume:
A Materialist Encounter

Joel Reed

Considering Althusser's critique of empiricism in *Reading Capital,* Gregory Elliott's question, toward the end of his essay on Althusser and contingency, "how does his own position differ from the kind of empiricist common sense of English historians?" seems to require only one answer: in all ways![1] Althusser lampooned the "obviousness" of common sense and of its recourse to experience as the basis for knowledge: "The proof of the pudding is in the eating," the pragmatic empiricist declares, but Althusser responds: "So what! We are interested in the *mechanism* that ensures that it really is a pudding we are eating and not a poached baby elephant, though we *think* we are eating our daily pudding!"[2] Althusser urges us to work our way out of the ideological circle which encloses idealism and empiricism alike through a particular combination of theory and practice in which the truth of the theory precedes the reality it analyzes, though the results of analysis are fed back into the theory itself. "Theoretical practice is indeed its own criterion" he argues (*RC* 59), thus distinguishing it from an empiricism that would find its criteria of truth outside of itself, in an experience that precedes systems of knowing it or of drawing principles to describe it. How, then, can we seriously entertain Elliott's question about the relationship between Althusser's work and that of the English empiricists, or the related question Callinicos posed to Elliott: "Is there . . . a precedent for Althusser's concerns in non-Marxist, Anglophone philosophy of history?"[3] What kind of empiricism could we find Althusser supporting?

The answer, I suggest, is a Humean one, but to call Althusser a Humean would ignore a series of disavowals, statements that are as critical of Hume as is his more extended critique of empiricism. In the early essay on content in Hegel (1947), Althusser traces the Hegelian contradiction, a "profound dismemberment characteristic of the understanding," to Kant and Hume before him, where the act of reflecting on a series of oppositions reaffirms only the primacy of the reflective philosopher.[4] The 1953 text "On Marxism" ends by quoting Lenin's dissociation "in the most emphatic and irrevocable manner . . . from philosophical idealism and the sophistry of the followers of Hume and Kant" (*SH* 256), a passage which echoes through "Lenin and Philosophy" and which Althusser again approvingly quotes toward the end of "Is it Simple to be a Marxist in Philosophy?"[5]

In these places, Althusser is returning to an old problem in Hume studies, the very framework of which fell out of fashion in nearly all but one orientation in the history of philosophy: whether Hume is to be considered a materialist or an idealist. Through the Marxist tradition, this debate became entwined with critical inquiries into ideology, and more specifically with the modality of change, and was transported from the nineteenth century into the twentieth. Do, as those members of the "various schools of materialism" who regard "nature as primary" would have it, the rules of history reveal themselves through the study of the matter of things or, from "the camp of idealism," by determining guiding principles first, and then applying those principles to the physical world?[6]

At least since T. H. Huxley, Hume has been seen as someplace in between the two poles of materialism and idealism, or as occupying both positions in the debate and therefore no position at all. According to Huxley, in Hume, "realism and idealism are equally probable hypotheses."[7] Hume's analysis of the origins of mental impressions is not fundamentally materialist, since he fails to prove that physical changes in the brain produce thoughts and perceptions, but he argues such a conclusion cannot be disproven, either, and that the reason for drawing a causal connnection between physiological motion and mental effect is as sound as that for making any other causal link between action and reaction. Locating the origin of ideas in physical matter, as Huxley points out, "is what is commonly called materialism" (78). Yet, he adds, "it is nevertheless true that the doctrine contains nothing inconsistent with the purest idealism" (78), since the physical body is only perceived through the impressions we form of it. At the moment the materialism/idealism dichotomy was taking on world-historical significance through Marx and Engels' insistence that only historical materialism could provide a correct analysis of capitalism, Huxley's discussion of Hume suggests a deconstruction of the opposition—not a privileging of idealism over materialism but a hint that the pursuit of the latter leads to a justification of the former. "The more completely the materialistic position is admitted, the easier it is to show that the idealistic position is unassailable" (80).

It seems that through his analysis, Huxley has converted to the "agnosticism" he finds in Hume, where there is an "incapacity to discover the indispensable conditions of either positive or negative knowledge" (58). If agnosticism is an improvement over a blind fideism, replacing faith with an empirically based skepticism, for those materialists intent on changing the world, rather than interpreting it, this ambiguity is as damning as confirmed idealism. While rejecting Huxley's sympathy with Hume, Engels adopts his language in his reference to the "agnostics" who resurrect Hume in a move that is "scientifically a regression and practically merely a shamefaced way of surreptitiously accepting materialism, while denying it before the world."[8] Lenin picked up this language as well, first in asking:

> Does the lecturer acknowledge Engels' fundamental division of philo-
> sophical systems into *idealism* and *materialism,* Engels regarding those
> intermediate between these two, wavering between them, as the *line* of
> Hume in modern philosophy, calling this line "agnosticism"?[9]

And later, referring both to Huxley and Engels, Lenin dismisses Hume and his adherents as agnostics, postitivists, and reactionaries.[10]

The material/ideal dichotomy that Huxley brought to his analysis of Hume conformed well to the polemical contexts faced by Engels and Lenin, where debates about philosophical materialism directly impacted the outcomes for the historical-materialist critique of capitalism. Althusser, too, devoted to developing *the class struggle in philosophy* in the late twentieth century, returned to these debates. By refunctioning those polemics, Althusser made sure that Marxism not "fall behind history" but rather produce "new knowledge, about imperialism *and* the State *and* ideologies *and* socialism *and* the Labour movement itself," and in the process he carried their frameworks and targets into the present.[11] This long and even passionate context for rejecting Hume only reaffirms the absurdity of suggesting that his work might provide a precursor for an Althusserian theory of contingency.

Yet Althusser's single extended treatment of Hume suggests that things might not be so clear. In the final course in his series on philosophy for scientists, "The Directions of Philosophy" ("Du côté de la philosophie"), from 1967, Althusser characterizes two forms of empiricism. He argues that in the philosophical representation of scientific knowledge, Truth is found in the equation of subject and object, and empiricism suppresses one of these terms. In most cases, empiricism suppresses the subject to locate truth in the object itself. But Hume presents the opposite, an almost antiempiricist empiricism, in which it is the *object* that is suppressed. Hume's skepticism denies us knowledge of the object but shifts its truth to the subject's experience of it. Althusser calls this a "subjective empiricism," a kind of special case that departs from the fundamental objective-empiricist variation.[12] While Hume is not the only subjective empiricist—Althusser includes Condillac and Rousseau in this category as well—this discussion logically follows from the earlier designation of Hume as an "agnostic." Denying that knowledge of a thing is inherent within it, Hume nonetheless asserts that the object does have true qualities at the same time as he argues that those qualities are derived from the subject's sensations of them. So Hume falls, again, in between the great camps of idealism and materialism, but Althusser's analysis in this text reveals something exceptional about that agnosticism, which, while not endorsing it, nonetheless treats it without the polemical tone of his other references to Hume.

Perhaps the odd denomination of "subjective empiricism" hints at something to be gained in paying more attention to Hume in order to develop an effective, historically refunctioned, materialist critique. A long footnote in the English translation of Engels's *Ludwig Feurbach* also suggests this possibility, though such a conclusion is antithetical to the note's purpose:

> Engels calls the philosophy of Hume agnosticism. The agnostic says: *I do not know* whether there is an objective reality which is reflected by our senses. Engels calls Kant an agnostic also, who, it is true, admits of objective reality, the "thing-in-itself," but maintains that this "thing in itself" is beyond our ken. Engels therefore remarks: "To this, Hegel, long since, has replied: If you know all the qualities of a thing, you know the thing itself; nothing remains but the fact that the said thing exists without us; and when your senses have taught you that fact, you have grasped the last remnant of thing thing-in-itself, Kant's celebrated unknowable *Ding an sich.*" (22)

Within the dismissal of Hume as insufficiently materialist is the suggestion of a model historicism, for here we are led to conclude that Hegel's materialism is less historical than Hume's agnosticism. Hume never claims knowledge of an object whose qualities transcends history, only knowledge of how the subject has experienced the object. These experiences have occurred at particular times, and their repetition leads subjects to claims about the things themselves. This Humean experience is much closer to the "practice" that Lenin, through reference to Engels and Marx, argues is crucial to a historical-materialist epistemology, than to the agnosticism he rejects (*MEC* 155); indeed, it takes the same form as the materialism that Lenin *opposes* to Hume (*MEC* 189).

It would be stretching things to argue that the tonal variation in

Althusser's attention to Hume signals a significant break or rupture; after all, "The Directions of Philosophy" was delivered eight years before Althusser repeated the Leninist dismissal of Hume in "Is it Simple to be a Marxist in Philosophy?" Yet the absence of a sustained, overt engagement with Hume in Althusser's oeuvre seems to be in keeping with the very lineage of aleatory materialism traced by his unfinished "The Subterranean Current of the Materialism of the Encounter." There Althusser writes that "from Epicurus to Marx has always subsisted, though covered again, by its "discovery" a profound tradition which finds its materialist place in a philosophy of the encounter."[13] Althusser invites us to recover a "materialism of the encounter" from within a series of denegations, condemnations, and forgettings; from within philosophy this form of materialism rejects the presence that Reason, Origin, and End have maintained throughout philosophy, including, he suggests, throughout the history of materialism. Even in the classic texts of Marx, Engels and Lenin, Althusser finds "a materialism of necessity and of teleology, that's to say a transformed and disguised form of idealism" ("SC" 540). The themes of this discovery are familiar, though the critique here of even Marxist theories of materialism less so. Yet in *Materialism and Empirio-Criticism*, we find Lenin arguing that "Engels does not admit even the shadow of a doubt as to the existence of objective law, causality and necessity in nature" (178); against this "materialism of the essence" ("SC" 569), in which a transcendental purposiveness cloaks an analysis of the pure "being" of nature, Althusser proposes a materialism attentive to contingency or accidents, to dumb luck, even when it goes bad, and which is ungoverned by any sense or reason that we ascribe to it, even though in doing so he may veer toward an idealism that in refusing to hold nature accountable to the laws we derive from it may deny the very notions of necessity and causality that flow from those laws. Careening through philosophy the way the atoms of Epicurus and Lucretius careen through the void, Althusser's materialism of the encounter, he writes, "escapes from the classic criteria of all materialism" ("SC" 543).

Its refusal of necessity and determinism relate this text to Althusser's "classic" complications of the problem of determinism: the notion of overdetermination, where he reads Mao's theory of contradiction into Freud's work; the work on structural causality in *Reading Capital*, developed in direct distinction from mechanistic and spiritual notions of determinism and influenced by Jacques-Alain Miller's work; the call in the "Ideological State Apparatuses" essay to move through the metaphoricity of the base/superstructure model toward an analysis of the determining force of cultural and ideological phenomenon on the reproduction of the "material" conditions of production. In each of these formulations Althusser works beyond the metaphysical assumptions that have organized our categories of analysis, even of Marxist analysis, drawing on a range of material from the history of philosophy and from his contemporaries that would include the process of that analysis in its conclusions about the relationships between culture and economy. I'm sure it's no coincidence that at each of these moments Althusser staged an encounter between Marxist and psychoanalytic theory, for the latter provided not only a critical theory of subjectivity but also a model for a non-Hegelian dialectics that in being attentive to the historical life-world of the thinker would refuse the purity of a materialist essence; as Warren Montag wrote, "Lacan as dialectician does not intervene from a position outside of philosophy. . . . For the effects of the spontaneous materialism of psychoanalytic practice on philosophy can be realized only insofar as Lacan enters the philosophical domain."[14] Rather than operate on a system from the outside, in the model of cause-and-effect Althusser condemned as mechanistic, Lacan dismantles philosophy from within, confronting its idealisms with the reality of the unconscious which he too understood as a materialist form of encounter: Rejecting the notion that psychoanalysis leads "in the direction of idealism," he suggests (in *The Four Fundamental Concepts*) that "what we have in the discovery of psycho-analysis is an encounter, an essential encounter . . . *the encounter with the real.*"[15]

Lacan's "encounter" challenges a materialism that would insist on a purely physical or objective grounding for analysis, or which would find in the physical world of nature and objects the cause or determination of human behavior, to account for human development that progresses not through stages but rather through a series of accidents—the real is the encounter with trauma, the "knock" that comes haphazardly in the night and which the subject is inclined to relive or repeat. In Althusser's terms, the "knock" or *tuché* is a "deviation which produces the *clinamen*" (540), the accident that tilts history without reason or cause and which then survives or repeats itself in the social unconscious, and *its* analysis would be the most material thing, just as it represents for Lacan the heart of the real. Etienne Balibar made this point while discussing the role of Lacan's "imaginary" and "Real" in Althusser's theory of ideology, where "'Real' and 'Imaginary' . . . are not opposites, they are inseparable one from another: thinking the real is part of the real, in an infinite process."[16] If, from a doctrinal perspective, such a collapse of "real" and "imaginary" seems like a new version of the agnosticism that refuses to prioritize either material or ideal origins of mental impressions, it is at the same time absolutely necessary in understanding how individuals suture themselves into the symbolic practices of collective, historical institutions.[17] An aleatory materialism recognizes that the analysis of the determining force in history is made only after the fact, following the events that have come together into a pattern or structure of *repeated* elements: "all determination of these elements can only be assigned in the retrospective return of the result within its becoming, in its recurrence" ("SC" 566).

Similar to the young Marx's "detour" through Hegel, Althusser, then, has taken his own detours in his attempts to accomplish this critique, through psychoanalytic theory, structuralism, Spinoza, and, in his "materialism of the encounter," through a neo-Epicurean atomism and its manifestations in a counter-tradition that reverses the idealism disguised within materialism. Sketching out this counter-tradition, he writes that "from Nietzsche to Deleuze and Derrida, English empiricism (Deleuze) or Heidegger (Derrida helps) we are henceforth becoming familiar and productive in all understanding, not only of philosophy, but of all its pretended 'objects' (whether science, culture, art, literature, or all other expressions of existence), [with] the essentials of the materialism of the encounter, disguised as they are under species of other concepts" (562). It appears that we can add Deleuze's first book, *Empiricism and Subjectivity: An Essay on Hume's Theory of Human Nature,* to the list of his early works which Ted Stolze suggests "Althusser and his circle seem to have been quite favorably disposed toward."[18]

My brief survey of Hume's critical reception reinforces my sense that he's a perfect figure on whom Althusser could hinge an aleatory materialism. As we have seen, his previous readers—Marxists and non-Marxists alike—find that his work tends toward a materialism extraordinarily situated between idealism and materialism. At first glance, Hume is the archetypal materialist, rooting all knowledge in the nature of things and situating his epistemology in observations and experiments. But this materialism shifts as soon as we attend to his simultaneous emphasis on our *experience* in developing a theory of knowledge, and slips further when we find him concentrating on the perceptions and interpretations of experience, not the experience itself; indeed, the object-world of material things yields to the way the subject mentally works on this world. Against our lay-understanding of empiricism as the philosophy of experience, Deleuze reads Hume, and Kant's commentary on Hume in *The Critique of Pure Reason,* to demonstrate that "empiricism is a philosophy of the imagination and not a philosophy of the senses."[19] Inserting Hume into the tradition of the materialist encounter I earlier discussed in reference to Lacan's *Four Fundamental Concepts* lets us expand that psychoanalytic framework toward one more broadly psychological, and reminds us that a materialism that ignores the role of human agency and thought not only succumbs to the "false philosophy" that Hume indicts, "when we transfer the determination of the thought to external objects," but, for all the good it does, might as well focus on geology as on social change, while this attention to the imagination simultaneously alerts us to the naiveté of pretending that agency is a purely *rational* response to external stimuli or conditions.[20]

Hume's consideration of causality in his *Treatise of Human Nature* (1739–40) is a perfect place to view both the relationship between event and interpretation and his connection to Althusser's aleatory materialism. In the materialism of the encounter, "one never finds there Cause which precedes these effects . . . all the elements are here and at the same time beyond" ("SC" 546). In his *Treatise of Human Nature,* Hume presents necessity as a determination of cause conditioned by the repeated conjunction of two events; from the series of repetitions and the association between these events we therefore become habituated to making, we determine that the second event is dependent on the first and conclude that a *necessary* relation between them exists, though this determination is always based only in habit, not in any verifiable fact of the relationship. That a thing is or things are, that "*il y a,*" as Althusser phrases it in reference to the aleatory, Hume doesn't dispute; it is only the *meaning* of the thing, and of a relationship between two things, that seems troubling to him, for the thing itself has no essence or internal purpose that would give us the basis for moving past it: "*there is nothing in any object, consider'd in itself, which can afford us a reason for drawing a conclusion beyond it*" (*T* 139). Similarly, a relationship between two things is not sensible through an internal law of necessity but only through the association that we make between them, an association that we reinforce each time we repeat it (*T* 130). Presenting these objects historically, as events, makes no difference in the rule: "the supposition, *that the future resembles the past,* is not founded on arguments of any kind, but is deriv'd entirely from habit, by which we are determin'd to expect for the future the same train of objects, to which we have become accustom'd" (*T* 134). The high-flying Reason, Origin, and End that Althusser rejects in classical materialism is for Hume the mere force of habit, a "train of objects" whose relationship custom, not internal purposiveness, determines and then denominates as necessity.

Hume well knows that this analysis of necessary causes flies in the face of common materialism. "What!" he imagines his critic crying, "the efficacy of causes lies in the determination of the mind! As if causes did not operate entirely independent of the mind. . . . Thought may well depend on causes for its operation, but not causes on thought. This is to reverse the order of nature" (*T* 167). But Hume responds that cause and necessity are categories of analysis, not of nature—that just as there are no innate qualities separate from our ideas of those qualities, ideas which are always subjective, rather than based in demonstrable fact, there can be no innate relationships between things aside from the conclusions about those relationships we derive from the impressions that a repeated association of the things has made on us. Thus the idea of necessary cause "is impossible and imaginary" (*T* 158).

Hume's attention to these relationships, then, leaves innate qualities behind in order to focus on the processes by which they are formed, and, as Deleuze suggests in his book on Hume's *Treatise,* these processes occur through two different types of spontaneity: "spontaneity of relation," in which the accident of contiguity suggests a connection between two things or events, and a "spontaneity of disposition," the natural tendency or inclination that provides the limit to the pure accident of contiguity (*ES* 96–97). Now Althusser's reference to Deleuze's work on English empiricism makes more sense because the relationship between the aleatory and the *clinamen* is at the heart of the materialism of the encounter.

While it is easy to see how "relations" of contiguity can be spontaneous or unmotivated—when things happen to fall next to each other, raining down into the void, as Althusser suggests on the first page of his text, like the atoms of Lucretius and Epicurus, the notion of a spontaneous disposition is paradoxical, or even oxymoronic: it might be termed an "unconstrained constraint." Yet, with this oxymoron Hume is pointing to the ways a particular association erupts from the field of the possible. Deleuze observes that while this field is "natural," we come to understand it as especially irrational—dispositions are for him passions both grounded in the body and somehow free of the body as well: hunger, thirst, sexual desire, but also pride and humility, love and hatred, joy and sadness (*ES* 97). Double-spontaneity is the supplement to the reasonable association we make, following the recurrence of a chain of events or things, that leads us to determine one as the cause and the other as the effect, or to claim a necessary relationship between them. Helping us link this problem in the philosophy of causality to the problem of subjectivity, Deleuze writes that "association gives the subject a possible structure, but only the passions can give it being and existence. In its relation to the passions, the association finds its sense and destiny" (*ES* 120). And bringing this theory of subjectivity back to the social world, he adds: "Association . . . defines a set of possible means for a practical subject for which all real ends belong to the moral, passional, political, and economic order" (*ES* 121).

Another way to grasp the links between the subject, the politico-economic order, and Hume's critique of necessity is to pay attention to the terms he associates with it: at one place, "*efficacy, agency, power, force, energy, necessity, connexion,* and *productive quality*" (*T* 157), and at another, "cause, and effect, and necessity, and liberty, and chance" (*T* 407). Through these associative chains, the problem of causality connects directly to those of the nature of power itself and of social change. The quality of one thing to cause another is a power, as Hume points out, but by his system of analysis, that power exists only in associations we draw between the two things, not as an inherent quality of the thing. Power flows from the "multiplicity of resembling instances" (*T* 163) that leads us to create the association. What happens if we shift this sense of power into the political realm? We would find that power is not innate or inherent in any thing, party, class, or mass—"energy lies not in any of the known qualities of matter" (*T* 161) —but is constituted in a process by which the matter makes an impression on us that we, through custom or habit and following the double-spontaneity of relation and disposition, form into an idea. The "idea" is always mediated through the "impression" for Hume—it never refers directly to the object, much less emanates from the object. Thus he claims that "we never therefore have any idea of power" (*T* 161) itself or in itself distinct from this aleatory process of forming an idea.

Althusser's discussion of Machiavelli helps us relate this skeptical theory of power to the social field. In that discussion Althusser suggests that Machiavelli was another theorist of aleatory materialism for the ways he sketched out the role of the Prince as a unifying force for the Italian state, yet refused to determine which prince would fulfill this role: "unity will occur if it encounters a man without a name who will have enough chance and virtue for installing himself in some way, in a corner of Italy *without a name* . . . This reasoning is completely aleatory" ("SC" 544). Unity is the result of chance, or of a "deviation" from history, not a historically determinable or predictable matter. Althusser moves close to the version of political change we see in Laclau and Mouffe's understanding of hegemony (in *Hegemony and Socialist Strategy*), where any group or party is equally likely, or has an equal chance, to seize power, and away from their understanding of political change as well. That is, his reading of Machiavelli avoids a purely volunteerist idealism, for the "elements" which produce historical effects must be in place. In some ways, then, rather than the volunteerism of Laclau and Mouffe, Althusser's reading of Machiavelli suggests an understanding of the nation-state closer to Balibar's analysis of the "relative indeterminacy" of its process of development. Explicitly against a sense of "linear development schemas," Balibar demonstrates that the nation form was never "necessary" or destined but rather was the contingent outcome of particular conditions and events.[21] In another text on Machiavelli, Althusser writes of his

> simultaneously necessary and unthinkable hypothesis that the new state could begin anywhere, *on the aleatory character of the formation of national states*. For us, they are drawn on the map, as if for ever fixed in a destiny

that always preceded them. For him, on the contrary, they are largely
aleatory, their frontiers are not fixed, there have to be conquests, but
how far? To the boundaries of languages or beyond? To the limits of
their forces?[22]

So a particular political formation is both preconditioned and is
beyond determination or necessity as well. Explaining the concept of the
"conjuncture" that dominates Machiavelli, Althusser writes: "in order to
give laws to men it is necessary to hold the greatest reckoning of the manner in which the *conditions* present themselves, of the '*il y a*' which is this
and not that . . . of the conditions and their history, that's to say of their
'being-becoming'" ("SC" 559). History and the social field presents the
conditions within which an accident occurs and within which power shifts,
and if we can grasp that balance of the aleatory and necessity, or of relation and disposition, then we can think "in the horizon torn between the
aleatory of the Encounter and the necessity of Revolution" ("SC" 560)
while rejecting an essence of power in a particular "subject of history."
    In his essay "Of the Rise and Progress of the Arts and Sciences,"
Hume himself brings the debate about power, chance, and necessity to
the modality of political change: "*What depends upon a few persons is, in a
great measure, to be ascribed to chance, or secret and unknown causes: What arises
from a great number, may often be accounted for by determinate and known
causes.*"[23] The multiple, repeated occurrences that in the *Treatise* were necessary for the creation of an idea of causal determination here is converted into a *multitude* of actors, or a mass which is "less subject to accidents, and less influenced by whim and private fancy," and thus to Hume
produce "the gradual revolutions of a state [which are] a more proper
subject of reasoning and observation, than the . . . violent, which are commonly produced by single persons." When in his essay on the materialism
of the encounter Althusser discusses specific political change, in recount-
ing Machiavelli's and Hobbes's contributions to the tradition he remains
close to this Humean sense of chance: The chance encounter, the *tuché* of
atomic forces, introduces the deviation which tilts the system toward one
Prince or another or shifts the power field. In some ways, however, Hume's
system is more materialist than Althusser's aleatory materialism, or is less
agnostic, anyway, for at least in its terminology it suggests a faith in the necessity of the masses to change history. Althusser's text suggests a loss of
such faith; toward its end he contrasts a series of historical revolutions,
from the French Revolution to the Paris Commune and the revolution of
1917 to the events of May 1968, where "an enduring encounter was not
produced . . . when the long parallel processions of the workers and the
students, who could have been joined crossed but *without uniting*" ("SC"

569). This loss of faith may be the price of a materialism of the encounter: In its rejection of metaphysical Reasons, Origins, and Ends, it leads us to view more skeptically the necessity of radical social change; or, on the other hand, it may point to the ways in which necessity is a prop that a strategy toward change cannot afford, though one form of theoretical necessity may remain: At the end of "On Contradiction," Mao calls on his comrades to "demolish dogmatist ideas . . . to organize their experience into principles and avoid repeating empiricist errors."[24] Althusser's aleatory materialism, a kind of Humean empiricism against itself, may be following in this tradition.

Notes

I am grateful to Gregg Lambert for our discussions about this essay's argument and for help with translations.

1. Gregory Elliott, "The Necessity of Contingency: Some Notes," *Rethinking Marxism* 10.3 (1998), 78.

2. Louis Althusser, *Reading Capital*, trans. Ben Brewster (London: Verso, 1979), 57; hereafter *RC*.

3. Elliott, "Necessity of Contingency," 78.

4. Louis Althusser, *The Spectre of Hegel*, trans. G. M. Goshgarian (London: Verso, 1997), 76–77; hereafter *SH*.

5. Louis Althusser, "Lenin and Philosophy," *Lenin and Philosophy and Other Essays*, trans. Ben Brewster (New York: Monthly Review Press, 1971), 60–61; Louis Althusser, "Is It Simple to be a Marxist in Philosophy?" *Essays in Self Criticism*, trans. Grahame Lock (London: New Left Books, 1976), 193.

6. Frederick Engels, *Ludwig Feuerbach and the Outcome of Classical German Philosophy* (1888), ed. C. P. Dutt (New York: International Publishers, 1996), 21.

7. Thomas Huxley, *Hume* (New York: Harper and Brothers, 1879), 72.

8. Engels, *Ludwig Feuerbach*, 23.

9. V. I. Lenin, "Ten Questions to a Lecturer" (1908), in *Materialism and Empirio-Criticism* (Peking: Foreign Language Press, 1976), 1; hereafter *MEC*.

10. Lenin, *MEC*, 22–26, 236.

11. Althusser, "Simple to be a Marxist?" 195.

12. Althusser, "Du côté de la philosophie," *Écrits philosophiques et politiques*, ed. François Matheron (Paris: STOCK/IMEC, 1995, 1997), II: 277, 275.

13. Althusser, "Le courant souterrain du matérialisme de la rencontre," *Écrits philosophiques et politiques*, ed. François Matheron (Paris: STOCK/IMEC, 1994) I: 561; hereafter "SC."

14. Warren Montag, "The Emptiness of a Distance Taken: Freud, Althusser, Lacan," *Rethinking Marxism* 4.1 (1991), 36.

15. Jacques Lacan, *The Four Fundamental Concepts of Psychoanalysis*, trans. Alan Sheridan (New York: Norton, 1981), 53.

16. Etienne Balibar, "The Non-Contemporaneity of Althusser," *The Althusserian Legacy,* eds. E. Ann Kaplan and Michael Sprinker (London: Verso, 1993), 10.

17. Cf. Balibar, "The Non-Contemporaneity of Althusser," 12.

18. Ted Stolze, "Deleuze and Althusser: Flirting With Structuralism," *Rethinking Marxism* 10.3 (1998), 51.

19. Gilles Deleuze, *Empiricism and Subjectivity,* trans. Constantin V. Boundas (New York: Columbia University Press, 1991), 110; hereafter *ES.*

20. David Hume, *A Treatise on Human Nature,* ed. P. H. Nidditch (Oxford: Clarendon Press, 1978), 168; hereafter *T.*

21. Etienne Balibar, "The Nation Form," in Balibar and Immanuel Wallerstein, *Race, Nation, Class: Ambiguous Identities* (London: Verso, 1991), 88, 90–91.

22. Louis Althusser, *Machiavelli and Us,* trans. Gregory Elliott (London: Verso, 1999), 125–26.

23. David Hume, "On the Rise and Progress of the Arts and Sciences," *Essays Moral, Political, and Literary,* ed. Eugene F. Miller (Indianapolis: Liberty Press, 1987), 112.

24. Mao Tsetung, "On Contradiction," *Five Essays on Philosophy* (Peking: Foreign Language Press, 1977), 72–73.

Loving the Impossible: Derrida, Rousseau, and the Politics of Perfectibility

Penelope Deutscher

Could an unconditional hospitality ever be possible? Posing the question in recent work, Jacques Derrida asks whether a pure hospitality is possible. The language of purity circulates in his recent work, pure hospitality or the pure welcome. Pure hospitality is impossible, he argues. Yet this does not mean that it has no place as a referent (of impossibility) in Derrida's work. Consider its repetition in a sequence of four passages from his "Manifesto for Hospitality" of 1999:

> A pure welcome would consist not only in not knowing, acting as if one did not know, but in avoiding all questions about the other's identity, desires, rules, language, capacity for work, adaptation, insertion . . . [F]rom the moment I ask such questions and pose these conditions . . . the ideal situation of non-knowledge is broken.[1]

He writes of how social and political problems may be caught between "this idea of pure hospitality, this poetics of unconditional hospitality . . . and . . . the stakes of conditions, frontiers and ethnicity" (*MH* 98). For, he acknowledges, although there may be contexts in which pure hospitality is a social or political ideal, in fact "it is difficult to translate the purity of an ethics of hospitality into the body of the law" (*MH* 99).

The language of purity returns in Derrida's contemplation of the impossible rigor which would be required by a pure hospitality without limit. Those whom I welcome might violate, might be assassins, might bring disorder to my place of dwelling—none of these possibilities could be excluded. The risk that one might be overwhelmed or overtaken would have to be accepted, indeed affirmed (*MH* 100). For, Derrida continues, "this menace inhabits, in an essential and irreducible fashion the pure principle of hospitality" (*MH* 100). And so he concludes that we need to theorize a concept of responsibility "at the heart of conditional hospitality, in such a way that this might be the best possible. Responsibility would consist, then, in giving the best possible conditionality and the best possible laws or legality to a hospitality we hope might be as large as possible" (*MH* 101). Similarly in *Sur Parole*, he writes quite simply that "political responsibility consists in finding the best or the least bad legislation . . . in a concrete, determinate situation—for example France today . . . the best legislation so that hospitality can be respected in the best possible manner."[2]

Readers of his most recent work have been struck by Derrida's willingness to refer to his hopes for a better politics—for example, in such contexts as immigration policy. As a way of thinking about the direction taken by this material, I propose a focus on the interconnection of three terms in his recent work: purity, pervertibility, and perfectibility. Passages from "Manifesto for Hospitality" bear witness to the intermittent use of purity as a reference for impossibility in certain recent works. In conjunction, references to the pervertibility of any possible purity have been seen as in the comment, "there is no model hospitality, only processes in the throes of their own perversion" (*MH* 105). To give one example, Derrida describes the xenophobia lurking behind claims that one's home is one's own, even in the context of welcoming others into that home. Such implicit xenophobia lurking behind claims to protect one's own home and hospitality is, he writes, evidence of "the perversion and pervertibility of this law (which is also a law of hospitality)."[3] Pure hospitality is inherently pervertible. In other words, the status of the pure is that there is no such thing, only its contamination. The law of pure hospitality is that there could be no pure hospitality, only its perversion. Even if we could pass laws authorizing unrestricted immigration, for example, we could never perfectly comply with a (an impossible) pure hospitality.

In that case, is it meaningful to think of conditional hospitality as a perversion of a (an impossible) pure hospitality? Derrida has long reflected on the inevitable perversion and pervertibility of ideals of purity, and his writings on hospitality allow him to continue this reflection. But the third term which intertwines with purity and perversion in this recent material is perfectibility. Derrida comments, perhaps most surprisingly, "Hospitality is immediately pervertible and perfectible: there is no model hospitality, only processes, the constant being in the process of perverting and, improving, with this improving carrying with it the risks of perversion" (*MH* 105), and elsewhere, "I believe in . . . the infinite perfectibility of law."[4]

In the words of Catherine Malabou,[5] Derrida has changed. In a recent forum with him, she commented, "You don't challenge logocentrism in the same way anymore, or perhaps you no longer challenge the *same* logocentrism."[6] Malabou's suggestion that Derrida is no longer challenging the same logocentrism can be usefully considered in the context of this interconnected series of terms of purity, pervertibility, and perfectibility, as they operate in his recent work on hospitality. For Derrida's readers have seen this interconnected series before, in the period of Derrida's most unambiguous challenges to logocentrism, the period of *Of Grammatology*.[7] Derrida's analysis in that work of Jean-Jacques Rousseau's references to nature and the natural are based around his discussion of the paradoxical status of Rousseauist nature as pure, pervertible, and perfectible. For this reason Derrida's most recent return to the series, purity, pervertibility, and perfectibility, provides a context for assessing the transformation in his work over two decades. In considering his different relationship to this series of terms in these two periods of his work, we can consider the suggestion that Derrida is either no longer challenging logocentrism in the same way, or perhaps no longer the same logocentrism.

To this end, let's recall that operative slippage[8] in Rousseau's work across the multiple connotations of nature, so relentlessly and with such plasticity depicted as a good. Sometimes Rousseau associates nature with the countryside, opposed to the devalued city life of salons, artificiality, and false values. Rousseau's depictions of Emile and Julie connect their potential for honesty, simplicity, and authenticity to their metonymic proximity to the pastoral, or the garden. Rousseau's nature is also a law with whose dictates we should comply. It is often represented as a voice to which we should listen with our hearts, minds, or consciences. However, nature's voice is muted by civilization. Our faculty for listening—our heart, conscience, or will to listen to the dictates of nature—may be corrupted. Rousseau also refers to a hypothetical state of nature. This is a conceptual though not historical possibility of that which would have existed prior to culture. The variations in Rousseau's depictions of the state of nature in works such as *Discourse on the Origin of Inequality, Essay on the Origin of Languages,* and elsewhere are widely discussed.

However, *Of Grammatology* argues that despite the inconstancy of its definition, nature is a structural invariant in Rousseau's work. Derrida reminds that "one can vary the facts without modifying the structural invariant" (*OG* 252). Rousseau systematically posits nature as anterior to the civilization which constitutes its inevitable degradation (and evolution). Nature always connotes authenticity. It always signifies purity in opposition to what is devalued as unnatural. A pastoral community obeys the dictates of nature while a highly cultivated, denatured city does not. True, the pastoral community is not to be equated with a state of nature. It could even be considered a perversion of nature, although Rousseau does not say so. It is still closer to nature than a highly artificial city-life.

That the pastoral community might be considered a perversion of nature when compared to a hypothetical state of nature, but still connotes authenticity when opposed to the highly unnatural, perverted mores of city life, shows how variable is the content of the term "nature." But for all this variability, nature remains a structural invariant in Rousseau's work insofar as it systematically signifies anteriority. Although a state of nature would be anterior to a pastoral community, the latter remains anterior—and so natural—when opposed to city life.

Derrida emphasizes that another structural invariant about Rousseauist nature is the inevitability of its perversion. The hypothetical state of nature is structurally pervertible. This destabilizes Rousseau's opposition between nature and perversion. In Derrida's well-known formulation from this period in his work, Rousseau describes what he does not declare. His text describes what he does not wish to say (*OG* 229). Rousseau associates nature with a hypothetical point of purity. He opposes it to the corruptions of humanity: our vain and arrogant quest for more knowledge than we need, our invasive mining of the earth (deemed by Rousseau a rape of nature), our vanity, greed, and artificiality. But his work also describes the perversion of nature as inevitable. Hypothetical states of nature, though their details may vary in Rousseau's work, are depicted in terms of their own inevitable mutation. Isolated humans will group together, grunting humans will develop language, men and women who copulate randomly will develop forms of love and tenderness and form couples, humans originally indifferent to the suffering of others find that their empathy, pity, and imagination are aroused by that suffering. Eventually humans will enclose a plot of land and take it into their heads to say, "*this is mine.*"[9] The inevitability of progress lies at the heart of the very nature that Rousseau also opposes to progress. If nature is associated with the pure in Rousseau's work, in opposition to the perversion of nature, nature is also depicted as inherently pervertible. Nature is both opposed to perversion and incorporates pervertibility—the inevitability of its own denaturalization. Rousseauist nature is that which denatures.

This does not minimize the rhetorical depiction of nature in terms of a lost or impossible purity. A pure nature (one which did not denature) is, according to the terms of Rousseau's analysis, impossible. But this does not inhibit his reverie for what we never could have had. For this reason, the state of nature is where we might have spent our days "insensibly in peace and innocence" ("Origin" 54) despite Rousseau's simultaneous definition of humans in terms of their own plasticity and capacity for modification and adaptation. Our perfectibility inevitably draws us out of any original state in which we might have spent our days "insensibly in peace and innocence." We never could have so passed our days. Our perfectibility would always have necessitated our own transcendence of that state.

Pervertibility and perfectibility dissolve into each other in Rousseau's work. Perfectibility (imagination, empathy, the forming of social bonds) leads eventually to the development of reason and to the arrogant acquisition of excessive knowledge, wealth, and property. So perfectibility does open the way to the vice and error which are associated with pervertibility and which do not belong in Rousseau's hypothetical state of nature. But, as Dent summarizes, "Perfectibility may open the way to vice and error; but without it there can be no virtue or wisdom either."[10] As Rousseau formulates this point:

> It would be sad for us to be forced to agree that this distinctive and almost unlimited faculty [perfectibility] is the source of all man's misfortunes; that this is what, by dint of time, draws him out of that original condition in which he would pass tranquil and innocent days; that this is what, through centuries of giving rise to his enlightenment and his errors, his vices and his virtues, eventually makes him a tyrant over himself and nature. ("Origin" 45)

Perfectibility relies on the pervertibility of nature and vice versa. But since the collapse from a state of nature is structurally inevitable, perfectibility also represents our only hope of redemption. We need our capacity for self-improvement, our plasticity, our capacity for modification and adaptation. Perfectibility invariably draws us out of any original state in which we might otherwise have spent out days "insensibly in peace and innocence" and eventually makes us tyrants over nature. But only because of perfectibility do we have the potential for the imagination, memory, reflection, and regulated rationality that allow us to understand ourselves as a perversion of nature's dictates. This understanding is necessary to our attempt to establish a human life in accordance with the dictates of nature.

Having read Rousseau's concept of perfectibility with acuity in *Of Grammatology* in the late sixties, Derrida has turn around more recently, in 1999, to declare his own passion for perfectibility: "I love the process of perfectibility."[11] While his interest in perfectibility has been widely expressed in recent work including *Specters of Marx* (1994),[12] my focus here is directed to occasions on which this is expressed as part of a chain of concurrent references to pervertibility and purity, as seen in the discussions of hospitality.

How does Derrida differently return to the interconnection he had earlier established between a philosopher's references to perfectibility and to impossible purity? Despite the chasm between Rousseau's discussion of nature and Derrida's discussion of hospitality,[13] I discuss them as a conjunction which allows us to reflect on what I take to be Derrida's altered relation to logocentrism in his recent work.

In relation to the impossible pure hospitality discussed by Derrida, all acts of hospitality can only be considered perversions. Pure hospitality is always already its own perversion. Since there could never be a pure hospitality, one might question its very status as a referent. Though it is impossible, it still prompts the speaker to rhetorically qualify as impure (by contrast) all acts of hospitality open to us. In his early work Derrida exposed the sleight of hand by which corruption is designated by contrast to a nature figured as pure. This was considered a sleight of hand because the pure enfolds its own potential for corruption. The opposition between pure and perversion does not stand up to scrutiny.

Because of the constancy of his early exposures of philosophers who refer to points of purity (*logos, eidos,* intention, nature, the savage, and so on) and whose coherence their own texts also undermine, we would not expect Derrida to indulge a reference to the pure. Yet the language of a (an impossible) pure hospitality has enormous currency in Derrida's later work, the very word "pure" repeatedly sounding like a bell in "Manifesto for Hospitality," so there could be no mistake about it.

Let's imagine a philosopher impassioned by the idea of unconditional hospitality. He dreams of open boundaries: subjective boundaries, national boundaries without limit, a generalized openness in all ways to all things. Our encounters with others would not be subject to questions such as: Who are you? Can you work? Have you money? Do you speak our language? Are you reasonable? Humanitarian? Male/female/human? We'd be open to the possibility of the not necessarily human, the radically other, or the unexpected. Come! Come! we'd say, gladly, with no idea for what we were waiting, and to whom or to what we were saying come. Figured in Derrida's work is the question—in that sense, the (im)possibility—of saying, in this sense, come.

Anyone who dreamt of such radical openness must realize its impossibility. Thus Derrida tells us on the one hand that "I try to think pure and unconditional hospitality, the idea of a pure welcoming of the unexpected guest, the unexpected arriving one" (*DE* 98). It could also be said that we are always thinking about the (im)possibility of unconditional hospitality in all our gestures of conditional hospitality: "I cannot think of a conditional hospitality without having in mind a pure hospitality" (*DE* 98). But Derrida means without having it in mind *as impossible.* In this sense, every act of impure hospitality—every act of hospitality, in other words—could be thought of as the presence of the absence of (the trace of) an impossible, pure hospitality.

Because the pure—(impossible) unconditional hospitality—does remain in Derrida's texts as a reference, as a result impure, conditional hospitality is depicted as less than we might have dreamed for:

> We have to improve the conditions of conditional hospitality, we can change, we should change the laws on immigration, as far as possible . . . We have the desire for this perfectibility. . . If we have a concept of conditional hospitality, it's because we have also the idea of a pure hospitality, of unconditional hospitality. (*DE* 101)

True, we have this idea as impossible—but still, we have it.

Someone comes along and says to our imaginary, dreaming philosopher: "Isn't your unconditional hospitality always already the necessity of its own perversion? Your unconditional hospitality is infinitely deferred in dreams and ideals. Your unconditional hospitality will always have been contaminated by the virus of conditional hospitality!" In other words, Derrida's legacy is that his readers can't hear the expression "pure hospitality" without incredulity. When the sanitary cordon is drawn around a field represented by the word "pure," and we are told that contamination comes from elsewhere—in fact, Derrida emphasizes that pure and impure hospitality are radically heterogeneous, although also inseparable[14]—don't we look suspiciously for the inevitable contamination at the heart of the pure? The point of Derrida's reading of Rousseau, for example, was precisely to argue that the necessity for the supplement lay at the heart of what he figured as original: "The supplement to Nature is within Nature as its play" (*OG* 258).

When Derrida comes to redeploy the series purity-pervertibility-perfectibility in his discussions of hospitality is he, to return to Catherine Malabou's question, no longer challenging logocentrism? Conditional hospitality is figured as perversion by Derrida's by contrast to an ideal field positioned as pure: pure hospitality. This despite the fact that the same author who appeals to the ideal of pure hospitality also depicts its impossibility.

Critical to an understanding of Derrida's different relationship to the series purity-pervertibility-perfectibility as analyzed in his earliest work, and redeployed more recently, is a comparison of the work on hospitality with *Of Grammatology*. Derrida's suggestion that Rousseau's texts describe something other than they declare reverberates through the last third of that work. Rousseau declares that pervertibility is not natural, at least insofar as he opposes perversion to nature. Undermining this declared content, his corpus describes the implicit pervertibility, or unnaturalness, of nature. Rousseau's texts capitalize on nature as a referent of the pure through their devalorizing denunciations of the unnatural. These denunciations lose the semblance of coherence in the light of the concurrent depiction of perversion as lying at the heart of nature, inevitable to it.

Willfully appealing to a point, concept, ideal, or law repeatedly depicted as pure, Derrida uses this appeal, and this referent, differently from Rousseau. His reference to the pure occurs specifically in the context of an overt, declared argument that the pure needs its own perversion, that pervertibility does lie at the heart of the pure. If his invocation of purity is not the same logocentrism, perhaps it is because Derrida willingly declares what he describes. Unlike Rousseau, Derrida both declares and describes that the pure would always be its own perversion.

Let's think back to his comment, "in fact, it is difficult to translate the purity of an ethics of hospitality into the body of the law" (*MH* 99). If his were a repetition of the logic of supplementarity, we'd expect Derrida to say that the Law of pure hospitality is coherent even in the absence of conditional hospitality. By contrast, Derrida insists that any pure hospitality, any Law of hospitality, always contains the possibility of its own perversion.[15] Without conditional hospitality, he writes, an "unconditional Law of hospitality would be in danger of remaining a pious and irresponsible desire, without form, and without potency" (*CF* 23). Any law of unconditional hospitality is meaningless except in the context of its perversion by conditional laws. If the Law of hospitality seems to be "above" laws of hospitality, it also requires them:

> But even while keeping itself above the laws of hospitality, *the* unconditional law of hospitality needs the laws, it requires them. This demand is constitutive. It wouldn't be effectively unconditional, the law, if it didn't *have to become* effective, concrete, determined, if that were not its being as having to be. It would risk being abstract, utopian, illusory, and so turning over into its opposite. In order to be what it is, *the* law thus needs the laws, which however, deny it, or at any rate threaten it, sometimes corrupt or pervert it. And must always be able to do this. (*OH* 79)

To distinguish Derrida's deployment of a concept of the pure from the logocentric Rousseauist logic of supplementarity, I have suggested that Derrida declares what he describes. That the pure requires its own perversion (and in this sense is already its own perversion) is not disavowed by Derrida. By contrast, when in *Of Grammatology* Derrida analyzes the interconnection between pervertibility and perfectibility in Rousseau's work, this is how he depicts it: "What should never have happened had to come to pass . . . . But Rousseau does not *affirm* it . . . . He resigns himself to it" (*OG* 259–60). Does Derrida resign himself to, or affirm, the necessary perversion of any unconditional law of hospitality by impure laws of hospitality? He takes some pains to affirm this necessity, hence perhaps his startling declaration of love for perfectibility.

Finally, then, the status of perfectibility in Derrida's later work can be compared with his analysis of it as a Rousseauist term in *Of Grammatology* in his earlier work. In Rousseau's work perfectibility should connote the infinite transformability of the human. Instead it has the status of restitution. Despite the unviability of any (hypothetical) original state, Rousseau mourns it, at least insofar as he writes of the peace, innocence, and tranquil days in which we would have remained were that not impossible and incoherent. What is Rousseau anticipating? With his love of perfectibility it should be the future, each moment containing new possibilities for human development. While inseparable from pervertibility, perfectibility also makes possible the knowledge, virtue, and wisdom which allow a transgression of the corrupt, avaricious, worldly existence in which we find ourselves. Perfectibility should allow a passion for the future. Its effect should be equal to our nostalgia for any impossible, lost, hypothetical original. But in Rousseau's work, these affects are not equally balanced. His love of the future is no openness to the new. If Rousseau loves perfectibility, it is only because it enables us to listen to the dictates of nature. By contrast, we have Derrida's love—or so he depicts it. He adds to his declaration: "I love the process of perfectibility" the rejoinder "I'm for progress, I'm a 'progressist.' I think the law is perfectible and we can improve the law" (*DE* 100).

Derrida's passion for perfectibility is a passion for the future which has little in common with Rousseau's restitutive nostalgia. Rousseau should have loved an unpredictable future, but he did not. Though the state of nature would have been impossible, he mourns what could not have been: A state we might not have had to collapse inevitably out of. Rousseau's future is no state of nature, but it is described as a more natural, less artificial state of humanity.

And what does Derrida love? Certainly a future he knew he loved, or waited for, would not be the future but the projection of the present. Derrida anticipates the new. The future is deemed impossible, in terms described as messianic: "What I mean by 'messianicity' is the general structure of our relation to what is coming. Usually, we call this the future [in French, *l'avenir*]" (*DE* 67). The messianic structure is, he reminds, "the relation . . . to the unexpected surprise. . . . If I could anticipate, if I had an horizon of anticipation, if I could see what is coming or who is coming, there would be no coming" (*DE* 67–68). And in these terms he speaks of democracy "to come," "as opposed or as different to what we know today under the name of democracy" (*DE* 68): "For democracy remains to come. . . not only will it remain infinitely perfectible, hence always insufficient and future, but, belonging to the time of the promise, it will always remain, in each of its future times, to come."[16]

By contrast, I have suggested that Rousseau knows too well the future he anticipates. Works of imagination, he writes in the *Dialogue on the Subject of Romance*,

> must . . . reduce all things to a state of nature, make mankind in
> love with a life of peace and simplicity, destroy their prejudices and
> opinions, . . . keep them distant from each other, and instead of exciting
> people to crowd into large cities, persuade them to spread themselves all
> over the kingdom . . . to convince mankind that in rural life there are
> many pleasures which they know not how to enjoy; that the pleasures
> are neither so insipid nor so gross as they imagine.[17]

Rousseau knows what he anticipates in the sense that he can name the idyll that might arise from our cultivation of the capacity to listen to nature. Rousseau is waiting for a future which is natural, a future he can already easily describe. While the future would not restore the state of nature, it would restore the natural.

If nature, even in the future, must always already be pervertible, Rousseau can acknowledge this only with difficulty. Responsible for the inevitable collapse out of the state of nature, would perfectibility not also be responsible for an inevitable progression beyond any idyll we might establish in the future in accordance with the dictates of nature? For this reason, we can see how problematically static is Rousseau's depiction of his idyll. If only humans would listen to nature, he thinks, love peace and simplicity, destroy prejudice, pride, and opinion, avoid large cities, spread over the kingdoms and learn to enjoy the pleasures of rural life, perfectibility/pervertibility would seemingly propel them to a renewal of inevitable corruption. The Rousseauist future should be, but is not, an endless process. In this sense, Rousseau is not anticipating an unknown future, but the restoration of what we already know if we listen to our hearts and to the voice of nature. In this sense, Rousseau knows too well the future he anticipates.

The form of this interconnection of purity, pervertibility, and perfectibility in Rousseau's work helps us to understand better what occurs when this interconnection is borrowed and redeployed by Derrida—otherwise—in his recent work. Derrida does not know too well the future he anticipates, as he emphasizes: "Future, 'l'avenir' is an ambiguous name because if by 'future' one understands the modality of the present, the present of tomorrow, then we would find again some reduction to the living present that I would like to avoid. So that's why I say: 'to come' (in French, *à-venir*) rather than the future." (*DE* 67).

But this causes some tension with the supposition that he is anticipating the good, or at least the better, that anticipation so heavily emphasized by his use of the term perfectibility. On the one hand, deconstruction is tirelessly, in Derrida's recent writing, associated with the good. It is associated with progress and with gestures toward a democracy to come, gestures toward legal reform in terms of greater hospitality in contexts of asylum and immigration, for example:

> For instance, the Declaration of the Rights of Man has been improved for the last two centuries, there have been a series of declarations which have added new rights for the workers, for women and so on and so forth. So we can improve the law, the legal system, and to improve means to deconstruct. It is to criticize a previous state of the law and to change it into a better one. That is why the law is deconstructible. (*DE* 87)

So, he goes on to affirm: "I think the law is perfectible and we can improve the law. We have to improve the conditions of conditional hospitality, we can change, we should change the laws on immigration, as far as possible" (*DE* 100).

These heavily underscored references to progress suggest Derrida's confidence that reformed immigration laws are better. In other words, he professes with alacrity to recognize progress. But when asked, as he was in 1999 by Genevieve Lloyd, "can reflection on the messianic structure of consciousness help us live more constructively with uncertainty?"(*DE* 68), Derrida responds in the negative. He elaborates, "Then the problem would be solved, we would know how to live constructively with uncertainty, there would be no uncertainty, or the uncertainty would be under control. Messianicity means that the uncertainty is not and will never be under control" (*DE* 68).

Apparently, then, Derrida would have us suppose both that perfectibility takes us in the direction of progress but also that this is in no way ensured. His recent work is founded on this contradiction. But he does affirm this tension rather than disavow it. How readily he tells of his love for progress and legal reform, and yet how readily that we cannot, by definition, anticipate the future we think we anticipate. We think we know the good (at least the better). We have to think the good is what's to come, that we can identify progress. We may think of the future in terms of progress, but the future is also impossible; it is also the radically unanticipated. This is a contradiction and, Derrida affirms, an ethically critical one.

So is it that Derrida no longer challenges logocentrism—or is it no longer the same logocentrism? His references to the good, the better, to progress, to the pure, to perfectibility, to democracy to come, appear to be flagrant appeals to logocentrism. Yet this same material affirms that both the pure and the future are impossible. It is Derrida who writes that he wants to liberate the messianic from any "dogmatics and even from any metaphysico-religious determination, from any messianism."[18]

According to Derrida, we differ from those who wait for the Messiah, for example, in that we do not know what we anticipate. But according to Derrida, the assumption that we do know what we anticipate is also unavoidable: We anticipate the good, legal reform, democracy to come. Derrida does not pretend he is not dogmatic. I love progress, he says. And simultaneously he undermines it: I anticipate progress. By definition I can't anticipate progress. These two movements have to be understood as operating together. For if not, Derrida either does not know the future he anticipates (which is hardly coherent; he believes it's the good, or at least something better) or he does: which is incoherent, for he has defined the future as that which could not be anticipated. His recent work relies on that double movement.

The most straightforward reading of Derrida's work would be to argue that the appeal to the future as the "to come" is not logocentric. The *à venir* is not a presence beyond the horizon, a point in the future of static ideal democracy or utopia. It is for this reason that John Caputo has, for example, argued that Derrida's is a religion without religion,[19] and we could add that it is a faith in progress without faith in progress, and so on. But what of the suggestion that Derrida has engaged with a different logocentrism? Taking up this suggestion, I'd like to focus more closely on the way in which Derrida's is a logocentism which cancels itself out. It cancels itself out, but it is generated out of that canceling. This is a different interpretation from those who have argued that only a misreading could see Derrida as turning to logocentrism and Enlightenment values in his later work. While it is crucial not to overlook Derrida's emphasis on impossibility, it is also important to appreciate the stakes of a philosophy of impossibility. Doesn't a philosophy of impossibility rhetorically profit by naming the impossible?

For example, in thinking pure hospitality, we have to think it *as* impossible and as always impure. But for a fraction of a moment, one thinks pure hospitality—although so as to think its impossibility. Infinestimally it is given the status of a possibility, just as that possibility is cancelled out.

Insisting that pure hospitality is impossible, these writings nevertheless derive the fractional, unstable, affective profit from the writing of the (im)possibility of any pure hospitality.

In Derrida's early deconstructive readings of philosophers such as Plato and Rousseau, he demonstrated the impossibility of logocentric purity. In exposing an always contaminated ideal, as Derrida exposed the status of Rousseau's nature or Plato's *eidos*, I would not argue that his own writing gained any rhetorical profit from the argument that pure nature is impossible, nor from the argument that a pure *eidos* is impossible. By contrast, the politics of demonstrating that pure hospitality is impossible are, I am arguing, quite different. According to his later work: "the experience of the impossible is not simply the experience of something which is not given in actuality, not accessible, but something through which a possibility is given" (*DE* 64), and in this vein he affirms: "Unconditional hospitality can't be an establishment, but it may happen as a miracle . . . in an instant, not lasting more than an instant, it may happen. This is the . . . possible happening of something impossible" (*DE* 102).

Derrida writes that the purely other is impossible to us: "When I see the other appear, I am already mourning his absence."[20] In *The Prayers and Tears of Jacques Derrida,* John Caputo has stressed that Derrida is saying "come, come" to the purely other. But what must not be decoupled from this is Derrida's concurrent argument that the purely other is impossible for us. It is not that Derrida is drawing a boundary around our own possibilities, on the other side of which lies a self-present, pure other or a field of pure hospitality to which he is saying: come. If ever we say come to the other, to the future, or to an unconditional hospitality, it is also only insofar as it is also impossible to do so. If Derrida speaks of the pure—be this relentlessly, in his recent work—it is to rewrite purity; it is to say that the pure could never be. One would always be mourning the pure as impossible. As Caputo formulates this point, "The advent of the other . . . is to be distinguished, Derrida says, from a 'theological' order . . . where . . . the theological means the God-given, pre-given order of what is already there. For such an invention there is little to do save 'supplement' God's work" (*Prayers* x). Derrida's other is not a pregiven order, and conditional hospitality is not the supplement.

In discussing Derrida's recent material, Caputo makes a welcome reference to Luce Irigaray's work. One need not, he cautions, "turn the figure of Woman into a religion, unless of course religion is reinterpreted as a desire for intimacy, and that, I think, corresponds nicely to what Irigaray means by the divine and to what Derrida has recently called a "religion without religion" (*Prayers* 144). His brief juxtaposition of Derrida's recent work and Irigarayan feminism provokes a question not widely asked in recent debate about deconstruction and feminism:[21] What would a feminism of hospitality be? What would the implications of hospitality be for a feminist politics of sexual difference? Luce Irigaray could be said to anticipate a new permutation of sexual difference, which she takes to be impossible.[22] Anticipating an excluded possibility for sexual difference, she does not know, by definition, what she anticipates. This need not mean that sexual difference as what she anticipates is posited as having a pregiven identity. True, in anticipating I designate an other. True, designating the other sexual difference is misleading, since it assumes we know what we anticipate. By definition we would not recognize the sexual difference we anticipate. When we say that ours is a politics of sexual difference, in other words, we project the present into the future.[23]

For to return to John Caputo's discussion, "the figure of the future is an absolute surprise, and as such . . . something monstrous. To prepare for the future, were that possible, would be to prepare for a coming species of monster, it would be to welcome the monstrous *arrivant,* to welcome it, that is, to accord hospitality to that which is absolutely foreign, or strange."[24] "We always try to domesticate this monster," adds Caputo, but "the *tout autre* for Derrida is always, more importantly, structurally outside, out of place, out of power, im-possible, to-come. If the Messiah ever actually showed up, if you ever thought that justice had come—that would ruin everything" (*Prayers* 74).

To be sure, Irigaray's waiting for sexual difference is a domestication of the monster. The point is the inevitability of this domestication. We love perfectibility; we anticipate the other, the future, the new, or even sexual difference. In other words, much as Derrida once affirmed that he never said there was no subject, we might see him now as "never having said there were no politics." We are constantly saying "yes, come." We can't do so without anticipation, even though anticipation is impossible, the taming of the monster. Sexual difference, as with anything we designate the radically other, is impossible. It is not an identity lying on the other side of our field of expectation, not a pregiven order. In writing about this material one inevitably lends identity to that other anticipated by Derrida and Irigaray: the future, the new democracy, sexual difference, as when we say, as if we know what this means: that Derrida is saying come to the radically other.

"It" cancels itself out as it says itself. There is no it, but as we say it, for that brief moment, that impossible has an infinestimal possibility as impossible, in its self-canceling. Another way of putting it might be that we don't know what we're waiting for, but we know that we're waiting. So of course Irigaray loves sexual difference, and Derrida progress. They've got nothing to lose, and not doing so is not an option. You may as well love it: I love progress, declares Derrida. I love progress toward sexual difference, declares Irigaray. But these are, at the same time, those inevitable domestications of the monster from lovers of the impossible. Is Derrida "no longer challenging logocentrism in the same way anymore?" As Caputo points out, "Derrida's interest in unmasking the tensions within 'hospitality' is not aimed at cynically unmasking it."[25] To understand this, compare, I have suggested, the stakes of Derrida's discussion of Rousseauist pure nature as impossible (which could be described as an unmasking), and more recently of pure hospitality as impossible. Derrida attributes the radically other with (non-) presence just long enough to say this is impossible. To whatever extent he does so, he says "this is monstrous" at the same time as, infinestimally, he tames the monster. But to whatever extent this is so: "a possibility is given."

Notes

1. Jacques Derrida, *Manifeste pour l'hospitalité*, ed. M. Seffahi (Paris: Editions Paroles d'aube, 1999), 98. Hereafter *MH*.

2. Jacques Derrida, *Sur parole–Instantanés philosophiques* (Paris: La Tour d'Aigues, Editions de l'aube, 1999), 71.

3. Jacques Derrida, *Of Hospitality: Anne Dufourmantelle Invites Jacques Derrida to Respond*, trans. Rachel Bowlby (Stanford: Stanford University Press, 2000), 53; hereafter *OH*.

4. Jacques Derrida, "Fidelité à plus d'un," *Cahiers Intersignes* 13 (1998): 221–265, especially 258.

5. Coauthor with Derrida of the collaborative work *La Contre-allée* (Paris: Quinzaine littéraire–Louis Vuitton, 1999).

6. C. Malabou, "Toucher sans prêter main-forte," unpublished manuscript, 2000: 3.

7. See Jacques Derrida, *Of Grammatology* (corrected edition), trans. Gayatri Chavravorty Spivak (Baltimore: Johns Hopkins Press, 1997); hereafter *OG*.

8. The analysis of this as an operative slippage is pursued further in Penelope Deutscher, *Yielding Gender: Feminism, Deconstruction and the History of Philosophy* (New York: Routledge, 1997).

9. Jean-Jacques Rousseau, "Discourse on the Origin and Foundations of Inequality Among Men," in *The Basic Political Writings of Jean-Jacques Rousseau* [*PW*], trans D. A. Cress (Indianapolis: Hackett, 1987), 23–109, especially 60; hereafter "Origin."

10. N. J. H. Dent, *A Rousseau Dictionary* (Oxford: Blackwell, 1992), 191.

11. Jacques Derrida, *Deconstruction Engaged: The Sydney Seminars*, ed. Paul Patton and Terry Smith (Sydney: Power Publications, 2001), 100; hereafter *DE*.

12. See Jacques Derrida, *Specters of Marx: The State of the Debt, the Work of Mourning, and the New International* (New York: Routledge, 1994).

13. This said, texts such as Rousseau's "Discourse on Political Economy" ad-

dress themes of justice in relation to national boundaries. For example, considering the body politic as "like a body that is organized, living and similar to that of a man," a "moral being which possesses a will," Rousseau acknowledges that "this rule of justice, on a firm footing with all citizens, can be defective with regard to foreigners" (*PW* 111–38, especially 114). In the "Social Contract" (*PW* 139–227) he qualifies this by saying that the foreigner is not part of the social body but an external factor in relation to which a people "becomes a simple being, an individual" (from which the foreigner is excluded) (149). In "Political Economy" he also raises the issue of whether human virtues are naturally extended to foreigners in distant lands: "It seems that the sentiment of humanity evaporates and weakens in being extended over the entire world, and that we cannot be affected by the calamities in Tartary or Japan the way we are by those of a European people" (121). We seek, and rightly seek, the happiness of others, but not the happiness of those who are far from us or foreign to us, who are also not understood as sharing the common interest. Furthermore, Rousseau associates the foundation for my love of my country with the fact that what my country extends to me is precisely not extended to foreigners. How, he asks, could I love a country which extends to me only what it would extend to any foreigner? (122)

14. See Derrida, *Sur parole*, 73; and Derrida, *Deconstruction Engaged*, 87.

15. Jacques Derrida, *On Cosmopolitanism and Forgiveness*, trans. Mark Dooley and Michael Hughes (New York: Routledge, 2001), 17; hereafter *CF*.

16. Jacques Derrida, *The Politics of Friendship* (London: Verso Books, 1997), 306.

17. Jean-Jacques Rousseau, *A Dialogue Between a Man of Letters and Jean-Jacques Rousseau on the Subject of Romance*, in Jean-Jacques Rousseau, *Eloisa, or a Series of Original Letters*, trans. William Kenrick (2 vols.; Oxford: Woodstock Books, 1989), 1:xi–xlii, especially xxviii.

18. Derrida, *Specters*, 89.

19. This expression provides the subtitle of John Caputo's *The Prayers and Tears of Jacques Derrida* (Bloomington: Indiana University Press, 1997); hereafter *Prayers*.

20. Derrida, "Fidelité à plus d'un," 227.

21. For example, it is not a question asked in essays included in the recent anthologies on Derrida and feminism edited by N. J. Holland [*Feminist Interpretations of Jacques Derrida* (University Park: Pennsylvania State University Press, 1997)]; and E. K. Feder, M. C. Rawlinson, et al. [*Derrida and Feminism: Recasting the Question of Woman* (New York: Routledge, 1997)]; nor is it discussed in D. Elam, *Feminism and Deconstruction: Ms. en abyme* (New York: Routledge, 1994). However, in a recent unpublished essay, "Universality, Singularity and Sexual Difference" (2000), Diane Perpich explores the connections between Irigarayan feminism and Derrida's latest work.

22. She specifically calls hers a politics of the impossible; see Luce Irigaray, *I Love To You: Sketch of a Possible Felicity in History* (New York: Routledge, 1996), 10.

23. Of course I do not mean that Irigaray hopes for a culture in which sexual difference means what it does now. To the contrary, Irigaray hopes precisely for a

culture of sexual difference which would be other than any sexual difference we now know. But insofar as she names the future in terms of a new or another sexual difference, the point would be that she still projects the present into the future.

24. Caputo, *Prayers*, 74; citing Jacques Derrida, *Points . . . Interviews, 1974–1995*, ed. Elisabeth Weber (Stanford: Stanford University Press, 1995), 386–7.

25. John D. Caputo, *Deconstruction in a Nutshell: A Conversation with Jacques Derrida* (New York: Fordham University Press, 1997), 112.

"What We Cannot Say": Gadamer, Kant, and Freedom

Dennis J. Schmidt

> Diese Erhebung des allertiefsten Centri in Licht geschieht in
> keiner der uns sichtbaren Creaturen ausser im Menschen. Im
> Menschen ist die ganze Macht des finstern Princips und in eben
> demselben zugleich die ganze Kraft des Lichts. In ihm ist der
> tiefste Abgrund und der höchste Himmel, oder beide Centra. . . .
> Der Mensch hat dadurch . . . der Geist. Denn der ewige Geist
> spricht die Einheit oder das Wort aus in die Natur. Das
> ausgesprochene (reale) Wort aber ist nur in der Einheit von
> Licht und Dunkel.
>
> Schelling, *Philosophische Untersuchungen über das Wesen der*
> *menschlichen Freiheit*

My intention in what follows is to ask about the kinship of language and
freedom. More precisely, it is to ask a two-part question. First, to what extent does the word (that is, language or speech) open the experience of
freedom? And second, is it possible to speak of freedom? As you will see, I
am not interested in the question of "free speech" here. I am, however, interested in asking whether the "fact" of language illuminates something of
the "fact" of freedom and how the meaning of freedom divides itself as we
try to elucidate this fact. As the title of my paper might indicate, I will suggest that it is in approaching the limits of language that this question becomes most interesting. One might say that the point most in need of being
spoken about in the matter of freedom is the point at which we cannot
speak. Or, put even more paradoxically, I want to suggest that the proper
expression of freedom, however it is conceived, is the existence of language
itself, but that freedom is not able to be expressed as a proposition in language. Finally, I want to suggest that this paradox of the kinship of language

and freedom has some significant consequences for what it means for us to try to speak of moral life, that is, to speak of human freedom.

This question, at least as I want to pose it, has two distinct philosophical heritages inspiring it. The concern with the theme of freedom has its roots in Kant and German Idealism (Schelling most of all), while my interest in the theme of the limits of language is indebted chiefly to Heidegger and Gadamer. But the impulse driving this effort to unite these two themes belongs to the future of philosophy, not its past: I believe that it is necessary for those of us who work out of this tradition inaugurated by Heidegger and Gadamer to find a way to speak more directly to questions that are traditionally taken as matters of moral philosophy (and lest there be any confusion about this matter, let me say here that I take "moral philosophy" to be that form of thinking which is centered above all on the enigma of human freedom; it is *not*, at least as I understand it, a form of thinking which is bent upon setting up prescriptions for human behavior). While I confess that the questions of moral life have not been central to the tradition of hermeneutics, which has been more identified with the question of truth than of freedom, I nonetheless believe that in the future hermeneutics will come to be seen as marking an original achievement in the field of moral philosophy. My hope is to begin to open avenues for this achievement to become more visible. One way for this to come to pass is to begin to understand how it is that the relation of thinking and language which has formed the center of the tradition of hermeneutics speaks, quite directly, to the relation of thinking and moral life as it has been unfolded by Kant and his immediate successors.

To begin this project, I argue that Kant's moral philosophy, which operates by unpacking the relation between reason and freedom, assumes (without ever *thematizing*) a quite distinct conception of language. It is the conceptualizing possibilities of the word that underpins Kant's efforts to grant an essential place to the juridical meaning of freedom in any understanding of human experience. In short, Kant privileges what one might call not simply a metaphysical conception of language but, more so, the language of metaphysics itself. However, the reflections on language that we find in Heidegger and Gadamer include a sharp and, to my mind, persuasive critique of such a conception of language. This "hermeneutic theory" of language undermines the presumptions of privilege that might be said to belong to the language of metaphysics—in fact, here we see that it is another sort of relation to the word, one which is more the province of poetry than of philosophy, that drives us to the deepest forms of the experience of language.

But here my question begins. I find Kant's arguments about the kinship between thinking and freedom compelling and I believe that an effort to grant freedom a place in how we think of human experience must be central to all philosophizing worthy of its name. I believe that he is simply right when he suggests that only by acknowledging this issue of freedom, of the unconditioned, do we come to understand the moral weight of experience. But I find the treatment of language in Heidegger and Gadamer equally compelling and just as central to any possible conception of human experience; and yet, as I will argue, this conception of language undermines much of what Kant will come to conclude regarding the moral law, and it will shift how we need to think of the meaning of freedom as the basis of this law. So my question is this: What might we say, if anything, about the riddle of moral life, the enigma of freedom, in light of the remarks on language which have been so central to the hermeneutic tradition?

My remarks here are divided into two parts. In the first part, which focuses chiefly on Kant's *Grundlegung*, my intention is to outline what one might call a "juridical" answer to this question about the kinship of language and moral life. This answer has provided a justification in the history of philosophy for the authority of philosophic language in matters of moral life. But it is precisely this answer which I believe is no longer tenable in light of what has been learned about language from hermeneutics. In the second part, which takes Kant's third critique as a point of departure, my intention is to outline what I take to be a more interesting answer to this question, an answer which Gadamer has done much to open. Because I am most interested in what I take to be the progressive possibilities which emerge from the "hermeneutic" approach to this question, the second part of my paper is given more attention.

To clarify what I am calling the juridical account of the moral significance of the fact of language, four points need to be established: First, that in the history of philosophy the governing consensus is that truth is what we most desire and what language is most in need of saying; second, that the proper language of philosophizing is, in some manner or other, conceptual, and that the concept marks the summit of the possibilities of the word; third, that by virtue of its relation to truth and to the conceptualizing power of language philosophy must understand itself as bearing a unique duty to the law; fourth, that the desire, language, and duty of philosophy are understood as needing to be secured by being grounded in the act whereby philosophizing takes possession of itself. While a thorough treatment of my question would need to elaborate upon all four of these points, the second and third points here—namely, the claim that the concept is the preeminent possibility of language, and the claim that the relation between the language of philosophy and the foundations of law is a privileged one—will serve as the center of my remarks since together they ground what has long been assumed to be the legislative function of philosophy. Most notable here is that the moral meaning of the fact of language is understood in this juridical account in the way that language introduces the possibility of law, instead of serving (as in the hermeneutic account) as testimony to the actuality of freedom.

We already find the argument for the legislative function of philosophy more or less explicitly formulated in Plato and Aristotle. Each suggests that philosophy has a fundamental authority in matters concerning human affairs. But it is Kant who first formulates the reason that philosophizing needs to arrogate to itself this privilege of being the supreme arbiter of moral life. He does this in the arguments on behalf of the categorical imperative in which the link between the speaking and thinking of universals and the possibility of a moral law is explicitly formulated (for what, if not this potential of language, does Kant mean when he speaks of our relation to universalizability?) A simple trope of a possibility belonging to the word grounds moral reason: the law of universalization is grounded in the universalizing potential that is retained in the kinship of thinking and language. Respect for law shows itself to emerge from a possibility of language. Even the "imperative," the "force," of conceptual, categorical reasoning is explained by noting that it, like language, is able to maintain itself in a relation to what is external to it. Though Kant himself will not say so (it will be left to Hegel to make this point), the structure of the moral law has its foundation in the structure of human language, and the highest accomplishment of language is found in the language of philosophy. We are moral beings because we can philosophize, and because we can philosophize our moral life is necessarily to be thought according to law. In the end, when we speak we lay down the law: *jus dicere*.

But, of course, even if to speak is always, in some sense, to speak the law, not all speech qualifies as *true* to the law. Such speech (in Kant's language, such "willing") is defined solely by its relation to the idea proper to law, the idea of universality, and this idea is the province of the language of metaphysics, which is defined by its self-reflexive commitment to the universalizing potential of language. The task of philosophy is to speak in a manner which opens this formal realm of the universal. The basis of any possible metaphysics of morals is rooted in the moral privilege of the metaphysical relation to the universalizing potential of language. Moral life is thoroughly committed to the dream of the universalizability of the law, and the "grounds" of this law show themselves to be an expression of what is understood as the preeminent possibility of the word, namely, the law of universalizability governing the formation of concepts. In the end, moral life is defined and determined by the jurisdiction of the language of metaphysics. One of the revealing ways in which this thoroughgoing commitment to the universal is evidenced for Kant is found in his treatment of the role of the "example" in moral questions. Though each of our acts carries the burden of being exemplary, that is, of being simultaneously unique and universal in character, Kant resists the notion that examples could ever be enlisted as a means of grounding moral life.[1] In the end, thinking and speaking of moral life are rigorously submitted to the authority of the language of metaphysics, the language of the concept, which preserves the possibility of universality. The idiom of philosophy, the concept, binds human freedom to its own nature in the form of the moral law. A different sort of language—the language, for instance, of stories—cannot serve a fundamental role in the task of negotiating freedom.

But my purpose is not to rehearse the details of Kantian ethical theory. Rather, my intention is simply to suggest that a certain conception of language operates, however covertly, in Kantian moral philosophy (and I believe that it could be shown to be a widespread tendency in moral philosophy generally). While Kant will draw upon this assumption (but without ever naming or acknowledging it) in trying to understand what can be said philosophically about moral life, it is Hegel who will be the first to explicitly name this assumption as a truth when he speaks of the "divine nature" of language as "inherently universal" and when he claims that "what is called unutterable is nothing else than the untrue."[2] Hegel will see history as the process, even the progress, of freedom, but, in the end, freedom is submitted to the jurisdiction of the concept and the law of universalization which is proper to the concept. Furthermore, Hegel, like Kant, will see in this so-called truth of language a sort of moral vocation being expressed: This promotion to the universal is what Hegel refers to as "*Bildung*." One who weds oneself to particularity, one who lacks the powers of abstraction and universalization, is "*ungebildet*," and such a failing can be understood only as a moral failing. This process of *Bildung*, which repeatedly requires the sacrifice of particularity,[3] is, Hegel reminds us, not only a theoretical process but equally a practical one—and the path of this process is the path of philosophy. Gadamer's remarks on *Bildung* in the first part of *Wahrheit und Methode* emphasize the role of the concept of *Bildung* in the humanistic tradition, and he does this most of all by highlighting the conception of universality which governs that concept and the role of language in its formation.

Kant's efforts to ask what philosophy might say about the riddles of moral life struggle to keep freedom, the basic "fact" of reason, as the unassailable center of any possible theorization of moral life. But the moment we begin to speak of freedom—that is, the instant it becomes a matter for theory and enters the field of conceptuality, the law of this field (namely, of that which is bound to the imperative of law as such)—is enforced. In this way the language which we enlist to speak of the presence of freedom converts freedom into a problem of law. Freedom ceases to be what dispenses relations and becomes instead the problem of how we are to regulate those relations.

Such, in broad outline, is what I have referred to as the juridical account of the moral significance of the fact of language. It is a point of view which holds that the significance of language for moral life is found first and foremost in the capacity of language to universalize, to conceptualize. However, the understanding of the nature of language operating in this view is thoroughly problematic. After one grants that language resists and exceeds, rather than founds, the process of universalization, the transformation of the question of moral life into the question of law becomes problematic. When the ineluctable finitude of language, rather than its conceptualizing potential, is acknowledged, a different sense of the moral meaning of language begins to emerge.

One of the chief contributions of hermeneutics to contemporary philosophizing has been its ability to open thinking to this finite being of the word. But while it seems relatively clear that a hermeneutic conception of language does not lend itself to the view which finds the greatest potential of the word in its capacity to lay down the law, it still remains to be seen just what a hermeneutic conception of language might mean for the task of understanding moral life. In what follows, my intention is to indicate a few of the avenues down which such an understanding might be found.

The universalization constitutive of the formulation of the moral law operates on a conception of language that regards the concept as the highest achievement of the word and the language of metaphysics as the proper form of the language that address the life of free beings. Though it remains an unannounced assumption, for Kant the way we understand our freedom is shaped in an essential way by the way we understand the formal possibilities opened by the language we speak. The form of the moral law is rooted in an understanding of those formal possibilities of language which culminate in the concept. Likewise, this understanding of language lies at the basis of Kant's conception of freedom as an originally juridical matter rather than as an experience of openness. But hermeneutics has demonstrated in several ways—here one thinks of themes such as translation, silence, the workings of language in the poem, metaphor—that the finitude of language cannot be held fast for the operations of such universalization and conceptualization. Consequently, when we grant the elemental sameness of thinking and language, we need to grant as well that the workings of the word do not permit such universalization, such a formalization in law, of the freedom that remains always as the unassailable fact of reason. I believe we have seen that Kant draws some important moral conclusions— conclusions about the nature of our freedom—from the fact that we are speakers of language. The question remains whether we can still draw any meaningful conclusions about our moral being from this fact of language when we think of language from a hermeneutic point of view.

The path to answering this question, at least as Gadamer has opened it for us, begins, curiously, with Kant. But with a "different Kant" than the Kant who formulates the categorical imperative; namely, with the Kant who interrogates the character of aesthetic judgment in the third critique. There Kant struggles to come to terms with an experience that is strictly untranslatable into the language of the concept. When Kant defines the judgment of taste, he notes that it is by nature without any relation to a concept and that it must retain this reserve.[4] This resistance to the concept is the chief defining feature of aesthetic judgment, and it is the feature which most clearly distinguishes such judgment from moral judgment which is, ultimately, guided by the concept in two ways: in the formulation of the law as well as by the concept of the good itself. But Kant's investigations into aesthetic experience bring him two surprises: first, that this experience harbors an a priori, and second, that this experience is relevant for our understanding of our moral life. When Gadamer takes up the achievement of Kant's third critique in the first part of *Wahrheit und Methode,* he turns his attentions primarily to the first of these points, which concerns the connection between aesthetic experience and truth. My intention in what follows is to trace in more detail the second of these discoveries, namely, the discovery of the way that the nonconceptualizable experience of the beautiful illuminates something of moral life.[5] In doing this I depart from Gadamer's interpretation of Kant in two crucial ways: first, I suggest that Kant's third critique does not mark the subjectivization of aesthetics but that it goes far toward dislodging our understanding of experience from any conception of the subject and the human; and second, I argue that the chief ethical insight of the third critique emerges out of an understanding not of the work of art but of the experience of nature, and that in this way Kant's moral philosophy moves away from the humanistic tradition. But both of these points are seen most clearly by beginning with some remarks on the quiet, but decisive, role of language in the third critique.

Kant does not make the role of language a theme in the *Kritik der*

Urteilskraft but, as with the treatment of the categorical imperative in the *Grundlegung*, the question of language haunts all that is said here since the analysis of aesthetic experience shows it to be simultaneously communicable and nonconceptual.[6] This time, however, a different sort of language shapes the issues. In the strict sense the language of aesthetic experience is the language proper to what withholds itself, to what we cannot say, to what cannot be told. It is, one might be tempted to say, the language of the secret. Kant tries to speak of this strange language in two ways. First, when asking about the genius, he speaks of the *aesthetic ideas* which guide thinking for the genius; second, when speaking of the presentation of beauty, he speaks of *symbolic hypotyposis*, which is the language of taste. It is in speaking of the language of the symbol that Kant begins to clarify how the moral weight of aesthetic experience is presented to us.

Despite its importance, Kant's discussion of the symbol is remarkably brief and does not easily carry the burden which this notion must bear in the work as a whole. However, Gadamer's discussion of the symbol in "Die Aktualität des Schönen"[7] helps clarify the meaning of the symbol. Beginning by noting that the word "symbol" is originally a Greek word which referred to a fragment that served as a reminder of a hidden or forgotten connection between individuals, Gadamer moves to a discussion of Aristophanes' speech in the *Symposium* where a link is drawn between the symbolic and the erotic. In that lovely speech Aristophanes suggests that each of us is but the *symbolon* of a human being, and that we each pursue the never-ending search for the *symbolon* of ourselves. What becomes especially clear in drawing these ancient Greek senses of the symbolic into the operations of the symbolic that Kant describes is that in the symbol we are presented simultaneously with a knowledge of ourselves and of what exceeds that which we define and can know (which is why Kant suggests that the symbolic is always tinged with a sense of the divine).[8] In other words, in the symbol I experience myself as finite and yet, by virtue of the way that finitude is presented to me, as belonging to what exceeds my finite being and its cognitive possibilities. In the symbol the *aporias* of finite life are presented, not effaced.

What is significant here is that the symbolic ruptures the economy and the logic of identity governing the operations of the concept. Furthermore, the symbol is not able to be deciphered; it infinitely eludes translation into any form other than itself. It is a hieroglyph for which no code can be found since the symbol comes into its own nature only in belonging to that which withholds itself from any direct presentation. Thus though the form of the symbolic marks the summit of the knowledge won in aesthetic experience, the symbol simultaneously stands as a memento of the *limits* of what can be said, what can be known, conceptually. The significance of this shift from the concept to the symbol as the summit of the formal possibilities of the language which arises out of experience becomes most clear when we remember that while the truth of the concept expresses itself as *law*, the truth of the symbol finds itself in the *openness* of the mind that knows itself to be finite. Here we begin to see why Kant refers to beauty as the *symbol* of morality, and we begin to see how dramatic this shift in the form of the presentation proper to the moral—the shift from the conceptual to the symbolic—is.

But perhaps the most important feature of the symbolic—one might even say the most original element of the third critique—has to do with the role of *nature* here. Unfortunately, this is also the least recognized and understood dimension of the third critique. There are two ways in which the central role of nature is effaced in most readings of Kant: first, the first part of the *Kritik der Urteilskraft* is taken as a text concerned with the work of art rather than with a form in which nature is presented; second, the second part of the text—namely, the treatment of judgment with respect to nature—is simply ignored.[9] Missing the force of what nature means in the third critique, one misses the most original moment of that work with respect to its contribution to the questions of moral life, since it is ultimately in our relation to nature that we truly understand ourselves as moral beings. The moral life of a finite being finds its truth and its greatest task in finding its place in the life of nature. Here we begin to see how far the third critique moves away from a view of moral life that thinks within the orbit of humanism. It is precisely the nonhuman, that which comes without human bidding, that orients the moral judgment outlined in the third critique. Furthermore, this disclosure of nature as a sort of magnetic north for our moral compass can be understood only according to the workings of the symbol. The language of moral life is symbolic. This is a decisive point, the importance of which can be made clear by remembering that the symbol itself, the form in which the supreme experience of nature is expressed, must be understood as natural—in other words, it must be understood as exceeding the conceptual, cognitive, reach of the finite mind. This is why, as Gadamer points out, the symbol must be distinguished from allegory, which is an invention of the human mind.[10] The symbol is the form in which we communicate with that which is not designed by human purposes. In the symbol something is given which cannot be known otherwise. In the end, nature, which is the site and the form of the symbolic, shows itself to be the supreme riddle for judgment, and we learn that it is only judgment which has indexed itself to the original experience of nature that earns the name of "good" judgment.

But my purpose is not to investigate the relation of nature and judgment for Kant (though I would like to suggest that this issue is central for any thorough reflection on the theme of human freedom). Rather, my purpose is to indicate what I take to be an original, and yet to be explored, avenue for thinking through the riddle that freedom poses for a finite being. This is the avenue opened by the analysis of judgment that we find in Kant's third critique. There, in the possibilities opened by his reflections on nature and above all on the language of the symbol, I believe that Kant offers a genuine alternative to the manner of thinking of human freedom that does so with reference to the law. I have tried to suggest as well that each of these alternative routes to understanding freedom owes much to the differing conceptions of language operating in them: The lawfulness of the conception of moral life outlined in the second critique rests upon an understanding of the formal possibilities of the language of the concept, whereas the openness that characterizes moral life that is exposed in the third critique rests upon an understanding of the finite possibilities of the language of the symbolic. However, Kant never fully thinks through the way in which the relation of language and freedom shapes how freedom is understood. In the end, the treatment of the workings of the symbolic are never fully explored in Kant, and this, I believe, is why some of the richest implications of the relation of freedom and nature remain unexamined by him. Ultimately, Kant lacks an adequate conception of the dynamics of the finitude of the disclosure proper to the symbolic. But this is the point at which the hermeneutic conception of the finitude of language can advance the route which Kant begins in the third critique.

In the final part of my paper my intention is to indicate some of those dimensions of a hermeneutic theory of language which can enrich the discussion of freedom that Kant outlines.

The *Kritik der Urteilskraft* plays a decisive role in the problematic that is outlined in *Wahrheit und Methode;* consequently, the range of issues broached in the third critique, especially the most original issues such as the manner in which the question of freedom is opened anew in the formal possibilities of the symbol, can be wedded nicely with the insights of *Wahrheit und Methode.* However, in large measure because Gadamer focuses on the question of the work of art rather than of nature for Kant, the problem of freedom which Kant exposes in connection with the experience of nature is never given its due in *Wahrheit und Methode.*[11] Despite this, the understanding of language that Gadamer develops there is especially helpful in advancing the question of freedom that Kant announces but never fully articulates. The chief contribution in this regard of Gadamer's insights into language is that they give us a way of understanding the relation of thinking and language that preserves the original, even the abyssal, force of freedom for us. The finitude of the word, above all the poetic word, which Gadamer describes mirrors the logic of the symbol which Kant describes only in rough contour. We thus learn something about the paradox of trying to speak about the nature of human freedom. In this way a hermeneutic sense of the workings of the word can say much about how it is that we can begin to speak of freedom without thereby converting it, from the outset, into a question of law. From Gadamer we can come to understand that the deepest moral significance of the "fact" of language is that it is a witness to the special character of human freedom. Speech, rather than serve as the ground of the formation of law, is the preeminent form of the practice of freedom. In the word, what Schelling described as "the most abyssal center,"[12] which is full of both light and dark, is brought into the world. When we constitute the world linguistically, we constitute it as saturated with freedom. With the word, freedom is set loose in the world.

My contention has been that conceptions of language which take language to have conceptualization as its highest possibility invariably ossify the openness of the experience of freedom by turning it into a question of law. This assumption about the nature of language, one which governs the language proper to metaphysics, leads to an understanding of the moral weight of the word in the world: There it is assumed that with the word, the maxim of lawfulness is grounded. But the hermeneutic conception of language, which understands that the word is not able to be contained in the concept, deepens the experience of freedom by recognizing that in language we are reminded that we live in a world larger than that which we can either define or control. In other words, we live in a world defined first and foremost by the experience of radical openness. Not surprisingly, the conception of freedom which emerges here does not take freedom as an originally juridical matter but as an originary openness.

Most important here is understanding the finitude proper to the word since it is in the finite nature of language that freedom is preserved as this openness to a world. Above all, one ought not conceive of this finitude as a sort of shortcoming of language, as if it meant something like the non-*sensical* commonplace which suggests that words cannot say everything. The finitude of language is not even found in the fact that all language solicits itself, that our speech always asks for a *counterword* and so always appears in the world as incomplete, as a request.[13] Rather, the finitude of the word, like that of the symbol, is found in the capacity of the word to unfold itself beyond the boundaries of the thinkable and of what is present without itself disappearing *as* word. As Gadamer has shown, this self-surpassing capacity of language does not *sublate,* or efface, itself in a transcendence that ends up in the abstraction of a universal. Rather, the density of the word, its linguistic being, serves as an intransitive residue that weds the word to the mystery of its own being. This, in part, is what Schelling means when he says that "*[d]as ausgesprochene (reale) Wort aber ist nur in der Einheit von Licht und Dunkel.*"[14] Language in the poem—in which metaphor and symbolic language, even sound, are decisive—is most adept at presenting this finite character of the word, and so it is no surprise that poetic language has been the focus of some of Gadamer's most extensive and original reflections on the nature of the word. The resistance of the word to abstraction becomes powerfully evident in the materiality, the real concretion and finitude of langauge. It is precisely because language possesses this finite nature, this double being, that we are able, with our words, to grope in the region of our ignorance and learn.

But let me conclude by bringing these remarks back to my original concern with the question about the relation of language and freedom. I have proposed that a hermeneutic theory of language such as we find in Gadamer offers original and productive avenues for thinking through the riddles our human freedom. While the central role of the notion of *phronesis* in Gadamer's work is well known (if still underappreciated) and is one obvious way in which many of the concerns of moral philosophy enter into hermeneutic theory, the moral force of the being of language which is disclosed there is still to be explored. To that end, I have merely made the suggestion that Gadamer's sensitivities to the finite character of the word open possibilities that escape the legislative impulses of a juridical conception of language. Such a hermeneutic conception of language does this insofar as it undermines the claims to conceptuality governing the language of metaphysics. In so doing we are reminded that in our words we "elevate the deepest center of life"—namely, freedom—into the light. Speech, above all speech that knows itself to be finite—namely, poetic speech—bears witness to this freedom. In this way, I believe that a hermeneutic theory of language helps us to find a way to preserve the fact of freedom, which needs to be a dominant concern of all philosophizing. It also serves as a reminder that poetic language might well merit the claim to be the most original language of moral life—even more so than the language of metaphysics.

But the ethical possibilities opened by hermeneutic theory can still be enriched by taking to heart Kant's insights into the kinship of moral life and the experience of nature, and this I believe is the line of questioning which the hermeneutic tradition would do well to pursue. The experience of nature, and the effort to speak of that which comes to us unbidden and without reference to human purposes, poses a crucial question for any possible understanding of moral life. But a new beginning toward understanding the roots of this moral life—its roots in freedom—can be made if we take seriously the insight that perhaps nothing comes so directly into the world from out of the experience of freedom as the word. Properly heard, the word is the most faithful affirmation, the most intimate experience for us, of the freedom from which the word is born.[15] But what we learn from the hermeneutic conception of the finitude of language is that freedom, which dispenses the word, is itself not fully *sayable*. The meaning of this is still to be explored, but when it is addressed, it will, I believe, place us before the paradoxical question of how we are to understand freedom simultaneously as absolute, as "the basis of all reality,"[16] and as shadowed always by its own *unpresentability* and unfreedom. This, of course, is the question of moral life.

Notes

1. Cf. Kant, *Grundlegung*, Akademie edition, 408. It is this paradox of exemplarity that leads Kant to the final description of human moral being as simultaneously exposing each individual as sovereign and subject, and to the peculiar concept of autonomy which is proper to such individuals.

2. Hegel, *Phaenomenologie des Geistes*, paragraph 110.

3. *Ibid.*, paragraph 807.

4. Cf. Kant, *Kritik der Urteilskraft*, Ak. ed., 219.

5. For a fuller treatment of these questions see my "Lyrical and Ethical Subjects," in *Internationale Zeitschrift für Philosophie*, Heft 1, 1995, 147–58.

6. Though as Gadamer rightly notes this does not mean that aesthetic experience is to be understood in an abstract opposition with conceptual knowing. Cf. his *Gesammelte Werke*, Bd. 8, 192.

7. *Ibid.*, 122–30.

8. Cf. Kant, *Anthropologie*, paragraph 38.

9. But the case is quite clear: The beauty of nature is superior to the beauty of works of art. Cf. for instance Kant, *Kritik der Urteilskraft*, Ak. 299–300. It is worth noting that this exclusion of the question of nature seems to begin already in Hegel, for whom the beauty of nature is manifestly inferior to that found in the artwork. Adorno is right when he says that since Hegel natural beauty has been illegitimately dropped from the agenda of aesthetics; cf. his *Aesthetische Theorie*, chapter 5, where he makes some gestures toward remedying this problem. Here Gadamer's otherwise remarkably sensitive reading of Kant, especially in *Wahrheit und Methode*, must be included in this problem.

10. Curiously, Kant himself does not do this. In fact, the example he gives of a symbol—the pepper mill and the despot—really qualifies more as allegory than as symbol. The truly symbolic is much more akin to what Aristotle means by metaphor in the *Poetics*. On this, see my "Stereoscopic Thinking and the Law of Resemblances," in *American Continental Philosophy* (Bloomington: Indiana University Press, 2000). See also J.-F. Courtine, *Extase de la Raison* (Paris: Galilée, 1990), 45–68.

11. The question of freedom appears only briefly in *Wahrheit und Methode* and then chiefly in the context of the theme of universal history, not as a problem of moral life.

12. See the epigraph to this paper.

13. On this, see especially Gadamer's treatment of the "logic of question and answer" in *Wahrheit und Methode*, 375–86.

14. See the epigraph to this paper.

15. This is the point at which the uncompromised need for free speech is to be thought.

16. Schelling, *Philosophische Untersuchungen über das Wesen der menschlichen Freiheit*, 351.

The Art of Begetting Monsters: The Unnatural Nuptials of Deleuze and Kant

Constantin Boundas

Thinking of Deleuze today and of his encounters with philosophers of old brings to mind first and foremost his sustained dialogue with Bergson, Nietzsche and Spinoza. His early work on Hume is practically overlooked, while his fruitful discussion of Leibniz is thought to be too demanding and, therefore, capable of being visited only by the hardiest of his commentators. When it comes to his writings on Kant, with rare exceptions we seem to do what Deleuze warned us against—we take what he said for what he actually did. And, since what Deleuze said about his texts on Kant is that he wrote them with the intention of showing how the system of a *"frère-enemi"* works, we rarely place these early texts in the context of his others, missing therefore the challenge and the surprise of the realization that Deleuze's entire work seems to be deployed with the specter of Kant, the brother enemy, peering over Deleuze's shoulder. Kant becoming Deleuze as Deleuze becomes Kant or rather both of them becoming that which cannot be either one of them—isn't this the sort of unnatural nuptials that Deleuze stages for the sake of a becoming which would not be the mere preamble to being?

This essay has three parts: I begin with a straightforward report on Deleuze's reading of Kant. I then trace the slidings and the twistings to which Deleuze subjects the Kantian organic body—slidings and twistings which allow him to provide his own work with an architectonic strikingly similar to Kant's own, with one important exception: This architectonic is now placed in the service of assembling the Deleuzean corpus without organs. The third part of this essay builds upon the first and second parts in an effort to display and elucidate Deleuze's reasons for his (minor) deconstruction of the *history* of philosophy and his substitution of it with what he calls "philosophy's own *becoming*."

Deleuze Reads Kant

Deleuze published a small book on Kant in 1963, under the title *La Philosophie critique de Kant: Doctrine des facultés,* which did not become available to English readers until 1984.[1] In the same year, 1963, he also published in *Revue d'Esthétique* an important essay, *L'Idée de genése dans l'esthétique de Kant,* which has only recently become available in English.[2] Since then, there have been scattered references to his encounter with Kant (for example, in his letter to Michel Cressole[3] and in the 1988 special issue of the *Magazine Littéraire* dedicated to his work);[4] frequent and important rereadings of Kant in *Difference and Repetition,*[5] *The Logic of Sense,*[6] and *What is Philosophy?*;[7] the strikingly simple and direct introduction to the English translation of his 1963 book on Kant under the title "On Four Poetic Formulas which Might Summarize the Kantian Philosophy" (*KCP* vii–xiii); and the 1978 Seminar on Kant held at the Université VIII of Paris, in Saint Dennis, where he taught until his retirement.[8]

In the early references, one can detect a certain polemic disposition. A passage from his letter to Cressole is typical of this kind of disposition, and I offer it here, in its entirety, for the significance it will assume in our discussion of Deleuze's complex position in the face of the history of philosophy.

> My book on Kant is different; I like it, I did it as a book about an enemy and tried to show how his system works, its various cogs—the tribunal of reason, the legitimate exercise of the faculties (our subjection to these made all the more hypocritical by our being characterized as legislators). But I suppose the main way I coped with it at the time was to see the history of philosophy as a sort of buggery or (it comes to the same thing) as immaculate conception. I saw myself as taking an author from behind and giving him a child that would be his own offspring, yet a monstrous one. It was really important that it be his own child, because the author had to actually say all I had him say. But the child was bound to be monstrous too, because it resulted from all sorts of shifting, slipping, dislocations and hidden emissions that I really enjoyed.[9]

This passage reads as if the shiftings, slippings, dislocations, and hidden emissions in producing a monstrous child were all on Deleuze's initiative and for his pleasure—the time of coping with an oppressive history of philosophy. But not all of Deleuze's references to Kant resonate this tone. When, for example, in the preface to the English translation of his book on Kant and the doctrine of the faculties, Deleuze hails the philosopher of Königsberg as the Hamlet, the Rimbaud, and the Kafka of philosophy; it sounds as if it is Kant this time who crept up behind Deleuze and gave him strange and monstrous children. One wonders: Should the privilege of a bugger who cannot be buggered that Deleuze once attributed to Nietzsche also be assigned to Kant? Or, would it be more in line with Deleuze's reading of others, as I tend to think, that we think of a general economy of "unnatural nuptials" in the context of which everyone begets and gives birth to a monstrous child? Suppose that we leave this question of nuptials against nature open for now, together with the corresponding question of whether anyone is ever immune to them. For the time being, I want to turn attention to Deleuze's reading of Kant, as if a report of this reading can be made without my intervention which would only turn the report of the already unnatural nuptials into a banal *menage à trois*.

Despite its determination to articulate a theory of rationality that would establish a consensual harmony among mental faculties for the sake of a harmonious republic of ends, the Kantian narrative, Deleuze claims, deconstructs itself into two distinct subtexts. One of them culminates in ideas without adequate intuitions to fill them (ideas of speculative reason), whereas the other ends with an intuition missing an adequate idea or concept (the aesthetic instance of the sublime). Given the Kantian ambition to offer *a system* of reason, the tension between these two texts remains intolerable. How is this tension created? Why does the one Kantian text split into two subtexts?

The Kantian tribunal of reason sits in judgment of faculties, but "faculty" in the Kantian narrative has two different senses. In the broad sense of life praxis, Kant recognizes three faculties: cognition, desire, and feeling of pleasure and pain. In the more narrow sense of "mental faculty," the term ranges from passive, intuitive sensibility to active imagination, understanding, and reason. Since philosophy in Kant's book is the science that relates all life praxis to the essential ends of reason, the tribunal of reason raises two fundamental questions: (a) can the faculties, in the first sense, find in themselves the supreme law of their own exercise and their superior form?; and (b) assuming that the tribunal can find these immanent superior forms, how do faculties, in the second sense, cooperate among themselves in order to bring about the realization of the supreme law of faculties in the first sense?

Kant chooses to call "speculative interest" the supreme law of the faculty of knowledge, and "practical interest" the supreme law of the faculty of desire. The faculty to feel pleasure and pain, to the extent that it functions as the handmaid of the other two, has no supreme law of its own. Kant goes on to explain that the faculty of knowledge, in light of its speculative interest, makes the known object conform to the a priori representations of transcendental subjectivity, under strict rational guidelines for the continuing totalization of knowledge. As for the faculty of desire, it finds its own superior form in the respect it has for its own law and in the practical interest in trying to realize the totality symbolized by the kingdom of ends. However, the interests of reason would be mere pious wishes if Kant could not explain how mental faculties are coordinated for the sake of these interests. Reason, in order not to be a house divided, must establish a *sensus communis* that will express the harmony of mental faculties inside each and every interest. An a priori agreement among faculties that differ in nature is what Kant needs in order to establish that the interests of reason do not contradict the tendencies of faculties.

This feat is accomplished as follows: For the production of knowledge to be possible, understanding legislates, imagination synthesizes, and reason totalizes. But the economy of mental faculties is not the same in all three domains of life praxis. The *sensus communis moralis* permits reason to legislate directly upon its objects, whereas understanding, in harmony with reason, judges and symbolizes. On the other hand, inside the faculty of feeling pleasure and pain, imagination (with the cooperation of the other two faculties) takes center stage. Between imagination and understanding there is a free and undetermined agreement; and reason, in the case of the sublime at least, gives imagination its *cogitandum*—that which imagination cannot grasp in its empirical exercise and yet that which constitutes its own superior form.[10]

Deleuze, in fact, thinks that he can bring out the tension between the two Kantian narratives even more effectively if he examines them from the vantage point of the functions they assign to reason. Without constituting objects of knowledge, speculative reason by means of its ideas is brought to bear upon the matter of experience. Phenomena must correspond to the ideas of reason, although this correspondence is only postulated. The fact is that ideas have an objective value. Although indeterminate in their objects, they are determinable by analogy with the objects of experience; they are also the focus of an infinite determination in relation to the concepts of the understanding. The *sensus communis logicus* depends upon the fulfilment of these conditions. Common sense—moral in this case—is also present in the faculty of desire. In this case, reason legislates directly and understanding symbolizes as it extracts from the law of nature an analogue for the sake of suprasensible nature. On this point Deleuze notes that it is a mistake to think that Kantian ethics is not interested in its realization. The noumenal world must be realized in the sensible, and the realization of the moral good presupposes an affinity between the phenomenal and the noumenal. There must be, therefore, within the phenomenal world, conditions that permit understanding to express and symbolize the noumenon. The end of the second *Critique* makes it clear that the interests of reason are determined in terms of one final end: Reason proposes the realization of the moral end to phenomenal nature. Not only are the two interests—speculative and practical—coordinated but also the speculative is subordinated to the practical. The sensible world would have no speculative interest if, from the point of view of a higher interest, it did not testify to the possibility of the realization of the suprasensible world.[11]

The possibility of this realization is what the third Kantian *Critique* argues. But in its pages, surprises await the reader. The faculty of feeling pleasure and pain has also a superior form, and judgment legislates within it. Understanding, imagination, and reason cooperate in order to bring about an aesthetic common sense; but the latter, far from merely completing the list of common senses, grounds the other two and renders them possible. And here is how: Aesthetic judgment is brought to bear upon forms, that is, upon the design and composition of objects, and the form is the reflection of a singular object in the imagination. It is the reflected representation of the form which, from the point of view of the aesthetic judgment, is the cause of superior pleasure in the face of something beautiful. All this is the work of imagination; but the objectivity of the aesthetic judgment presupposes that pleasure is communicable, to the extent that, for Kant, the understanding as faculty of rules is the source of communicability. The communicable, superior pleasure of the beautiful is possible because of the agreement between imagination reflecting on the beautiful and understanding, the source of an unspecified legality. As a result, a free and undetermined harmony between two faculties has been reached, for the first time, in the Kantian system.

In the case of the sublime—that is, the formless, the malformed, and the immense—imagination is confronted with its own limit; it suffers a kind of violence which brings it to the end of its power. In the preface to the English translation of his book on Kant, Deleuze puts it this way:

> [The sublime] brings the various faculties into play in such a way that they struggle against one another, the one pushing the other towards its maximum or limit, the other reacting by pushing the first towards an inspiration which it would not have had alone. Each pushes the other to the limit, but each makes the one go beyond the limit of the other. . . . The faculties confront one another, each stretched to its own limit, and find their accord in a fundamental discord. . . . At the end Kant discovers discord which produces accord. (*KCP* xii, xiii)

Deleuze finds in Kant's text one more way of introducing the sublime. In order to apprehend something, a successive synthesis of its parts is required. This synthesis in turn presupposes the discovery of a unit of measurement. But in situations in which the objects to be apprehended are radically different from one another, a common unit of measurement is not available. In such circumstances, Deleuze argues, "underneath the contemplated synthesis which seems to belong to the order of reason, there is an aesthetic comprehension requiring an apprehension of a rhythm."[12] The fact is that, in the case of the sublime, one fails to discover the rhythm and, as a result, one fails to apprehend the parts and to recognize the object. In all this, it is reason that forces the imagination off its hinges and gives it a task far exceeding its empirical exercise. The sense of the sublime is engendered in us in a way which suggests a higher purpose and which prepares us for the advent of the moral law.

With the beautiful, on the other hand, the picture changes. Although itself not an object of interest, the beautiful can enter a synthesis with a rational interest, which is brought to bear on our capacity to produce beautiful forms. This interest in the beautiful form has a contingent relationship with the materials that Nature disposes for the production of those objects capable of being formally reflected in the imagination. We experience therefore a rational interest in the contingent agreement between the products of Nature and our disinterested pleasure. The transcendental genesis of the aesthetic idea of the beautiful makes evident a kind of symbolization, which is the work of reason. The materials of Nature—the colors and the sounds—are not simply related to the concepts of understanding; they transcend the understanding and offer it objects to thought, which goes beyond the jurisdiction of the concept. In this manner, the understanding finds that its own concepts broaden, and imagination liberates itself from the grip of a hegemonic understanding to which it was subjected throughout the first *Critique*.

This is the maxim that Deleuze draws from all this: whenever we find the harmony of faculties to be the product of the hegemonic determination of one among them, we presuppose that they all are able to enter freely into harmonious relations, without which their alternating hegemonic determinations would not be possible. But, at the same time, in the Kantian system the free agreement of mental faculties must show that reason is destined to play a determining role in the face of the practical interest. And this is precisely Kant's achievement when he allows the beautiful to symbolize the good. The third *Critique* discovers a free and undetermined agreement among faculties as the condition for the possibility of all their determined relations. The rational idea was presented all along as a concept with no intuition adequate to it. But the final *concordia discordata* shows the aesthetic idea to be an intuition with no concept adequate to it. And yet, this aesthetic idea expresses what could not be expressed in the rational idea. It looks as if the *cogitandum* and the *sentiendum* have both been named.

Nevertheless, this Kantian line of flight is really blocked—and Deleuze deplores the blockage. One final review of the Kantian strategy makes the reason for this clear. The interest of speculative reason is to regulate the understanding for the sake of totalizations. But there would be no reason to think that there is an agreement between mental faculties in the domain of knowledge, if imagination were not able to schematize. Moreover, the schematism of the imagination would not permit speculative reason to find a real application if it were not for the discordant harmony between reason and imagination in the third *Critique*. Finally, the coordination of the first and the second *Critiques,* based upon the subordination of the speculative interest to the practical, would have been a pious wish were it not for the symbolizations of the *Critique of Judgment*. Not until the third *Critique* is it revealed how imagination is trained in order to educate sensibility, understanding, and reason.

But the problem with Kantianism is that sensibility is not really ever trained, resigned as it is to receptivity and passivity. The sensible manifold of the first *Critique* remains isolated from the *sentiendum* of the third. And this brings us full circle back to the divided Kantian narrative. The coordination of the cognitive, the praxiological, and the ludic that Deleuze reviewed barely conceals the tension between, on the one hand, a critical/revolutionary discourse fastened upon the primacy of the categorical imperative as the supreme form of the praxiological interest and as the summoner of the cognitive and the ludic to its own side; *and,* on the other, a reassuring discourse promising the coexistence of science, morality, and art, unproblematically sharing among themselves the regions of the real. The first narrative establishes the primacy of the ethico-political end of reason; it solicits factual knowledge for the sake of the realization of this end and canvases the ludic for its ability to provide practical reason with an analogue for the end that praxis seeks. As for the reassuring narrative, it tends to foreground the Kantian "as if" to lodge it solidly in the interstices between science, morality, and art, thereby making it dispensable whenever the revolutions of the historical render the counterfactual as fair game for instrumental rationality.

Deleuze's Becoming Kant

The Kantian sublime asks the imagination to train sensibility and yet, given the form that the object $= x$ takes in the first *Critique*, this assignment cannot be completed. Deleuze then, in his writings, undertakes to complete precisely what Kant had already thought but never dared to bring about; that is, the coordination of the sensibility involved in the cognitive experience *with* the sensibility present in the appreciation of artworks.[13] After all, *aisthesis* is the ground common to both. The results of this undertaking are indeed surprising. The unnatural nuptials that Deleuze celebrates, in the space of becoming, understood as a creative and innovative process, seem to give monstrous children to Deleuze—of a Kantian paternity this time. Readers often comment on Deleuze's effort to thoroughly displace and dismember the Kantian text, as if no alternative to the Kantian narrative could stand without the sinews and syntheses of this narrative being undone and deconstructed; but most surprising of all is that, as he labors to minorize Kant, Deleuze retains and in fact repeats the Kantian architectonic, with a fidelity unparalleled by anyone else of his generation. As we could expect, this repetition makes all the difference.

The fidelity is revealed in a striking display when we put *Kant's Critique of Pure Reason* and Deleuze's *Difference and Repetition* side by side. In his search for the conditions of all possible experience, Kant postulates the cooperation between the forms of sensibility (space and time), the forms of the understanding (categories), and the regulative ideas of reason. Deleuze aptly remarks that this cooperation hinges on schematism, that is, on the demonstration that the two different realms of determination (the spatio-temporal and the conceptual) are made to fit into each other. He also notes that, as Kant discusses the cooperation among faculties, he meticulously exposes the illusions, antinomies, and paralogisms to which thought falls victim each time that it mistakes ideas for concepts. The mistaken, constitutive use of the ideas exposes reason to the sterility of its dialectic. The denunciation of this mistake and the exposure of the fraudulent employment of reason do not eliminate these illusions once and for all—the illusions are transcendental, that is, deep-seated errors against which we can protect ourselves without nonetheless refraining from thinking them or from experiencing their pull. Finally, he notes that cooperation among faculties requires that Kant establish the unity of apperception on the side of the subject; and, on the side of the object, the a priori form of object-ness (the object = x). The mistaken, constitutive use of the ideas exposes reason to the sterility of its dialectic.

Deleuze retains the Kantian form of the transcendental illusions, but he changes their content.[14] He shares Kant's insight that we are the victims of transcendental illusions and that, although we should be able to monitor them, we cannot eliminate them altogether. In fact, he praises Kant for having demonstrated with his dialectic that error is a much more serious affair than the traditional image of thought had allowed it to be:

With Kant, the source of error has been located inside thought; thought has discovered that its internal enemies are much more formidable than the mere misrecognition and misrepresentation of entities dimly entering our perceptual field from outside—the kind of error that had been the preoccupation of philosophers before Kant. Even the most diligent exercise of our faculties cannot eliminate the sources of these errors. Yet, Deleuze chooses to emphasize a set of illusions that do not duplicate Kant's own. They include the misrecognition of the role that intensity plays in the constitution of the real and the false primacy that we tend to assign to extensive magnitudes; the license we give the traditional postulates of thought to construct an almost incorrigible image of thought; and the misdirected attempt to think of time by means of spatial terms.

In the Kantian text, the dialectic not only is shaking a disapproving finger but also is invited to show, by contrast, the legitimate and necessary use of the ideas. Deleuze, too, assigns this function to dialectics, albeit with two important differences that radically transform the Kantian critique and contribute to the pedagogy of the concept. Ideas do not totalize experience, nor are they the sole prerogatives of reason. They belong to all faculties and provide the impetus necessary for the creation of concepts. They give sensibility its superior form, forcing it to sense what ought to be sensed; they present imagination with what ought to be imagined, memory with what ought to be remembered, and thought with what ought to be thought. *Sentiendum, memorandum, cogitandum*—instead of *sensa,* memories and *cogitationes.*[15] With this one stroke, it looks as if the sublime has come to inhabit each and every faculty. Ideas exercise a sort of violence upon the faculties, forcing them to grasp what cannot be given to their normal, empirical exercise. The education of sensibility, for the sake of its higher vocation, will no longer be pursued by proxy, with the responsibility of its being assigned to another faculty. Its education will be the task of all faculties whose cooperation will go on being—as Kant had wanted it—a *concordia discordata*—a forced resonance, felt at the level of the transcendental exercise of each one of them. In this way, and by means of moving about Kantian blocks in a non-Kantian way, the section of the first *Critique* which was demarcating the domain of reason from the other faculties is opening, building bridges and establishing connections between one faculty and another. The result is that the Kantian dialectic of pure reason has in Deleuze invaded the erstwhile inviolable precinct of the transcendental analytic. Ideas generate concepts under actual conditions that can always be specified, and Deleuze repeats the Kantian architectonic, including its effort to show the fitness between conceptual and spatio-temporal determinations—always with a minor twist. Whereas Kant's concepts had to be schematized, with Deleuze ideas must be dramatized. The actualization of ideas is now determined by dynamic processes. Akin to, albeit more successful than, Kantian schemata, says Deleuze, such processes constitute a time for actualization or differentiation as much as they outline spaces of actualization. Dramatization is the differentiation/ actualization of the idea that is already differentiated.[16]

With similar determination, Deleuze's Kantian becoming taps into the resources of Kant's analytic. Indeed, Deleuze starts by giving Kant full credit: Of all the novel creations that Kant introduced to philosophy, he singles out the one that revolves around the problematics of time.[17] Here he finds an entirely new conception of time, decisive for the formulation of a modern consciousness of time as opposed to what is classic or ancient. In his Seminar on Kant, Deleuze clearly makes this point: "With Kant, it is an indescribable novelty. This is the first time that time gets to be free, relaxed, being no longer a cosmological or psychological entity . . . and becomes a pure form, a deployed pure form. This is going to be for modern thought a phenomenon of extreme importance."[18] In the case of Kant, we are told, "deployment" must be taken in the strictest sense: Time is uncoiled, it loses its circular form. It becomes time in itself and for itself, pure and empty time. It no longer measures anything. It comes off its hinges; that is, it is no longer subordinated to nature—rather, nature is subordinated to it. Far from being an obstacle to thought, time is the limit that erodes thought from within. Unlike classical philosophy that had designated space as the external limit of thought, the liberation of time from space makes time the limit inherent in thought. It is as if in thought there is something that can no longer be thought.

However, Deleuze's daring reconfiguration of the Kantian analytic still lies ahead. In the anticipations of perception of the Kantian analytic, quanta of extended magnitudes and degrees of intensity fill the space and make the phenomenal real. With Deleuze, intensity does not peaceably sit next to extension; it is the *ratio essendi* of the real, that is, it is that which makes the (extended) real exist in the first place. The world of extended objects in extended space is the result of intensive quanta of energy, captured in the process of slowing and cooling down. This process is always already reversible thanks to new stirrings of intensity.[19] The full impact of this reconfiguration of the Kantian analytic takes a while to be revealed.

To say that transformation, change, and motion implicate at least two different intensive forces is neither new nor surprising. But what is not so obvious is Deleuze's characterization of intensive magnitudes in terms of incommensurability, inequality, and indivisibility. For, although intensive forces seem to be divisible into parts, the parts obtained through division differ in kind from each other. In an important sense, therefore, intensive magnitudes are indivisible because, unlike extended magnitudes, not one of their parts preexists the division or retains the nature that it used to have before the division. This permits Deleuze to conclude that the sufficient reason for the order of becoming (and there is no other order than this) lies in the interaction of differential intensities, which are incommensurable with respect to each other, indivisible in themselves, but not at all, for these reasons, indeterminate (*DR* 232–46).

And there is still more in this Kantian becoming of Deleuze. In Kant, the unity of apperception is the bandage over the wound[20] that Kant inflicted on the subject—this wound being the result of his daring reconfiguration of time and the ensuing separation of the I from the ego. With Deleuze, the wounded subject (the cracked I) has no longer any reason to conceal its wound. It is indeed in the Kantian narrative that Deleuze discovers the philosophical origins of the "alienated" I. A quotation from the preface to the English translation of his book on Kant makes the point eloquently:

> "I is another"—this formula from Rimbaud can be seen as the expression of another aspect of the Kantian revolution. . . . Kant explains that the Ego itself is in time, and thus constantly changing: it is a passive, or rather receptive, Ego, which experiences changes in time. But, on the other hand, the I is an act which constantly carries out a synthesis of time, and of that which happens in time, by dividing up the present, the past and the future at every instant. The I and the Ego are thus separated by the line of time which relates them to each other, but under the condition of a fundamental difference. (*KCP* viii)

With Kant, something begins that is absolutely new—the I is another. The subject is cracked, traversed by the line of time. The crack is the result of the fact that the Kantian subject is the synthesis of two forms— the form of receptivity and intuition and the form of spontaneity and thought—two forms which are irreducible to each other. The two forms correspond to each other (since there would be no knowledge in the absence of some correspondence between spatio-temporal and conceptual determinations); but the fact remains that the I is an act represented in and by an ego that stays passive.

It is not therefore surprising to find in the trajectory of Deleuze's Kantian becoming the reconfiguration of the a priori form of object-ness (the object = x). For, as Deleuze argued in his essay on Michel Tournier,[21] a reconfiguration of the Self always repeats a reconfiguration of the Other. In the Kantian text, the object = x is the cipher of objectivity which supports the entire deduction of transcendental subjectivity and of the union of apperception. As such, the object = x is, therefore, the ultimate foundation for the categorial repetition of the same, for the recognitive and representational character of Kant's epistemology, and for his tender love of empirical objects. But the object = other (the discourse of the other or the other discourse) is a cipher with an entirely different function. It signifies the inadequacy of concepts to ever fully realize the idea—its function is, therefore, antirepresentational and antirecognitive; it testifies to the destiny of every solution to ever fall short vis-à-vis the requisites of the problem. At the same time, however, it makes possible a kind of thinking that patterns itself after the progressive specifications of a problem rather than models itself after the logic of solutions that tends to discard the problems which are not yet solved. It prevents language from ever closing upon itself; politics from ever coinciding with the political; time from ever dilating to a mere succession of immobile space-like cuts; natural perception from ever catching up with the *sentiendum;* central organizations from ever completely blocking the lines of flight; and decentered subjects from ever reaching the unity of apperception of the Kantian transcendental ego (*KCP* passim).

It is a mistake, often made, to think that the Kantian becoming of Deleuze has nothing more to show for itself than the expropriation/appropriation of the first *Critique* that I have outlined so far. All this is true: Deleuze's minoritarian reading of the Kantian narrative begins with the message of the third *Critique;* the sublime represents an intuition seeking, but not finding, an idea that could be adequate to it. But since this intuition, together with the aesthetic ideas, symbolizes the end of the praxiological interest, for the narrative to hold together, this intuition must somehow be coordinated with the ideas of reason, which were left suspended in earlier Kantian texts, without an adequate intuition. For this coordination to become possible, imagination must be assigned the task of training sensibility, memory, and understanding. This in turn requires the removing of the Kantian protective barriers from the cognitive, practical, and aesthetic interests and a fair redistribution of the insights of discordant reason among all faculties.

The important thing is that, with the message of the third *Critique* in mind, Deleuze comes to the second *Critique* looking for the foundation upon which the praxiological interest rests, and finds in it reason directly legislating upon the life praxis constituted by desire. He finds also that desire desires this auto-legislation and aims at the realization of what it proposes. From these two Kantian admissions, Deleuze deduces that desire is not chasing after mere phantasms but rather is producing the real in the domain of praxis. This deduction, of course, is not original; one thinks of Fichte, at this point, and perhaps of Hegel and surely of Spinoza. But a long line of theorists have conditioned us to think of desire as an intentional process extended between an original lack and an appropriation of whichever lack is to be satisfied. Between the pain of lack and the satiation of pleasure, desire has been the captive of an incessant cyclical process and, therefore, unable by itself to carry the weight of an emancipatory interest. *Kinesis* rather than *energeia*—to borrow key Aristotelian notions[22]—desire is deemed to be pathological. As a consequence of this reading of desire, and in order to assist desire in the production of the real, the Kantian narrative found it necessary to build over desire the edifice of a law extrinsic to it.

If this reading of desire is correct, desire must be allowed to construct the real. Desire will be its own law as it seeks more links, connections, and arrangements. It will be truly an anthropogenic and socializing force—our force to exist as we encounter others. Far from being a passive state of being, it will be an act, enhanced by joy, capable of generating adequate ideas and annexing Being. And if desire is an annexation of Being—rather than the dream of this annexation—it follows that desire is power and empowerment.

The Becoming of Philosophy

Anyone coming to Deleuze for the first time, and witnessing the shiftings, slippings, and dislocations with the help of which he celebrates his unnatural nuptials with Kant, is likely to conclude, with Guy Lardreau, that Deleuze, disguised as an historian of philosophy, "infests the system that he presents with his own system, abandoning therefore the requisites of objectivity: it is *his own* thought that [this] historian proposes in his examination of an earlier philosophy; it is his own thought that he essays, improves little by little, rectifies and expands through the exposition of a doctrine that is only *nominally* foreign to him."[23] In other words, he is likely to conclude that Deleuze, as a historian of philosophy, is a forger.

The trouble with this verdict is that it attributes to Deleuze a role and a function that he did not want—that of the historian of philosophy. In this section of my paper, I want to appeal to Deleuze's reading of Kant (section one) and to the impact that Kant had on the rhizome named "Deleuze" (section two) in order to explain Deleuze's displacement of the history of philosophy in favor of what he calls "philosophy's own becoming." I argue that this displacement colors his encounter with Kant and strikes the unprepared reader as a mixture of fidelity and forgery. I then go on to argue that this mixture, which is present in every encounter between Deleuze and his others, reminiscent as it might be of Derrida's "double séance," is not due to the play of language. It is dictated by the nature of becoming, as Deleuze understands it, and by the stratigraphic time that this nature entails.

I begin with a remark made by Deleuze (in his letter) to Michel Cressole: "I belong to a generation, one of the last generations, that was more or less bludgeoned to death with the history of philosophy. The history of philosophy plays a patently repressive role in philosophy; it's philosophy's own version of the Oedipus complex."[24] In his *Dialogues* with Claire Parnet, Deleuze returns to this theme.

> The history of philosophy has always been the agent of power in philosophy, and even in thought. It has played the repressor's role: how can you think without having read Plato, Descartes, Kant and Heidegger, and so-and-so's book about them? A formidable school of intimidation which manufactures specialists in thought—but which also makes those who stay outside conform all the more to this specialization which they despise. An image of thought called philosophy has been formed historically and it effectively stops people from thinking. . . . For thought borrows its properly philosophical image from the state as beautiful, substantial or subjective interiority. . . . It involves a properly spiritual State, as an absolute state, which is by no means a dream, since it operates effectively in the mind. Hence the importance of notions such as universality, method, questions and answers, judgment, or recognition of just correct, always having correct ideas. Hence the importance of themes like those of a republic of spirits, an enquiry of the understanding, a court of reason. A pure "right" of thought, with ministers of the Interior and bureaucrats of pure thought. . . . The Ratio as tribunal, as universal state, as republic of spirits (the more you are subjected, the more you are legislators, for you are only subject . . . to pure reason).[25]

From this long quotation I want to retain its provocation: *The history of philosophy as the oppressor of thought.* Why is that? Deleuze has also said that "the history of philosophy is completely without interest if it does not undertake to awaken a dormant concept and to play it again on a new stage, even if it comes at the price of turning it against itself" (*WP* 83). Which notion of the history of philosophy could justify this admonition and necessitate such an advice? After all, it wasn't exactly yesterday that we learned to eschew the role of curators of *musées imaginaires* and to laugh at our earlier beliefs that to read the texts of yesteryear requires, if these texts are ever going to speak to us, the obliteration of our prejudices. Which notion, indeed? The answer must stay in the shadows for a little while longer. But it is not difficult to see that the above quotation targets

Kant, as if the image of thought he bequeathed philosophy was the point on which the entire history of philosophy had to converge. The image of thought, displayed and criticized in *Difference and Repetition,* and the postulates that render it canonic fit the Kantian critical philosophy like a glove.[26] They fit it in its conclusions, without depriving his thought of the possibility of new beginnings, which are hidden among its premises. The postulates of common and good sense, of representation and recognition, and of the privileged space of solutions strengthen Kant's system, despite the problem-inducing presence of a time having gone off its hinges, of an I which is always already another, and of Ideas as the source of problems.

Speaking from a space already beyond the history of philosophy, Deleuze has this to say:

> One always writes in order to give life, to free life out of the space where it was imprisoned, one writes in order to trace lines of flight. To do this, language must no longer be an homogeneous system, but an always heterogeneous (open system) in disequilibrium: style hollows in it differences of potential between which something may pass, may happen, a lightning may surge up from within language and make us see and think what was in the shadows around the words, or discern entities the existence of which we barely suspected.[27]

This claim raises more questions than it answers, for it seems now that the history of philosophy is being scolded for not tracing "lines of flight," for not making things visible which are nevertheless there. We do not yet see where these lines of flight are going, nor do we begin to discern the site of what may become visible. But we can, at least at this point, remind ourselves of the importance that Deleuze assigns to lines of flight.[28] They are the lines of transformation, intrinsic to the domain they are in the process of transforming, and yet always in need of being traced and retraced. The tensions between what I call "premises" of Kantianism and what I call "conclusions" generate and feed lines of flight capable of metamorphosing a critical philosophy turned timid. This is also the point to remind ourselves of Deleuze's clear preference for Leibniz's vicediction: An attentive gathering of the components of a concept (its actualized cases) is the correct way to seize, through a backward assent, its condensed intensity.[29] This condensed intensity will not just be another case; the key to Kantianism will not be a part of its system. Nevertheless, its lines of flight are more promising clues regarding the wherefrom and the whereto of critical philosophy. To the extent that lines of flight are the becoming and the transformation of "assemblages," the philosopher who does not want to perpetuate the oppression exercised by the history of philosophy must initiate and pursue vice-dictory strategies.[30] And the hints keep coming: "The history of philosophy," writes Deleuze in "*Signes et événements,*"

> is not a particularly reflexive discipline. It is rather like the art of the por-trait in painting. These are mental, conceptual portraits. As in painting, one must feign resemblance (*il faut faire ressemblant*), but with dissimilar means, with different means: resemblance must be produced; it must not be a means of reproduction (in which case, one would be satisfied in retelling what a philosopher did say). Philosophers bring in new con-cepts, they expose them, but they do not say (at least not entirely) the problems to which these concepts respond. . . . The history of philos-ophy must not repeat what a philosopher did say, but rather what he was necessarily assuming, what he was not saying and, nevertheless, what was present in what he did say.[31]

No claim in this passage is exactly new—with one exception: "*one must feign resemblance, but with dissimilar means.*" We should retain this claim and come back to it later; it requires a firmer grasp of Deleuze's project than the one we can claim to have at this moment.

The right question at this point seems to be the following: What is philosophy, for Deleuze, for whom the history of philosophy represses thought and its liberation presupposes its transformation into blocks of becoming? This question receives in his works the following answer. Being neither reflective (one is perfectly capable of reflecting without philos-ophy) nor communicative (communication arrives either too early or too late), philosophy is creative—creative of concepts. The concepts that it creates are neither abstract ideas nor universals—they do not name the essence of things. They are about the circumstances of the emergence of a thing (the "how," the "when," the "where," the "particular case"). Con-cepts have component elements—each one of which is a singularity in its own right—but they are nonetheless *concepts* to the extent that they stand for a point of coincidence or condensation of these components; their in-ternal consistency depends on these points.[32] A concept condenses the conditions of the actualization of an entity. Unlike extended magnitudes, concepts cannot be decomposed to their constituent singularities[33] with-out becoming different concepts—and this is precisely what makes a con-cept an intensity. Deleuze has an interesting way of making this point and of advancing the discussion of philosophy's calling to create concepts. He says that a concept is both relative and absolute: relative with respect to its component elements, other concepts, the "plane of consistence" which defines it, and the questions/problems it supports or resolves. But it is absolute in terms of its condensation, the place it occupies within the plane, and the conditions it assigns to the question/problem. Philosophical constructivism, according to Deleuze, links together the relative and the absolute (*WP*21). Moreover, although the conditions they express are incarnated in actual (sensible, particular) bodies, concepts are not reducible to the states of affairs of these bodies or to their interactions. They are virtual conditions, with no spatio-temporal coordinates—mere intensive ordinates. Concepts are best thought of as expressing events—virtual and yet real events—in the process of actualization.

We may conclude, therefore, that between Kant, the curator of the a priori concepts of pure reason, and Deleuze, the constructivist, the difference of point of view is glaring. They share between them, of course, the view that concepts are not mere abstractions; concepts condition the cases which actualize them. But in insisting that concepts must be conditions of the actual—and not of the possible, as Kant had it—Deleuze launches a grand quest for the transcendental genesis of the actual states of affairs. The task of philosophy now is to draw out concepts from states of affairs inasmuch as it extracts the event from them. To the extent that Deleuze intends these directives to be directives for a (new) thought without image, they are bound to regulate his approach to the "history of philosophy" as well. From Deleuze's point of view, Kant's system is one state of affairs among many, a case of a concept ("Kantianism") conditioning its actualization without being identified with it. Indeed, Deleuze will demand that conditions must not resemble the conditioned, just as problems do not resemble their solutions. If resemblance is maintained, then the grandiose claims made on behalf of the transcendental ground would turn out to be fraudulent: The so called transcendental ground would merely repeat and unnecessarily duplicate the empirical.[34] Nevertheless, in our effort to avoid the unnecessary duplication, we are not free to conclude that between condition and conditioned there is no relation whatsoever; the condition differs from the conditioned, without the conditioned differing from it.[35]

This is then the justification of the imperative that we encountered already: *one must feign resemblance, but with dissimilar means.* If, as Deleuze suggests, the "historian of philosophy" should separate the concepts that her predecessors created from the plane of immanence that she constructed as their horizon, the aura of familiarity and congeniality that the history of philosophy invariably brings about will dissipate. Why not think of the "historian of philosophy" as a painter and of her labor as a deformation of the material she works with, undertaken in order to reveal the fluidity of it and the primacy of flux over the ephemeral concretions? "The history of philosophy," says Deleuze, "is comparable to the art of the portrait. . . . These are mental, noetic, and machinic portraits. Although they are usually created with philosophical tools, they can also be produced aesthetically."[36]

Returning for now to the Deleuzean event, it must be said it has generated a lot of discussion and controversy. That this event is not to be confused with states of affairs is by now common knowledge; but then the temptation to think of the event as transcendent to the states of affairs that actualize it is not easily controlled, as even of one of his best readers (Alain Badiou) has shown.[37] The fact is that Deleuze left behind ample warnings against this temptation: It is the structure of the event that is double; it is the nature of time to be crystalline. As he writes,

> Every event can be said to have a double structure. On the one hand, there is necessarily the present moment of its actualization: the event "happens" and gets embodied in a state of affairs and in an individual. . . . Here the time of the event, its past and future, are evaluated from the perspective of this definitive present and actual embodiment. On the other hand, the event continues to "live on," enjoying its own past and future, haunting each present.[38]

To reduce events to states of affairs and assign them to the rupture points of a continuum is "to grant an unwarranted normative status to that state and to posit the break with it in terms that are both blind and transcendent."[39] Events are virtual and, therefore, real; states of affairs are actual and either possible or real. "The task of philosophy," write Deleuze and Guattari, "is always to extract an event from things and beings, always to give them a new event: space, time, matter, thought, the possible as events" (*WP* 33); the greatness of a particular philosophy depends on the number of concepts it creates and the events it succeeds in expressing by means of them.

Someone may say at this point that, if this is what philosophy is, to expect from the historians of philosophy to be creators of concepts, instead of submitting themselves to a decorous recollection of concepts, is to invite arbitrariness. We may of course reply that this objection regresses behind the imperatives of Gadamer's "effective history" and its moderate stance in favor of fused horizons. But this will not be Deleuze's riposte. For him, if the history of philosophy oppresses thought, it is because it sacrifices the virtual to the possible and the actual. To assume that our reading of Kant has been done as soon as we are able to determine what he actually said, and how what he actually said links up with what his predecessors did actually say, is perhaps to do history of philosophy, but this has nothing to do with philosophy's becoming. The latter, as with any other becoming, goes from the actual to the virtual and then back again to the actual—never from one actual to another (*DR* 208–14). Kant's critical philosophy (the actual) is a solution to problems which cannot be correctly grasped by looking at the questions and the problems that those who came before him left without answer and without solution. The conditions for the actualization of critical philosophy rest with the virtual events which ultimately govern its transcendental genesis. The counter-actualization of Kant's state of affairs, which is another way to refer to the Leibnizean vice-diction, is the only strategy possible for reaching the event, that is, philosophy's own becoming.

Nothing said so far precludes concepts from having a history:

> We say that every concept always has a history, even though this history zigzags, though it passes, if need be, through other problems or onto different planes. In any concept there are usually bits or components that come from other concepts, which correspond to other problems and presuppose other planes. This is inevitable because each concept carries out new cut-outs, takes on new contours, and has to be reactivated or recut. (*WP* 18)

Consequently, to be with Kant or to flirt with him today makes sense: His concepts can still be reactivated for the sake of our problems. And this raises the question of the historical evolution of concepts. Deleuze quotes Robbe-Grillet pithily yet approvingly for his answer to the question of whether there is progress in philosophy.[40] There is movement in philosophy, Robbe-Grillet used to say, but to try to do philosophy the way Kant did is senseless—not because we know better than Kant, but because Kant cannot be outdone or outsmarted; what he did, he did forever. The only choice is between the history of philosophy and Kant-grafts on problems which are no longer his own. *Remember:* A new philosopher arrives on the scene when the one before him has run out of problems.

Philosophy, then, is the invention of concepts and concepts are intensive singularities with histories of their own. But concepts are not floating on thin air. Philosophers have to lay out a plane of immanence as the horizon of the concepts that they create, provided that they do not confuse plane and method. "Plane" is not another word for method; planes are systems, already presupposed by the concept—systems of coordinates, dynamisms, and orientations in thinking. The plane of immanence functions like a sieve over chaos. Since concepts are events and their invention marks the beginning of philosophy, the plane is the horizon of these events and is prephilosophical. "Prephilosophical" here does not mean that the plane exists outside philosophy; it exists within philosophy in the sense that philosophy constantly presupposes it. As for concepts—given their dependence on the plane within which they exist, and given that planes do change—they themselves have their own history.[41] It seems to me that between Deleuze's plane of immanence and Foucault's *epistemes* there is a definite family resemblance. This prephilosophical horizon seems to play the same role that visibility and sayability play in Deleuze's book on Foucault: It renders things visible and sayable.[42] It is the a priori responsible for concepts clustering into assemblages rather than having no relation whatsoever with one another. The plane itself has to be constructed but, just as do concepts, it has to be constructed along preexisting lines and "with dissimilar means."

It is not worth letting go Deleuze's scepticism about our ability to justify a progressivist outlook on planes without remark. I quote him:

> Is there one plane that is better than all the others, or problems that dominate all others? Nothing at all can be said on this point. Planes must be constructed and problems posed, just as concepts must be created. . . . Of course, new concepts must relate to our problems, to our history, and, above all, to our becomings. But what does it mean for a concept to be of our time, or of any time? . . . If one concept is "better" than an earlier one, it is because it makes us aware of new variations and unknown resonances, it carries out unforeseen cuttings out, it brings forth an Event that surveys . . . us. But did the earlier concept not do this already? (*WP* 27–28)

It seems to follow that the becoming of philosophy, unlike its history, has nothing to do with the nostalgia of the archaeologist or the impatience of the eschatologist. As the case is with every other Deleuzean becoming, the only historico-philosophical repetition possible is the repetition of differences. One more reason for denouncing the oppressive image of the dominant historico-philosophical thought; with its continuist and progressivist postulates, it obliterates differences. The only way to tackle the question of "progress" intelligently is to adapt a stratigraphic perspective of time, and to do *geology rather than history*—in which case, becoming has effectively replaced history. This is what Deleuze has to say on this subject:

> We can only make headway with these questions if we give up the narrowly historical point of view of before and after in order to consider the time rather than the history of philosophy. This is a stratigraphic time where "before" and "after" indicate only an order of superimpositions. Certain paths (movements) take a sense and direction only on the short-

cuts and detours of faded paths . . . a stratum or layer of the plane of immanence will necessarily be above or below in relation to another, and images of thought cannot arise in any order whatever because they involve changes in orientation that can be directly located only on the earlier image. . . . Mental landscapes do not change haphazardly through the ages. . . . It is true that very old strata can rise to the surface again, can cut a path through the formations that covered them. (*WP* 58)

But how is this stratigraphic time to be understood, and to which problem is it the answer? A recent, very well written book on Deleuze—Keith Ansell-Pearson's *Germinal Life*—gives me the clues that I need for this discussion. Deleuze, as is true of Nietzsche before him—claims Ansell-Pearson—writes for a transhuman tribe that does not yet exist.[43] "When [Deleuze and] Nietzsche ask [their] great question, what may still become of man [they are] speaking of a future that does not cancel or abort the human, but one which is necessarily bound with the inhuman and the transhuman."[44] Of course, to think and to actualize the transhuman requires the dissolution of the form that the human presently exhibits—a form that is the result of the present configuration of forces. To think the transhuman is to think of a "higher human nature through an adequate comprehension of nature as well as the raising of physics to a higher plane (a metaphysics) by showing that bodies are capable of a potentially infinite becoming and modulation within finite limits."[45]

Constructivist to the very end, Deleuze will attempt to think the task of bringing about the transhuman by means of a creative evolution that will never lose sight of the two grand parallel lines of the virtual and the actual. Poised between subjective voluntarism and mechanistic determinism, Deleuze will look for a solution that taps the resources of the virtual in its process of being actualized. And since the actual is the present that passes, and the virtual, the past that conserves itself in its entirety, the construction of the transhuman will require an answer to the enigma of time. It is here that Bergson will find a very special place in Deleuze's thinking. It is from Bergson, not from Kant, that Deleuze learns to think of philosophy as the thought, beyond the human condition, of an intense life that is germinal and nonorganic. It is from him that he learns that time as duration prevents becoming from being configured as a mere succession of "still lives" and that makes it possible to think of movement without the customary appeal to invariable substances.[46] It is Bergson who persuades Deleuze that phenomenology is always an epiphenomenology, that things are always mixtures of actualized virtual tendencies, and that, therefore, a transcendental empiricist approach to the actual must aim beyond it, toward the conditions of its actualization. The significance of the Bergsonian emphasis on virtual tendencies cannot be overestimated, since "the dynamic and inventive condition of the possibility of evolution as a creative process" depends totally on those tendencies. For Bergson, the future of creative evolution does not belong to molar species and organisms but to the individuals and the singularities subtending them. In Bergson's thinking of time as duration, the emphasis is on its virtual character, in particular on time's past, which always "grows without ceasing" and which possesses an infinite capacity for novel reinvention.

We are now better situated to answer the questions that we raised earlier and to shed some light on the distinction between the history of philosophy and the becoming of philosophy which is Deleuze's own. We saw that Deleuze attributes to the history of philosophy the tendency to oppress thought. Unless it becomes capable of creating or awakening concepts and of tracing lines of flight and transformation, the history of philosophy serves only conservative interests. This accusation levelled against the history of philosophy is intelligible only against the background of Deleuze's "revisionist" view of philosophy and of its function. According to Deleuze, only philosophy creates concepts, lays out the horizon of these concepts, and dramatizes their movement through the choice of conceptual personae. The concepts that philosophy creates express intensive singularities or events. Now, this "revisionist" view of philosophy presupposes Deleuze's master project—the awakening of a thought capable of advancing the cause of the transhuman, and the articulation of an ethics worthy of this thought. Philosophy must create concepts which help to intensify the thought of the transhuman and contribute to its actualization. The ethical dimension of this creation and this thought is evaluated according to the intensity and the quality of the contribution.

The fact is that the history of philosophy cannot create concepts or trace lines of flight that could intensify the thought of the transhuman, and to this extent the history of philosophy is an obstacle to thought. The reason for its inability to create is that the history of philosophy lacks the notion of the virtual, without which philosophemes are nothing but the dialectical movement between the possible and the actual. But without the virtual, the dynamic and inventive conditions of becoming as a creative process will stay hidden. The predilection of the history of philosophy for the organic and for tree-like growth is not suited for the germinal life and its rhizomatic expansion. What is called forth, therefore, is the replacement of the history of philosophy with *philosophy's becoming* which would presuppose a new reading of time (Deleuze calls it "stratigraphic time"), permit experimentation with, and creation of, concepts, and represent (ethico-politically) the requisite resistance to the present. What history grasps of the event is its actualization in states of affairs or in lived experience, but the event in its becoming, in its self-positing as concept, escapes history. But with the stratigraphic sense of time that Deleuze introduces with the help of Bergson (and Nietzsche and Proust), he is able to say that a concept has also a becoming that involves its relationship with concepts situated on the same plane.[47] Here concepts link together, support one another, coordinate their contours, articulate their respective problems, and *belong to the same philosophy, even if they have different histories.* "Philosophical time," writes Deleuze, "is a grandiose time of coexistence that does not exclude the before and after, but *superimposes* them in a stratigraphic order. It is an infinite becoming of philosophy that crosscuts its history without being confused with it" (*WP* 59). Philosophy is becoming, not history; it is the coexistence of planes, not the succession of systems.

> It is less history and more geology or geography because geography
> wrests history from the cult of necessity in order to stress the irreducibil-
> ity of contingency. It wrests it from the cult of origins in order to affirm
> the power of a "milieu". . . . It wrests it from structures in order to trace
> the lines of flight that pass through. . . . Finally, it wrests history from
> itself in order to face becomings that do not belong to history even if
> they fall back into it. It is true that without history, becoming would re-
> main indeterminate and unconditional, but this does not mean that we
> should confuse becoming and history. The actual without the virtual is
> blind; but the virtual without the actual is empty. The problem with his-
> tory is that it is not experimentation, it is only the set of almost negative
> conditions that make possible the experimentation of something that
> escapes history. Don't you ever interpret; experiment! For, experimenta-
> tion always bears on the new, the actual and the emerging. (*WP* 96)

Becoming, unlike history, reveals the conditions for experimentation. "The creation of concepts in itself calls for a future form, for a new earth and people that do not yet exist" (*WP* 108). And the race summoned forth is not the one that claims to be pure but rather an oppressed, bastard, low, anarchical, nomadic and irremediably minor race—the kind of race that Kant excluded from the pages of his critical philosophy (*WP* 109).

Ultimately, the displacement of the history of philosophy in favor of the becoming of philosophy is a political decision: What is lacking today is not reflection, communication, or history, says Deleuze; it is resistance—resistance to the present. To create is to resist. To create the concept is always untimely, in the same sense that Péguy attributed to the event when he designated it as "aternal" (*internel*) (*WP* 113). Indeed, Péguy, to whom Deleuze often refers, had two ways of thinking of the event: one consisted of going through its actualization in history, its conditioning and deterioration; the other consisted of reassembling the event, installing oneself in it as if in a becoming, going through all its components or singularities. Péguy used to say—and the Stoic in Deleuze concludes likewise—that it may be the case that nothing changes or seems to change in history, but everything changes, along with us, in the event.

Notes

1. *La Philosophie critique de Kant. Doctrine des facultés* (Paris: Presses Universitaires de France, 1963); *Kant's Critical Philosophy: The Doctrine of the Faculties*, trans. Hugh Tomlinson and Barbara Habberjam (Minneapolis: University of Minnesota Press, 1984); hereafter *KCP*.
2. *Revue d'Esthétique*, 16:2 (Avril–Juin 1963), 113–36.
3. Michel Cressole, *Deleuze* (Paris: Editions Universitaires, 1973), 107–18; trans. Martin Joughin, "Letter to a Harsh Critic," in Gilles Deleuze, *Negotiations. 1972–90* (New York: Columbia University Press, 1995), 3–12.
4. "Signes et événements" (entretien), *Magazine Littéraire*, 257 (September 1988): 16–25; trans. Martin Joughin, "On Philosophy," *Negotiations 1972–90*, 135–55.
5. *Difference and Repetition*, trans. Paul Patton (New York: Columbia University Press, 1994); hereafter *DR*.
6. *The Logic of Sense*, trans. Mark Lester with Charles Stivale; ed. Constantin V. Boundas (New York: Columbia University Press, 1990).
7. Gilles Deleuze and Felix Guattari, *What is Philosophy?* trans. Hugh Tomlinson and Graham Burchell (New York: Columbia University Press, 1994); hereafter *WP*.
8. http://www.imaginet.fr/deleuze/TXT/140378.html; http://www.imaginet .fr/deleuze/TXT/210378.html; http://www.imaginet.fr./deleuze/TXT/280378.
9. Deleuze, "Letter to a Harsh Critic," 6.
10. "Cogitandum," being a gerund, suggests that something ought to be thought; the "ought" of the gerund is the mark of Deleuze's transcendental empiricism. See *infra*, note 16.
11. This is Fichte's entry point to transcendental philosophy and of his resolve to deduce the a priori of pure reason from the a priori determinations of practical reason; see his *Vocation of Man*, trans. William Smith (Chicago: Open Court, 1965).
12. Gilles Deleuze, "Troisième leçon sur Kant," March 28, 1978: http://www .imaginet.fr/deleuze/TXT/280378.html.
13. On this point, compare the previous essay by Dennis Schmidt in this volume.
14. For a discussion of Ideas and transcendental illusions, see *Difference and Repetition*, chapter 4; see also pp. 240–41.
15. "Transcendental empiricism" is the expression Deleuze chooses for the method which searches for the being of what is sensed, remembered, and thought. See *Difference and Repetition*, 139–47. Transcendental empiricism has generated

many discussions; the best one continues to be Bruce Baugh's "Deleuze and Empiricism," *The Journal of the British Society for Phenomenology* 24 (1993): 15–31. See also his "Transcendental Empiricism: Deleuze's Response to Hegel," *Man and World* 25 (1992): 133–48.

16. On Deleuze's dramatization and the role it is asked to play in the context of Kant's schematism, see "La Méthode de dramatisation," *Bulletin de la Société Française de Philosophie* 61, no. 3: Seance of January 28, 1967.

17. Deleuze repeatedly acknowledges Kant as the one who liberated time from its subordination to movement and, as a result, as the one who revolutionizes philosophy. See, for example, Deleuze: "Deuxième leçon sur Kant," March 21, 1978: http://www.imaginet.fr/deleuze/TXT/210378.html.

18. "Deleuze—Kant: synthèse et temps," March 14, 1978: http://www.imaginet.fr/deleuze/TXT/140378.html.

19. On Deleuze's views on intensity (intensive magnitude), see *Difference and Repetition*, 230–46; see also the excellent book of Juliette Simont, *Essai sur la quantité, la qualité, la relation chez Kant, Hegel, Deleuze* (Paris: L'Harmattan, 1997), especially chapters 4 and 5; see also my essay "An Ontology of Intensities," *Epoché* 7 (2002): 15–38.

20. On Deleuze's "cracked I" which replaces the classical robust subject, see *The Logic of Sense*, 154–55.

21. "Michel Tournier and the World without Others," *Logic of Sense*, 301–21.

22. I find it useful to think of the Deleuzean desire on the basis of Aristotle's theory of pleasure, without of course confusing the two. For Aristotle's discussion of pleasure, see Aristotle, *Nichomachean Ethics*, X: 1–5 (and VII: 11–14).

23. Guy Lardreau, *L'Exercise différé de la philosophie. A l'occasion de Deleuze* (Paris: Verdier, 1999), 34–35.

24. Deleuze, "Letter to a Harsh Critic," 5.

25. Gilles Deleuze and Claire Parnet, *Dialogues*, trans. Hugh Tomlinson and Barbara Habberjam (New York: Columbia University Press, 1987), 23.

26. Deleuze denounces the (traditional) image of thought and the postulates on which it rests in *Difference and Repetition*, chapter 3.

27. *Magazine Littéraire*, 257 (September 1988), 19.

28. On the lines of flight, see "Many Politics," *Dialogues*, 124 ff.

29. For a discussion of vice-diction, see *Difference and Repetition*, 189–91.

30. Strategies of vice-diction may bear a superficial resemblance to Gadamer's hermeneutic demand that the reader be allowed to bring her prejudices to the text she reads (see Hans-Georg Gadamer, *Truth and Method*, trans. Joel Weinsheimer and Donald G. Marshall [New York: Crossroad, 1989], 265–99) but it is not to be confused with them. Vice-diction gathers together the cases of the event, not the subject's responses to states of affairs.

31. *Magazine Littéraire*, 257 (September 1988), 16.

32. All these points concerning philosophy as the discipline creating concepts, the function of concepts, and their relation to the event are fully discussed in *What is Philosophy?* Part One.

33. Singularity is a concept having extension = 1; the term is used by Deleuze as a variant of the Leibnizean "monad." See *Logic of Sense*, 100–9.

34. Only when the conditions do not resemble the conditioned, the project of transcendental genesis can come to fruition. See Juliet Simmont's *Kant, Hegel, Deleuze*; and my essay "An Ontology of Intensities."

35. This is Deleuze's characterization of difference in itself. See on this point *Difference and Repetition*, 28–29.

36. *What Philosophy?* 55; see on the next page Deleuze's machinic portrait of Kant.

37. Alain Badiou, *Deleuze: The Clamor of Being*, trans. Louise Burchill (Minneapolis: University of Minnesota Press, 2000).

38. Keith Ansell-Pearson, *Germinal Life: The Difference and Repetition of Deleuze* (New York: Routledge, 1999), 124.

39. Ansell-Pearson, *Germinal Life*, 132.

40. *Magazine Littéraire*, 23.

41. For a helpful discussion of the plane of immanence, see *What is Philosophy?* 35–60.

42. See Gilles Deleuze, *Foucault*, trans. Seán Hand (Minneapolis: University of Minnesota Press, 1988), 108 ff.

43. Ansell-Pearson, *Germinal Life*, 43.

44. Keith Ansell Pearson, *Viroid Life: Perspectives on Nietzsche and the Transhuman Condition* (New York: Routledge, 1997), 163.

45. Ansell-Pearson, *Germinal Life*, 13.

46. Deleuze's admiration for Bergson is well documented. A long essay, "La Conception de la différence chez Bergson" (1956), and a chapter, "Bergson 1859–1941" in *Les Philosophes célèbres*, edited by Merleau Ponty (1956), were followed by an anthology of Bergson's writings, *Henri Bergson, Mémoire et vie* (1957) and then by a book, *Le Bergsonisme* (1966). Later references to Bergson can be found in almost all Deleuze's books. See my essay "Deleuze-Bergson: an Ontology of the Virtual," in *Deleuze: A Critical Reader*, ed. Paul Patton (Oxford: Blackwell, 1996), 81–106.

47. I find the recent discussion of stratigraphic time by Ronald Bogue very helpful. See Ronald Bogue, *Deleuze on Cinema* (New York: Routledge, 2003), 135–63.

Index

205–6; Leibniz on, 135; Spinoza on, 67–68, 97, 117–21, 124–25
Sufficient reason, principle of, 129–37, 146
Suicide, 164
Supplementarity, 12, 99, 230, 235
Symbol, 247–51
Symbolic order, 84, 88
Sympathy, 202–3

Taoism, 114–15; Valley Girl, 115–21, 125
Teleology, 103, 106
Testimony, 31–33
Thales, 43
Thomas Aquinas, 169, 173
Time, 9, 121–24, 141–42, 263, 275–76, 278–79
Tocqueville, Alexis de, 77
Todorov, Tzvetan, 195
Tournier, Michel, 264
Transcendence, 116–20, 124, 144
Truth, 241; Althusser on, 212; Levinas on, 21–35
Tully, James, 155, 157, 160, 169
Turgot, Anne R. J., 183

"the Unconscious," 49, 141–42, 147, 215

Vacuum, xiv, 59–69, 214
Valley Girl, see Taoism
Value, 174–75, 178; Hume on, 201
Veluti, 70, 72
Vico, Giambattista, xviii, 3, 182
Vice-diction, 268, 272, 278
"the Virtual," 121–23, 125, 141, 270–72, 274–76
Virtue, 41–42
Void, see Vacuum
Voltaire, F. M. Arouet de, 134, 183

Wahl, Jean, 198
Weber, Max, 173
Weierstrass, Karl, 138
White, Hayden, xviii
Whitman, Walt, 205–6
Will, 142
Wisdom, 44
Wonder, xiv, 36, 48, 53–55
World, 144–45, 163, 166
Work, see Labor

Zeus, 9, 50

Contributors

Katherine Arens is a professor of Germanic Studies at the University of Texas in Austin. She is the author or editor of eight books that focus on eighteenth- and nineteenth-century intellectual history, including *Structures of Knowing: Psychologies of the Nineteenth Century*.

Etienne Balibar is a professor of political and moral philosophy at the Université de Paris X Nanterre and distinguished professor in Critical Theory at University of California Irvine. He is the author of numerous books and critical essays on political philosophy and Marxism, including *Spinoza and Politics* and *Spinoza: From Individuality to Transindividuality*.

Robert Bernasconi is the Moss Professor of Philosophy at the University of Memphis. His writings focus on recent continental philosophy, Hegel, and race theory, and include *Derrida and Différance* and *The Question of Language in Heidegger's History of Being*.

Constantin Boundas is a professor of philosophy at Trent University in Ontario. He edited *The Deleuze Reader* and (with Dorothea Olkowski) *Gilles Deleuze and the Theater of Philosophy*. He also translated Deleuze's *Logic of Sense* and *Empiricism and Subjectivity*.

Jay Conway is currently completing his doctorate in philosophy on Deleuze's metatheory and the history of philosophy at the University of California at Riverside.

Stephen H. Daniel, professor of philosophy at Texas A&M University, focuses mainly on seventeenth- and eighteenth-century philosophy. He has written four books, including *The Philosophy of Jonathan Edwards*; *Myth and Modern Philosophy*; and *Contemporary Continental Thought*; and edited three others, including *New Interpretations of Berkeley's Philosophy*.

Anthony David completed his studies for the Unitarian Universalist ministry at Meadville Lombard Theological School (Chicago) in 2003 and is now Senior Minister of Pathways Church in Keller, Texas. His publications include an essay on Lyotard's interpretation of Kant.

Penelope Deutscher teaches philosophy at Northwestern University. A specialist in twentieth-century French philosophy, she is author of *Yielding Gender: Feminism, Deconstruction, and the History of Philosophy*; *A Politics of Impossible Difference: The Later Work of Luce Irigaray*; and *How to Read Derrida*.

Susan James, professor of philosophy at Birkbeck College, University of London, has published on modern philosophy, political thought, and feminist legal theory. She is the author of *Passion and Action: The Emotions in Seventeenth-Century Philosophy,* and editor of the political writings of Margaret Cavendish.

Leslie MacAvoy teaches philosophy at East Tennessee State University, where she specializes in nineteenth- and twentieth-century continental thought. Her published work focuses on issues of subjectivity and alterity in phenomenology, especially in the work of Heidegger and Levinas.

Pierre Macherey is a professor of philosophy at the Université de Lille III. A major contributor to discussions of contemporary Marxist critique, he is the author of numerous works, including *Avec Spinoza: études sur la doctrine et l'histoire du spinozisme* and *Introduction à l'Ethique de Spinoza.*

Todd May is a professor of philosophy at Clemson University. He has written books on Michel Foucault, anarchism, and other topics in contemporary continental philosophy. His publications include *The Moral Theory of Poststructuralism; Reconsidering Difference: Nancy, Derrida, Levinas, and Deleuze;* and *Gilles Deleuze.*

Warren Montag is a professor of English and Comparative Literary Studies at Occidental College. A specialist in eighteenth-century literature, political philosophy, and contemporary Marxist theory, he is author of *Bodies, Masses, Power: Spinoza and His Contemporaries* and *Louis Althusser,* and is editor of *The New Spinoza.*

Joel Reed, in several published essays, has developed a Marxist critique of early modern British nationalism, histories of language, and natural history. He has taught at Syracuse University and Skidmore College and is Associate Director of the Saratoga County Arts Council in upstate New York.

Dennis J. Schmidt, professor of philosophy at Pennsylvania State University, has written extensively on Gadamer and Heidegger and is author of *Of Germans and Other Greeks: Tragedy and Ethical Life* and *Lyrical and Ethical Subjects: On the Periphery of the Word, Freedom, and History.*

Daniel W. Smith teaches in the Department of Philosophy at Purdue University, where he specializes in contemporary European philosophy. He is the translator of Gilles Deleuze's *Francis Bacon: The Logic of Sensation* and *Essays Critical and Clinical* (with Michael A. Greco).

Miguel Vatter is a member of the Department of Political Science at Northwestern University. He is the author of *Between Form and Event: Machiavelli's Theory of Political Freedom* and articles on contemporary democratic theory and recent continental philosophy.

I CAC 00 0110398 V

B
791
.C87
2005